Please remember that this is a library book,
and that it belongs only temporarily to each
person who uses it. Be considerate. Do
not write in this, or any, library book.

STUDENT PERCEPTIONS
in the CLASSROOM

STUDENT PERCEPTIONS
in the CLASSROOM

Edited by
Dale H. Schunk
Judith L. Meece
University of North Carolina at Chapel Hill

WITHDRAWN

LEA LAWRENCE ERLBAUM ASSOCIATES, PUBLISHERS
1992 Hillsdale, New Jersey   Hove and London

Lawrence Erlbaum Associates, Inc., Publishers
365 Broadway
Hillsdale, New Jersey 07642

Library of Congress Cataloging-in-Publication Data

Student perceptions in the classroom / [edited by] Dale H. Schunk,
    Judith L. Meece.
        p.   cm.
    Includes bibliographical references and indexes.
    ISBN 0-8058-0981-3. — ISBN 0-8058-0982-1 (pbk.)
    1. Students—United States—Self-rating of.   2. Motivation in
education.   3. Learning, Psychology of.   4. Academic achievement-
-United States.   I. Schunk, Dale H.   II. Meece, Judith L.
LB1117.S84   1992
370.15′23—dc20   91-29235
                                                                            CIP

Printed in the United States of America
10 9 8 7 6 5 4 3 2 1

Contents

PART II: SOCIAL PERCEPTIONS

PART IV: GOAL PERCEPTIONS

Preface

Student perceptions are thoughts, beliefs, and feelings about persons, situations, and events. A book devoted to student perceptions underscores the importance of the topic in current educational theory and research. Such a book would have been less likely in the past when research was based largely on behavioral theories emphasizing environmental stimuli and reinforcement history as influences on behavior.

In contrast, contemporary cognitive theories of learning, motivation, and instruction assume that students are active processors of information rather than passive recipients of knowledge and that there is no automatic relation between information presented and how it is perceived by students. These theories view perceptions as factors that are influenced by personal attributes and situational cues and that affect one's own behaviors and the perceptions and actions of others in the environment. Research conducted in the past few years supports the idea that student perceptions help to explain achievement-related outcomes beyond the effects of student abilities and environmental factors (e.g., rewards, instructional materials).

As the chapters in this book make clear, there are many types of student perceptions that operate in classrooms. Self-perceptions involve perceptions of students' own abilities, self-concepts, goals, competence, effort, interests, attitudes, values, and emotions. Social perceptions refer to students' perceptions of their peers' abilities, self-concepts, goals, and so forth, as well as to perceptions of various qualities of teachers (e.g., attitudes, competence, goals, opinions of students' abilities). Also important are students' perceptions of tasks and other classroom factors (e.g., task difficulty, effective learning strategies, environmental factors that help and hinder learning).

This book grew from our desire to have leading researchers describe their theoretical positions on the role of student perceptions in education and to present supporting research. We felt that this type of book would be timely and would make a significant contribution to the literature. Although most books on learning, motivation, and instruction discuss the role of student perceptions, they typically do so briefly and not in sufficient depth for readers to develop conceptual understanding. We thought that professionals and students alike would be highly interested in a book that provided in-depth reviews of theory and research on student perceptions and discussed their role in learning, instruction, and motivation.

Our goal in producing this type of volume led to several decisions that we felt would increase the book's impact in the field. We solicited chapters from individuals actively engaged in research on student perceptions. We felt this diversity would highlight the importance and role of student perceptions in many aspects of classroom life. At the same time, we wanted an integrated series of chapters that surveyed the field rather than a loosely linked collection of chapters summarizing individuals' research programs. Accordingly, we asked authors to follow a common chapter format of presenting relevant theoretical ideas, discussing research evidence bearing on these ideas, suggesting future research directions, and describing implications for educational practice. In short, we wanted contributors not only to discuss the current status of their ideas but also to provide a forward look in terms of research and practice.

For organizational purposes we subdivided the book into four sections: Issues in the Study of Student Perceptions, Social Perceptions, Ability-Related Perceptions, and Goal Perceptions. Chapters in the Issues section do not follow the preceding format but rather discuss general issues relevant to the study of student perceptions. The placement of each of the remaining chapters in one of the other three sections identifies the chapter's major focus, although many chapters cut across sections.

This book is designed for persons interested or working in the field of education. Professionals should appreciate the book's compilation of current theory and research and their implications for educational practice. The book is appropriate as a text for graduate students in schools of education or related disciplines, as well as for advanced undergraduates interested in education. It is assumed that students using this book possess minimal familiarity with psychological concepts and research methods. Contributors were asked to address their chapters to a general audience by defining and explaining technical concepts and by discussing research findings in nonstatistical language.

ACKNOWLEDGMENTS

There are many people we wish to acknowledge for making this book a reality. We express our sincerest gratitude to our contributors. Despite the press of busy academic schedules that befit active researchers, they worked on this task diligently, which made our jobs as editors personally and professionally satisfying. We also express our appreciation to many professional colleagues and students with whom we have had stimulating discussions over the years. In particular, we have benefited from our activities in the American Educational Research Association Motivation in Education Special Interest Group. With respect to the production of this book, we thank Hollis Heimbouch, our editor at Lawrence Erlbaum Associates, and her assistant Kathy Dolan, for their support, patience, and editorial guidance. Finally, we wish to thank Caryl and Laura Schunk for their encouragement and understanding throughout this project.

Dale H. Schunk
Judith L. Meece

	I

Issues in the Study of Student Perceptions

1

Theory and Research on Student Perceptions in the Classroom

DALE H. SCHUNK
University of North Carolina at Chapel Hill

Researchers studying students' classroom behaviors are focusing increasingly on the influence of students' thoughts, beliefs, and feelings about themselves, other persons, and events. This focus on *student perceptions* assumes that students are active information processors who affect classroom events as much as they are affected by them (Pintrich, Cross, Kozma, & McKeachie, 1986). Current theories of learning and motivation portray students as individuals who formulate achievement goals, selectively attend to events, engage in activities, and employ strategies they believe will help them attain goals, process (organize, transform, code) information in meaningful ways for storage in memory, and create and maintain a positive psychological climate for accomplishing goals (Weinstein & Mayer, 1986).

This view contrasts with earlier, behavioristic views of learners as passive recipients of information whose responses are affected by their reinforcement histories and stimuli in the present environment (Skinner, 1953). As Zimmerman (1989) noted, this view also contrasts with theories postulating that student learning, motivation, and achievement depend heavily on abilities and other individual differences. Although such variables as intelligence and socioeconomic status (SES) may affect students' academic behaviors, the former do not completely explain the latter. For example, students within any given ability level differ in their motivation, achievement, and ability-related perceptions (Bandura, 1986; Schunk, 1989).

The contributors to this volume diverge in many ways: theoretical perspective, types of perceptions addressed, and methodological considerations (tasks, subjects, procedures). Despite these differences, they share the belief that student perceptions represent complex processes that are influenced by a variety of factors and that have diverse effects in school. In this chapter I initially provide a historical perspective on the role of student perceptions in the disciplines of teaching and instructional processes, learning, and motivation. I then discuss the chapters within an organizational framework comprising four sections: Issues in the Study of Student Perceptions, Social Perceptions, Ability-Related Perceptions, Goal Perceptions. I conclude with suggestions for future research.

HISTORICAL PERSPECTIVE

Theory and research in various disciplines have influenced the current emphasis on student perceptions. I have chosen to discuss the contributions from the fields of teaching and instructional processes, learning, and motivation. These domains are relevant to the book's focus and reveal a similar progression in the importance of student perceptions in educational settings. Space limitations preclude an in-depth review of the contributions from other domains (e.g., counseling and psychotherapy, developmental and social psychology).

Teaching and Instructional Processes

Researchers currently investigate student perceptions to determine their relation to teaching and student behaviors (Brophy & Good, 1986), but historically perceptions received little research attention. A sense of this changing emphasis is evident from examining the three volumes of the *Handbook of Research on Teaching* edited by Gage (1963), Travers (1973), and Wittrock (1986a). Neither the first nor second handbook includes a chapter exclusively devoted to student perceptions. The first handbook contains a chapter by Stern (1963) on noncognitive variables. *Noncognitive* is defined as, "measures of individual differences in attitudes, values, interests, appreciations, adjustments, temperament, and personality" (p. 400), although attitude is the primary measure for which research on students is summarized. The second handbook includes a chapter on teaching of affective responses (Khan & Weiss, 1973). *Affective* is defined as, "the evaluative component of attitudes associated with a feeling core of liking or disliking for social and psychological objects" (p. 760), and the chapter focuses on attitudinal research.

The third handbook (Wittrock, 1986a) contains a chapter on students' thought processes (Wittrock, 1986b). The first sentence of this chapter highlights the importance of student perceptions:

> The recent research on students' thought processes studies the effects of teachers and instruction upon the student perceptions, expectations, attentional processes, motivations, attributions, memories, generations, understandings, beliefs, attitudes, learning strategies, and metacognitive processes that mediate achievement. (p. 297)

Research is summarized on the influence in classrooms of student perceptions of self-concepts, expectations, teachers and teacher behaviors, instructional processes, cognitive and metacognitive processes, attributions, and learning strategies. This research shows that student perceptions can mediate the relationship of teacher behaviors to student achievement: Teaching can influence student perceptions, which in turn can affect achievement.

One limitation of historical work is that attitudes and other student beliefs were viewed as products of observable actions by teachers and students. Although student beliefs are influenced by classroom events, the chapters in this volume make it clear that student perceptions also affect classroom events. In short, research on teaching historically offered a limited view of the role of student perceptions in the classroom.

In addition to research on attitudes, another historical line of investigation that contributed to the present emphasis on student perceptions is research on self-concept. *Self-concept* refers to one's collective self-perceptions that are formed through experiences with, and interpretations of, the environment, and that are heavily influenced by reinforcements and evaluations by significant other persons (Marsh & Shavelson, 1985; Shavelson & Bolus, 1982). Little educational research investigated self-concept prior to 1950, but since then work has accelerated (Wylie, 1961, 1979). Wylie (1961) devoted four pages to educational factors affecting self-concept and the role of self-concept during learning, but her 1979 volume contains 53 pages addressing the relation of self-concept to achievement. Hansford and Hattie (1982) conducted a meta-analysis of 128 studies that investigated self-concept and achievement and that involved over 200,000 subjects.

Current research on teaching and instructional processes explores student perceptions of control, competence, attributions, teachers, peers, and metacognitive (higher-order) processes, among others.

Researchers assess student perceptions with oral or written measures, by asking students to recall what they were thinking about at various points during a lesson (possibly after watching videotaped portions of the lesson), and by having them verbalize aloud as they work on academic tasks (*think-aloud procedure*). A goal of many researchers is to integrate findings from research on teaching with those from the learning literature to formulate a unified model of classroom teaching and learning (Winne, 1985).

Learning

Although the focus was short-lived, perceptions formed an integral part of some early learning research. In 1879 Wundt established a psychological laboratory in Leipzig, Germany. Titchener, a student of Wundt's, subsequently became the director of the psychological laboratory at Cornell University (Mueller, 1979). The experimental method used by Wundt, Titchener, and many others of the period was *introspection,* a form of observation involving people's perceptions. Subjects in experiments reported their immediate experiences following exposure to objects or events (e.g., if shown a table they might verbalize their perceptions of shape, size, color, texture, etc.). They were not to label (say "table") or report knowledge about it or meanings of their perceptions; these activities implied that subjects were attending to the stimulus rather than to their conscious processes, which defeated introspection's purpose of studying the structure of mental processes.

Introspection was highly regarded by many psychologists because it helped demarcate psychology from other sciences. Unfortunately, introspection often was problematic and its results unreliable. Forcing people to ignore meanings is an unnatural exercise that provides an inaccurate picture of the mind's structure (Schunk, 1991). Led by Watson (1914), behaviorists criticized introspection and urged psychologists to study behavior.

Through the work of Thorndike, Guthrie, Hull, Skinner, and others, behaviorism dominated American psychology until the early 1960s. Behaviorists do not deny the existence of mental processes, but they contend that these processes do not explain behavior because the causes of behavior reside primarily in the environment. To change behavior, one should alter environmental cues and consequences of actions.

With the domination of behaviorism, learning researchers did not study perceptions. One exception was Gestalt psychologists (Kohler,

1947/1959). Originally a theory of perception, Gestalt theory viewed learning as the organizing of perceptions into meaningful configurations (Schunk, 1991). As a formal view of learning, Gestalt theory was thought provoking but generated little research and did not develop into a major theory.

Various factors contributed to the decline of behaviorism, but a major cause was that its principles had difficulty explaining research findings involving complex learning. The cognitive conceptions of learning that began to appear in the 1960s stressed that learning involves the acquisition of knowledge and knowledge structures and occurs as a result of information being mentally processed (Atkinson & Shiffrin, 1968). Although early information-processing research was primarily oriented toward factors related to learning (e.g., knowledge states, memory), interest in learning processes has grown since 1975 (Shuell, 1986).

From an information-processing perspective, student perceptions are types of *metacognitive* processes. Two types of metacognitive processes are involved in learning (Shuell, 1986). One type helps to regulate activities necessary for learning; examples are planning, organizing information, and monitoring one's level of understanding. The second type is concerned with what learners do and do not know about the material being learned and the processes involved in learning it. Subsumed under the second type is metacognitive knowledge about persons, tasks, and strategies (Flavell, 1985). The persons category includes knowledge of similarities and differences among persons, as well as knowledge of one's own skills and beliefs (e.g., "I'm better in math than in English"); the tasks category comprises information about how task demands can influence performance (recognizing information is easier than recalling it); the strategies categories includes knowledge about the potential value of different strategies for successfully completing tasks (rehearsal is a good strategy for memorizing).

Social cognitive theory also stresses the importance of student perceptions during learning with its emphasis on the idea that people often acquire knowledge, rules, skills, strategies, beliefs, and attitudes, by observing others (Bandura, 1986). Individuals learn the functional value and appropriateness of modeled behaviors by observing their consequences, and they act in accordance with their beliefs concerning the expected outcomes of actions.

Two types of student perceptions are outcome expectations and perceived self-efficacy. *Outcome expectations* are beliefs about anticipated outcomes of actions. People select actions they believe will be successful and attend to models who they think will teach them valued skills. Outcome expectations sustain behaviors over long periods when people believe their actions will eventually produce desired outcomes (Bandura, 1986). *Perceived self-efficacy* refers to judgments of one's capabilities to organize and implement actions necessary to attain designated performance levels. Self-efficacy can influence choice of activities, effort expended, and persistence. Although these outcomes typically are associated with motivation, they also affect learning (Schunk, 1989).

Current learning research explores the role of student perceptions in the acquisition, retention, and use of knowledge. A particularly active area of research is concerned with teaching students to use *learning strategies,* or systematic cognitive plans that assist the acquisition of information and task performance (Borkowski, 1985; Pressley et al., 1990). Researchers are showing that learning is a complex process affected by personal and contextual variables and that students' perceptions of themselves, teachers, and peers are influential during learning (Pintrich et al., 1986).

Motivation

The role of student perceptions in motivation theory and research has evolved since the early experimental studies of motivation in the 1930s (Weiner, 1990). Early behavioral theories explained motivation in terms of responses elicited by stimuli (classical conditioning), emitted in the presence of stimuli (operant conditioning), or produced by drive and habit strength (systematic behavior theory). In classical conditioning, the motivational properties of an unconditioned stimulus are transmitted to a conditioned stimulus through repeated pairings. This is a passive view of motivation because once conditioning occurs, the conditioned response is elicited by the conditioned stimulus. In fact, conditioning is complex and depends on information conveyed to the individual about the likelihood of the unconditioned stimulus following presentation of the conditioned stimulus (Rescorla, 1972).

In operant conditioning, motivated behavior is an increased rate of responding or a greater likelihood that a response will be made contingent on a stimulus (Skinner, 1953). Motivated behavior is a function of the individual's reinforcement history and cues presently in the environment. According to systematic behavior theory (Hull, 1943), needs produce drives that energize individuals. Responding that results in reinforcement creates a habit, and habit strength increases with reinforced stimulus–response pairings. Learning represents increased habit strength; motivation is, "the initiation of learned, or habitual, patterns of movement or behavior" (Hull, 1943, p. 226).

Various lines of evidence caused difficulty for these views, but especially important was research on reinforcement. Tolman and Honzik (1930) demonstrated the phenomenon of *latent learning* (learning in the absence of reinforcement), which contradicted the notion that behavior change occurs only through reinforcement. Some time later, Bandura (1969) showed that much learning occurs through observation in the absence of reinforcement and performance by observers. Although there is ample evidence that reinforcers can influence what people do, it is not reinforcement that affects behavior but rather people's beliefs about reinforcement. People engage in activities when they believe they will be reinforced and they value that reinforcement (Bandura, 1986). When reinforcement history conflicts with beliefs, people act based on their beliefs (Brewer, 1974). In short, behavioral views offer incomplete accounts of motivation because they ignore the influence of cognitive processes.

Important early cognitive perspectives on motivation emerged from work by Lewin, Dembo, Festinger, and Sears (1944) on *level of aspiration* (the goal one is attempting to attain), and by Atkinson (1957) on *achievement motivation* (the striving to perform difficult tasks as well as possible). Atkinson's expectancy-value theory postulated that achievement behaviors represent a conflict between the tendencies to approach (hope for success) and avoid (fear of failure) achievement situations. Achievement actions carry the possibilities of success and failure. Whether one approaches or avoids a situation depends on the motive to succeed or avoid failure, the subjective probability of success or failure, and the incentive value of succeeding or avoiding failure. Achievement motivation is determined by the relative weights of the tendency to approach the goal and the tendency to avoid it.

Recent cognitive approaches to motivation highlight the importance of perceived control, goal setting, self-evaluation, expectations, and attributions. *Perceived control* is an umbrella term that has been defined in various ways. Rotter's (1966) *locus of control* emphasizes perceived control over outcomes. Students differ in whether they believe that outcomes either occur independently of how they act and are due to luck, chance, or fate (external control) or are highly contingent on their actions (internal control). A related construct is *learned helplessness,* or a psychological state involving a disturbance in motivation, emotion, cognition, and behavior, which results from a perceived independence between responses and outcomes (uncontrollability) (Seligman, 1975). The model of perceived control by Skinner and her colleagues comprises *strategy* beliefs (extent that potential causes produce given outcomes), *capacity* beliefs (whether the student has or can acquire the potential causes), and *control* beliefs (whether the student can produce desired outcomes without reference to any particular means) (Skinner, Wellborn, & Connell, 1990).

In social cognitive theory (Bandura, 1986), motivation is goal-directed behavior instigated and sustained by students' expectations concerning the anticipated outcomes of their actions, self-efficacy for performing those actions, and self-evaluation of goal progress. A perceived negative discrepancy between one's goal and present performance creates an incentive for change. As students work toward goals, they note their progress; the perception of progress sustains motivation and self-efficacy. Goal attainment validates students' self-efficacy and outcome expectations, and they may set new, challenging goals for themselves.

Attributions are perceived causes of outcomes. Attribution theories assume that people desire to explain the causes of significant events (Kelley & Michela, 1980; Weiner, 1985). In achievement settings, students often attribute successes and failures to such factors as ability, effort, task difficulty, and luck; attributions influence expectancies of future success (Weiner, 1979). Assuming that learning conditions are not expected to change much, students who attribute prior successes (failures) to such stable factors as high (low) ability or low (high) task difficulty are apt to hold higher (lower) expectancies for success than those who emphasize the variable factors of high (low) effort or good (bad) luck.

Goal theory represents the newest approach to studying motivation in achievement settings (Weiner, 1990). This view postulates important relationships between students' perceptions of their achievement goals (task/ego orientations, learning/performance goals), reward structures (competitive, cooperative, individualistic), attributions (ability, effort), types of comparisons for determining progress (self-, social), and achievement behaviors (choice of activities, effort, persistence, performance). Goal theory integrates many constructs postulated as important by other theoretical views of motivation. So much current research is based at least in part on goal theory that one section of this volume presents this work.

CHAPTER OVERVIEWS

For organizational purposes, the chapters in this volume are grouped by theme into four sections. The first section (Issues in the Study of Student Perceptions) includes this chapter and the chapter by Assor and Connell and discusses general issues that cut across themes. The remaining three sections refer to types of student perceptions: social, ability-related, and goal. Chapters are categorized according to their major focus; however, sections are not mutually exclusive and some chapters cut across sections. Although goal perceptions are ability-related perceptions, chapters that focus on goal perceptions are grouped together to highlight the current research emphasis.

Issues in the Study of Student Perceptions

Validity of Self-Reports. Student perceptions typically are assessed through questionnaires or interviews in which students are presented with items asking about their beliefs and they judge each item using a numerical scale or respond to it verbally. Much has been written about the process of accessing information in memory as input for self-report measures (Ericsson & Simon, 1980; Nisbett & Wilson, 1977). A major concern is whether such self-reports are valid indicators of students' perceptions that presumably can affect behavior.

Assor and Connell (chapter 2) address these perceptions, or *performance affecting self-appraisals,* as they relate to self-reports of academic competence. They present empirical evidence to support the point that self-reports of academic competence generally are valid measures of students' perceptions of competence. In arriving at this conclusion they examine two potential sources of invalidity of self-reports. One source is that subjects may not be able to accurately assess their own competence, as might happen with young children whose judgments depend heavily on salient performance outcomes and therefore might be unstable over time and poor predictors of performance. Assor and Connell review studies showing that, although some stability is evident in young children's judgments, greater stability and prediction of academic behaviors is found beginning in the third or fourth grade (ages 9–10).

A second source involves subjects who distort competence self-appraisals to maintain self-esteem or favorable judgments by others. Overestimating or underestimating what one can do should result in poor prediction of academic behaviors. Based on their review of studies, Assor and Connell report that moderate overestimating is associated with increased levels of task engagement and performance, high overestimating is associated with a leveling off or a decline, and underestimating relates to lower levels. The authors conclude by offering suggestions for improving the validity of self-reports, which researchers and practitioners interested in assessing students' perceptions should find helpful.

Social Perceptions

Influence of Friends.   Berndt and Keefe (chapter 3) address the influence of friends on adolescents' perceptions. There are theories on the role of friends' influence (Hartup, 1978), but there is little research on this influence in the classroom. Berndt and Keefe found that junior high school students report greater influence from parents than friends. When students believe friends have some influence on them or vice-versa, more often this influence is positive, rather than negative (e.g., correction of undesirable behavior). Berndt and Keefe also summarize research in which two friends were asked to discuss an issue and changes in students' perceptions were assessed. Shifts in decisions depended on how opinions were exchanged: The more information exchanged, the more likely a shift in opinion. Discussions generally increased the similarity of friends' beliefs.

A longitudinal study over a school year investigating class participation of junior high students showed that students who differ in participation draw away from one another and new friendships emerge based on common participation. Students with more satisfactory friendships show better school adjustment; friendships in the fall predict later changes in adjustment. These findings support the importance of friends in school and suggest that friends affect students' classroom perceptions and participation.

Perceived Intentionality and Aggression.   Graham and Hudley (chapter 4) explore aggression among African-American students. Although there are several factors that can promote aggression (e.g., poverty, single-parent families, assignment to remedial classes, exposure to violence), Graham and Hudley present an attributional model postulating that cues from an event are used to infer intentionality by the instigator. For example, if a student is pushed by an instigator while waiting in line and the student believes the instigator acted intentionally, then this belief may produce anger and aggression. The basic premise is that aggressive children display an attributional bias to ascribe hostile intent to others following negative events.

Graham and Hudley summarize research showing that aggressive students are more likely than nonaggressive students to believe that peers are intentionally malicious and that anger results from perceived intentionality and causes aggressive actions. In other words, aggressive students feel the way they think and act based on their feelings. The authors describe an intervention designed to change intentionality attributions of aggressive children. The intervention helps children attend to and properly interpret social cues. Particular attention is paid to situations offering ambiguous cues about intention. As a result of participating in the intervention program, children showed less perceived intentionality and anger. There also was evidence of generalization outside of the training setting, which has important implications for school-based treatment programs.

Teachers' Beliefs. Wigfield and Harold (chapter 5) discuss the influence of teacher beliefs on student perceptions. Much has been written on teacher expectations of student achievement (Brophy & Good, 1974), but Wigfield and Harold expand this focus to include teachers' beliefs about students' abilities, interests, and the value they attach to tasks. Wigfield and Harold summarize longitudinal research on the development and socialization of children's achievement perceptions. Consistent with other work (Harter & Connell, 1984; Stipek & Mac Iver, 1989), Wigfield and Harold found that students' perceptions of ability decrease across the elementary school years. They also found consistency between teachers' perceptions of students' abilities and students' self-ratings, especially in reading, mathematics, and sports.

This work has important implications for teacher–student interactions. Young children are not sophisticated in interpreting teacher evaluations, but with development, children receive more teacher feedback reflecting beliefs. By the mid-elementary years, teachers' beliefs about students' abilities in specific domains relate strongly to students' beliefs about their abilities in those domains. This heightened influence of teacher beliefs with development may stem from changes in children's thinking. Young children do not have a stable conception of ability but rather view it as roughly synonymous in meaning with effort. Around third grade, children begin to develop a conception of ability as a factor underlying performance, which implies that teacher beliefs then may become more influential.

Academic Help-Seeking. Newman and Schwager (chapter 6) explore the role of academic help-seeking to obtain information relevant to learning or mastering school tasks. Help-seeking involves asking direct questions of teachers and peers and is an effective component of classroom learning used often by high achievers. In deciding to ask for help students weigh and combine sources of information about task demands, personal resources, and costs and benefits, and they decide whom to ask, what to ask about, and how to do it.

Newman and Schwager summarize research showing that help-seeking depends on perceptions of ability, control, and goals. Children who perceive themselves as academically competent tend to view help-seeking as an effective learning strategy. Students who feel in control of their academic successes—they know what actions are required to perform well and believe they can accomplish them—are likely to seek help. Children with an intrinsic goal (mastery) orientation are more apt to seek help than those holding an extrinsic orientation. Help-seeking also can be affected by students' perceptions of such classroom factors as characteristics of potential help-givers, teacher involvement and liking, classroom goal orientation, structure of activities, and amount of teacher control. This chapter highlights the idea that many perceptions affect help-seeking and suggests ways to foster students' perceiving help in a positive light.

Ability-Related Perceptions

Motivation and Cognitive Engagement.   Pintrich and Schrauben (chapter 7) discuss the usefulness of motivational constructs for explaining students' cognitive engagement in academic tasks. They present an academic model that highlights motivation and cognitive components. Important motivation components include perceptions of self-efficacy, control, goal orientation, and task value. The authors focus their discussion on how these components relate to such learning strategies as rehearsal, elaboration, monitoring, and self-regulation. Pintrich and Schrauben summarize evidence on the links between these indexes of motivation and cognitive engagement. For example, among college-age and junior high school students strategy use relates positively to self-efficacy, perceived control, intrinsic (mastery) goal orientation, and perceived task value. Although data are correlational, they show important relations between students' perceptions and academic work.

This chapter represents a detailed inquiry into the links between motivation and cognitive engagement. Pintrich and Schrauben underscore the need for research exploring the mechanisms whereby students' perceptions and cognitive engagement affect one another and achievement outcomes. Research exploring the generality of their model will determine how well it applies across various domains and with students of different ages.

Self-Regulated Learning.   Zimmerman and Martinez-Pons (chapter 8) explore the relation between self-efficacy and learning strategy use during self-regulated learning. *Self-regulated learning* refers to learners' efforts to regulate their learning and performance metacognitively (use of higher-order strategies), motivationally, and behaviorally. They postulate three types of influences: behavioral (self-observation, self-judgment, self-reaction), environmental (academic outcomes), and personal (goals, self-efficacy, metacognition, knowledge, affect). They summarize data showing that students differ in efficacy and strategy use as a function of academic ability and grade level. Academically able students report greater use of effective learning strategies and hold higher verbal and mathematical self-efficacy compared with less academically able students. Students show an increase in strategy use and self-efficacy from the 5th to the 11th grade.

Zimmerman and Martinez-Pons underscore the point that students' academic work represents a complex process that is influenced by various perceptions and cognitions. The authors discuss the implications of their work for educational practice and emphasize that training programs must address behavioral, environmental, and personal factors in order to be effective.

Sex Differences. Meece and Courtney's (chapter 9) chapter examines sex differences in achievement perceptions with emphasis on mathematics. Their conceptual focus is an academic choice model, which postulates that sex differences result in part from students' expectations of success and the perceived incentive value of the task (Eccles et al., 1983). Research shows that boys often hold higher performance expectations in mathematics than girls and that gender-role identities and socialization practices can influence the value that children attach to tasks. Meece and Courtney review studies that support the model but also demonstrate some inconsistency in the relative influence of expectancy and value perceptions.

Meece and Courtney underscore the utility of their framework by noting that neither gender nor measures of ability adequately explain sex differences in achievement. They also point out that sex differences, when found, generally are not large, and urge that future research address such areas as developmental origins of differences, parental expectations, and classroom interaction patterns. The theory and research discussed in this chapter make it clear that teachers need to use materials and instructional practices that enhance both expectations and value perceptions in order to prevent and alleviate differential perceptions by male and female students.

Self-Efficacy and Career-Related Choices. The important role played by self-efficacy in career-related choices is discussed by Hackett and Betz (chapter 10). They present a model postulating that sex-typed childhood experiences limit acquisition of information to use in developing self-efficacy for certain occupational areas. Lower efficacy for given careers affects the types of occupational alternatives considered. For example, women who as children were dissuaded from studying science are likely to choose a nonscientific college major and occupation. Hackett and Betz present data showing that occupational self-efficacy is a strong predictor of career choice. They also summarize evidence supporting the idea that experiences affect self-efficacy and that vocational interests are influenced by self-efficacy.

The notion that self-efficacy may help explain the low incidence of women in many jobs and fields of study has important implications for classroom practice. Research shows that teachers often convey sex-typed feedback to students (Meece, Parsons, Kaczala, Goff, & Futterman, 1982). Such feedback may affect students' efficacy for various occupations. Teachers can help students by determining their sense of efficacy for various content areas and by ensuring that students have diverse experiences that expand their career choices.

Students With Learning Problems. Licht (chapter 11) examines self-evaluations of ability among students with learning problems. Licht notes that theory and research support the idea that many children who experience failures during their early school years develop perceptions of low ability. Low perceived ability can negatively affect effort, persistence, and achievement, and these outcomes substantiate children's perceptions of low ability. At the same time, developmental research shows that many young children do not respond in this fashion but rather maintain a high perception of their abilities even in the face of failure. Negative self-perceptions and low motivation and achievement often do not occur until children have been in school for a while, which suggests that negative outcomes may have to accumulate to exert their effects.

Licht argues that the latter evidence underestimates the vulnerability of children to school failure. She cites evidence showing that preschool and kindergarten children lower their self-evaluations of ability following failure and display motivational deficiencies. Whether learning problems lead to low perceptions and achievement may depend on such variables as parental encouragement of autonomy, classroom grouping practices, opportunities for social comparisons, and the presence of types of behavior problems. These and other ideas discussed by Licht have important implications for parents and teachers as they attempt to strengthen ability perceptions among students for whom classroom learning often is difficult.

Goal Perceptions

Theories About Education. Nicholls (chapter 12) postulates that students hold many theoretical ideas pertaining to education. Some of the most important relate to motivational orientations. Students with an *ego orientation* are concerned about their ability as it compares with that of other students. They feel successful when they perceive their ability as higher than that of others, and adopt performance goals of working well enough so teachers and peers will believe they are competent. Students with a *task orientation* are concerned about learning and improving their skills. They feel successful when they expend effort and believe they are improving. They adopt learning goals and think that ability is enhanced through effort. These two orientations are separate and often unrelated; they are not two ends of a continuum.

Nicholls summarizes evidence showing that students' theoretical ideas bear important relations with such other variables as use of reading strategies, higher-order mathematical knowledge, and endorsement of practices conducive to learning. Task and ego orientations also relate differently to beliefs about the purposes of education. These points have implications for educational planning. Children have theories about the nature and value of knowledge and how it should be acquired. Students' ideas usually are not considered when planning instruction. Nicholls suggests that educators would benefit by determining students' beliefs about school learning.

Multiple Goals. Wentzel (chapter 13) discusses the multiple goals that adolescents hold. Goals influence achievement behaviors, may conflict with or complement one another, and may relate to task mastery and reflect the processes of learning or be concerned with evaluation and social comparisons. Students also hold nonacademic goals—obtaining social approval, cooperating with others. Wentzel summarizes research showing that goals interact with one another, achievement, and classroom behavior. Goals relating positively to student achievement are: be a successful student, be dependable, be responsible, learn new things, understand things, do your best, and get things done on time. High achievers report frequent pursuit of mastery, evaluation, and social responsibility goals (i.e., be helpful to others, be cooperative and sharing). Social responsibility goals relate positively to social acceptance by peers and to teachers' preferences for students.

Wentzel notes that academic achievement is explained better by sets of goals than by single goals. Academic and social responsibility goals may affect achievement in additive fashion. Research needs to clarify the mechanisms whereby goals combine to influence achievement behaviors and to explore the generality of findings to younger and older students. Wentzel's work suggests that teachers emphasize that academic success depends on many factors and teach social responsibility along with academics.

Feedback and Social Comparison.   Jagacinski (chapter 14) explores the effects of task-and ego-involving conditions on students'
perceptions and behaviors and discusses the influential roles played by
feedback and social comparisons of one's performance with those of
others. Under task-involving conditions, high effort is positively related to perceived competence, pride, and a sense of accomplishment,
but under ego-involving conditions low effort is associated with these
outcomes. Social comparisons have greater effects on students' perceptions under ego-involving conditions than under task-involving
ones. Feedback sustains motivation to the extent it provides information relevant to the conception of ability employed. Task-involved
students are interested in assessing their improvement and mastery;
ego-involved students want to perform better than others.

Jagacinski's work shows that students react differently to task- and
ego-involving conditions. Classrooms can foster differential beliefs
among students depending on the conditions in effect. Emphasizing
normative evaluation may promote ego involvement, but the absence
of such evaluation does not necessarily increase task involvement.
Group projects and cooperative work in which students share the
responsibility for the final product are some ways to foster a task-
involved learning orientation.

Classroom Climate.   Ames (chapter 15) explores the relation between classroom climate and students' goals (mastery and performance). Mastery-oriented learners focus on developing skills and
derive satisfaction from participation. Effort is viewed as a way to
succeed. Performance-oriented students desire to protect their sense
of self-worth. They want to be viewed as having high ability, and they
do not necessarily value effort because to be judged as able requires
succeeding with little effort. Ames argues that these goal orientations
can arise from classroom conditions. Adoption of a goal orientation
depends in part on its salience in the classroom.

Ames describes a systematic intervention aimed at fostering a
mastery-goal orientation. Six features of the classroom can be structured to stress a mastery-goal orientation: task design, distribution of
authority, rewards, grouping, evaluation, time allocation. Data from
Ames's long-term project show that the mastery climate of classrooms
is increased when teachers implement these features during an academic year. These features also influence children's interest in learning, use of effective learning strategies, attitudes toward learning, and
perceived abilities. This type of intervention holds important promise
for educators who wish to foster a productive classroom environment.

CONCLUSION AND A LOOK FORWARD

Research on student perceptions is an active area and we can anticipate that research will continue to examine the variables that influence perceptions and the effects of perceptions in educational settings. In the remainder of this chapter I present some suggestions for future research. Being associated with this project for several months helped to clarify my thinking on the role of student perceptions in education. These suggestions derive from the recommendations discussed by the chapter authors and from my beliefs about topics that need to be addressed.

Student Behaviors

In much of the research summarized in these chapters investigators assessed student perceptions and related these to such measures as achievement, goals, and intentions to engage in activities or use strategies. These findings are informative and contribute to our understanding of the role of perceptions in educational settings. I recommend, however, that more researchers investigate how well perceptions translate into actual classroom behaviors. For example, researchers might examine to what extent students who report that they intend to use a particular strategy actually employ it while learning.

Such data can be collected by observing students in class, videotaping them as they work on tasks, using *think-aloud* protocols in which students verbalize aloud as they work on tasks, and asking teachers to rate students on frequency of strategy use. Investigators also might conduct experimental studies where they attempt to alter students' perceptions and see whether there are changes in behaviors, and longitudinal studies in which students are followed over time to assess the stability of their perceptions and determine when perceptions are most susceptible to change. We might draw teachers into the research process and have them implement treatments designed to affect students' perceptions and behaviors. Such studies sacrifice some experimental control but provide a wealth of knowledge on the operation of student perceptions.

Theory Development

Weiner (1990) noted that the large, formal theories that once dominanted the field of motivation (e.g., operant conditioning, Hull's systematic behavior theory) have been replaced by smaller scale cognitive theories emphasizing such interrelated constructs as self-efficacy, attributions, perceived control, and goals. Theorists typically hypothesize that these latter constructs are related, although how they are related often is not clearly specified. Weiner contended that, "The lack of theoretical elaboration reduces both the generality and the precision of these intertwined approaches" (p. 620).

The same issue is applicable to theories concerning student perceptions. The chapters in this volume represent such cognitive theoretical approaches as attribution theory, social cognitive theory, and goal theory. I am not calling for a return to global theorizing, which has its own set of problems; rather, I am recommending that investigators pay more attention to the generality of their theoretical ideas. In this regard, investigators should continue integrating constructs and testing integrated models in different contexts to determine their usefulness for explaining achievement behaviors.

Emotion

A third research direction is to explore the links between students' perceptions and emotions in achievement settings. Although many theoretical perspectives on student perceptions stress the role of emotion in achievement situations, little educational research is examining these links.

Weiner (1990) recommended research investigating the interrelationship of cognition, emotion, and motivation. I extend this recommendation to include exploring the relation of emotion to classroom learning and achievement. The research methodologies described in this book could be adapted to include affective variables, and the findings would have important implications for interventions designed to foster student learning and motivation.

Research Methods

These chapters highlight some methodological issues that need to be addressed. Many researchers have developed instruments specific to the domains being studied. At a minimum, researchers should report reliability and validity data. It also would be useful to include copies of instruments as appendixes to articles (for an example see Pintrich & De Groot, 1990).

We also need to consider alternative methods of data collection. Quantitative measures might be broadened from reliance on numerical scales to include qualitative indexes: Subjects could describe their perceptions in response to different scenarios. Rather than relying on self-report measures and relating these to outcomes in short-term studies, we could conduct longitudinal studies, case studies, and oral histories. Although such studies might include fewer subjects, they would yield rich data sources for examining the role of student perceptions in academic settings.

A Final Word

In this chapter I have provided readers with background information on student perceptions in educationally relevant research, along with an organizational framework and summary comments on the chapters in this volume. I hope this framework highlights the distinct features of chapters and their relationships to other chapters. As I noted at the outset, the contributors differ in many ways, but they share the belief that student perceptions are influenced by many factors and have diverse effects in educational settings. The scope and diversity of these chapters promise exciting research developments in the next several years.

ACKNOWLEDGMENT

I wish to thank Judith L. Meece for her helpful comments on an earlier draft of this chapter.

REFERENCES

Atkinson, J. W. (1957). Motivational determinants of risk-taking behavior. *Psychological Review, 64,* 359–372.

Atkinson, R. C., & Shiffrin, R. M. (1968). Human memory: A proposed system and its control processes. In K. W. Spence & J. T. Spence (Eds.), *The psychology of learning and motivation: Advances in research and theory* (Vol. 2, pp. 89–195). New York: Academic Press.

Bandura, A. (1969). *Principles of behavior modification.* New York: Holt, Rinehart & Winston.

Bandura, A. (1986). *Social foundations of thought and action: A social cognitive theory.* Englewood Cliffs, NJ: Prentice-Hall.

Borkowski, J. G. (1985). Signs of intelligence: Strategy generalization and metacognition. In S. Yussen (Ed.), *The growth of reflection in children* (pp. 105–144). New York: Academic Press.

Brewer, W. F. (1974). There is no convincing evidence for operant or classical conditioning in adult humans. In W. B. Weimer & D. S. Palermo (Eds.), *Cognition and the symbolic processes* (pp. 1–42). Hillsdale, NJ: Lawrence Erlbaum Associates.

Brophy, J., & Good, T. (1974). *Teacher-student relationships: Causes and consequences.* New York: Holt, Rinehart & Winston.

Brophy, J., & Good, T. (1986). Teacher behavior and student achievement. In M. C. Wittrock (Ed.), *Handbook of research on teaching* (3rd ed., pp. 328–375). New York: Macmillan.

Eccles, J. S., Adler, T., Futterman, R., Goff, S., Kaczala, C., Meece, J., & Midgley, C. (1983). Expectancies, values, and academic behavior. In J. T. Spence (Ed.), *Achievement and achievement motives* (pp. 75–146). San Francisco: Freeman.

Ericsson, K. A., & Simon, H. A. (1980). Verbal reports as data. *Psychological Review, 87,* 215–251.

Flavell, J. H. (1985). *Cognitive development* (2nd ed.). Englewood Cliffs, NJ: Prentice-Hall.

Gage, N. L. (1963). *Handbook of research on teaching.* Chicago: Rand McNally.

Hansford, B. C., & Hattie, J. A. (1982). The relationship between self and achievement/performance measures. *Review of Educational Research, 52,* 123–142.

Harter, S., & Connell, R. (1984). A model of children's achievement and related self-perceptions of competence, control, and motivational orientation. In J. Nicholls (Ed.), *Advances in motivation and achievement* (Vol. 3, pp. 219–250). New York: JAI Press.

Hartup, W. W. (1978). Children and their friends. In H. McGurk (Ed.), *Issues in childhood social development* (pp. 130–170). London: Methuen.

Hull, C. L. (1943). *Principles of behavior: An introduction to behavior theory.* New York: Appleton-Century-Crofts.

Kelley, H. H., & Michela, J. (1980). Attribution theory and research. *Annual Review of Psychology, 31,* 457–501.

Khan, S. B., & Weiss, J. (1973). The teaching of affective responses. In R. M. W. Travers (Ed.), *Second handbook of research on teaching* (pp. 759–804). Chicago: Rand McNally.

Kohler, W. (1959). *Gestalt psychology: An introduction to new concepts in modern psychology.* New York: New American Library. (Original work published 1947)

Lewin, K., Dembo, T., Festinger, L., & Sears, P. S. (1944). Level of aspiration. In J. McV. Hunt (Ed.), *Personality and the behavior disorders* (Vol. 1, pp. 333–378). New York: Ronald Press.

Marsh, H. W., & Shavelson, R. (1985). Self-concept: Its multifaceted, hierarchical structure. *Educational Psychologist, 20,* 107–123.

Meece, J. L., Parsons, J. E., Kaczala, C. M., Goff, S. B., & Futterman, R. (1982). Sex differences in math achievement: Toward a model of academic choice. *Psychological Bulletin, 91,* 324–348.

Mueller, C. G. (1979). Some origins of psychology as a science. *Annual Review of Psychology, 30,* 9–29.

Nisbett, R. E., & Wilson, T. D. (1977). Telling more than we can know: Verbal reports on mental processes. *Psychological Review, 84,* 231–259.

Pintrich, P. R., Cross, D. R., Kozma, R. B., & McKeachie, W. J. (1986). Instructional psychology. *Annual Review of Psychology, 37,* 611–651.

Pintrich, P. R., & De Groot, E. V. (1990). Motivational and self-regulated learning components of classroom academic performance. *Journal of Educational Psychology, 82,* 33–40.

Pressley, M., Woloshyn, V., Lysynchuk, L. M., Martin, V., Wood, E., & Willoughby, T. (1990). A primer of research on cognitive strategy instruction: The important issues and how to address them. *Educational Psychology Review, 2,* 1–58.

Rescorla, R. A. (1972). Informational variables in conditioning. In G. H. Bower (Ed.), *The psychology of learning and motivation* (Vol. 6, pp. 1–46). New York: Academic Press.

Rotter, J. B. (1966). Generalized expectancies for internal versus external control of reinforcement. *Psychological Monographs, 80* (Whole No. 609).

Schunk, D. H. (1989). Self-efficacy and cognitive skill learning. In C. Ames & R. Ames (Eds.), *Research on motivation in education. Vol. 3: Goals and cognitions* (pp. 13–44). San Diego: Academic Press.

Schunk, D. H. (1991). *Learning theories: An educational perspective.* New York: Merrill.

Seligman, M. E. P. (1975). *Helplessness: On depression, development, and death.* San Francisco: Freeman.

Shavelson, R. J., & Bolus, R. (1982). Self-concept: The interplay of theory and methods. *Journal of Educational Psychology, 74,* 3–17.

Shuell, T. J. (1986). Cognitive conceptions of learning. *Review of Educational Research, 56,* 411–436.

Skinner, B. F. (1953). *Science and human behavior.* New York: The Free Press.

Skinner, E. A., Wellborn, J. G., & Connell, J. P. (1990). What it takes to do well in school and whether I've got it: A process model of perceived control and children's engagement and achievement in school. *Journal of Educational Psychology, 82,* 22–32.

Stern, G. G. (1963). Measuring noncognitive variables in research in teaching. In N. L. Gage (Ed.), *Handbook of research on teaching* (pp. 398–447). Chicago: Rand McNally.

Stipek, D. J., & Mac Iver, D. (1989). Developmental change in children's assessment of intellectual competence. *Child Development, 60,* 521–538.

Tolman, E. C., & Honzik, C. H. (1930). Introduction and removal of reward, and maze performance in rats. *University of California Publications in Psychology, 4,* 257–275.

Travers, R. M. W. (1973). *Second handbook of research on teaching.* Chicago: Rand McNally.

Watson, J. B. (1914). *Behavior: An introduction to comparative psychology.* New York: Henry Holt.

Weiner, B. (1979). A theory of motivation for some classroom experiences. *Journal of Educational Psychology, 71,* 3–25.

Weiner, B. (1985). *Human motivation.* New York: Springer-Verlag.

Weiner, B. (1990). History of motivational research in education. *Journal of Educational Psychology, 82,* 616–622.

Weinstein, C. E., & Mayer, R. E. (1986). The teaching of learning strategies. In M. C. Wittrock (Ed.), *Handbook of research on teaching* (3rd ed., pp. 315–327). New York: Macmillan.

Winne, P. H. (1985). Cognitive processing in the classroom. In T. Husen & T. N. Postlethwaite (Eds.), *The international encyclopedia of education* (Vol. 2, pp. 795–808). Oxford, England: Pergamon.

Wittrock, M. C. (1986a). *Handbook of research on teaching* (3rd ed.). New York: Macmillan.

Wittrock, M. C. (1986b). Students' thought processes. In M. C. Wittrock (Ed.), *Handbook of research on teaching* (3rd ed., pp. 297–314). New York: Macmillan.

Wylie, R. C. (1961). *The self-concept. Vol. 1: A review of methodological considerations and measuring instruments.* Lincoln, NE: University of Nebraska Press.

Wylie, R. C. (1979). *The self-concept. Vol. 2: Theory and research on selected topics.* Lincoln, NE: University of Nebraska Press.

Zimmerman, B. J. (1989). Models of self-regulated learning and academic achievement. In B. J. Zimmerman & D. H. Schunk (Eds.), *Self-regulated learning and academic achievement: Theory, research, and practice* (pp. 1–25). New York: Springer-Verlag.

2

The Validity of Students' Self-Reports as Measures of Performance Affecting Self-Appraisals

AVI ASSOR
Ben-Gurion University

JAMES P. CONNELL
University of Rochester

Students' appraisals of their scholastic competence and efficacy are assumed by many theorists to be major determinants of achievement motivation and behavior (cf. Bandura, 1977, 1983; Covington & Beery, 1976; Deci & Ryan, 1985; Dweck & Elliot, 1983; Harter, 1985; Schunk, 1989, 1990; Skinner, Wellborn, & Connell, 1990). Yet, the measurement of self-appraisals has long been viewed as problematic, particularly in children (Arkin, 1980; Bandura, 1983; Nisbett & Wilson, 1977; Wilson, 1985; Wylie, 1974, 1979). One major concern is that the self-reported appraisals provided by students in interviews or on questionnaire instruments are not the same appraisals that affect their performance (i.e., the internal appraisals that are accessed or activated before and during achievement activities). These critics caution that students' self-reports may be a random product of deficient self-knowledge (see Wilson, 1985) or, more problematically, a product of systematic bias due to impression and emotion management efforts (Schlenker, 1980; Schneider & Turkat, 1975). Thus, it is argued that students' reports of their competence and efficacy are not valid indicators of students' performance affecting self-appraisals (PASAs).

Given the theoretical centrality of PASAs such as perceived efficacy and perceived competence in theoretical models in developmental, social, and educational psychology (cf. contributors in this volume), the issue of whether student self-report measures of PASAs are valid or not is of obvious relevance. This chapter seeks to address this issue in

25

three ways. First, we attempt to define criteria for assessing the validity of measures of performance affecting self-appraisals. Specifically, we use a theoretical framework (Connell, 1990) to specify what we should and should not expect students' self-reports to predict if indeed they are valid. Second, we review existing evidence for the validity of children's and adolescents' self-reports of academic competence and efficacy as measures of performance affecting self-appraisals. We survey our own and others' findings that relate student self-reports of perceived competence and efficacy to subsequent achievement-related behaviors (including engagement in academic work and measures of classroom and test performance). In this review, we also draw heavily on our recent research on the issues of accuracy and bias in self-evaluation (Assor & Connell, in prep.; Assor Flum, & Meir, 1989; Assor, Ilardi, & Lin, in prep.; Assor & Nadav, in prep.; Assor, Orr, & Priel, 1989; Assor, Tzelogov, Thein, Ilardi, & Connell, 1990; Connell & Ilardi, 1987; Hagay, 1989). We conclude from this review that self-reported appraisals of competence and efficacy are in fact valid measures of performance affecting self-appraisals in the academic domain. Finally, we suggest ways to obtain more valid self-report measures of children's PASAs.

VALIDITY OF PERFORMANCE AFFECTING SELF-APPRAISALS: DEFINITIONS AND THEORETICAL CONSIDERATIONS

We define PASAs as cognitive, emotional, and perceptual appraisals of self that are accessed or activated before and during achievement activities. These PASAs can be in relation to a particular activity (doing a math problem) or a particular set of activities (school work). In this chapter we restrict ourselves to self-appraisals of competence or efficacy in the academic domain. Competence-related PASAs in this domain are defined as perceptions of one's capacity to achieve desired academic outcomes and avoid negative academic outcomes. For example, "can I do this task?", "can I get good grades?". According to a theoretical framework derived from Connell (1990), these appraisals of perceived efficacy or competence directly affect the degree and quality of engagement and disaffection in the achievement-related activity. According to Connell (1990), engagement refers to patterns of behaviors, emotions, and orientations that reflect commitment to and acceptance of the goals of the enterprise, in this case schooling. The model also specifies that PASAs indirectly affect student performance (such as grades and achievement test scores), but only to the extent that these measures are associated with the degree and quality of the student's engagement in the activity. By defining particular sets of PASAs (e.g., those associated with perceived competence or efficacy) and by specifying their direct and indirect relations to particular consequences (e.g., engagement and academic performance, respectively) we avoid the looming tautology that PASAs are only identifiable once you know they affect performance.

In our definition, PASAs are restricted to appraisals of self in relation to the activity. Appraisals other than PASAs also affect school performance; for example, children's appraisals of what the teacher said to do in order to solve a math problem will presumably affect how children do the math problem. Appraisals such as these would not be included in our definition of PASAs because they have no direct reference to the self and thus, according to the theoretical model, are not expected to regulate the child's engagement or disaffection with the activity. However, if the child's appraisal of the teachers instruction is followed by appraisals such as "I can't do that!" or "I don't know what she's talking about!", these appraisals would be included in our definition of PASAs. These latter appraisals are predicted to affect the child's degree and quality of engagement in the activity: (a) because they involve appraisals of self, and (b) because they refer to the child's experience of competence (unable to do . . ., confused . . .). Whether or not these appraisals actually affect the child's engagement (behavior, emotion, or orientation) is an empirical question. One major benefit of using the theoretical model is that it allows us to make empirical predictions about the role of PASAs in regulating student engagement and performance.

The theoretical model also puts constraints on what should be expected when attempting to validate self-reports by relating them to academic performance. Specifically, to the extent that engagement versus disaffection does not affect assessed performance, the prediction of performance assessments by self-reports of perceived competence will be attenuated—not due to the invalidity of the self-reports but due to the lack of linkage between the activity that PASAs are thought to regulate (engagement vs. disaffection) and the culturally defined assessment of educational performance.

We also constrain our definitions of what constitutes a valid measure of PASAs when we recognize that by focusing on a single set of PASAs, such as those related to perceived competence or efficacy, we are ignoring other sets of PASAs that may be equally predictive of performance. For example, in the full Connell (1990) model, three sets of what he called self-system processes are specified. In addition to perceived competence, self-appraisals of autonomy and relatedness are also hypothesized to regulate student engagement in school and to predict academic performance through their relations to engagement. Thus, according to the model, the indirect effect of self-reported perceived competence on educational performance is an attenuated estimate of the total indirect effect of PASAs on educational performance because the two other sets of PASAs are omitted.

Consistent with the Connell (1990) model, many other theories of achievement motivation and behavior also assume that students' appraisals of their academic competence or efficacy influence variables included under the broader construct of engagement (Bandura, 1977, 1983; Covington & Beery, 1976; Deci & Ryan, 1985; Dweck & Elliot, 1983; Eccles, 1983; Harter & Connell, 1984; Meece, Blumenthal, & Hoyle, 1988; Meece, Wigfield, & Eccles, 1990; Schunk, 1989, 1990; Skinner et al., 1990; Zimmerman & Martinez-Pons, 1990). These variables include degree of persistence, effort, and engagement with the task, strategies of regulating one's learning, and ways of responding to obstacles and failures. Many of these same theorists also assume that self-appraisals influence the acquisition of skills, knowledge, and subsequent achievement through a variety of mediating processes (Eccles, 1983; Meece et al., 1988, 1990; Schunk, 1989, 1990; Skinner et al., 1990; Zimmerman & Martinez-Pons, 1990) and some hypothesize that self-appraisals of competence and efficacy are not the only, or even the major, cognitive-affective process influencing achievement-related behaviors. These other constructs, such as the perceived value (importance) of the relevant task or achievement domain, the types of achievement goals, naive theories of intelligence, schema of effort-ability relations, and locus of causality could all be considered PASAs by our definition.

POTENTIAL SOURCES OF INVALIDITY IN CHILDREN'S SELF-REPORTS

Given these qualifying conditions on what we might expect from valid measures of PASAs, we can then proceed to specify potential sources of invalidity in children's self-reports of perceived competence and efficacy. As stated earlier, invalidity occurs when what subjects report regarding their perceptions of competence or efficacy is not the same as the appraisal they make at the time they are engaging in achievement-related activity.

One potential source of invalidity is that subjects may not be able to accurately assess their own competence or efficacy. This threat to valid assessment of PASAs is clearly more serious in younger and less cognitively able subjects who may need to rely on local and proximal cues to activate and calibrate the appraisal process (Marsh, 1990; Morse & Gergen, 1970; Suls & Mullen, 1982). Bandura (1983) stated that young children's self-appraisals are apt to be heavily dependent on immediate and salient outcomes and hence will tend to be relatively unstable. The second potential source of invalidity is when subjects are consciously or unconsciously distorting information regarding their competence as a function of needs to maintain or enhance esteem in their own or others' eyes (Connell & Ilardi, 1987) or to manage impressions being made on self or others.

If these two sources of invalidity are at work what are the empirical consequences? If subjects are not able to appraise their own competence or efficacy without a lot of contextual support then we would expect self-reports of these appraisals, in the absence of rich contextual cues, to show considerable intra-individual lability and low inter-individual stability over time. If, on the other hand, a systematic bias is at work we might expect it to be persistent over time and thus contribute to greater stability of inter-individual differences among students. In either case, both sources of invalidity would be expected to attenuate the relations of self-reports of perceived efficacy to engagement in academic tasks and academic performance.

In the next section of the chapter we review the status of empirical relations among self-reports of competence and efficacy and student engagement and performance. The purpose of this review is to see whether the empirical findings more generally conform to a pattern suggesting invalidity or validity of children's and adolescents' self-reports as measures of their performance affecting self-appraisals of competence and efficacy.

EMPIRICAL EVIDENCE FOR THE VALIDITY OF SELF-REPORTS

Stability

Research with adults suggests that people are often unable "to tell what they know about themselves" (Arkin, 1980; Nisbett & Wilson, 1977; Wilson, 1985). Work with children suggests that children are often unable to verbalize and describe the ideas and principles directing their decisions and behavior (Bearison & Isaac, 1975). Young children who may possess fairly stable PASAs, may be unable to describe these appraisals accurately, because, in part, their self-reports of these appraisals are strongly influenced by recent and salient environmental cues (Bandura, 1983). As stated earlier, if subjects are not cognitively able to generate self-reports that reflect PASAs, we should see low levels of inter-individual stability as a function of the random or highly context-dependent nature of these self-reports.

Despite these less than sanguine views of children's self-reports, results up to this point suggest that if we confine ourselves to looking at stability over several months, beginning in the third or fourth grade, moderate levels of inter-individual stability in these self-reports exist (Harter, 1982; Rholes, Jones, & Wade, 1988; Rholes & Ruble, 1984). According to Rholes et al. (1988), beginning in middle elementary school, most children actually begin to view their behaviors as reflecting general stable traits. Research by Harter (1982) and Connell (1985) has shown that, beginning in the third or fourth grade, children's self-appraisals of their academic competence and perceived control show moderate correlations over periods of months and even years.

The self-appraisals of young children tend to be much less stable, and the concept of a general, stable trait is merely nascent in young children's thinking. Yet, when the self-appraisals of young children are measured carefully, with special attention to the limitations and demands imposed by children's age, some stability can be demonstrated (Eder, 1990).

The findings of moderate stability of self-reported appraisals of competence and efficacy make it less plausible that children cannot access and report PASAs. However, the degree to which capacity constraints undermine the validity of students' self-reports can best be tested by examining whether children's self-reports of perceived efficacy and competence show relations to subsequent achievement behavior. We now turn to this issue.

Do self-reports of efficacy and competence predict subsequent engagement and performance? Before reviewing the empirical evidence on this issue, a caveat is required. In the earlier discussion of the theoretical constraints on establishing criteria for validity of self-reported appraisals, two specific issues were left unresolved. First, we still need to know what magnitude of prediction we should expect in order to be confident that our self-report measure is indeed a valid indicator of PASAs. Second, we need to know whether and how we can increase our confidence in these self-reported appraisals by putting further demands on their relations with academic engagement and school performance.

With respect to the magnitude issue, the degree of predictive validity is the degree to which the observed strength of the relationship approaches the theoretically expected magnitude. As most theories do not presently specify expected magnitudes of these relations, specific estimation of *degree* of validity is not possible. However, what we can do is decrease the plausibility that our measures of PASAs are *in*valid by establishing their empirical relations to academic engagement and school performance across developmental periods, across student populations, and across different measures of PASAs, engagement, and student performance.

The second issue is conceptually more difficult. It is our view that once bivariate predictive relations (simple correlations) are established between self-reported appraisals and academic engagement and performance, they should then be embedded in theoretically meaningful networks of other constructs and examined longitudinally. Appropriate statistical tests should then be performed to test for relations between the self-reported appraisals and their designated outcome variables when these other variables are included in longitudinal models. The simplest example of such a refined test of validity is to ask whether *change* in self-reported appraisals is associated with *subsequent change* in engagement and performance (e.g., Sheirer & Kraut, 1979). Typically, this question is addressed by partialling earlier measures of engagement or performance from intervening self-reported appraisals and then asking whether the self-reported appraisals still predict future engagement and performance (i.e., a semi-partial correlation of self-reports with academic engagement and performance). (Other more direct approaches to answering this question are also available, see Connell & Skinner, 1990, for descriptions of how "growth curve analysis" can be used to address these issues.)

Data bearing both on the simple bivariate correlations and the semi-partial correlations between self-reported perceived efficacy and competence and subsequent academic engagement and student performance are presented in the next section of the chapter.

Correlations Between Self-Reports and Future Engagement and Performance

Barbara M. Byrne (1984) reviewed evidence concerning general and academic self-concepts as predictors of future academic achievement. The review shows that, in general, self-judgments of competence (particularly academic competence) are positively and significantly related to future achievement. Although most of the research focused on elementary and high school students, studies by Wattenford and Clifford (1964) and Lamy (1965) show that self-perceptions measured in kindergarten can predict reading achievement a year or two later.

Table 2.1 summarizes the findings of studies examining the effects

Table 2.1

Studies Examining Effects of Self-Reported Academic Competence on Later Engagement and Performance

Study	Grade Level	Sample Size	Measure of Self-Reported Competence	Later Engagement and Performance Measures			
				Preferred Difficulty Level	Course Enrollment Plans	Persistence and Engagement	Grades and Achievement Test Scores
Bierer (1981), cited in Harter & Pike (1984)	1–2	Unknown	Perceived cognitive competence	$r = 42^{**}$			
Harter (1979), cited in Harter (1982)	6	$n = 49$	Perceived cognitive competence	$t = 3.6^{**}$			
Eccles (1983)	5–12	$n = 668$	Self-concept of math ability		$r = .35^{**}$ with intention to take more math a year later	$r = .39^{**}$ with math grade a year later	
Newman (1984)	2, 5, and 10	$n = 75$	One item self-rating on math ability				$r_{2,5} = .24$ (self-concept in second grade with achievement test in fifth (grade) $r_{5,10} = .45^{*}$ to $.51^{*}$
Meece et al. (1988)	5–6	$n = 275$	Perceived cognitive competence Harter (1982)			$r = .23^{***}$ with effort to attain mastery $r = -.22^{***}$ with avoidance of work	

Chapman (1988)	6–7	$n = 149$ (78 learning disabled [LD]; 71 non-LD)	Perception of ability scale for students (70-item scale)	$r = -.26^{***}$ with superficial engagement $r = +.16^{**}$ with active engagement $r_1 = .60^{**}$ $r_2 = .64^{**}$ with grades 9 and 21 months later, respectively (NLD) $r_1 = .42^{**}$ $r_2 = .44^{**}$ with grades 9 and 21 months later (LD)
Assor, Ilardi, & Lin (in prep.)	High school	$n = 1,422$	Capacity to complete college (CCC)	$r = .48^{***}$ with achievement test score 2 years later
Pokay & Blumenfeld (1990)	High school (80% in 10th grade)	$n = 283$	Algebra or geometry self-concept (ASC or GSC)	$r = .38^{***}$ ASC with geometry Test 1 $r = .44^{***}$ ASC with geometry Test 2 $r = .62^{***}$ GSC with geometry Test 2
Meece et al. (1990)	7–9	$n = 250$	Math ability perception scale (Eccles et al., 1986)	$r = .33^{***}$ to $.41^{***}$ with final math grade

*$p < .05$; **$p < .01$; ***$p < .001$.

of self-reported appraisals of academic competence on later engagement and performance. Only studies conducted since 1984 that were
not included in Byrne's (1984) review are presented. In most of the
studies, the outcome measures were assessed at least half a semester
after the self-report measure. In the two large-scale studies (Assor,
Ilardi, & Lin, in prep.; Eccles, 1983) outcomes were assessed 1 and 2
years later, respectively.

The data summarized in Table 2.1 clearly support the notion that
self-reported appraisals of academic competence and efficacy have
significant, positive, and linear relations to future achievement-related
behaviors and performance.

Alexander and Entwistle (1988) did find that, for 5- to 8-year-olds,
self-reported expectations of future success in school (as measured by
a scale of two to three items) were rather weak predictors of subsequent
academic success. However, these findings were not included in Table
2.1 because the self-report variable was not perceived competence or
efficacy. As pointed out by Bandura (1977), Meece et al. (1990), and
Dweck and Elliot (1983), expectancies of success are influenced by
other factors in addition to perceived competence or efficacy, and
therefore cannot be equated with these constructs.

Given that Table 2.1 presents only one study that supports the
validity of self-reported appraisals of competence in first and second
graders (Harter & Pike, 1984), and in view of the well-known positivity
bias of young children, it seems safe to conclude that self-reports of
competence and efficacy can be viewed as reasonably valid measures
of PASAs for children 9–10 years and older.

The second, more demanding criterion for establishing the validity
of self-reported appraisals as measures of PASA is the detection of a
significant positive semi-partial correlation between self-reports of
academic competence and efficacy and measures of future engagement and performance when earlier measures of these outcome
variables are statistically controlled. It should be noted that Byrne's
(1984) review, although supporting the presence of simple correlations between self-reports and outcomes, does not directly address the
second criterion. Table 2.2 summarizes studies that controlled for the
effect of earlier academic achievement in predicting future engagement or performance from intervening self-reports of academic
competence.

Table 2.2 reveals that in five of the six studies reported, self-reported
appraisals of acadmic competence and efficacy had direct or indirect
effects on future achievement and on enrollment plans. In four of these
six studies, self-reported appraisals had a significant direct effect on

future performance when differences in earlier achievement were removed. Only in one study (Meece et al., 1990) was the effect indirect. The lack of direct effect in this particular case may be because the regression procedure controlled not only for earlier achievement, but also for expectancies, importance, and anxiety. At least two of these variables (importance and anxiety) are conceptually related to our definition of engagement, so it is not surprising that when they are controlled for, no direct effect of self-reports on performance is obtained.

The negative findings reported by Newman (1984) suggest that, when the second criterion for the validity of self-reports is applied, the support for the validity of self-reports is less consistent. However, because of the large time gap between measurements (3 and 5 year differences), the application of this criterion may be too stringent. As noted previously, earlier self-reported appraisals can continue to be valid indicators of later PASAs over time only if the PASAs themselves remain stable. The expectation that comparative self-concept of math (PASA) will remain stable from Grade 2 to Grade 5 or from Grade 5 to Grade 10 (across different educational contexts) may be unrealistic. In fact, Connell and Furman (1984) reported that the stability of children's self-reported appraisals of their perceived control over academic outcomes is lower across educational transitions (e.g., from elementary to junior high school) than it is across the same length of time when a transition is not present (e.g., from fourth to sixth grade). The results of Newman (1984) and Connell and Furman (1984) suggest that the time span and the stability (or instability) of educational contexts are important factors to consider when constructing longitudinal models of how self-report measures of PASAs influence later engagement and performance.

Finally, the results of the Assor, Ilardi, and Lin study based on the High School and Beyond national database reveal significant partial correlations between self-reported appraisals of competence early in high school and subsequent performance on achievement tests 2 years later. Connell, Clifford, and Crichlow (1992) reported similar findings with a sample of African-American urban adolescents. The Assor, Ilardi, and Lin study included statistical controls on the student self-reports not only for early achievement test performance but also for parents' evaluations of students' competence and students' grades in school.

To summarize, the findings presented in Table 2.2 indicate that, based on our second validity criterion, self-reported appraisals of academic competence can be viewed as valid measures of PASAs.

Table 2.2

Studies Examining Effects of Self-Reported Academic Competence on Future Engagement and Performance: Earlier Ahievement Statistically Controlled

Study	Grade Level	Sample Size	Future Engagement and Performance Measures	
			Enrollment in difficult courses	Grades or scores on Achievement tests
Eccles (1983)	5–12	$n = 156$	Beta = .41** with intention to take math, controlling for math achievement	Beta significant at p < .02 with math grades 2 years later, controlling for math achievement and other variables.
Newman (1984)	2, 5, 10	$n = 75$		Beta predicting math achievement 3–5 years later not significant.
Chapman (1988)	6–7	$n = 149$		Self-concept with next year's grades, controlling for present year's grades. Beta(non-L.D.) = .39** Beta(L.D.) = .22*
Meece et al. (1990)	7–9	$n = 250$	Effect of self-concept (SC) in Year 1 on enrollment intentions (EI) in Year 2 mediated by importance of math (IMP) in Year 2. Beta$_{(SC \rightarrow IMP)}$ = .39* Beta$_{(IMP \rightarrow EI)}$ = .49*	Effect of SC Year 1 & on grades in Year 2 is mediated by expectancies in Year 2 (EXP) Beta$_{(SC \rightarrow EXP)}$ = .31* Beta$_{(EXP \rightarrow GR)}$ = .50*
Pokay & Blumenfield (1990)	High school	$n = 283$		Beta$_{GSC \rightarrow Geometry\ GR}$ = .37* (controlling for earlier geometry and algebra grades)
Assor, Ilardi, & Lin (in prep.)	High school	$n = 1,422$		Beta = .13*** (CCC → ACH2; controlling for AHC1) Beta = .08** (CCC → ACH2; controlling for ACH1, Grades 1 and parent perception of ability 1)

*p < .05; **p < .01; ***p < .001.

Validity of Inaccurate (Biased) Self-Reports of Competence and Efficacy

Processes in which self-descriptions are used to manipulate others' perceptions or expectations and one's own mood and emotions have received considerable attention in the psychological literature. These processes have been described using the terms *impression management* (Schlenker, 1980), *tactical self-presentation* (Jones & Pittman, 1982; Schneider & Turkat, 1975), *self-enhancement* (Greenberg & Pyszczynski, 1985; Shrauger, 1975; Wylie, 1979), *security operations* (Sullivan, 1953), and *wishful thinking and confusion between real and ideal self* (Harter & Pike, 1984; Stipek, 1984). Positive and negative biases (overrating and underrating) have also been observed among elementary school children by us and other researchers (Assor et al., 1990; Connell & Ilardi, 1987; Covington & Beery, 1976; Harter, 1985; Phillips, 1984, 1987). This section of the chapter examines whether positively and negatively biased self-reports, irrespective of their functional and socioemotional antecedents, can still be considered valid assessments of PASAs. Do biased reports of competence and efficacy still predict later engagement and performance? In order to address this issue we briefly review findings from our own and our colleagues' work on discrepancies between children's reports of their perceived academic competence and their actual school performance.

Although the validity of extremely "inflated" or "deflated" self-reports as measures of PASA seems prima facae problematic, our theoretical framework allows for these self-reports to affect subsequent performance through their effects on the emotional and motivational component of engagement. From our motivational perspective, enhanced feelings of competence and efficacy, however nonveridical they may be, could increase engagement. We introduce this hypothesis in order to balance the view that bias or inaccuracy in self-report measures is by definition damaging to their validity. We now summarize a series of studies that examined relations between inflated and deflated self-reports of perceived competence and efficacy in relation to later engagement and school performance.

The empirical tests of the validity of these inflated and deflated self-reports are more complicated than either of the first two tests of validity (simple correlation and semi-partial correlations with subsequent outcome measures). These validity tests will proceed in two steps. First, we offer three possible interpretations of the inaccurate component of the discrepant self-reports, each of which has different implications for the validity of these self-reports. Next, we link each inter pretation to a predicted set of empirical relations between different degrees of discrepancy and subsequent engagement and performance.

According to the first interpretation of self-reports that diverge from objective standards, the entire inaccurate component is due to error in the measurement of PASA. The empirical prediction is that persons with inaccurate versus accurate self-appraisals should be very similar on the subsequent educational outcomes because their true score on perceived competence and efficacy (their PASA) is exactly the same. This same prediction of "no differences" would hold both for overraters and underraters.

According to the second interpretation, the entire inaccurate component of the self-reported appraisal accurately reflects the person's PASA. According to this interpretation, persons with extremely inflated or deflated self-reports access (or generate) internal self-appraisals that are much more positive or negative than the internal self-appraisals of persons whose self-reported appraisals are accurate or only moderately inflated or deflated. The empirical prediction from this interpretation is that there should be a direct linear relation between degree of discrepancy in self-reported competence appraisals and observed levels of the outcome variables, such that extreme overraters would show higher levels of engagement and performance outcomes than do "moderate overraters" or "accurate self-reporters"; and, conversely, extreme underraters would show lower levels of achievement motivation than moderate underraters or accurate reporters.

According to the third interpretation, part of the inaccurate component affects engagement and part does not, and the part that does affect engagement and performance does so in either a linear increasing or decreasing fashion depending on the direction of the bias. The "inert" part of the inaccurate component may have emotion and/or impression management effects on behaviors unrelated to engagement and performance or be pure error. The prediction from this interpretation is that extreme overraters will manifest a higher level of engagement than do accurate perceivers, but they will not necessarily show a higher level than "moderate" overraters. Extreme underraters should show a lower level of achievement and engagement than do accurate perceivers, but not necessarily lower than moderate underraters.

Evidence for the Validity of Inflated Self-Reports. Table 2.3 presents the three interpretations and the three patterns of prediction with respect to the engagement and performance variables for inflated self-reports only. These predictions are restricted to subgroups of children all of whom score equally low on earlier achievement. The importance of controlling for level of achievement when making the between group comparisons such as these is discussed at length in Assor et al. (1990).

One low achieving group includes students who rate themselves as low on academic competence and therefore can be viewed as relatively *accurate perceivers* (ACCs). The second group includes students who rate themselves as moderately competent, and because their level of actual achievement is low, they can be classified as *moderate overraters* (MORs). Members of the third group rate themselves as highly competent, and given their low achievement level, they can be viewed as a group of *extreme overraters* (EORs).

Table 2.3 also presents findings pertaining to the validity of extremely inflated self-appraisals. Table 2.3 classifies research findings as supporting one of the three possible patterns. Because the dependent measures used in these studies varied, they are listed under the column that reflects the obtained results.

Inspection of Table 2.3 shows that in three laboratory studies (Hagay, 1989; Harter, 1985) EORs did not show a higher level of preferred difficulty than did ACCs. These initial findings suggest that the inflated component of the self-reports of extreme overraters is not valid as a measure of PASA. In contrast, results of larger scale field studies by Assor and Connell (in prep.), Assor et al. (1990), and Assor, Ilardi, and Lin (in prep.) indicate that EORs perform better on an achievement test taken 2 years later, show more engagement, more internalized motivation, and more constructive coping with academic failures than do ACCs, but not MORs.

The general pattern of relations between the degree of discrepancy and the engagement and performance variables is a curvilinear pattern, with the sharpest increases in engagement and performance associated with moderate overrating and either a leveling off or a slight decrease in the outcome variables associated with extreme overrating. This pattern was first detected by Assor and his colleagues (Assor et al., 1990). Assor and Connell (in prep.) obtained the same pattern for the dependent measure of teachers' ratings of student engagement.

In formulating an overall opinion regarding the validity of extremely inflated self-reports as measures of PASA, the results obtained by Assor, Ilardi, and Lin (in prep.) are crucial. These results indicate that self-reported appraisals of competence that are positively biased (inflated) relative to multiple criteria of academic performance have a significant positive influence on achievement 2 years later! Therefore, although these self-reports did not match with the social "reality" of achievement test scores, grades, and parental evaluations, they do

Table 2.3

Predicted and Obtained Results Comparing Degrees of Overrating of Perceived Cognitive Competence on Later Engagement and Performance

Study	Grade Level	Sample Size	Predicted Relations of Accuracy Groups on Engagement & Performance		
			Inflated Component is Partially Valid	Inflated Component is Valid	Inflated Component is an Error
			MOR ≥ EOR > ACC	MOR < EOR > ACC	MOR = EOR = ACC
Hater (1985)	Middle elementary	Unknown			Preferred Difficulty
Harter (1985)	Middle elementary	Unknown			Preferred Difficulty
Hagay (1989)	Middle elementary	48			Preferred Difficulty
Assor et al. (1990)	Middle elementary	102	Internalized academic motivation Constructive coping with failure		
Assor & Connell (in prep.)	3–8	283	Internalized academic motivation Constructive coping with failure Teacher rated engagement		
Assor, Ilardi, & Lin (in prep.)	High school	1,422	Scores on achievement test taken 2 years later		

meet our criteria for being valid measures of PASAs. According to Assor, Ilardi, and Lin these "inflated" self-reports are not merely defensive reactions to low achievement, nor are they detrimental to later educational performance; on the contrary, relative to accurate appraisals, positive appraisals of efficacy in the face of below average performance appear to enhance future performance. The results of this study appear to be particularly robust for several reasons: first, the sample in this study was larger than the samples of all other studies combined; second, the outcome measure, an achievement test, was taken 2 years later; third, this is the only longitudinal study presented in Table 2.3; and finally, this study employed multiple standards to assess the degree of discrepancy in the self-reports.

Assessing the Validity of Extremely Deflated Self-Reports. Studies of how different degrees of underrating are related to subsequent engagement and performance in relatively high achieving groups show very consistent and powerful evidence for the validity self-reported appraisals of competence as measures of PASAs. In the findings of all the studies we reviewed, extreme underrating children and adolescents showed significantly lower levels of engagement and performance. In addition, studies that included a moderate underrating group showed that extreme underraters differed significantly in the expected negative direction from this group as well. These results clearly indicate that extremely deflated self-reports of academic competence should be viewed as valid measures of PASA. Two additional studies (Assor, Flum, & Musrat, in prep.; Assor & Nadav, in prep.) have shown that extreme underrating in middle elementary school children is also associated with a great deal of isolation and lack of popularity among peers, and with the inability to make ideological or occupational commitments several years later. Thus, our conclusions that extreme underrating is problematic with respect to academic outcomes can be extended to socioemotional outcomes as well (Canavan-Gumpert, Garner, & Gumpert, 1977; Covington & Beery, 1976; Phillips, 1984, 1987).

SUMMARY OF EMPIRICAL FINDINGS

Surveys of relevant research findings clearly demonstrate that, beginning in the third and fourth grade and extending through high school, in populations ranging from upper middle-class Caucasian American youth, to lower and middle-class Israeli children, to primarily poor

African-American adolescents, there is no empirical justification for viewing self-reported appraisals of academic competence and efficacy as invalid measures of performance affecting self-appraisals. Across recent studies of these variables, empirical relations between self-reports of competence and efficacy and subsequent engagement and performance outcomes were found both before and after controlling for earlier achievement scores. As a further check on the validity of students' self-reports, we examined two kinds of self-reports whose validity as measures of PASAs has often been questioned: extremely inflated and extremely deflated self-reported appraisals. Surveys of relevant research findings showed that extremely deflated self-reports can be viewed unequivocally as a valid measures of PASA across the school-age years. As for extremely inflated self-reports, this type of self-report appears to be at least partially valid beginning in junior high school.

SUGGESTIONS FOR IMPROVING THE VALIDITY OF CHILDREN'S SELF-REPORTS

Over the past 15 years of our research on children's and adolescents' self-perceptions, we and our colleagues have tried to enhance the quality of our measurement techniques. The following are some lessons we have learned about how to optimize the validity of children's self-reports.

1. Remember that when we refer to *accuracy* of self-reports we mean that we want children to tell us what they truly believe about their sense of their competence and efficacy (or autonomy, or theories of intelligence, etc.). We are not asking for a veridical assessment of their competence. "Actual performance," "academic achievement," "teachers', parents', and observers' perceptions of the child's competence" are theoretical constructs in their own right and should not be equated conceptually or operationally with children's perceived competence and efficacy. This may be an obvious point to the readers of this volume but this insight has not been incorporated fully into the broader arenas in which this research is used and, unfortunately, misused at times.

2. We need to ask young subjects questions in a way that *helps* them *understand* what we are after. The strategy of trying to hide what we are really after in our research should be left in deception studies and in projective test assessments. If we do not make it clear what information we want from child and adolescent subjects, and if we do not check

whether they understand what we want, our assessments can easily go awry. If a child does not understand the question, he or she will typically answer it anyway, and either respond randomly or make up a question to answer and then answer it. In either case accuracy is gone.

3. We should make every effort (without protesting too much) to convince our child subjects that any answer they give to our questions are acceptable as long as they are telling us what they really believe. Susan Harter's (e.g., 1982) structured alternative format is one strategy for doing so. Sets of instructions should be designed to put children at ease and should encourage children to use the full range of responses on the questions. Statements such as "there are no right or wrong answers to these questions" are helpful, as are walking through sample items like "I really like spinach" where many children will be able to endorse heartily the "negative" end of a Likert-type scale.

4. Children (like adults) want to feel valued as reporters, they want to know why we are asking them all these questions, and they want to know what we are going to do with their answers to these questions. How this information is communicated to them will depend on the purposes of the study and the developmental level of the children. But, we have found that this sharing of "what we are going to do with this stuff" is important even with young children in order for them to fully engage in the research process.

5. Administration procedures, whether group or individual, are crucial to obtaining accurate appraisals. We prefer to administer the questionnaires or interviews without a "known" adult present (no teachers, parents, or principals). In group administrations we have one person from our research team read the questions to pace the group and another person "cruise" to answer individual questions and to help assure subjects are staying on task.

6. It is important for children to know who is going to see and, more importantly, who is not going to see their responses to our interview or questionnaire assessment. We tell the children that only the computer will see their individual responses and only results from "the fifth-grade classes in lots of different schools" will be shared with teachers and parents. We use a master list of subject names and subject codes to distribute questionnaires with only the subject code on the questionnaire itself.

7. What type of scale should be used to assess these appraisals: true–false, forced choice, or Likert-type scale? How many points on a scale? There is considerable disagreement among psychometricians on most of these issues. We do not know of any saint who has actually done comparative validity studies on all of these issues. Our sense is

that Likert-type scales of 4 points do a good job with children as young as kindergarten (when supported by pictorial information as in Harter & Pike, 1984); and, that older children and adolescents continue to give good information on 4-point scales all the way through high school. Four points on a scale forces a discrimination between the first two and the second two choices (vs. leaving the middle option open) and six choices hasn't bought us any additional precision at least on our self-report measures.

8. Groups of over typical class size (> 25–30) are generally problematic for survey administration. Individual administration is more effective for earlier elementary children (K–2) and with special education children, but may be less effective for older children and adolescents. Unless we have a chance to develop a personal relationship with the older child, we find that child subjects older than 8 or so become very self-conscious when presented with survey questions by an unfamiliar adult in a one-on-one setting. Group administrations of questionnaires actually offer more anonymity and privacy and thus may generate more accurate self-reports from older children.

9. Interviews and questionnaires do not and should not be expected to yield the same information even when the questions are relatively similar. These two measurement strategies are usually confounded with individual versus group administration, but even when they are not, they typically yield different results and their cross-method correlations are not always high. Our experience is that when we are looking to get responses to structured questions, well-constructed questionnaires given in a well-monitored group setting yield better information than individually interviewing children about the same questions. When we are looking for the unexpected, or trying to generate new items, establishing a relationship with a child subject and then letting them "fly," an open-ended, individual interview is the way to go.

10. If we need to ask a lot of similar questions in order to obtain adequate estimates of internal consistency, we do it; but, we also tell the young subjects why we are doing it. Children as young as 8 years old can understand why it is important to get more than one measure of their opinions about themselves. Redundancy is also reduced by spreading out the similar items and asking the same question in different ways. Length of these questionnaires or interviews is a more serious concern. Many times, we may not even recognize that children disengage when the assessment is too long. We suggest going no more than 40 minutes in one sitting, and trying to break these sessions up with a 2–5 minute break doing something that the child subjects find entertaining (Simon Says for younger subjects, "brain teasers" for older subjects).

REFERENCES

Alexander, K. L., & Entwisle, D. R. (1988). Achievement in the first 2 years of school: Patterns and processes. *Monographs of the Society for Research in Child Development, 53.*

Arkin, R. M. (1980). Self presentation. In D. M. Wegner & R. R. Vallacher (Eds.), *The self in social psychology* (pp. 158–182). New York: Oxford University Press.

Assor, A., & Connell, J. P. (in prep.). *Over- and underrating of academic competence in children, and its relationship with academic motivation and coping.* University of Rochester, Rochester, NY.

Assor, A., Flum, H., & Meir, Y. (1987). *Correlates of extreme over- and underrating.* Paper presented at the 1987 convention of the Israeli Psychological Association (Hebrew).

Assor, A., Flum, H., & Musrat, J. (in prep.). *Extreme over- and underrating of academic competence as predictors of structure and content of self descriptions and identity formation status among pre-adolescents.* Ben Gurion University, Israel.

Assor, A., Ilardi, B., & Lin, Y. C. (in prep.). *Overrating of academic competence among American youth: Inconsequential, damaging, or beneficial?* University of Rochester, Rochester, NY.

Assor, A., & Nadav, M. (in prep.). *Over- and underrating of academic competence and its relationship with popularity among peers and perceptions of friendships.* Ben Gurion University, Israel.

Assor, A., Orr, E., & Priel, B. (1989). Correlates of over- and under-estimation of cognitive competence in kindergarten children. *Psychology in the Schools, 26,* 337–345.

Assor, A., Tzelgov, J., Thein, R., Ilardi, R., & Connell, J. P. (1990). Assessing the correlates of over- and underrating of academic competence: A conceptual clarification and a methodological proposal. *Child Development, 61,* 2085–2097.

Bandura, A. (1977). Self efficacy: Toward a unifying theory of behavioral change. *Psychological Review, 84,* 191–215

Bandura, A. (1983). Self referent thought: A developmental analysis of self efficacy. In J. H. Flavell & L. Ross (Eds.) *Social cognitive development* (pp. 200–239). Cambridge: Cambridge University Press.

Bearison, D. J., & Isaacs, L. (1975). Production deficiency in children's moral judgments. *Developmental Psychology, 11,* 732–737.

Byrne, B. M. (1984). The general/academic self concept nomological network: A review of construct validation research. *Review of Educational Research, 54,* 427–456.

Canavan-Gumpert, D., Garner, K., & Gumpert, P. (1977). *The success fearing personality.* Lexington, MA: Lexington Books.

Chapman, J. W. (1988). Cognitive-motivational characteristics and academic achievement of learning disabled children: A longitudinal study. *Journal of Educational Psychology, 80,* 357–365.

Connell, J. P. (1985). A new multidimensional measure of children's perceptions of control. *Child Development, 56,* 1018–1041.

Connell, J. P. (1990). Context, self and action: A motivational analysis of self-system processes across the life span. In D. Cicchetti & M. Beeghly (Eds.), *The self in transition: Infancy to childhood.* Chicago: University of Chicago Press.

Connell, J. P., Clifford, E., & Crichlow, W. (1992). *Why do urban students leave school? Neighborhood, family, and motivational influences.* Paper presented at Research Conference on the Urban Underclass, Chicago, IL.

Connell, J. P., & Furman, W. (1984). The study of transitions: Conceptual and methodological issues. In R. Ende & R. Harrison (Eds.). *Continuity and discontinuity in development* (pp. 153-173). New York: Plenum Press.

Connell, J. P., & Ilardi, B. C. (1987). Self system concomitants of discrepancies between children's and teachers' evaluations of academic competence. *Child Development, 58,* 1297-1307.

Connell, J. P., & Skinner, E. A. (1990). *A growth curve approach to studying trajections of children's engagement and disaffection.* Paper presented at the American Education Research Association meeting, Boston, MA.

Covington, M. C., & Beery, R. (1976). *Self worth and school learning.* New York: Holt, Rinehart & Winston.

Deci, E. L., & Ryan, R. M. (1985). *Intrinsic motivation and self determination in human behavior.* New York: Plenum.

Dweck, C. S., & Elliot, E. S. (1983). Achievement motivation. In E. M. Hetherington (Ed.), *Handbook of child psychology: Socialization, personality, and social development* (Vol. 4, pp. 643-691). New York: Wiley.

Eccles, J. (1983). Expectancies, values, and academic behaviors. In J. T. Spence (Ed.), *Achievement and achievement motives: Psychological and sociological approaches* (pp. 75-146). San Francisco: Freeman.

Eder, R. A. (1990). Uncovering young children's psychological selves: Individual and developmental differences. *Child Development, 61,* 849-863.

Greenberg, J., & Pyszczynski, T. (1985). Compensatory self inflation: A response to the threat to self regard of public failure. *Journal of Personality and Social Psychology, 49,* 273-280.

Hagay, I. (1989). *Positivity and accuracy of self evaluation as predictors of coping with academic failure in children.* Unpublished Master thesis, Ben Gurion University, Israel.

Harter, S. (1982). The perceived competence scale for children. *Child Development, 53,* 87-97.

Harter, S. (1985). Competence as a dimension of self-evaluation: Toward a comprehensive model of self-worth. In R. Leahy (Ed.), *The development of the self.* New York: Academic Press

Harter, S., & Connell, J. P. (1984). A model of children's achievement and related self perceptions of competence, control, and motivational orientation. In J. Nichols (Ed.), *Advances in motivation and achievement (Vol. 3): The development of achievement motivation.* Greenwich, CT: JAI.

Harter, S., & Pike, R. (1984). The pictorial scale of perceived competence and social acceptance for young children. *Child Development, 55,* 1969-1982.

Jones, E. E., & Pittman, T. S. (1982). Toward a general theory of strategic self presentation. In J. Suls & A. Greenwald (Eds.), *Psychological perspectives on the self* (pp. 231-262). Hillsdale, NJ: Lawrence Erlbaum Associates.

Lamy, M. W. (1965). Relationship of self perceptions of early primary children to achievement in reading. In I. J. Gordon (Ed.) *Human development: Readings in research.* Chicago: Scott, Foresman.

Marsh, H. W. (1990). Influences of internal and external frames of reference on the formation of math and English self concepts. *Journal of Educational Psychology, 82,* 107-116.

Meece, J. L., Blumenfeld, P. C., & Hoyle, R. H. (1988). Students' goal orientations and cognitive engagement in classroom activities. *Journal of Educational Psychology, 80,* 514-523.

Meece, J. L., Wigfield, A., & Eccles, J. S. (1990). Predictors of math anxiety and its influence on young adolescents' course enrollment intentions and performance in mathematics. *Journal of Educational Psychology, 82,* 60-70

Morse, S., & Gergen, K. J. (1970). Social comparison, self consistency, and the concept of self. *Journal of Personality and Social Psychology, 16,* 148-156.

Newman, R. S. (1984). Children's achievement and self evaluations in mathematics: A longitudinal study. *Journal of Educational Psychology, 76*, 857–873.

Nisbett, R. E., & Wilson, T. D. (1977). Telling more than we can know: Verbal reports on mental processes. *Psychological Review, 84*, 231–259.

Phillips, D. (1984). The illusion of incompetence among academically competent children. *Child Development, 55*, 2000–2016.

Phillips, D. (1987). Socialization of perceived academic competence among highly competent children. *Child Development, 58* (5), 1308–1320.

Pokay, P., & Blumenfeld, P. C. (1990). Predicting achievement early and late in the semester: The role of motivation and use of learning strategies. *Journal of Educational Psychology, 82*, 41–50.

Rholes, W. S., Jones, M., & Wade, C. (1988). Children's understanding of personal dispositions and its relationship to behavior. *Journal of Experimental Child Psychology, 45*, 1–17.

Rholes, W. S., & Ruble, D. (1984). Children's understanding of dispositional characteristics of others. *Child Development, 55*, 550–560.

Scheirer, M. A., & Kraut, R. E. (1979). Increasing educational achievement via self concept change. *Review of Educational Research, 49*, 131–150.

Schlenker, B. R. (1980). *Impression management: The self concept, social identity, and interpersonal relations.* Belmont, CA: Wadsworth.

Schneider, D. J., & Turkat, D. (1975). Self presentation following success or failure: Defensive self esteem models. *Journal of Personality, 43*, 127–135.

Schunk, D. H. (1989). Self efficacy and cognitive skill learning. In C. Ames & R. Ames (Eds.), *Research on motivation in education: Vol. 3. Goals and cognitions* (pp. 13–44). San Diego, CA: Academic Press.

Schunk, D. H. (1990). Introduction to the special section on motivation and efficacy. *Journal of Educational Psychology, 82*, 3–6.

Shrauger, J. S. (1975). Responses to evaluation as a function of initial self perceptions. *Psychological Bulletin, 82*, 581–596

Skinner, E. A., Wellborn, J. G., & Connell, J. P. (1990). What it takes to do well in school and whether I've got it: A process model of perceived control and children's engagement and achievement in school. *Journal of Educational Psychology, 82*, 22–32.

Stipek, D. J. (1984). Young children's performance expectations: Logical analysis or wishful thinking? In *Advances in motivation and achievement (Vol. 3): The development of achievement motivation* (pp. 33–56). Grenwich, CT: JAI.

Suls, J., & Mullen, B. (1982). From the cradle to the grave: Comparison and self evaluation across the life span. In J. Suls & A. Greenwald (Eds.), *Psychological perspectives on the self* (Vol. 2, pp. 97–125). Hillsdale, NJ: Lawrence Erlbaum Associates.

Sullivan, H. S. (1953). *The interpersonal theory of psychiatry.* New York: Norton.

Wattenford, W. W., & Clifford, C. (1964). Relation of self concept to beginning achievement in reading. *Child Development, 35*, 461–467.

Wilson, T. D. (1985). Strangers to ourselves: The origins and accuracy of beliefs about one's own mental states. In J. H. Harvey & G. Weary (Eds.), *Attribution in contemporary psychology* (pp. 9–36). New York: Academic Press.

Wylie, R. C. (1974). *The self concept* (Vol. 1). Lincoln, NE: University of Nebraska Press.

Wylie, R. C. (1979). *The self concept* (Vol. 2). Lincoln NE: University of Nebraska Press.

Zimmerman, B. J., & Martinez-Pons, M. (1990). Student differences in self regulated learning: Relating grade, sex, and giftedness to self efficacy and strategy use. *Journal of Educational Psychology, 82*, 51–59.

II

Social Perceptions

3

Friends' Influence on Adolescents' Perceptions of Themselves at School

THOMAS J. BERNDT
Purdue University

KEUNHO KEEFE
California State University, Fullerton

Many educators and social scientists have expressed concern about the influence of peers on adolescents' attitudes and behavior. In the 1970s, Bronfenbrenner (1970) argued that adolescents often conform to pressure from peers to engage in undesirable behavior. He said that "where the peer group is to a large extent autonomous—as it often is in the United States—it can exert influence in opposition to values held by adult society" (p. 189). More recently, Bishop (1989) argued that many high school students are not motivated to achieve academically, in part because they give in to peer pressure against working hard in school (see also Coleman, 1961; Steinberg & Silverberg, 1986).

The negative view of peer influence presented by Bronfenbrenner, Bishop, and other writers has often been challenged (Hartup, 1983; Kandel & Lesser, 1972). Most researchers now assume that peers can have either a negative or a positive influence on adolescents' attitudes and behavior. In particular, peers can either encourage adolescents to view their school experiences positively, or encourage them to see school as an uninteresting or hostile place. The outcomes for any specific adolescent depend on the characteristics of the peers with whom the adolescent spends most of his or her time. Those peers are usually the adolescent's close friends. Several researchers (e.g., Davies & Kandel, 1981; Epstein, 1983) have shown that adolescents whose friends perceive school positively and behave appropriately in school improve over time in their own perceptions and behavior. Conversely, adolescents whose friends dislike school or are disruptive in school decrease over time in their own adjustment to school.

There is surprisingly little research on how the characteristics of friends influence adolescents' perceptions and behavior. Researchers have more often tried to measure the outcomes of friends' influence than to examine the processes of influence. Some researchers who assume that these outcomes vary, depending on the friends an adolescent has, also assume that direct pressure (e.g., threats of punishment for nonconformity) is one way that friends influence each other. Occasionally, however, researchers have suggested that friends' influence may result from processes of observational learning or social reinforcement rather than coercive pressure (Davies & Kandel, 1981; Kandel & Andrews, 1987).

Still, most researchers assume that these various processes lead to the same result: Friends adopt ever more similar attitudes and behaviors. In other words, all the processes are linked to social-psychological theories that explain how individuals can influence each other so that they become more similar over time. In that sense, hypotheses about peer pressure, observational learning, and reinforcement all deal with the same general pathway by which friends with specific characteristics influence adolescents and vice versa.

There is another important perspective on both the outcomes of friends' influence and the processes or pathway of influence. Many theorists have suggested that close and supportive friendships have unequivocally positive effects on students' behavior and adjustment. Piaget (1932/1965) was apparently the first major theorist to advocate this perspective. He proposed that peer relationships are critical for the development of a mature morality. Later, Harry Stack Sullivan (1953) emphasized the importance of close friendships in later childhood and early adolescence for the development of self-esteem and social understanding.

More recently, many theorists have suggested that friendships or other close relationships provide support for people faced with stressful events and help them cope more effectively (e.g., Cohen & Wills, 1985; Sarason & Sarason, 1985). In short, these supportive relationships improve people's psychological adjustment. Other researchers have argued that close and harmonious relationships with peers can improve adolescents' social and academic adjustment to school (e.g., Damon, 1984; Furman & Gavin, 1989). This theoretical perspective implies that adolescents with closer and more supportive friendships should have more positive perceptions of school and their place in it. As a result, they should be more motivated to achieve and show better classroom behavior.

Hypotheses about the positive effects of friendship refer not to the characteristics of friends, as in the first pathway of influence, but to the features of their friendships. For example, Piaget (1932/1965) argued that interactions with friends have positive effects on adolescents' development when their friendships are based on mutual respect and collaboration. Sullivan (1953) proposed that friendships have positive effects on adolescents when they are highly intimate and involve a high degree of mutual support.

Some adolescents have intimate, supportive friendships based on mutual respect. Other adolescents do not. If Piaget's and Sullivan's hypotheses are correct, variations in the positive features of adolescents' friendships should be related to variations in the adolescents' psychological adjustment, and their adjustment to school in particular.

We argue that researchers should also pay attention to the negative features of adolescents' friendships. Some friendships are marred by frequent conflicts, rivalry, or other types of negative interactions. Just as friendships with positive features may have positive effects on adolescents, friendships with negative features may have negative effects on them. And although friendships with more negative features might have fewer positive features, variations in the two types of features could have different effects on the school-related perceptions of adolescents. Thus, to understand the effects of friendship—and to fully explore the second pathway of friends' influence—both the positive and the negative features of friendships must be considered.

For several years, we have used this model of two distinct pathways of influence as the basis for research on friendship and school adjustment. In this chapter, we summarize the findings of our research. We show that adolescents are influenced by their friends' characteristics, as hypotheses about the first pathway of influence imply. For example, adolescents' perceptions of school and of their own behavior in school become more similar, over time, to those of their friends. We also show that adolescents' perceptions of themselves at school are influenced by the positive and negative features of their friendships, as hypotheses about the second pathway of influence imply. Thus, hypotheses about the two pathways of influence are complementary rather than contradictory. Both pathways must be considered to fully account for the influence of friends and friendships on adolescents.

The studies that are the focus of this chapter differed in their central issues and in their research designs. Some studies dealt primarily with the first pathway of influence, or the processes by which friends with specific attitudes and behaviors influence adolescents. Other studies dealt more equally with both pathways of influence. The studies also differed greatly in techniques of measurement, ranging from interviews to direct observations to group-administered surveys. Taken together, the studies clarify the distinction between the two pathways of influence. They also suggest when friends have a positive influence, and when they have a negative influence, on adolescents' perceptions of their school experiences.

ADOLESCENTS' PERCEPTIONS OF FRIENDS' INFLUENCE

We begin with two studies in which we adopted an unusual strategy for examining questions about friends' influence (Berndt, Miller, & Park, 1989). Most previous researchers inferred the effects of friends' influence from adolescents' responses to questionnaires about their own attitudes or behaviors and their friends' attitudes or behaviors. By contrast, we asked adolescents directly about their perceptions of their friends' influence on them. Adolescents' perceptions of friends' influence are worth exploring for at least two reasons.

First, these perceptions may clarify how friends actually influence each other. Brown, Clasen, and Eicher (1986) found that adolescents' perceptions of pressure from peers were related to their reports on their actual behavior. For example, adolescents who perceived more peer pressure to engage in misconduct reported more misconduct themselves. Although adolescents' perceptions may not be entirely accurate, they may clarify both the processes and the outcomes of friends' influence.

Second, perceptions of friends' influence provide a novel perspective on adolescents' social cognition, or their interpretation of the social world. O'Brien and Bierman (1988) found an increase between middle childhood and adolescence in beliefs that peer groups influence attitudes, personal appearance, and antisocial behaviors. Thus, these researchers showed that awareness of social influences increases with age.

Our studies focused on adolescents' perceptions of their friends' influence on school-related attitudes and behaviors. Our first study included 55 Grade 7 students (26 girls and 29 boys) from a junior high school in a rural school district. Each student was interviewed individually. The students first named their best or closest friend. Then they answered questions about the friends' influence on their liking for school, their behavior in school, their effort on schoolwork, and their grades. For example, one question was "Does your friend have any effect on how much effort you put into your schoolwork?" The students answered comparable questions about their parents' influence on their attitudes and behavior in school. The interview concluded with the general question, "Of all the people you know, who do you think has the greatest effect on how well you do in school?"

Note that our questions about friends' and parents' influence were completely open-ended. They did not imply, by their very wording, that we expected affirmative answers. By contrast, Brown et al. (1986) asked adolescents how strongly friends pressured them to engage in various behaviors. O'Brien and Bierman (1988) asked adolescents to describe ways that peer groups influence adolescents. Both types of questions imply that peers exert pressure or actually do influence adolescents.

The answers of the Grade 7 students to our more open-ended questions were surprising. Most students denied that their friends had any effect on their attitudes toward school and behavior in school. Students gave a "yes" answer to only 35% of the questions about their friends' influence on them. Yet these students were not generally unwilling to acknowledge the influence of other people. They gave a "yes" answer to 60% of the questions about their parents' influence on them. And on the question about who had the greatest influence on their school performance, most students (53%) answered "parents"; only 20% named their best friend or other peers. These percentages did not differ significantly for the two genders.

Because the students' answers were inconsistent with common assumptions about peer influence in adolescence, we examined the same issues in a second study with a larger sample. The second study included 114 Grade 7 students (74 girls and 40 boys) from a junior high school in a small town. The students again were interviewed individually. This time, however, each student was asked about the influence of up to three close friends, not just one best friend. Also, students were asked whether they influenced their friends as well as vice versa. For example, they were asked "Have your friends changed your feelings about school?" and "Do you think you have changed your friends' feelings about school?"

Most importantly, students were asked to explain their answers to these questions. If they said their friends had not changed their feelings about school, or vice versa, they were asked why not. If they said their friends had changed their feelings, or vice versa, they were asked how they had done so.

As in the first study, the Grade 7 students in this study most often denied that their friends had any influence on their attitudes toward school and behavior in school. The students gave a definite "no" answer to 63% of the questions about friends' influence. They gave a definite "yes" answer to only 28% of the questions. Again, these percentages were similar for boys and for girls.

The students most often gave three types of reasons for the lack of influence of friends. These reasons reflect what might be described as three truths about the processes of peer influence.

First, students said that they and their friends not only were independent in their thinking and behavior, but also respected one another's independence. One student said "I have my own ideas and he has his, and we don't try to change each other's ideas." Such statements about friends' independence may illustrate the mutual respect that Piaget (1932/1965) ascribed to peer relationships in adolescence (see also Youniss, 1980). Mutual respect rules out the attempt to make another person believe or behave the same way you do. It certainly rules out the use of pressure to change another person's attitudes and behavior.

Ethnographic studies of peer groups in natural settings confirm that group members rarely exert overt pressure on each other (Suttles, 1968). Even decisions to engage in antisocial behavior, like vandalizing property, are rarely the result of pressure by some group members on the rest of the group. Thus, popular ideas and theoretical assumptions about the importance of coercive pressure for friends' influence are misleading.

Second, students said that they and their friends did not influence each other because both they and their friends were already positively oriented toward school. Thus, in their view, no further influence was possible. They said, for example, "He likes school, and so do I, so we can't change each other." For the moment, we leave aside the curious assumption, implicit in the student's comment, that friends' influence can only lead to more positive attitudes toward school. Instead, we want to focus on another implication of the comment. The student obviously believed that he and his friend had similar attitudes toward school.

This belief was widely shared by the students in our studies. In this study and the previous one, we asked students directly about their attitudes toward school and their perceptions of their friends' attitudes. The two types of measures were strongly correlated. In the first study, students who were more accepting of misbehavior in class perceived their friends as more accepting of misbehavior. In the second study, students who said they were more interested and involved in school also perceived their friends as more interested and involved.

The students' belief that their friends' attitudes toward school were similar to their own probably had a basis in reality. Several researchers have found moderate correlations between the self-reports of students and their friends about their attitudes toward school and performance in school (e.g., Epstein, 1983; Ide, Parkerson, Haertel, & Walberg,

1981). In our second study, we also found significant correlations between the report card grades of students and their friends. Yet the more important question is why this similarity exists.

Some years ago, Kandel (1978) noted that friends may be similar for two reasons: (a) They may have influenced each other after they became friends, so their attitudes became more similar; or (b) their attitudes may have already been similar when they became friends. Indeed, they may have selected each other as friends partly because they recognized their attitudes were similar. When the students in our study said they and their friends did not influence each other because they already shared a positive attitude toward school, they implied that they had similar attitudes when they selected each other as friends.

Third, students said that they and their friends did not influence each other's attitudes toward school because they had little interest in, or opportunities for, influencing each other. Students said, for example, that "We hardly talk about school." These responses probably reflect the true state of affairs for many adolescents. After extended observations in schools, Everhart (1983) concluded that schoolwork and the academic dimensions of the school experience are not salient issues for many adolescents. Thus, friends may not try to directly influence each other's positions on these dimensions.

Yet for each of the three truths implied by students' comments about a lack of friends' influence, there is an opposing view that may also capture part of the truth. First, adolescents' respect for each other's independence rules out overt coercive pressure. But other processes of influence may operate in friendship groups. Kelman (1958) noted that conformity need not be the result of compliance to overt pressure. Conformity may result from identification with a person or group. Kelman defined *identification* as admiration or liking for another person that makes people accept what the other person recommends. Adolescents, in particular, may be influenced by friends because they respect their friends and they tend to adopt the opinions of people they respect.

Conformity may also result from a process of internalization. According to Kelman (1958), *internalization* refers to the acceptance of others' opinions because those opinions seem to fit one's own value system. Thus, unlike identification, internalization depends more on the content of another person's opinions than on who the other person is. For example, students may be persuaded by their friends' opinions not because the opinions are those of friends, but because those opinions make sense to them.

This point relates to the second one. Adolescents may be short-sighted when they assert there is no possibility of influence because they and their friends already have positive attitudes toward school. When adolescents make this assertion, they are ignoring the possibility that their interactions with friends could anchor or strengthen their positive attitudes. Through processes of identification and internalization, interactions with friends may make adolescents feel more certain of their attitudes toward school and more resistant to changes in these attitudes.

Third, the comments that friends have no interest in, or opportunity to, influence each others' attitudes must be placed in perspective. Only a fraction of the adolescents in our study made such comments. For some adolescents, typically those most successful academically, school-related issues are of great interest and are important topics of conversation (Ball, 1981). Adolescents less interested in school may assert that they "hardly talk about school," but this assertion may actually mean that they tell each other that schoolwork is not worth talking about. Such offhand comments that denigrate the value of schooling are likely to have a negative influence on adolescents' perceptions of school. Conversations with such friends are likely to reinforce indifference toward school, even if the friends do not extensively discuss the reasons for their alienation from school.

Finally, it is important to remember that a minority of the students in both studies reported that their friends had an influence on them or vice versa. Some students in the second study described cases in which they had a positive influence on friends. They said, for example, "If they're messing around, I tell them to quit goofing off." They also described cases in which their friends had a negative influence on them. For example, "They'd start talking about how they're going to be bad in school and I'd start going along with it." The students more often reported positive influences of friends on them, or vice versa, than negative influences. This finding is consistent with the evidence of Brown et al. (1986) that adolescents perceive peers as exerting more pressure toward desirable conduct than toward misconduct.

Yet before drawing firm conclusions about the outcomes of friends' influence, we need data not based solely on adolescents' perceptions of influence attempts and their effectiveness. We need to assess the effects of interactions with friends directly. In our next study, we examined the effects of actual discussions with a friend on adolescents' motivation to do well in school.

EFFECTS OF DISCUSSIONS WITH A FRIEND

As we mentioned earlier, most previous researchers created indices of friends' influence from adolescents' responses to questionnaires administered on one or more occasions (e.g., Epstein, 1983; Kandel, 1978). The purpose of our study (Berndt, Laychak, & Park, 1990) was to examine the influence of friends directly, by seeing how a discussion with a friend influenced adolescents' decisions about how much effort to expend on schoolwork.

The study included 118 eighth graders (74 girls and 44 boys) from a county school district. The students first named their best friends and reported how much they liked each of the other students of the same gender in their grade. Using this information, we identified the friends of each student. Then we paired each student with one close friend.

Each pair of friends was randomly assigned to an experimental condition or to a control condition. Pairs in the experimental condition first completed a pretest for which they made decisions on several dilemmas related to academic achievement motivation. The following is an example:

> One of the most popular rock groups is coming to town to give one performance. You have eagerly awaited their visit and have already purchased your ticket. Then you learn that the concert is on the night before a big exam. You don't really feel prepared for the exam and you have been having difficulty with the subject. Because of other commitments, this night will be the only opportunity to see one of your favorite groups in concert. You must decide whether to go to the concert or to stay home and study.

For the pretest, each student indicated what he or she would do if faced with this decision by checking one point on an 11-point scale. On the scale, *0* represented one alternative, *5* represented *not sure,* and *10* represented the other alternative. These alternatives were later re-coded so higher scores always reflected higher achievement motivation, or more positive perceptions of the value of working hard to do well in school.

Then the pair of students discussed each dilemma. They were asked to try to agree on one decision, and all pairs did so on all dilemmas. After their discussions, all students took a posttest in which they responded to the same dilemmas again. The experimenter told students to decide for themselves how to answer the dilemmas, without considering how they had answered them before.

The pairs of students in the control condition also had a pretest and posttest on the motivation-related dilemmas. They also had a discussion between the pretest and the posttest, but their discussions focused on topics unrelated to school. They talked, for example, about where they would like to spend their summer vacation.

In analyzing the results, we first examined whether discussions with a friend affected the average scores of individual students on the motivation-related dilemmas. In other words, we asked if the discussions led to an increase or a decrease in students' expressed motivation to work hard on their schoolwork. We found that the discussions did not have a noticeable effect on these scores. In both conditions, students' scores on the pretest were close to the *not sure* point on the response scale. Scores on the posttest were close to the same point, or equally ambivalent, in both conditions. The lack of a significant shift between the pretest and the posttest shows that the friends' discussion did not produce a general change in adolescents' expressed motivation. That is, the friends' discussions did not make adolescents shift toward either more positive or less positive perceptions of the value of working hard in school.

A large amount of research with adults suggests that a discussion should cause shifts toward more extreme opinions on dilemmas like the ones we used (see Isenberg, 1986; Lamm & Myers, 1978). In particular, pairs of friends who initially favor the low-motivation alternatives on the dilemmas should favor those alternatives even more after discussion. Conversely, pairs of friends who initially favor the high-motivation alternatives should favor those alternatives even more after discussion. Note that this hypothesis could be supported even if there was no shift in mean scores for the group as a whole.

Further analyses of the results did not confirm this hypothesis. Even the pairs of friends with relatively extreme pretest decisions did not shift toward more extreme decisions after the discussions. On the contrary, the pairs of boys with relatively extreme pretest decisions shifted toward more neutral or ambivalent decisions. The mean decisions by pairs of girls did not shift significantly, regardless of the extremity of their pretest decisions.

The boys' shifts were related to the content of their discussions. The boys who favored the low-motivation alternatives on the pretest expressed opinions supporting those alternatives during the discussions about as often as they expressed opinions favoring the high-motivation alternatives. Conversely, the boys who favored the high-motivation alternatives on the pretest expressed opinions supporting those alternatives about as often as they expressed opinions favoring the low-motivation alternatives. Thus, the biases in the boys' pretest decisions were not evident during their discussions. And without a bias in the discussions, the bias in individual students' decisions disappeared.

These findings imply that shifts in decisions depended on the exchange of opinions during the discussions. In other words, they imply that the friends' influence on each other was based heavily on the information they provided to each other. As mentioned earlier, some researchers imply that social pressure is more critical to peer influence during adolescence than a rational discussion of opinions and reasons (e.g., Steinberg & Silverberg, 1986). We did not directly compare the effects of information exchange between friends with those of friends' pressure on each other. Even so, our data and other research suggest that influence among adolescents depends heavily on information exchange, just as is true among adults (Berndt, McCartney, Caparulo, & Moore, 1983–1984; Isenberg, 1986).

In the study of friends' discussions, we also examined the results for a second measure. This measure was for the discrepancy in the decisions of each pair of friends. Pairs received high scores on the measure when the two students in the pair chose very different responses to a dilemma. For example, one student might choose the 0 on the response scale, indicating a certain choice of one alternative, whereas the other student chose 10, indicating a certain choice of the other alternative. Discrepancy scores were calculated for each pair in each condition on the pretest and the posttest.

In the experimental condition, the discrepancies in the decisions by pairs of friends decreased significantly between the pretest and the posttest. In the control condition, the discrepancies in decisions changed little between the two tests. Thus, the friends' decisions on motivation-related dilemmas were more similar after they discussed them than before. The discussions, in short, increased the similarity of friends' decisions.

As mentioned earlier, previous studies (e.g., Epstein, 1983; Ide et al., 1981; Kandel, 1978) had suggested that processes of influence typically lead to an increase in friends' similarity. The findings of our study strengthen and extend this conclusion. They show with an experimental design that adolescents' discussions with friends increase the similarity in their decisions about academic achievement motivation.

In addition, we had observers rate each pair's discussions for their liveliness, cooperation, and aggression. The similarity in friends' decisions increased most in pairs whose interactions were rated as most cooperative and least aggressive. These findings are consistent with the hypothesis of Hallinan (1983) that friends' influence is enhanced when the friends have a close and harmonious relationship.

We also asked students to complete a brief questionnaire after they finished the posttest on the motivation-related dilemmas. The questionnaire included several items about how often students had conflicts with the friend who was their partner in the study. Pairs who reported the fewest conflicts in their friendships increased most in the similarity of their decisions after discussing them with each other. This finding is especially intriguing because it suggests a link between the two pathways of influence we described earlier.

Conflicts between friends are relevant to the second pathway of influence, which emphasizes the effects of the positive and negative features of friendships. Increases in friends' similarity in achievement motivation are relevant to the first pathway of influence, which emphasizes the increasing similarity in friends' characteristics. However, our findings, and Hallinan's (1983) hypothesis, imply that the features of adolescents' friendships affect how much they are influenced by their friends' characteristics.

From a broader perspective, the results of our experimental study have implications for the debate about the outcomes of peer influence during adolescence. One result that bears repeating is that discussions with a friend did not have uniformly negative effects on decisions about achievement motivation. Even the students more alienated from school, who expressed less motivation to achieve on the pretest, did not develop more negative attitudes after discussing school-related decisions with a friend. This evidence and comparable data from previous research (e.g., Brown et al., 1986) suggest that fears about the negative influence of peers on adolescents are exaggerated. Of course, friends' discussions did not have uniformly positive effects on their achievement motivation, either. The effects of the discussions depended on the particular friend with whom each adolescent was paired.

Of course, the results of our experiment must be interpreted cautiously. We looked at the effect of a single interaction between a pair of friends over a short time in a structured setting. We need to know more about the effects of multiple interactions between groups of friends over long periods in natural settings.

FRIENDS' INFLUENCE DURING A SCHOOL YEAR

Our next study (Berndt, Keefe, & Laychak, 1991) had a short-term longitudinal design. The study included 297 students (194 girls and 103 boys) from the seventh and eighth grades in three junior high schools. During the fall semester, and again late in the spring, students reported their involvement in school. For example, they noted how often they participated in class discussions and did extra effort on school activities outside class. They also reported on their disruptive behavior. They said, for example, how often they interfered with the work of classmates or talked when they shouldn't be talking. In addition, two of the students' teachers rated their involvement in class and their disruptive behavior.

In both the fall and the spring, students also named up to three close friends. Most students named friends who were in the same school and the same grade. Thus, we could determine the actual scores of an adolescent's friends on the same measures as for adolescents themselves.

Friends' Similarity and the First Pathway of Friends' Influence

Most of the correlations between students' scores and their friends' scores were significant in both the fall and the spring. On most measures, however, the correlations were larger in the spring than in the fall. Thus, friends' similarity increased during the year. The increase was significant for the measures of self-reported disruptive behavior and teacher-rated involvement. These increases are preliminary evidence that friends influenced each other so that they became more similar over time.

We should treat an increase in a similarity correlation as a sign of friends' influence only if students kept the same friends throughout the year. This was true for the measure of self-reported disruption, or adolescents' perceptions of their behavior in school. For students with stable friendships, the similarity correlations for self-reported disruption increased significantly between the fall and the spring. By contrast, the similarity correlations did not increase significantly when students' friendships were unstable.

The correlations imply that students with stable friendships were influenced by their friends, and vice versa, so that their level of disruptive behavior became more similar over time. Many teachers have assumed that disruptive students have a negative influence on the other students who are their friends. Our study is among the first to provide evidence for this assumption.

We found a different pattern of results for the measure of teacher-rated involvement. The correlations for friends' similarity in involvement only increased significantly during the year when students' friendships were unstable. There was little increase in similarity for students with stable friendships. These findings suggest that friendships often ended during the year when students were dissimilar in involvement. Then students formed new relationships with other students more similar to themselves. In other words, the increased similarity in teacher-rated involvement should be attributed not to friends' influence but to processes of friendship selection.

These results raise an intriguing question for future research. What characteristics do adolescents consider when they select friends, and on what characteristics do friends influence each other? For most psychological characteristics, it is difficult to judge, a priori, whether friends' similarity is due mostly to influence or mostly to selection. For example, we know that friends usually are similar in their achievement in school (Epstein, 1983; Ide et al., 1981). Although this similarity might result from their influence on each other, it could also reflect patterns of ability grouping that bring together students similar in ability (Bossert, 1979; Hallinan & Sorensen, 1985).

Researchers have tried with longitudinal designs to discover to what degree friends' similarity depends on influence and on selection. So far, however, the findings are scanty and inconsistent (Berndt, 1988; Wilcox & Udry, 1986). Epstein (1983), for example, reported an increase in friends' similarity in grades over a 1-year period that seemed to result from friends' influence on each other. In our longitudinal study, by contrast, friends' similarity in grades did not increase between the fall and the spring of the same year. Thus, additional data on the sources of friends' similarity are greatly needed. Those data would not only clarify how much adolescents are influenced by their friends' characteristics. They also would show what characteristics of adolescents have an impact on friendship selection or the formation of friendships.

Friendship Features and the Second Pathway of Friends' Influence

The students in our longitudinal study did more than name their best friends in the fall and the spring. They also reported on the positive and negative features of these friendships (see Berndt & Perry, 1986). Their reports allowed us to test hypotheses about the second pathway of friends' influence, the effects of supportive and conflicted friendships.

The students answered standard, close-ended questions about several positive features of friendship. For example, one question about a friend's efforts to encourage positive moods was "How often would [name of friend] try to make you feel better when you are sad or upset?" Other questions dealt with the benefits of intimate self-disclosure to friends, and the frequency of prosocial behavior by friends toward each other.

The students also responded to standard questions about the negative features of their friendships. For example, one question was "How often do you and [name of friend] get into fights or arguments with each other?" Other questions dealt with other types of conflicts, and with rivalry or unpleasant competition between friends.

The students answered separate sets of questions about the features of their relationships with up to three close friends. Then we computed mean scores for the positive features and the negative features of each student's best friendship. We also computed mean scores for the positive and negative features of all the close friendships named by each student.

Students' reports on their friendships were related to their perceptions of their involvement and behavior in school. Students who described their friendships more positively described themselves as more involved in school at each time. Their teachers also rated them as more involved. Students who described their friendships more negatively also described themselves as more disruptive in school at each time. These correlations suggest that students with better friendships had more positive perceptions of school and their own behavior in school. They also were viewed more positively by their teachers.

Taken together, the correlations establish that problems in friendships and problems at school are not independent. Instead, good friendships and a satisfactory adjustment to school go together. Because most adolescents formed friendships with their classmates, the correlations further suggest that having good friendships with classmates makes students perceive their school experiences more positively and behave more positively in school.

Yet such correlational data cannot prove that the features of students' friendships have a direct impact on their school adjustment. That is, they cannot tell us if there is a true pathway of influence between friendship features and school adjustment. Additional analyses addressed this issue. We used multiple regression analyses to see if the features of students' friendships in the fall of a school year predicted the changes in their adjustment during the year.

The measures of students' adjustment in the spring of the year were the criteria in these analyses. The corresponding measures of students' adjustment in the fall were the first predictors. Then we determined if the measures of friendship features accounted for additional variance. When done in this way, multiple regression analyses provide an indication of the relation of friendship features to changes in students' adjustment between the fall and the spring.

These analyses showed that the features of students' friendship in the fall influenced the changes in their school adjustment, especially as they reported it. Students who described their fall friendships more positively showed an increase, over time, in their reported involvement in school. Conversely, students who described their fall friendships more negatively showed an increase, over time, in their reported disruptive behavior.

The two findings suggest that the second pathway of friends' influence can account for both positive and negative effects of friendship.
As previous theories implied, positive or supportive friendships enhance adolescents' adjustment to school. Supportive friendships appear to influence attitudes or motivation most directly; they have less
effect on disruptive behavior or academic achievement.

Problems with friends may have even stronger effects than friends'
support, but these effects are also linked to specific outcomes. Fights
or arguments with friends are associated with, and contribute to,
disruptive behavior in the classroom. Thus, the behaviors that increase
conflicts with friends also increase conflicts with classmates and teachers.

SUGGESTIONS FOR FUTURE RESEARCH

The distinction between the two pathways of friends' influence clarifies
the contrasting assumptions of theorists and researchers about the
processes and outcomes of influence. Yet currently, too little is known
about each pathway. Three general questions call for more complete
answers.

The first question focuses on the outcomes of friends' influence.
Under what conditions does this influence have positive effects, and
negative effects, on adolescents' perceptions and behavior? Previous
research provides a partial answer to questions about the first pathway
of influence, the effects of friends' characteristics. Friends most often
have a positive influence when they have desirable characteristics, for
example, when they like school and perceive schoolwork as valuable.
Friends are likely to have a negative influence on an adolescent when
those friends have undesirable characteristics, for example, when they
dislike school and perceive schoolwork as worthless.

Yet some adolescents are more influenced by their friends than vice
versa. Other adolescents have more influence on their friends than vice
versa. More research is needed on the social and personality characteristics that make some adolescents more influential and other adolescents more susceptible to influence. Limited data suggest that more
intelligent, physically attractive, and athletic adolescents are especially influential in friendship groups. By contrast, adolescents who are
marginal members of their peer group are more susceptible to influence (Berndt & Savin-Williams, in press; Steinberg & Silverberg, 1986).
Yet these data come from very few studies, often studies of a small
number of adolescent groups. Additional research could confirm or
qualify these conclusions. Additional data could also reveal other

characteristics that affect adolescents' tendencies to influence or be influenced by their friends.

Besides exploring the characteristics of individuals that affect the outcomes of influence, researchers should explore the social conditions that affect these outcomes. Our studies included samples of adolescents from fairly traditional schools that were in small towns or rural areas. Scattered data suggest that the characteristics of schools and of the communities from which they draw their students can have an impact on the nature of friends' influence. Several researchers have suggested, for example, that ability grouping of students has a dramatic effect on peer influence (e.g., Ball, 1981; Schwartz, 1981). Peers in high-ability groups encourage learning, and thus have a generally positive influence on each other. Peers in low-ability groups have less positive perceptions of school and attitudes toward school. They also have a generally negative influence on each other.

In some communities, most adolescents do not see schooling as a likely route to success and attractive adult roles, so they have little motivation to do well in school. In other communities, most adolescents place a high value on doing well in school (see Cauce, 1987; Eckert, 1989). These contrasts affect the general climate of a school. This climate may bias the outcomes of friends' influence in the same direction, and make friends who share the prevailing view more influential than those who do not. But support for this conclusion is tentative. Most evidence comes from case studies or speculative interpretations of other data. Direct tests of these hypotheses are required before they can be taken as valid.

If we turn to the second pathway of influence, the effects of the features of adolescents' friendships, questions about outcomes are even more open and more difficult to answer. Much of the existing evidence on the effects of friendship features comes from research with correlational designs (Savin-Williams & Berndt, 1990). As mentioned earlier, these designs provide weak tests of hypotheses about the effects of variations in friendship features. More data from longitudinal studies are needed. In addition, researchers might use a new design, experimental interventions to improve adolescents' friendships (Berndt & Savin-Williams, in press). If interventions that increase friends' support or decrease conflicts between friends also improve other aspects of adolescents' adjustment, arguments for the influence of friendship features would be strengthened.

The second general question for future research concerns the processes by which friends influence each other. How do friends with specific characteristics, or friendships with specific features, cause changes in adolescents' perceptions, attitudes, and behavior? Researchers who focus on the first pathway of influence have often suggested that this influence depends on some form of social pressure. Yet our studies, and ethnographic research (e.g., Suttles, 1968), suggest that direct pressure is seldom the primary process of influence. Our study of friends' discussions suggested that information exchange that leads to the internalization of new beliefs is another process by which friends influence each other. Our study was not designed to provide definitive evidence on processes of influence, however. More research is needed that includes careful assessments of influence processes in experimental and natural settings (cf. Eder, 1990; Savin-Williams, 1987).

The processes linked to the second pathway of influence, the effects of friendship features, also require more careful, focused study. Current theories differ in their assumptions about how close and supportive friendships affect people's adjustment (see Savin-Williams & Berndt, 1990). Some theorists believe that adolescents who feel supported by friends benefit just from having such a relationship. For example, adolescents may feel more positively about school when they can look forward to interacting with friends who accept and value them. Other theorists believe that adolescents benefit from interactions that are explicitly intended to be helpful or supportive. For example, when an adolescent does poorly on a test, a friend may try to boost his or her self-esteem by offering hope for better performance next time. To understand more about exactly how supportive friendships help adolescents, researchers might ask adolescents themselves about how close friends help them cope with the daily lives. Ethnographic studies would also illuminate this issue.

The third general question for future research relates to social development. Do friends have more influence on the perceptions and behavior of adolescents than of children or adults? Our research focused on early adolescence, or the middle school years, because we assumed that these ages are "prime time" for friends' influence. Other research suggests that the characteristics of friends and the features of these friendships have more influence during early adolescence than during middle childhood (Berndt & Perry, 1990). But this conclusion rests upon very few studies. Researchers who include multiple age groups in their studies of friends' influence can begin to close this gap in our knowledge.

IMPLICATIONS FOR EDUCATIONAL PRACTICE

The distinction between the two pathways of friends' influence has important implications for educational practice. Some of our findings regarding the first pathway of influence may not be surprising to teachers. As mentioned earlier, our data confirm the assumption of many teachers that disruptive students have a negative influence on the behavior of their friends.

But how should teachers react to this information? According to Epstein (1983), "Many school policies are based on the suppression of peer relations in classrooms" (p. 245). For example, some teachers do not let children sit with their friends. Some teachers change seat assignments so that students who are disruptive or who often talk to each other are not allowed to sit together (Bossert, 1979).

These strategies can be effective (Ball, 1981), but they are largely reactive and can have negative side effects. They are likely to weaken existing friendships and make it difficult for students to make new friends. These strategies may also result in the social isolation of some children, leaving them without any friends among their classmates. Our evidence on the second pathway of influence suggests that these children may, in turn, form less positive perceptions of their school experience. In addition, they may reduce their motivation and performance in school.

Other strategies are more likely to enhance the positive effects of friends and friendships on school-related perceptions, motivation, and performance. Placing students in cooperative learning groups can foster positive relationships between classmates. Systematic use of cooperative learning can also improve students' attitudes toward school and raise their level of academic achievement (Epstein, 1983; Furman & Gavin, 1989; Slavin, 1983). Moreover, programs of cooperative learning can reduce the number of students who are socially isolated and help classmates make friends with each other (Hansell & Slavin, 1981).

Cooperative learning programs may be beneficial for many reasons. Our studies suggest one possible reason that has not been emphasized in previous writings. These programs contribute to conditions in the classroom that encourage the formation of supportive friendships between classmates. When engaged in cooperative activities, students act in generous and helpful ways toward classmates, rather than seeing their classmates as competitors. Cooperative learning programs give students time to interact with classmates. During this time, students find out how they are similar to classmates and share enjoyable experiences. These experiences are the foundation for making good friendships.

Besides the varieties of cooperative learning (see Epstein, 1983; Slavin, 1983), other programs have been designed to foster positive relationships among classmates. Vorrath and Brendtro (1974) devised an intervention program based on "positive peer culture." In this program, adults try to reduce deviant behavior by increasing adolescents' concern for others, including their concern for their friends. Adults also try to increase adolescents' trust and support for one another.

Kohlberg and his colleagues tried to establish what he called Just Communities in schools (see Power, Higgins, & Kohlberg, 1989). The teachers and students who join these communities agree to act according to principles of mutual respect for other members of the community. They also agree to act to improve the welfare of other community members. Thus, the goal of this program is to establish supportive relationships among students and between teachers and students.

The advocates of all these programs reject the idea that teachers should suppress or ignore peer relationships in classrooms. They argue that teachers should care about peer relationships not just because these relationships are important to students, but also because these relationships affect a teacher's ability to meet academic goals. As our final study showed, students who have many conflicts with friends also tend to have conflicts with teachers and to be disruptive in class. Changing these students' friendships in a positive way could have beneficial effects on other aspects of their adjustment. Such a change could, in particular, improve the students' perceptions of school and their behavior in school. Then teaching these students could become more pleasant and more successful.

Of course, programs like cooperative learning that are directed at an entire classroom are not effective in changing the behavior of all students. Some students need an intervention directed specifically at them. One type of intervention that teachers should consider is structured training in social skills. Many researchers have devised interventions to increase the social skills of students who lack friends or are rejected by many of their peers.

Students who have poor relationships with classmates often are socially withdrawn or aggressive (Asher & Coie, 1990). In social skills training programs, these students learn to initiate positive interactions with peers, to resolve conflicts without using aggression, and to think about the likely consequences of their behavior before acting (Ladd & Mize, 1983; Price & Dodge, 1989). These interventions are most successful when (a) they focus on skills or abilities that particular students need to master, and (b) they involve peers in the intervention, so peers can see the improvement in the trained students' social skills and behavior firsthand.

The effectiveness of social skills training may depend partly on the social organization of a classroom. Individual training may work best if trained students are placed in classrooms that allow peer interactions, so the students can practice the skills trained. The teachers in these classrooms should also encourage cooperation and helping by class-mates, so trained students receive positive responses when they apply the new skills they have learned. Thus, programs that focus on the relationships among all students in a classroom are a valuable com-plement to those focusing on individual students. A combination of both types of programs should help teachers maximize the positive influence of friends, and friendships, on students' perceptions of school and behavior in the classroom.

ACKNOWLEDGMENT

The research reported in this chapter was supported in part by a grant from the Spencer Foundation. Their support is gratefully acknowl-edged.

REFERENCES

Asher, S. R., & Coie, J. D. (Eds.). (1990). *Peer rejection in childhood.* Cambridge, England: Cambridge University Press.

Ball, S. J. (1981). *Beachside comprehensive.* Cambridge, England: Cambridge University Press.

Berndt, T. J. (1988). The nature and significance of children's friendships. In R. Vasta (Ed.), *Annals of child development* (Vol. 5, pp. 155–186). Greenwich, CT: JAI Press.

Berndt, T. J., Keefe, K., & Laychak, A. E. (1991). *Friends' influence on adolescents' achievement motivation: A longitudinal study.* Unpublished manuscript, Purdue Uni-versity.

Berndt, T. J., Laychak, A. E., & Park, K. (1990). Friends' influence on adolescents' academic achievement motivation: An experimental study. *Journal of Educational Psychology, 82,* 664–670.

Berndt, T. J., McCartney, K., Caparulo, B. K., & Moore, A. M. (1983–1984). The effects of group discussions on children's moral decisions. *Social Cognition, 2,* 343–360.

Berndt, T. J., Miller, K. E., & Park, K. (1989). Adolescents' perceptions of friends' and parents' influence on aspects of their school adjustment. *Journal of Early Adolescence, 9,* 419–435.

Berndt, T. J., & Perry, T. B. (1986). Children's perceptions of friendships as supportive relationships. *Developmental Psychology, 22,* 640–648.

Berndt, T. J., & Perry, T. B. (1990). Distinctive features and effects of early adolescent friendships. In R. Montemayor, G. R. Adams, & T. P. Gullotta (Eds.), *From childhood to adolescence: A transitional period?* (pp. 269–287). Newbury Park, CA: Sage.

Berndt, T. J., & Savin-Williams, R. C. (in press). Variations in friendships and peer-group relationships in adolescence. In P. Tolan & B. Cohler (Eds.), *Handbook of clinical research and practice with adolescents.* New York: Wiley.

Bishop, J. H. (1989). Why the apathy in American high schools? *Educational Researcher, 18,* 6–10.

Bossert, S. T. (1979). *Tasks and social relationships in classrooms.* Cambridge, England: Cambridge University Press.

Bronfenbrenner, U. (1970). Reaction to social pressure from adults versus peers among Soviet day school and boarding school pupils in the perspective of an American sample. *Journal of Personality and Social Psychology, 15,* 179–189.

Brown, B. B., Clasen, D. R., & Eicher, S. A. (1986). Perceptions of peer pressure, peer conformity dispositions, and self-reported behavior among adolescents. *Developmental Psychology, 22,* 521–530.

Cauce, A. M. (1987). School and peer competence in early adolescence: A test of domain-specific self-perceived competence. *Developmental Psychology, 23,* 287–291.

Cohen, S., & Wills, T. A. (1985). Stress, social support, and the buffering hypothesis. *Psychological Bulletin, 98,* 310–357.

Coleman, J. S. (1961). *The adolescent society.* New York: The Free Press.

Damon, W. (1984). Peer education: The untapped potential. *Journal of Applied Developmental Psychology, 5,* 331–343.

Davies, M., & Kandel, D. B. (1981). Parental and peer influences on adolescents' educational plans: Some further evidence. *American Journal of Sociology, 87,* 363–387.

Eckert, P. (1989). *Jocks and burnouts: Social categories and identity in the high school.* New York: Teachers College, Columbia University.

Eder, D. (1990). Serious and playful disputes: Variation in conflict talk among female adolescents. In A. D. Grimshaw (Ed.), *Conflict talk: Sociolinguistic investigations of arguments in conversations* (pp. 67–84). Cambridge: Cambridge University Press.

Epstein, J. L. (1983). The influence of friends on achievement and affective outcomes. In J. L. Epstein & N. L. Karweit (Eds.), *Friends in school* (pp. 177–200). New York: Academic Press.

Everhart, R. B. (1983). *Reading, writing, and resistance: Adolescence and labor in a junior high school.* New York: Routledge & Kegan Paul.

Furman, W., & Gavin, L. A. (1989). Peers' influence and adjustment and development: A view from the intervention literature. In T. J. Berndt & G. W. Ladd (Eds.), *Peer relationships in child development* (pp. 319–340). New York: Wiley.

Hallinan, M. T. (1983). Commentary: New directions for research on peer influence. In J. L. Epstein & N. L. Karweit (Eds.), *Friends in school* (pp. 177–200). New York: Academic Press.

Hallinan, M. T., & Sorensen, A. B. (1985). Ability grouping and student friendships. *American Educational Research Journal, 22,* 485–499.

Hansell, S., & Slavin, R. E. (1981). Cooperative learning and the structure of interracial friendships. *Sociology of Education, 54,* 98–106.

Hartup, W. W. (1983). Peer relations. In E. M. Hetherington (Ed.), *Handbook of child psychology. Vol. 4. Socialization, personality, and social development* (pp. 103–196). New York: Wiley.

Ide, J. K., Parkerson, J., Haertel, G. D., & Walberg, J. J. (1981). Peer group influence on educational outcomes: A quantitative synthesis. *Journal of Educational Psychology, 73,* 472–484.

Isenberg, D. J. (1986). Group polarization: A critical review and meta-analysis. *Journal of Personality and Social Psychology, 50,* 1141–1152.

Kandel, D. B. (1978). Homophily, selection, and socialization in adolescent friendships. *American Journal of Sociology, 84,* 427–436.

Kandel, D. B., & Andrews, K. (1987). Processes of adolescent socialization by parents and peers. *International Journal of the Addictions, 22,* 319–342.

Kandel, D. B., & Lesser, G. S. (1972). *Youth in two worlds: U.S. and Denmark.* San Francisco: Jossey-Bass.

Kelman, H. C. (1958). Compliance, identification, and internalization: Three processes of attitude change. *Journal of Conflict Resolution, 2,* 51–60.

Ladd, G. W., & Mize, J. (1983). A cognitive-social learning model of social-skill training. *Psychological Review, 90,* 127–157.

Lamm, H., & Myers, D. G. (1978). Group-induced polarization of attitudes and behavior. In L. Berkowitz (Ed.), *Advances in experimental social psychology* (Vol. 11, pp. 145–195). New York: Academic Press.

O'Brien, S. F., & Bierman, K. L. (1988). Conceptions and perceived influence of peer groups: Interviews with preadolescents and adolescents. *Child Development, 59,* 1360–1365.

Piaget, J. (1965). *The moral judgment of the child.* New York: The Free Press. (Original work published 1932)

Power, F. C., Higgins, A., & Kohlberg, L. (1989). *Lawrence Kohlberg's approach to moral education.* New York: Columbia University Press.

Price, J. M., & Dodge, K. A. (1989). Peers' contributions to children's social maladjustment: Description and intervention. In T. J. Berndt & G. W. Ladd (Eds.), *Peer relationships in child development* (pp. 341–370). New York: Wiley.

Sarason, I. G., & Sarason, B. R. (Eds.). (1985). *Social support: Theory, research, and applications.* Dordrecht, the Netherlands: Martinus Nijhoff.

Savin-Williams, R. C. (1987). *Adolescence: An ethological perspective.* New York: Springer-Verlag.

Savin-Williams, R. C., & Berndt, T. J. (1990). Friendships and peer relations during adolescence. In S. S. Feldman & G. Elliott (Eds), *At the threshold: The developing adolescent* (pp. 277–307). Cambridge, MA: Harvard University Press.

Schwartz, F. (1981). Supporting or subverting learning: Peer group patterns in four tracked schools. *Anthropology and Education Quarterly, 12,* 99–121.

Slavin, R. E. (1983). When does cooperative learning increase student achievement. *Psychological Bulletin, 94,* 429–445.

Steinberg, L., & Silverberg, S. B. (1986). The vicissitudes of autonomy in early adolescence. *Child Development, 57,* 841–851.

Sullivan, H. S. (1953). *The interpersonal theory of psychiatry.* New York: Norton.

Suttles, G. D. (1968). *The social order of the slum.* Chicago: University of Chicago Press.

Vorrath, H. H., & Brendtro, L. K. (1974). *Positive peer culture.* Hawthorne, NY: Aldine.

Wilcox, S., & Udry, J. R. (1986). Autism and accuracy in adolescent perceptions of friends' sexual attitudes and behavior. *Journal of Applied Social Psychology, 16,* 361–374.

Youniss, J. (1980). *Parents and peers in social development.* Chicago: University of Chicago Press.

An Attributional Approach to Aggression in African-American Children

SANDRA GRAHAM
CYNTHIA HUDLEY
University of California, Los Angeles

Social scientists are sometimes drawn to the study of particular topics within their discipline out of concern for the social problems associated with ethnic minority status in this society. Thus, for example, psychologists may investigate intelligence because of the chronic school failure of many African-American children, helping relationships given the negative consequences associated with welfare dependency, aggression due to the higher incidence of violent crimes among urban Black males, and so on.

As educational psychologists, our interest in aggression as a social problem grows out of our concern for the effects of deviant behavior on the school experiences of African-American youth. Although African-American children represent 25% of the national public school population, they comprise 40% of all suspensions and expulsions, most of which are prompted by school staff perceptions of excessive verbal and physical aggression (Reed, 1988). Furthermore, a large empirical literature has documented the stability of aggression from childhood to young adulthood (Loeber, 1982; Olweus, 1979), as well as its relation to a host of negative outcomes including low academic achievement (Quay, 1987); school dropout in adolescence (Cairns, Cairns, & Neckerman, 1989); rejection among peers (Coie, Dodge, & Kupersmidt, 1990); and juvenile delinquency (Loeber & Stouthamer-Loeber, 1987). It should come as no surprise that most of these known correlates of childhood aggression are disproportionately prevalent

75

among ethnic minorities, particularly African-American males (see Gibbs, 1988; Wilson & Herrnstein, 1985).

Recognizing the severity of this problem, in this chapter we describe our recent empirical work on school-based aggressive behavior among African-American youth. The conceptual framework guiding our research is attribution theory, which is concerned with perceptions about why outcomes occur (Graham, 1991; Weiner, 1985a, 1986). This theory has proved to be particularly useful for examining attributional thinking of Black students in the achievement domain (see Graham, 1988). Here we present our findings on causal inferences of African-American children labeled as aggressive and how these judgments then influence peer-directed aggression in school settings. Thus, our emphasis is in keeping with the focus in this volume on student perceptions, although here we are more concerned with perceptions of *social* rather than academic outcomes.

To establish a context for our research, we begin with a discussion of some of the antecedents to childhood aggression, focusing on those conditions that appear to be particularly prevalent in African-Americans. Explanations of deviant behavior have a long history in psychology and a number of comprehensive reviews are available (e.g., Parke & Slaby, 1983; Wilson & Herrnstein, 1985). Our discussion of these antecedents is therefore brief. Next, we turn to a social cognitive perspective on childhood aggression where we concentrate on a conceptual analysis of the problem provided by attribution theory. This is followed by a discussion of two empirical studies that apply principles of attribution theory to the study of aggression among African-American children. The chapter concludes with a discussion of the implications of our approach for intervention based on attributional change.

ANTECEDENTS OF CHILDHOOD AGGRESSION

In general, the determinants of aggression can be divided into two broad categories. On the one hand, there are constitutional or within-person variables that include gender, temperament, intelligence, and factors that emerge at birth. These can be contrasted with environmental or external variables such as family configuration, parenting styles, socioeconomic status (SES), schooling, and the mass media.

Among the constitutional factors, the clearest evidence relates to gender differences: Boys display more aggressive behavior than girls. This is a very robust finding that prevails across age, social class, and type of aggression (see Maccoby & Jacklin, 1980). Some temperament characteristics also appear to be precursors of antisocial behavior in childhood. Children who tend to be rated by caregivers as less adaptible, and more distractible, irregular, and intense are also more likely to be labeled as aggressive during the early school years (Parke & Slaby, 1983). Impulsivity and inability to delay gratification are closely related personality traits that are similarly linked to aggression. Children who get into trouble in school also have lower intelligence, as measured by the standard IQ tests (Quay, 1987). Measurement issues aside, however, it has been difficult to establish unequivocal IQ-aggression linkages because IQ is so confounded with SES, one of the most robust correlates of deviancy. Finally, certain perinatal factors, such as birth trauma or low birth weight, are believed to predispose particular children toward aggression, although the evidence on this constitutional factor is less clear (Mednick, Brennan, & Kandel, 1988).

The findings on environmental determinants of aggression in childhood are indeed complex, but we summarize here what is known about the major antecedents. No one disputes the fact that poverty is a major determinant of antisocial behavior in children, as is the closely related variable of family constellation. Poor children who are raised in families where only one parent is present, typically the mother, are more at risk for antisocial behavior than are their economically disadvantaged counterparts raised in two-parent families (see Jaynes & Williams, 1989). Moreover, certain dimensions of parenting put children at risk for later deviance. The child who is subjected to parental abuse (Widom, 1989) or to parents who use inconsistent or noncontingent discipline tactics (Patterson, 1986) is more prone to aggressive patterns of behavior at a relatively early age. Regarding the role of the school, some of the stigmatizing practices of teachers, such as assignment to remedial classes or academic tracking, also are correlated with aggression and delinquency (Reed, 1988). Finally, there is some evidence that excessive exposure to violence in the media at a young age, particularly television, is a reliable predictor of aggression in adolescence and even criminality in young adulthood (e.g., Eron, 1982; Friedrich-Cofer & Huston, 1986).

In summary, the impulsivity-prone male who: (a) is born prematurely to an unmarried mother who lacks adequate parenting skills, (b) scores poorly on IQ tests, and (c) prefers to stay home and watch TV rather than attend school, is the individual most at risk for childhood aggression. All of these eliciting factors are more prevalent in Blacks than Whites; it could hardly be otherwise as most are integrally related to SES.

AN ATTRIBUTIONAL APPROACH TO AGGRESSION

In contrast to these constitutional and environmental factors that have a long history in both basic and applied psychological research, a relatively recent approach to childhood aggression has been provided by psychologists working within a social cognitive perspective. These researchers have investigated how children's perceptions and infer-ences about others in social situations are related to subsequent aggressive behavior. Guided largely by the work of Kenneth Dodge and his colleagues, a number of studies report that aggressive children display a marked attributional bias to infer hostile intent following a peer-instigated negative event, particularly when the cause of the event is portrayed as ambiguous (see review in Dodge & Crick, 1990). Thus, for example, when a child is instructed to imagine that a peer spilled milk on him or her in the lunchroom, and no other information is given, the student labeled as aggressive is more likely to state that the peer did this "on purpose" than is his or her nonaggressive counterpart. Such biased intentionality inferences are then thought to lead to retaliatory behavior. Even among normal populations, the child who believes that another acted with malicious intent can feel justified in the endorsement of aggressive behavior. The problem with aggressive children, however, is that either through some process of social cue distortion or selective recall of available information, they often inap-propriately assume hostile peer intent in situations where the causes of outcomes are ambiguous.

Although this research capitalizes on an implicit attribution-behavior linkage, the processes relating intentionality perceptions to peer-directed aggression have yet to be fully explored. Why, for exam-ple, does perceiving a classmate as responsible for a negative event lead to hostile reactions? That is, what intervening thoughts and feelings might account for the cognition-to-action sequence suggested by Dodge's work? Dodge and others studying childhood aggression from a social cognitive perspective have not yet addressed this ques-tion. To elaborate our own approach to investigating the more com-plex thought processes leading to peer aggression, we turn now to attribution theory as conceptualized by Weiner (1985a, 1986). This theory has dealt extensively with perceptions of causal responsibility, and the related construct of causal intentionality.

Causal Attributions

"Why did I fail the test?" or "Why do the kids in my class pick on me?" The answers to such "why" queries are causal attributions. As implied in these examples, some categories of experience are particularly conducive to causal search. We are more likely to want to know *why* following negative, unexpected, or unusual events (Weiner, 1985b). Thus, the child who is the target of peer-instigated harm might particularly want to know why this negative and unanticipated outcome occurred. Causal search is therefore functional because it helps to impose order on an uncertain environment.

In achievement contexts, success and failure typically are ascribed to some ability factor that includes both aptitude and acquired skills, an exertion factor such as temporary or sustained effort, the difficulty (ease) of the task, personality, mood, and help or hindrance from others. Among these causal ascriptions, in this culture at least, ability and effort are most prominent. When explaining achievement outcomes, individuals attach the most importance to their perceived competencies and how hard they try. Similarly, in affiliative contexts, there are a few dominant causes for interpersonal acceptance or rejection, including physical characteristics and personality of the accepted or rejected individual. In general, however, relatively little research exists on perceived causes in domains other than achievement.

Causal Dimensions

Attributional judgments are phenomenological; they depict the causal world as perceived by the actor. Thus, attributional content will certainly vary between individuals and there may be an infinite number of perceived causes for achievement success and failure or peer acceptance and rejection. It has therefore been necessary for the theory to focus on causal *meaning* rather than particular causes per se. This enables contrasts and comparisons among causes both within a particular domain, like achievement, as well as between domains, such as achievement and affiliation.

It appears that meaning is determined in part by the underlying properties of perceived causes. Now what is meant by causal properties? Let us first illustrate with a nonsocial example. If we give students a variety of round objects that also differ in other ways such as color or size, and a variety of square objects that also differ in these other ways, and we ask our students to then sort these objects into two meaningful piles, it is likely that the round objects will be put in one pile and the square objects in another. Shape is therefore one of the perceived underlying properties of these objects.

In a similar manner, causes have underlying properties, although these are psychological rather than physical representations. Three such properties, labeled *causal dimensions,* have been identified with some certainty. They are locus, or whether a cause is internal or external to the person; stability, which designates a cause as constant or varying over time; and controllability (responsibility), or whether the cause is or is not subject to volitional control.

All causes are classifiable within one of the eight cells of a locus X stability X controllability dimensional matrix. For illustrative purposes, Table 4.1 shows the dimensional placement of effort and ability. It can be seen that effort is perceived as internal, unstable, and controllable. Failure ascriptions to lack of effort thus indicate a personal characteristic that is modifiable by one's own volitional behavior. The dimensional placement of ability, on the other hand, indicates that this cause is internal, stable, and uncontrollable. That is, when we attribute failure to low ability or aptitude, we tend to see this as a characteristic of ourselves, enduring over time, and beyond our personal control. The same dimensional placement applies to height (being too tall or too short) or racial identity (e.g., being Black rather than White) as a cause for interpersonal rejection. Thus, although aptitude and ethnicity obviously differ, they also share much in common when conceived in terms of underlying properties.

Causal inferences about others are subject to the same dimensional analysis. For example, others' efforts tend to be judged as controllable by them and their low abilities as uncontrollable. However, we prefer the label *responsibility* when referring to perceived controllability in others; this better captures the naive understanding of the construct when applied to other-perception rather than self-perception. Individuals typically view their own outcomes as personally controllable or not, whereas they tend to hold others responsible or not for what they do. We also do not distinguish between responsibility and intentionality, the preferred dimensional category in the childhood aggression literature. There is a good deal of theoretical overlap between these two causal constructs, the complexities of which need not concern us here (see Shaver, 1985).

Table 4.1
Effort and Ability Attributions Related to Causal Dimensions

	Causes	
Causal Dimensions	Effort	Ability
Locus	Internal	Internal
Stability	Unstable	Stable
Controllability	Controllable	Uncontrollable

The Consequences of Perceived Responsibility in Others

As a causal dimension, perceived responsibility has important consequences for both emotional reactions and behavior. According to attribution theory, responsibility inferences influence behavior toward others through the mediating influence of emotion. To illustrate, consider the evidence supporting these linkages that has been gathered in the domain of helping behavior. When people are perceived as not responsible for negative outcomes, this tends to elicit pity and prosocial emotions such as help (imagine a normal child's reaction to a retarded peer who continually experiences academic difficulty). In contrast, individuals judged as responsible for negative events often elicit anger and help tends to be withheld (consider the same child's reaction to the gifted peer who never completes assignments). Anger is therefore a moral emotion, often associated with judgments of "ought," "should have," or "could have." Furthermore, a very reliable finding in this attribution literature is that emotions of pity and anger, more so than responsibility attributions, directly influence helping behavior (see Graham & Weiner, 1991; Schmidt & Weiner, 1988). Thus, attribution theorists propose a particular thought-emotion-action sequence whereby causal thoughts determine feelings and feelings, in turn, guide behavior.

As indicated earlier, most of the empirical support for this proposed motivational role of emotion has come from research in the helping domain. However, we view aggression and helping behavior as theoretically complementary motivational domains, with the same attributional principles applicable to both. Applying these principles to the study of peer aggression, imagine a situation where a child experiences a negative outcome instigated by a peer, such as being pushed while waiting in line. To the degree that the peer provocation is perceived as intentional (i.e., the provocateur is responsible for the event), we would expect feelings of anger to be invoked and anger, in turn, to be directly related to retaliation. In contrast, to the degree that the damage is perceived as unintended, anger should be mitigated and hostile behavior less likely to be endorsed.

Figure 4.1 graphically depicts this thought-to-emotion-to-behavior motivational sequence, beginning with the antecedent cues (e.g., the recency of the event or the consistency of the provocateur's behavior) that elicit intentionality inferences. We already know from the research of Dodge and others cited previously that aggressive children often use such cues in a manner that biases then toward perceiving peer provocations as intentional (Linkage 1). But are feelings of anger systematically related to these attributional inferences (Linkage 2)? It might be that Linkage 2 does not accurately account for the feelings of socially deviant children. Perhaps such children get angry following peer provocation somewhat independently of perceived intent and the emotion of anger, in turn, accounts for higher levels of aggression. This would be consistent with the portrayal of aggressive children as having low thresholds for emotional arousal following negative social encounters (Parke & Slaby, 1983). A second possibility is that aggressive children's behavior is directly determined by their biased intentionality attributions (Linkage 4) without the mediating (and regulating) influence of emotion. Perhaps these children do not use their own emotional reactions, be they mild or intense anger, as guides to appropriate behavior.

We pursued these questions in two empirical studies with African-American youth. Our goal in the first investigation was to examine aggressive behavior within the framework of the motivational sequence proposed by attribution theory. The second study then focused on a particular step in this sequence (Linkage 2 in Fig. 4.1) with the development of an attributional intervention designed to alter the biased intentionality inferences of aggressive boys.

Testing Attribution–Emotion–Action Linkages in Peer Aggression

Our first study (Graham, Hudley, & Williams, in press) used a simulational or role-playing methodology. We wanted to document the understanding of the proposed thought–emotion–action linkages in a group of ethnic minority early adolescents, mostly African-American and almost exclusively male. The initial sample consisted of approximately 300 seventh and eighth graders attending junior high school in an economically depressed community of metropolitan Los Angeles. All of the children were drawn from average-ability math and English classes. From this initial pool, we identified a group of 44 aggressive young adolescents and a matched group of 44 nonaggressives using a

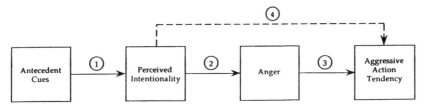

FIG. 4.1   An attribution–emotion–action temporal sequence in the domain of aggression.

combination of both peer nominations and teacher ratings as selection criteria. In the peer procedure, children nominated three students in their homeroom who best fit each of three aggressive behavior descriptions (e.g., starts fights, disrupts the group, has a very short temper) and three who best fit each of two prosocial descriptors (e.g., works well with others, is helpful to other students). Teachers, in turn, completed an eight-item aggression scale for each student in their homeroom (e.g., "This child threatens or bullies others to get his/her own way"), indicating the frequency of the target behavior. The 44 children in the aggressive group had the most number of peer nominations on the aggressive behavior descriptions, the least number of nominations on the prosocial items, and the highest scores on teacher ratings of aggression. Their nonaggressive counterparts were basically those children who had opposite scores on these same selection criteria.

These two groups of children were administered an attributional questionnaire developed for this study. In the questionnaire, participants read a series of short scenarios where they were asked to imagine that they experienced a negative outcome, such as damage to one's property or social rejection, that was initiated by a hypothetical peer provocateur. We then manipulated the intent of the peer provocation to be either prosocial, accidental, ambiguous, or hostile. For example, in the "homework paper" theme manipulated to be of ambiguous intent, participants read the following:

> Imagine that you are on your way to school one morning. You are walking onto the school grounds. At that moment, you happen to look down and notice that your shoelace is untied. You put the notebook that you are carrying down on the ground to tie your shoelace. An important homework paper that you worked on for a long time falls out of your notebook. Just then, another kid you know walks by and steps on the paper, leaving a muddy footprint right across the middle. The other kid looks down at your homework paper and then up at you.

Prosocial intent was communicated by the peer suggesting that he did this to keep the paper from blowing away, accidental intent was conveyed with the peer's apology that he did not see the homework paper lying there, and hostile intent was depicted by the peer who stepped on the paper and then laughed (see Graham et al., in press).

For each scenario, subjects made attributions about the peer's intent (e.g., did he or she do this "on purpose") and they indicated how angry they would feel if this outcome indeed happened to them. They also judged the likelihood that they would engage in each of six behaviors that varied along a continuum from prosocial ("do something nice for this other kid") to hostile ("do something to get even" and "have it out right then and there").

Let us offer one caveat about this methodology. We are asking children whether they would feel certain emotions or behave in a specific manner if particular conditions prevailed. We are measuring neither emotions during their state of activation nor actual behavior. These choices grow out of our belief that simulational studies are both useful and appropriate when one's goal is the testing of hypotheses or the development of theory. We believe that individuals' thoughts about feelings or their intentions to act in a particular way have a close correspondence with how they actually think, feel, and behave in real-world contexts. (See Cooper, 1976, or Forward, Canter, and Kirsch, 1976, for a more extended discussion of these issues.)

The analyses revealed that aggressive subjects were more likely to believe that the hypothetical peer acted with malicious intent (e.g., "he did it on purpose") than were their nonaggressive counterparts. Moreover, consistent with prior research, intentionality attributions of the two status groups only differed significantly when the causal situation was portrayed as ambiguous. Aggressive young adolescents also reported somewhat more anger overall and they were clearly more prone to endorse aggressive behavioral alternatives. Given a range of options, in other words, these children expressed a preference to "get even" or "have it out."

Next we examined the temporal relations between these variables. We have proposed that thoughts guide feelings and feelings, in turn, determine behavior. Are the data for aggressive and nonaggressives consistent with the model that views emotion as a direct determinant of behavior?

The top half of Table 4.2 shows the zero-order correlations between intent, anger, and the two aggressive action tendencies of "do something to get even" and "have it out right then and there" (combined to create one behavioral variable). The data are presented separately for the two status groups. Among nonaggressives, there were strong positive correlations between intentionality, anger, and likelihood of behaving aggressively. The more young adolescents perceive a peer as intentionally causing them harm, the more anger they feel and the greater their preference for hostile behavioral alternatives. All of these relations are in accord with attributional predictions. The same pattern of findings also prevails for aggressive subjects, although the magnitude of the correlations is not as great in this group.

To specifically examine the motivational role of anger, we then calculated partial correlations between intentionality and aggressive

Table 4.2
Zero-Order and Partial Correlations Between Intentionality, Anger, and Aggressive
Action, by Status Group

	Status Group	
Measure	Nonaggressive	Aggressive
Correlations		
Intent × Anger	.70***	.51***
Intent × Action	.61***	.33*
Anger × Action	.66***	.41**
Partial Correlations		
Intent × Action.Anger	.27	.16
Anger × Action.Intent	.41***	.30*

*$p < .05$; **$p < .01$; ***$p < .001$.

action, controlling for the influence of anger, and between anger and action, after partialing out the effect of perceived intent. Partial correlation is a reasonable statistical technique when the researcher's goal is to study the effects of one variable (intent) as it is mediated by another (anger). It does not completely rule out the possibility that other relations between these variables might exist, relations that do not imply causality (see Pedhazur, 1982). But with a sound theoretical model guiding the analysis, we see its application as valid in this case.

Applied here, the logic of partial correlational analysis is as follows: If anger mediates the relationship between perceived intent and action, then the correlation between intent and action (e.g., Linkage 4 in Fig. 4.1) should be greatly reduced once anger is partialed from the analysis. A zero or close to zero partial correlation between intent and action would lend support to our hypothesis of an "intent–anger–aggressive behavior" temporal sequence. Furthermore, if anger is a direct determinant of aggressive behavior (Linkage 3) then partialing intent from the anger-action relation should not greatly reduce the magnitude of that correlation.

The partial correlations shown in the bottom half of Table 4.2 support the role of anger as a mediator between thought and action for both status groups. When anger is statistically held constant, the correlation between intent and action is reduced to the point where it is no longer significant among aggressives as well as nonaggressives. But the relationship between anger and action remains significant even when intent is partialed out. Substantively, we interpret these findings as follows: When aggressive and nonaggressive young adolescents reason about social dilemmas with negative consequences, much of the relationship between what they think (e.g., "Did he do it on purpose?") and the way they intend to behave (e.g., "Should we have it out right here and now?") can be accounted for by how they feel (e.g., "How angry am I about this?").

Two major findings emerged from this study. First, we documented that African-American young adolescents labeled as aggressive do appear to have an attributional bias to infer hostile intent on the part of a peer provocateur. This was true particularly in situations of causal ambiguity. And second, there was evidence that thought, feeling, and action are systematically related in a manner proposed by attribution theory. Aggressive children feel the way they think and then act on the basis of their feelings.

These findings encouraged us to pursue the topic further and to think more concretely about attributional change. If attributions to intentionality instigate a set of reactions that leads to aggression, then it might be possible to train aggressive-prone children to see peer provocations as unintentional; this should mitigate anger as well as the tendency to react with hostility. The notion of altering causal thinking to produce changes in behavior has been the guiding assumption of attributional change programs in both the academic and clinical domains (Forsterling, 1990). So there are good theoretical and empirical precedents for considering attributional change as a way to alleviate peer-directed aggression.

Altering Intentionality Attributions

Guided by our own theoretical analysis as well as the clinical literature on the treatment of childhood aggression (e.g., Kazdin, 1985), we developed a school-based cognitive intervention program designed to alter the intentionality attributions of aggressive-prone children (Hudley, 1991). The intervention was a 6-week, 12-session program with activities designed to be appropriate for the late elementary grades. A variety of instructional strategies were employed, including group discussion, introspection, and paper-and-pencil exercises.

One component of the program was intended to strengthen aggressive children's ability to accurately detect intentionality. Through role-playing and discussion of personal experiences, the children were trained to search for, interpret, and properly categorize the verbal and behavioral cues emitted by others in social dilemmas. In addition, they produced short videotaped scenarios to demonstrate their understanding of the difference between prosocial, accidental, hostile, and ambiguous peer intent.

A second component was designed to increase the cognitive availability of attributions to unintentionality when the causal situation was portrayed as ambiguous. For example, children wrote endings to unfinished stories on social dilemmas of ambiguous causal origin, which then served as a vehicle for training them to judge accidental and uncertain outcomes as unintended by the peer. They were also given practice in the interpretation of ambiguous nonverbal social cues through use of photographs and pantomime games.

All 66 participants were African-American, Grade 5 and Grade 6 boys labeled as aggressive according to the criteria used in the prior study (i.e., peer nominations and teacher ratings). Approximately one third of these boys were targeted for the experimental intervention; one third participated in an attention training program of the same duration and scope as the experimental intervention, but not related to attributional change; and one third of the boys constituted the control group who participated in no intervention of any kind. Assignment of children to one of these three groups was done on a completely random basis. The experimental and attention training groups met twice weekly for 6 weeks in small groups of six to eight.

We collected pre- and postmeasures of children's intentionality attributions, emotional reactions of anger, and aggressive behavioral intent in hypothetical social dilemmas, much like those used in the previous study. The scenarios depicted negative outcomes that were manipulated to be of prosocial, accidental, ambiguous, and hostile intent, but here we focus only on the ambiguous stories because that is where the data were most clear. Prior to the intervention, we expected that all the children would respond like the aggressive sample in the first study; that is, they were expected to display a bias toward perceiving hostile intent on the part of a hypothetical peer provocateur. Following the treatment, however, we anticipated that only children in the attributional intervention would show meaningful changes in the direction of less perceived intentionality, with accompanying decreases in reported emotion and hostile behavioral intent.

Figure 4.2 shows the pre- and postexperimental data on attributions to intent, reported anger, and endorsement of aggressive behavior in hypothetical social dilemmas of ambiguous causality. Intent and anger judgments were made on 7-point rating scales, whereas behavioral choices were converted to 6-point scales. For the three variables, high numbers indicate greater perceived intent on the part of the peer provocateur, more anger, and more hostile behavioral preference.

It is evident that the attributional intervention had its intended effect. The first panel of data in Fig. 4.1 shows ratings of peer intent as a function of treatment group, both before and after the experimental intervention. All aggressive children perceived hostile intent on the part of the peer before the intervention. Posttest measures, however,

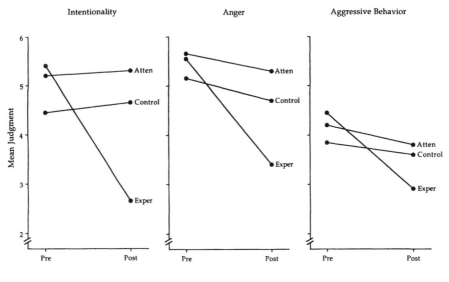

FIG. 4.2 Pre- and postexperimental intent attributions, anger, and aggressive action, by treatment group.

indicate that only the boys exposed to attributional change altered their judgments in the direction of less perceived intentionality. The same pattern prevailed for the anger and behavioral data, as shown in the second and third panels of Fig. 4.3. Following the intervention, only experimental subjects reduced the amounts of reported anger and endorsed hostile behavior. Across all three variables, the differences between experimental subjects compared to attention training and control groups were statistically significant, and in no case did the latter two groups differ from one another.

Did the attributional change program generalize to situations of actual behavior? Ethical constraints did not allow us to create *in vivo* the kinds of social dilemmas depicted in the hypothetical scenarios. Our compromise was to use a laboratory analogue task in the second part of this study that would simulate ambiguously caused peer provocation. We devised a situation where the aggressive child would communicate with an unseen peer whose actions resulted in the subject's failure to obtain a desired goal. The reasons for this outcome were designed to be perceived as ambiguous. Measures of perceived intent, amount of felt anger, and behavioral reactions were obtained.

More specifically, about 1 month after the training programs ended, all subjects participated in a problem-solving task that was supposedly unrelated to the earlier intervention. The task required the subject to communicate with an unseen peer who was seated on the other side of a barrier. Using simple grid maps, the peer was to give directions to the subject so that he could complete a maze, with the goal of winning a prize. But in fact, the task was designed to be frustrating. Unbeknownst to either child, the peer's map was different from the subject's. Thus, incorrect directions were necessarily given, the maze was not completed, and no prize awarded. While the two children engaged in the task, the experimenter unobtrusively observed and recorded the subject's behavior in the wake of non attainment of the goal. After the first trial, when it was clear that the subject had not successfully completed the maze, he was asked a series of questions about the outcome. Embedded in these questions were attributions about the unseen peer's intent (e.g., "Do you think your partner meant to give you bad directions so you wouldn't win a prize?") and feelings of anger toward the peer. These questions were answered using 7-point rating scales.

Aggressive children's intentionality attributions, reported anger, and recorded behavior during the frustrating task are reported in Table 4.3, as a function of experimental group. Notice that children who participated in the attributional intervention were significantly less likely than the other two groups to infer that the peer intentionally caused them to fail. They also expressed less anger, although the differences between groups on the emotion variable were less strong.

Verbal behaviors during the communications task were classified into one of four types: *neutral,* defined as nonjudgmental statements to the peer or adult experimenter (e.g., "That's not possible"); *complaining,* which captured negative comments directed toward the experimenter about the subject's own performance (e.g., "I can't do this");

Table 4.3

Attributions to Intent, Reported Anger, and Verbal Behavior in the Analogue Task, by Treatment Group

	Treatment Group		
Variable	Experimental (n = 20)	Attention Training (n = 24)	Control (n = 24)
Intentionality	2.3	4.5	4.7
Anger	1.7	2.5	2.6
Behavior (% total)			
Neutral	61%	29	31
Complaining	20	25	31
Criticizing	19	29	23
Insulting	0	17	15

Note: Rating scales for intentionality and anger range from 1 to 7. High numbers indicate greater perceived intent and more intense anger.

criticizing, defined as negative remarkes to the peer about his performance (e.g., "You obviously don't know how to read a map"); and
insulting, which described negative personal comments directed toward the peer (e.g., "You're dumb").

If boys who had participated in the attributional intervention inferred
less hostile intent and reported less anger, then they also should
engage in less of the kind of verbally aggressive behavior (i.e., criticizing and insulting) that might accompany goal frustration in this
context. The behavioral data in Table 4.3 show that this was indeed the
case. Neutral comments were far and away the preferred verbal behavior of experimental subjects (61%) and not one of these children
resorted to insult. For the two groups of nontrained aggressives, in
contrast, the four classes of behavior were more evenly evoked, with
about one of every six responses classified as an insult.

In summary, peer-directed aggression by young Black males is, to at
least a modest degree, predictable by these children's causal thoughts
and consequent emotions. Furthermore, it is possible to reduce their
tendency to respond with hostility by changing the way they causally
construe a social dilemma. We are really just beginning to explore the
causal thinking and behavior of African-American children labeled as
aggressive, but even these early findings are compelling and provide
direction for both our own research and for further intervention efforts
in school contexts.

IMPLICATIONS FOR ATTRIBUTIONAL
CHANGE PROGRAMS

The Targets of Attributional Change

It is evident that not all of the aggressive boys in our experimental
group benefited from the intervention. Thus, one goal for the future is
to identify the subtypes of socially deviant youth who can actually
profit from attributional change. A distinction between *reactive* and
proactive aggression discussed recently by Dodge (1991) appears
useful in this regard. A reactively aggressive boy responds to perceived
threat from others. The threat produces anger and hostility that then
"push" him to engage in retaliatory behavior. A proactively aggressive
boy, in contrast, more closely resembles the class bully; that is,
someone who engages in coercive and hostile behavior without immediate provocation. The anticipated rewards of acting aggressively
"pull" such an individual toward antisocial behavior. Although both
types of boys may be rated equally aggressive by teachers and peers,

we suspect that only reactively aggressive boys who respond to provocations from others would benefit from an intervention such as ours.

In a similar manner, we think it is necessary to consider more closely
the developmental level of our research participants. Because ethnic
minority males come to be labeled as aggressive often as early as first
grade, it is tempting to consider the possibility of attributional intervention in the very early elementary grades. This requires some
caution, however, inasmuch as children's conceptions of socially deviant behavior are known to change with age. First graders, for example, do not make clear distinctions between perceived aggressiveness
and other undesirable behaviors such as withdrawal (e.g., Younger,
Schwartzman, & Ledingham, 1986). From an attributional perspective,
moreover, children of this age have a less developed understanding of
the concept of intentionality (see Ruble & Rholes, 1981). Clearly, such
developmental differences in social cognition need to be considered as
we think about target populations for attributional interventions.

Changing More Than Causal Attributions

We focused on *attributional* change in the intervention described in this
chapter; that is, we trained aggression-prone boys to perceive peer
provocations as less intentional (Linkage 1 in Fig. 4.1). Yet when we
conceptualize peer-directed aggression as an attribution–emotion–action motivational sequence, then it evident that there are other places
along this temporal ordering of variables that also are amenable to
change.

Consider anger, for example. If children are trained to perceive
negative actions of others as relatively unintentional, then it follows
logically that feelings of anger should be mitigated (Linkage 2 in Fig.
4.1). Yet most interventions that focus on the anger component of
aggression have been fashioned after cognitive behavior modification
programs of Meichenbaum and others where aggressive children are
taught to control their anger by various self-talk strategies designed to
calm them down (e.g., Camp, 1977; Meichenbaum, 1985). Few, if any,
such programs relate feelings of anger back to their attributional
antecedents.

As our analysis indicates, an important dimension in interventions
that focus on the anger component of aggression might not so much be
training in anger *reduction,* as training children to realize that anger is
an appropriate emotional response only when a peer's negative actions
are clearly guided by hostile intent. If the attributional change agent
can help strengthen the relationship between emotion and its eliciting

causal thoughts in aggressive children, anger might be able to take on the more adaptive role of regulator, rather than instigator, of hostile behavior.

Even if the peer provocateur is perceived as intentionally causing one harm and anger is (appropriately) aroused, one could still intervene at the level of behavioral change. For example, children could be instructed in the costs (e.g., peer rejection) as opposed to the transitory benefits of aggression (Guerra & Slaby, 1990), or trained to consider other behavioral alternatives such as appealing to adults to settle conflicts among peers. In other words, the action tendencies of aggressive children might still be amenable to change, even if attributions to malicious intent and their emotional consequences have already been evoked. Given the modest success of the intervention reported here, we think such alternative approaches to attribution retraining programs are indeed viable and achievable in actual school settings.

A CONCLUDING NOTE

The popular press is increasingly portraying the African-American male as "an endangered species." Sadly, this is an apt metaphor; far too many young Black males are abandoning school at all levels of the educational pipeline; far too many swell the ranks of the unemployed; and far too many are lost to society through violent deaths, drug addiction, or incarceration. For untold numbers of these young men, their fates become sealed early in childhood. The 20-year-old dropout, addict, or criminal is often the 10-year-old labeled as aggressive by peers and teachers.

But social problems like childhood aggression are difficult to study. With so many interrelated factors contributing to its onset and such dire consequences likely to follow, researchers must grapple with enormous complexity to ascertain just what to study. We were drawn to attribution theory as a conceptual framework for examining aggression in Black male youth largely because it enabled us to manage this complexity. The theory allowed us to pose a reasonable set of researchable questions about antecedents and to explore the possibility of change. We would argue that an understanding of causal determinants and programmatic attempts at change based on this understanding are two important elements in the psychological study of social problems. But we remain humble in our claims. Neither the research that has been presented nor the theory guiding it has all or even most of the solutions to the problem of childhood aggression in African-American males. What it does offer us, however, is a framework to ask some of the right questions.

ACKNOWLEDGMENT

This chapter was written while Sandra Graham was a fellow at the Center for Advanced Study in the Behavioral Sciences, Stanford, California. Financial support during the fellowship year was provided by the Spencer Foundation and the Ford Foundation Postdoctoral Fellowships for Minorities.

REFERENCES

Cairns, R., Cairns, B., & Neckerman, H. (1989). Early school dropout: Configurations and determinants. *Child Development, 60,* 1437–1452.

Camp, B. (1977). Verbal mediation in young aggressive boys. *Journal of Abnormal Psychology, 86,* 145–153.

Coie, J., Dodge, K., & Kupersmidt, J. (1990). Peer group behavior and social status. In S. Asher & J. Coie (Eds), *Peer rejection in childhood* (pp. 17–59). New York: Cambridge University Press

Cooper, J. (1976). Deception and role playing: On telling the good guys from the bad guys. *American Psychologist, 31,* 603–610.

Dodge, K. (1991). The structure and function of reactive and proactive aggression. In D. Pepler & K. Rubin (Eds.), *The development and treatment of childhood aggression* (pp. 201–218). Hillsdale, NJ: Lawrence Erlbaum Associates.

Dodge, K., & Crick, N. (1990). Social information-processing bases of aggressive behavior in children. *Personality and Social Psychology Bulletin, 16,* 8–22.

Eron, L. (1982). Parent–child interaction, television violence, and aggression of children. *American Psychologist, 27,* 253–263.

Forsterling, F. (1990). Attributional therapies. In S. Graham & V. S. Folkes (Eds.), *Attribution theory: Applications to achievement, mental health, and interpersonal conflict* (pp. 123–139). Hillsdale, NJ: Lawrence Erlbaum Associates.

Forward, J., Canter, R., & Kirsch, N. (1976). Role-enactment and deception methodologies: Alternative paradigms? *American Psychologist, 31,* 595–604.

Friedrich-Cofer, L., & Huston, A. (1986). Television violence and aggression: The debate continues. *Psychological Bulletin, 100,* 364–371.

Gibbs, J. T. (Ed.). (1988). *Young, black, and male in America: An endangered species.* Dover, MA: Auburn House.

Graham, S. (1988). Can attribution theory tell us anything about motivation in blacks? *Educational Psychologist, 23,* 3–21.

Graham, S. (1991). A review of attribution theory in achievement contexts. *Educational Psychology Review, 3,* 5–39.

Graham, S., Hudley, C., & Williams, E. (in press). Attributional and emotional determinants of aggression among African-American and Latino young adolescents. *Developmental Psychology.*

Graham, S., & Weiner, B. (1991). Testing judgments about attribution-emotion-action linkages: A lifespan approach. *Social Cognition, 9,* 221–243.

Guerra, N., & Slaby, R. (1990). Cognitive mediators of aggression in adolescent offenders: 2. Intervention. *Developmental Psychology, 26,* 269–277.

Hudley, C. (1991). *The relationship between attributional bias and peer-directed aggression among elementary school African-American males.* Unpublished doctoral dissertation, University of California, Los Angeles, CA.

Jaynes, G., & Williams, R. (Eds.). (1989). *A common destiny: Blacks and American society.* Washington, DC: National Academy Press.

Kazdin, A. (1985). *Treatment of antisocial behavior in children and adolescents.* Homewood, IL: Dorsey Press.

Loeber, R. (1982). The stability of antisocial and delinquent child behavior. *Child Development, 53,* 1431–1446.

Loeber, R., & Stouthamer-Loeber, M. (1987). Prediction. In H. C. Quay (Ed.), *Handbook of juvenile delinquency* (pp. 325–382). New York: Wiley.

Loeber, R., & Stouthamer-Loeber, M. (1987). Prediction. In H. C. Quay (Ed.), *Handbook of juvenile delinquency* (pp. 325–382). New York: Wiley.

Maccoby, E., & Jacklin, C. (1980). Sex differences in aggression: A rejoinder and reprise. *Child Development, 51,* 964–980.

Mednick, S., Brennan, P., & Kandel, E. (1988). Predisposition to violence. *Aggressive Behavior, 14,* 25–33.

Meichenbaum, D. (1985). *Stress innoculation training.* New York: Pergamon Press.

Olweus, D. (1979). Stability of aggressive reaction patterns in males: A review. *Psychological Bulletin, 86,* 852–875.

Parke, R. D., & Slaby, R. G. (1983). The development of aggression. In E. Hetherington (Ed.), *Carmichael's manual of child psychology* (Vol. 4, pp. 547–642).

Patterson, G. R. (1986). Performance models for antisocial boys. *American Psychologist, 41,* 432–444.

Pedhazur, E. (1982). *Multiple regression in behavioral research.* New York: Holt, Rinehart & Winston.

Quay, H. C. (1987). Intelligence. In H. C. Quay (Ed.), *Handbook of juvenile delinquency* (pp. 106–117). New York: Wiley.

Reed, R. (1988). Education and achievement of young black males. In J. T. Gibbs (Ed.), *Young, black, and male in America: An endangered species* (pp. 37–96). Dover, MA: Auburn House.

Ruble, D., & Rholes, W. (1981). The development of children's perceptions and attributions about their social world. In J. H. Harvey, W. Ickes, & R. F. Kidd (Eds), *New directions in attribution research* (Vol. 3, pp. 3–36). Hillsdale, NJ: Lawrence Erlbaum Associates.

Schmidt, G., & Weiner, B. (1988). An attribution-affect-action theory of motivated behavior: Replications examining judgments of hel-giving. *Personality and Social Psychology Bulletin, 14,* 610–621.

Shaver, K. (1985). *The attribution of blame: Causality, responsibility, and blameworthiness.* New York: Springer-Verlag.

Weiner, B. (1985a). An attributional theory of achievement motivation and emotion. *Psychological Review, 92,* 548–573.

Weiner, B. (1985b). "Spontaneous" causal thinking. *Psychological Bulletin, 97,* 74–84.

Weiner, B. (1986). *An attributional theory of motivation and emotion.* New York: Springer-Verlag.

Widom, C. (1989). Does violence beget violence? A critical examination of the literature. *Psychological Bulletin, 106,* 3–28.

Wilson, J. O., & Herrnstein, R. J. (1985). *Crime and human nature.* New York: Simon & Schuster.

Younger, A., Schwartzman, A., & Ledingham, J. (1986). Age-related differences in children's perceptions of social deviance: Changes in behavior or in perspective? *Developmental Psychology, 22,* 531–542.

5

Teacher Beliefs and Children's Achievement Self-Perceptions: A Developmental Perspective

ALLAN WIGFIELD
University of Maryland

RENA D. HAROLD
Michigan State University

The literature on how teachers' expectancies influence students' achievement outcomes has flourished since the publication of Rosenthal and Jacobson's (1968) classic and controversial study of Pygmalion in the classroom. In that study elementary school teachers were given false information that some students in their classes would be "intellectual bloomers." Results showed that at some grades the children identified as bloomers performed much higher on a year-end intelligence test. Rosenthal and Jacobson concluded that teachers' expectancies about students, even if those beliefs are based on arbitrary information about children's intellectual capabilities, can influence children's achievement. Thus, teacher expectancies act as self-fulfilling prophecies because children's achievement comes to reflect the teachers' expectancies. This conclusion has been the subject of a heated and ongoing debate (e.g., Elashoff & Snow, 1971; Rosenthal, 1985; Thorndike, 1968). Since 1968 a great deal of research has ensued that attempted to determine when and how teachers' expectancies influence students' achievement, and whether those expectancies act as self-fulfilling prophecies (see Braun, 1976; Brophy, 1983, 1985; Brophy & Good, 1974; Cooper, 1979; Cooper & Good, 1983; Dusek, 1975, 1985; Rosenthal, 1974; West & Anderson, 1976, for reviews of this work). So much has been written in this area that readers may wonder what more needs to be said!

Much of the work in this area has focused on how teachers communicate their expectancies to children and treat them differentially, and how those processes influence children's achievement. In this chapter we approach this literature from a different perspective: How children may interpret teacher feedback, and how teachers' beliefs relate to children's developing self-perceptions. We use the term *teacher belief* rather than teacher expectancies in this chapter because beliefs other than teachers' expectancies for children's academic performance are discussed, including teachers' beliefs about children's effort, and the value children attach to different tasks. Most of the research discussed is with elementary school-aged children because that is the time in which children's achievement self-perceptions become established, and we highlight some of our own recent research on children's achievement self-perceptions. We begin by discussing prominent models of teacher expectancy effects.

MODELS OF TEACHER EXPECTANCY EFFECTS

Brophy and Good (1970, 1974) provided a comprehensive model of how teacher expectations could influence children's achievement. Their model posits that teachers' expectations indirectly affect children's achievement: "teacher expectations could also affect student outcomes indirectly by leading to differential teacher treatment of students that would condition student attitudes, expectations, and behavior" (Brophy, 1983, p. 639). The model includes the following sequence. Teachers form differential expectations for students early in the school year. Based on these expectations, they behave differently toward different students, and as a result of these behaviors the students begin to understand what the teacher expects from them. If students accept the teachers' expectations and behavior toward them then they will be more likely to act in ways that confirm the teacher's initial expectations. This process will ultimately affect student achievement so that teachers' initial expectancies are confirmed.

In discussing work related to this model, Brophy (1983) made several important observations about teacher expectation effects. First and foremost, he argued that most of the beliefs teachers hold about student are accurate, and so their expectations usually reflect students' actual performance levels. As a result, Brophy contended that self-fulfilling prophecy effects have relatively weak effects on student achievement, changing achievement 5% to 10%, although he did note that such effects usually are negative expectation effects rather than positive effects. Second, he pointed out that various situational and individual difference factors influence the extent to which teacher expectations will act as self-fulfilling prophecies. For instance, Brophy stated that expectancy effects may be larger in the early elementary grades, because teachers have more one-on-one interactions with students then, as they attempt to socialize children into the student role. In the upper elementary grades more whole-class teaching methods are used, which may minimize expectation effects. Some evidence supports this claim; expectancy effects in Rosenthal and Jacobson's (1968) study were strongest during the earlier grades. Raudenbush's (1984) meta-analysis of findings from different teacher expectancy studies in which expectancies were induced by giving teachers artificial information about children's intelligence showed that expectancy effects were stronger in Grades 1 and 2 than in Grades 3 through Grade 6, especially when the information was given to teachers during the first few weeks of school. These findings are particularly relevant to this chapter because they suggest that teacher beliefs about children may differentially affect children's achievement depending on the age of the child.

Most researchers (including Brophy and Good) have focused on the second part of the model, how teachers treat students differently based on their expectations for those students. In his model of how teacher expectancy effects operate, Rosenthal (1974) pointed to four main ways in which teachers differently treat students for whom they have high and low expectancies. Teachers may create warmer social-emotional relations with students for whom they have high expectancies (climate), give those students more information about their performance (feedback), and teach them more things (input). Finally, they may give those students more opportunities to interact in the classroom setting (output). Building on this model, Brophy and Good (1974) and Brophy (1983) listed a host of more specific ways in which teachers differentially treat high and low expectancy students. To name just a few, teachers may give lows less attention, give them less time to answer questions, and demand less of them. These differences in treatment (along with the others in Brophy's list) should be the basis by which students begin to understand what their teachers think of them.

In their model of expectancy effects, Cooper (1979) and Cooper and Good (1983) proposed that teachers' expectations lead them to attempt to control the timing, duration, and content of the interactions they have with students, especially students for whom they have low expectancies. Cooper (1979) posited that teachers try to maintain control over interactions with those students by limiting the frequencies of their public interactions, and instead interacting with them privately. He also suggested that teachers provide less emotional support for lows, and criticize lows more for lack of effort while praising their successful efforts less. Cooper claimed that this pattern of criticism and praise reduces the contingency between effort and outcome for those students, leaving them less certain that their efforts will produce positive achievement outcomes.

Cooper and Good's (1983) research confirmed several aspects of this model, although they found that highs were praised more for academic successes, whereas lows were praised more for following rules. They also found that students' *perceptions* of teacher behavior were more closely related to the students' perceptions of efficacy in school than were the actual frequencies of teachers' *behaviors*. Cooper and Good revised Cooper's (1979) model by adding students' perceptions of how teachers treat them to the model; they argued that it is not just what teachers do but how students view teachers' behaviors that relate both to students' own sense of efficacy and their school performance (see also Braun, 1976; Cooper, 1985). We turn next to a consideration of how students interpret differential teacher behavior.

STUDENTS' INTERPRETATIONS OF TEACHERS' DIFFERENTIAL TREATMENT

The models of Brophy and Good (1970) and Cooper and Good (1983) both give students' interpretations of teacher behavior a prominent role in mediating expectancy effects. However, they did not discuss systematically how students interpret teachers' behavior. Weinstein and her colleagues have done several important studies addressing this issue (e.g., Brattesani, Weinstein, & Marshall, 1984; Marshall & Weinstein, 1986; Weinstein, Marshall, Brattesani, & Middlestadt, 1982; Weinstein, Marshall, Sharp, & Botkin, 1987; Weinstein & Middlestadt, 1979; see Weinstein, 1983, 1985, 1989, for thorough discussion). They have been especially interested in how children understand teachers' behaviors toward different students in the classroom. Weinstein (1989) took a student mediational view of student achievement: "It is the students' perception—cognition that is ultimately the influential element on achievement" (p. 192), and so she has been most interested in how students understand teacher treatment.

Weinstein and Middlestadt (1979) developed a measure called the Teacher Treatment Inventory (TTI) to assess children's understanding of teacher behavior toward different students. The inventory contains four scales (see Weinstein et al., 1982): children's perceptions of teachers' negative feedback and directiveness; the supportive help teachers provide; how much teachers emphasize following rules and getting work done; and perceptions of teachers' expectancies, the opportunities they provide children, and choice allowed different students. One version of the scale has students rate teacher behavior toward hypothetical high and low achievers in their classroom, whereas another has students rate how teachers treat them on these dimensions.

In Weinstein and her colleagues' empirical work with the TTI children report that, compared to high achievers, low achievers receive more negative feedback and teacher directiveness, and more messages related to a work and rule orientation. By contrast, high achievers are seen as receiving more opportunities in the classroom, greater choice among alternative activities, and higher expectancies from the teachers. These differences are more pronounced in classrooms in which students see teachers treating high and low achievers quite differently (designated high differential classrooms) as compared to low differential classrooms in which teachers treat high and low achievers similarly (e.g., Weinstein et al., 1982; Weinstein et al., 1987; Weinstein & Middlestadt, 1979).

Differential teacher treatment also affects various student outcomes. In high differential classrooms, students' expectancies for themselves are more strongly associated with teachers' expectancies for them, and teacher expectancies for students' achievement explained more of the variance in students' year-end achievement than for students in low differential classes (Brattesani et al., 1984). Marshall, Weinstein, Sharp, and Brattesani (1982) reported that in high differential classrooms there are greater differences in orientation toward achievement tasks between high and low achievers than in low differential classrooms, with low achievers being less achievement oriented in the more differential classrooms.

One of the most striking findings emerging in these studies is that even children in the early elementary grades believe that teachers treat high and low achievers differently (e.g., Weinstein et al., 1987; Weinstein & Middlestadt, 1979). However, some interesting age differences have emerged in this work. Weinstein and Middlestadt (1979) found that although younger (Grade 1 through Grade 3) and older (Grade 4 through Grade 6) students believed teachers treat high and low achievers differently, their perceptions of these differences were not the same. The younger children believed teachers criticize high achievers more, whereas the older children thought low achievers receive more criticism. In the Weinstein et al. (1987) study, compared to older children, first graders were less accurate in their understanding of teachers' expectancies for themselves, and did not see as clearly how teachers' expectancies were tied to teachers' treatment of them. However, in high differential classrooms only, even first- and third-grade children for whom teachers had low expectancies had lower expectancies for themselves, suggesting that teacher evaluations already are a powerful determinant of children's expectancies at these ages. By Grade 5, children for whom teachers had low expectancies in both high and low differential classrooms themselves had lower expectancies.

This work has made an important contribution to the literature on teacher expectancy effects, showing clearly that children (even Grade 1 children) do understand that teachers treat high and low achievers differently. The findings support the contention by Brophy and Good (1970) and Cooper and Good (1983) that student perceptions should be included in models of how teacher expectancies affect student achievement. However, two limitations of this work should be noted. First, much of Weinstein and her colleagues' empirical work with the TTI is based on children's ratings of hypothetical high and low achievers in their classrooms. In the vignettes used to describe the students, their achievement level is portrayed very clearly; it is unclear whether information about "real" students' achievement is quite this clear (see Blumenfeld, Pintrich, Meece, & Wessels, 1982). Second, Brophy and Good (1970) proposed that students' interpretations of teacher behavior could influence outcomes such as motivation, performance, and behavioral conduct. The major achievement outcomes Weinstein and her colleagues have examined are students' expectancies for their own success and their year-end achievement. These clearly are crucial outcome measures, but particularly with respect to students' achievement-related beliefs and motivation there are other outcome variables that need to be considered. We discuss these beliefs next.

STUDENT ACHIEVEMENT SELF-PERCEPTIONS

Work on the development of children's achievement self-perceptions has burgeoned since the 1970s, and has shown that these beliefs are related to children's academic performance, persistence, and choice of different tasks. A complete review of this work is beyond the scope of this chapter; for reviews of different aspects of this work see Dweck and Elliott (1983), Eccles and Wigfield (1985), Nicholls (1984), Schunk (1984, 1990), Stipek and Mac Iver (1989), and Wigfield and Eccles (1989, in press), along with the chapters by Meece and Courtney, Pintrich and Schrauben, and Schunk in this volume. Although there are many important achievement beliefs, our perspective is that two major sets of beliefs are central to achievement motivation: individuals' beliefs regarding their ability and expectancies for success (see

Schunk, 1984, 1990, this volume for discussion of the related construct of perceived efficacy), and their beliefs regarding how much they value different tasks and their motivational orientation (e.g., see Eccles et al., 1983; Wigfield & Eccles, in press). Eccles and Wigfield (1985) proposed that these beliefs can be conceptualized in terms of two general questions children ask themselves: "Can I succeed on this task?" and "Do I want to succeed on this task?" To provide a context for how teacher beliefs influence children's developing achievement perceptions, we briefly discuss work relevant to these questions, focusing on our recent study of the development and socialization of these beliefs.

Can I Succeed: Children's Perceptions of Ability and Expectancies for Success

Children's perceptions of ability refer to children's sense of how good they are at different tasks. These perceptions change in several important ways over the elementary school years. First, children's understanding of what ability is appears to change. Nicholls (1978, 1984, this volume) argued that most young children have a mastery or learning view of ability, believing that increased effort can improve their abilities. By the late elementary school years, however, children understand how effort and ability can be inversely related (see Nicholls, 1978), and that if success requires a great deal of effort it may mean the individual lacks ability. This change leads some children to define *ability* as relatively stable and to judge it in comparison to others, and so have the notion of "ability as capacity" (see Dweck & Bempechat, 1983, for similar definitions of ability).

Another way children's perceptions of ability change is that they decline across the school years, and relate more closely to children's actual performance in school (see Stipek & Mac Iver, 1989). For instance, Marsh (1989) found that children's perceptions of ability in several domains declined linearly during the elementary school years. Similarly, Nicholls (1979) found that in Grade 1 most children ranked themselves near the top of the class in their reading ability, and there was essentially no correlation between those ability ratings and children's performance. By age 12, children's ratings were more dispersed, and the correlations between ability ratings and school grades were in the .70 range.

Expectancies for success are closely related to students' perceptions of ability (see Eccles & Wigfield, 1991), and they also undergo change during the elementary school years. Most studies show that young (4-

and 5-year-old) children's expectancies for success are overly optimistic, so that they nearly always think they will do well on the next task. This optimism holds even if young children repeatedly fail at a task, and so it appears that young children's expectancies are not grounded in the reality of their performance, but may reflect what outcome they hope to achieve. As children proceed through elementary school, their expectancies begin to correspond more closely to their previous performance, so that following success their expectancies increase, whereas following failure they decrease (see Parsons & Ruble, 1977; Stipek, 1984). Thus, expectancies for success appear to become more accurate or realistic as children get older, in the sense of relating more closely to their actual performance on different tasks and being more responsive to success and failure experiences (see Eccles, Midgley, & Adler, 1984; Stipek, 1984, for reviews of this work).

Do I Want to Succeed: Children's Achievement Values and Motivational Orientation

Children's achievement values refer to constructs such as their liking of different tasks, the importance of those tasks to them, and the potential usefulness of those tasks in the future (see Eccles et al., 1983; Wigfield & Eccles, in press, for theoretical views on the nature of children's achievement values). Like the literature on perceptions of ability, results of studies looking at changes in the mean level of children's values generally show that children value academic tasks less as they get older (see Eccles & Midgley, 1989; Eccles, Midgley, & Adler, 1984; Wigfield & Eccles, in press, for reviews). For instance, in studies of students' domain-specific achievement values, Eccles et al. (1983) and Wigfield (1984) examined how children's valuing of mathematics and English differed by age in a group of 5th- through 12th-grade students. Both studies showed that younger students valued math more highly than did older students. In contrast, students' valuing of English increased across age. Eccles et al. (1989) and Wigfield, Eccles, Mac Iver, Reuman, and Midgley (1991) looked at how the transition to junior high influenced children's valuing of different activities. They found that children's ratings of both the importance of math and English and their liking of these school subjects decreased across the transition from elementary to junior high school. In math, students' importance ratings continued to decline across Grade 7, whereas in their ratings of the importance of English the beliefs rebounded somewhat.

Studies of children's intrinsic versus extrinsic motivational orientation, which in this context is analagous to children's interest value, show that children become more extrinsically motivated as they get older; that is, they do tasks less because they like them and more because they are required. For example, in a cross-sectional study of children's intrinsic motivation Harter (1981) assessed different components of intrinsic motivation in third- through ninth-grade students. She found that older children's intrinsic motivation was much lower than younger children's on three of her intrinsic motivation subscales: preference for challenge, curiosity/interest, and independent mastery. Harter concluded that children's intrinsic motivation is stifled in important ways during the school years, an outcome she viewed as problematic.

A STUDY OF THE EARLY DEVELOPMENT OF CHILDREN'S ABILITY PERCEPTIONS AND VALUES ACROSS DIFFERENT ACTIVITY DOMAINS

A Brief Overview

Over the past several years, we have been examining the ontogeny of children's self and task beliefs that act as significant predictors of children's task choices and self-esteem. More specifically, we have studied the early development and socialization of children's ability perceptions and achievement values (and a host of other achievement-related beliefs and choices) across the elementary school years (see Eccles, Wigfield, Harold, & Blumenfeld, 1991; Harold et al., 1989; Wigfield et al., 1990, for reports on different aspects of this study). In this section, initial results from this project are presented that focus on the following broad questions: (a) how do children's achievement self-perceptions change over the elementary school years?; and (b) what do teachers perceive about children's abilities and interests in different activities, and how do those perceptions relate to children's beliefs?

The study has some unique features that differentiate it from other work in this area. First, we assessed the self-perceptions of children at least once each year over a 3-year period. Most studies of children's achievement self-perceptions reviewed earlier and studies of children's self-concepts (e.g., Harter, 1982, 1985; Marsh, 1989) have been cross-sectional. Second, we measured children's perceptions of ability and their achievement values in several different activity domains, including mathematics, reading, computers, music, sports, and social activities. With the important exceptions of Harter's work (e.g., Harter, 1982) and Marsh's work (e.g., Marsh, 1989; Marsh, Barnes, Cairns, & Tidman, 1984), few studies have looked at how children's self-perceptions vary across different activity domains, and even fewer have examined both ability perceptions and achievement values. Third, we obtained information from parents and teachers about the children, including their perceptions of children's abilities, interests, and activities. Thus, we have information about children from multiple informants.

This study also differs in regard to the kind of information that was gathered from teachers. Most research on teachers' beliefs about students has been limited to their perceptions of students' general academic performance. In this study, teachers were asked to assess children's ability, effort, and valuing of academic and nonacademic activities. These data allowed us to examine several specific questions following from the second broader question posed earlier (see Harold et al., 1989 for discussion of additional results from these data), including: (a) are there gender and age differences in teachers' ratings of children's abilities?; (b) what are the relations between teacher ratings of ability in various domains and actual aptitude measures given to children?; and (c) what are the relations between teachers' beliefs about children and children's self-perceptions?

Research Procedures

When the study began in 1987, participating children were in kindergarten, first, and third grades, and at the completion of data collection in 1990, the children were in Grade 3, Grade 4, and Grade 6. Data collected from children the first year included various academic and physical skills aptitude measures. Children first completed questionnaires assessing their achievement self-perceptions in the second year of the project (Spring 1988), when they were in Grade 1, Grade 2, and Grade 4. Children completed questionnaires again in the Springs of 1989 and 1990. The data we report regarding children's achievement beliefs come from children's responses to the Year 2 questionnaire.

There were approximately 850 child participants during the second year with almost equal gender representation; 275 of the children were in Grade 1, 313 in Grade 2, and 262 in Grade 4. The vast majority of the children are White and are from lower middle-class to middle-class socioeconomic backgrounds. The children attended 10 different elementary schools in four school districts near a large midwestern city.

Child Questionnaire. The child questionnaire assessed children's perceptions of ability and achievement values about mathematics, reading, computer, music, sports, and social activities, and many other constructs, including children's general self-esteem, which was assessed using items from Harter's (1982) general self-worth scale. Questions tapping children's perceptions of their ability in each domain included items assessing perceived competence, expectancies for future success, ease of learning new things, and perceptions of the difficulty of the activity; for example, How good are you at math? How good are you at music compared to other subjects?. Questions tapping achievement values assessed children's interest in the activity, how useful it would be for them in the future, and how important it was to be good at the activity; for example, How much do you like doing reading? How important is it to you to be good at sports?. The questions were modified from earlier questionnaires developed by Eccles et al. (1983) and Parsons (1980) that were used by Eccles and her colleagues in several previous studies of late elementary through high school aged-children (e.g., Eccles, Adler, & Meece, 1984; Eccles et al., 1983; Eccles et al., 1989; Meece, Wigfield, & Eccles, 1990; Parsons, Kaczala, & Meece, 1982; Wigfield et al., 1991; Wigfield & Meece, 1988). These questionnaires are described more completely in Eccles et al. (1991) and Wigfield et al. (1990), as are the procedures for pilot testing the questions for use with the younger children in this study.

Teacher Individual Assessment Questionnaire. Teachers completed individual assessment questionnaires on each participating child during the spring of each year of the study. They were asked to rate their students in the following domains: math, reading, social, sports, music, and art. For each domain, they were asked about several constructs; we focus here on their perceptions of children's talent or ability, effort, and the importance of quality performance to the child; for example, How important is it to this child to do well in art? How hard does this child try in math? The data we discuss come from the Year 1 and Year 2 teacher individual assessment questionnaires; that is, the year before children first completed questionnaires and the year they first did so.

Research Findings: Children's Beliefs

Structure of Children's Ability Perceptions and Values. Do young children discriminate between domains, and between ability and value? Factor analyses done for the whole sample and separately by grade on the items assessing children's beliefs about all the activities demonstrated that children's beliefs about each domain (math, reading, computers, music, sports, and social activities) formed separate factors. These six factors emerged in the analyses done at each grade level. Factor analyses done on the set of items within each domain showed that in most domains, children's perceptions of ability and valuing of the activity formed separate factors. These analyses indicate that children's self-perceptions are quite differentiated even at first grade, both for activities in different domains and for specific beliefs within an activity domain (see Eccles et al., 1991; Wigfield et al., 1990, for further discussion of these results, and their implications for theories of the development of children's achievement self-perceptions).

Gender and Age Differences in Children's Beliefs. Do children's beliefs differ by gender and/or age? Based on the results of the factor analyses, items were grouped into scales tapping children's perceptions of ability and valuing of each activity. The scales were analyzed for gender and grade effects. The means for all significant gender and grade effects are presented in Table 5.1. There were no interactions of gender and grade. Boys had higher ability perceptions for math, computers, and sports activities than did girls, whereas girls' ability perceptions were higher for music and social activities. Girls valued reading and music activities significantly more than boys did, whereas boys valued sports activities more than did girls.

Regarding the grade effects, for all activities but sports, younger children had more positive ability perceptions than did the older children, with the differences stronger between Grade 1 and Grade 4 children. Although there was no significant grade effect for sports ability perceptions, older children had slightly more positive ability perceptions in sports. Concerning values, the grade effects for achievement values were significant for reading, computers, music, and sports activities. For reading, computers, and music, younger children valued the activity more than those in Grade 4 did, whereas Grade 4 children valued sports the most.

These results demonstrate further that children's achievement self-perceptions, particularly their perceptions of ability, decrease across the elementary school years. They extend that work by showing how children's achievement values differ by age and gender during the early elementary school years, and also how children's beliefs vary across several different activity domains that are common to childhood. From that perspective these results show that age-related de-

Table 5.1

Means for the Significant Effects on Children's Perceptions of Ability and Valuing of
the Different Activities

Activity	Gender		Grade		
	Girls	Boys	1	2	4
Math SCA	5.38	5.67	5.69	5.49	5.38
Reading SCA			6.04	5.85	5.38
Reading value	5.84	5.34	5.76	5.62	5.38
Computer SCA	5.76	6.02	6.03	5.83	5.75
Computer value			5.99	5.98	5.70
Music SCA	5.15	4.41	5.26	4.78	4.26
Misic value	5.61	4.62	5.51	5.16	4.68
Sports SCA	5.22	6.18			
Sports value	5.66	6.19	5.76	5.98	6.02
Social SCA	5.88	5.34	5.77	5.61	5.46

Note: SCA = Self-concept of ability.

clines in achievement beliefs are quite general, with the exception of
beliefs about sports activities. These results paint a rather gloomy
picture of how children's perceptions of ability and valuing of academic activities change across the school years. In the early school
years children have quite positive perceptions of ability for different
academic activities, and value them highly. As they get older they
begin to value certain academic activities less, and generally their
perceptions of ability are lower. How might teachers' beliefs about their
students fit into this picture? We present results from our study
relevant to that issue next.

Research Findings: Teachers' Beliefs

*Gender and Age Differences in Teachers' Ratings of Children's
Abilities.*   Do teacher's ratings differ by gender and/or age? There
were no significant gender differences in teachers' ability ratings of
their students in math, reading, or in making friends at either Year 1 or
Year 2. However, boys were seen as being more talented in sports (at
Year 2), whereas girls were seen as having more ability in art (at Year 2)
and in music (both years). These findings are intriguing, given that
during the elementary school years there is little evidence for the
perceived differences in art and music, and the percent of variance
accounted for by actual performance in sports is not as marked as the
teachers' ratings might suggest. These differences in teachers' perceptions of sports and music ability for boys and girls parallel those
observed in children's own beliefs discussed earlier.

There were no significant grade differences in teachers' perceptions of talent either at Year 1 when the students were in Kindergarten, Grade 1, and Grade 3 or at Year 2 when they were in Grade 1, Grade 2, and Grade 4. These results differ from children's own beliefs, which showed that children's perceptions of competence decreased across grade. It is interesting that teachers do not share young children's optimistic ability perceptions; perhaps teachers' beliefs reflect the reality of children's performance more, a reality that only gradually influences children's own beliefs.

The Accuracy of Teachers' Perceptions of Their Students Across Domains. Are teachers' ratings of their students' ability congruent with the students' performance on aptitude measures? As mentioned earlier, in Year 1 of the project each child completed a battery of cognitive measures, a shortened form of the Bruininks–Oseretsky test of physical skills (Bruininks, 1977), and the Slosson I.Q. test. Correlations of teachers' ratings with these measures showed that teachers' perceptions of their students' abilities in math and reading were related moderately (r's about .40) to the children's IQ scores (i.e., students rated as doing well in math and reading scored highly on the Slosson test). Similarly, children's scores on the spatial skills measure correlated with teachers' ratings of their math ability ($r = .30$). Teachers' ratings of children's ability in sports were significantly related to the total Bruininks score and to the the large motor subtest scores such as running and broad jump, with the rs around .30. Teachers reported to us that they were much more confident of their ratings of their students' abilities in the two areas in which they had the most contact with the children, math and reading. They were hesitant to rate the children in the other domains. However, these data show that the teachers' ratings of the children's abilities are related to the children's actual performance on aptitude measures tapping math, reading, and sports.

Relations Between Teachers' Ratings and Children's Self-Perceptions. How closely related are teacher and student ratings of abilities and interests? Correlations were performed on teachers' ratings of children in the math, reading, sports, and social domains with children's achievement beliefs in those domains. These analyses were performed separately at each grade level. In general (especially for the older children), the significant correlations that emerged are between teachers' domain-specific beliefs about children and children's beliefs in that domain. However, these significant correlations (which are all positive) are relatively modest, ranging from .11 to .36.

In the analyses within each grade, for Grade 1, the two domains in which most of the significant relations occurred were reading and sports, and the significant correlations ranged from .11 to .30. For Grade 2, significant relations between children's beliefs and teachers' beliefs occurred in the math, reading, sports, and social domains (significant r's range from .11 to .30). Finally, for Grade 4, significant relations occurred in all domains but the social domain. The relations in the fourth-grade group (significant r's range from .11 to .36) between teachers' beliefs about children's academic abilities and children's academic self-perceptions are stronger than many relations in the Grade 1 group, but not markedly stronger than the relations at Grade 2.

Summary and Conclusions

Several conclusions can be drawn from these findings. Teachers appear to be reasonably accurate in judging children's ability in different domains, although the relations are moderate. Teachers' perceptions of children's talents did not differ for different-aged children, which contrasts rather sharply with the observed decline in children's own self-perceptions. However, teachers' beliefs about boys and girls did differ, as did boys' and girls' self-reports. The areas in which both children and teachers see boys and girls differing in ability were music and sports. As mentioned earlier, there likely is little or no performance difference between boys and girls in these areas at these ages and so the perceptions of differences in ability have little grounding in reality. Perhaps children and teachers infer ability differences in these areas because of children's expressed liking for these activities; from other questions on the child questionnaire that children answered we know that at all grades girls like music more than boys do, and boys like sports more than girls do (see Eccles et al., 1991). Each group may do the activity they like with more enthusiasm. The gender differences in teachers' beliefs about children and children's own beliefs also may reflect society's stereotypes about appropriate activities for boys and girls.

Regarding relations between teachers' and children's beliefs, there are domain differences in the pattern of relationships. In general, relations between teacher beliefs and children's beliefs are stronger in the math, reading, and sports domains (especially at Grade 2 and Grade 4) than in the social and music domains. If we assume that teachers are influencing children's beliefs by providing them feedback about their performance, these patterns suggest that teachers influence children's beliefs more in some areas than in others, with (as one would expect) the academic areas and sports being the ones in which teachers have the most impact. Further, the differences teachers see in boys' and girls' ability in sports may make that domain a particularly likely candidate for self-fulfilling prophecy effects to occur.

Although it seems plausible to assume that teachers are influencing children's beliefs, the analyses presented here are correlational and so, of course, causal direction cannot be inferred. It is very likely that children's performance and behavior influences teachers' beliefs about them too; the models of teacher expectancy effects reviewed earlier suggest children's performance is an important determinant of teachers' beliefs. This may be particularly true in the early elementary grades when teachers have relatively little information about children. Alexander and Entwisle (1988) have shown that parents' expectancies for their young children change in response to children's performance; this also may occur for teachers. As children go through school accumulating grades and test scores in their folders teachers may use that information to form impressions of children even before they interact with the children. Thus, it is important to acknowledge that relations between teachers' beliefs and children's beliefs likely are reciprocal. We plan to examine longitudinal relations between children's and teachers' beliefs to obtain a clearer understanding of the causal direction in these beliefs.

Although generally the relations between teachers' and children's beliefs are stronger in certain domains, there are some grade differences in the patterns of relations, with the Grade 4 children's beliefs in math and reading more closely related to teachers' beliefs in those areas than at the other two grades. This pattern likely occurred because Grade 4 students have received much more evaluative feedback from teachers in school, and would be predicted based on Nicholls' (1979) findings that children's perceptions of their reading attainment become increasingly highly correlated with their school grades as they get older. Our findings for Grade 4 are similar in magnitude to those Nicholls (1979) reported for the 10-year-olds in his study; for Grade 1 somewhat higher correlations in reading were obtained than Nicholls reported for the 6-year-olds in his study. Thus, our findings show that the magnitude of the relations between teachers' beliefs and children's beliefs increases somewhat across grade, and also that by Grade 4, children's ability perceptions in math and reading are more consistently related to teachers' perceptions of children's ability in those areas.

Children's general self-esteem did not strongly relate to teachers' beliefs about children; when significant relations emerged they only occurred in the Grade 1 group. The age differences in relations of self-esteem to teachers' perceptions may mean that younger children rely more on teacher evaluations in judging their overall self-worth, whereas older children do not. Although this possibility is intriguing, the relations between self-esteem and teachers' perceptions at Grade 1 are modest, and so we make this point cautiously. As mentioned earlier, Brophy (1983) suggested that teacher expectancy effects may have a stronger influence on younger children than on older children, and Raudenbush (1984) found some support for this claim in his meta-analysis of studies of induced teacher expectancy effects. Our findings regarding teacher beliefs and children's self-esteem provide some support for this claim; however, as just discussed, relations between children's beliefs and teachers' beliefs are somewhat stronger and more consistent across academic domains in the older than the younger children, which may suggest expectancy effects operate more at that time (see discussion later). If it is true, however, that Grade 1 self-esteem relates more to teachers' ratings, then the Grade 1 year could be considered a pivotal one in the development of children's sense of worth in school.

How might teachers' beliefs contribute to the decline in children's achievement self-perceptions? As noted earlier, teachers' domain specific-evaluations of children did not differ for children of different ages. Because by Grade 3 or Grade 4 children's academic beliefs begin to relate more to teachers' beliefs about them, perhaps teachers at all grades provide relatively consistent and realistic messages to children about their performance that take some time to be incorporated into children's self-perceptions. Another reason teacher beliefs could have more of an impact at this time is the shift in children's beliefs from viewing ability is modifiable to believing it is more stable (see Nicholls, 1978, 1984). For many children, perceptions of stable ability could deflate their estimates of ability in some areas, especially in areas in which they are not excelling. As children's ability perceptions for different activities decline, they also may begin to de-value those activities they do less well. This strategy may allow them to maintain their general self-esteem (see Harter, 1985, 1986).

Recall that Brophy (1983) claimed that teacher expectancy effects may be most likely to occur in the early elementary grades because of the kinds of teacher–student interactions that occur then. Raudenbush's (1984) meta-analysis suggested that effects of induced expectancies are strongest in Grades 1 and 2. In contrast, we would suggest that expectancy effects may be more likely to occur in the middle to later elementary grades, in part because of the changes in children's understanding of ability just discused. Brophy (1983, 1985) argued that most teacher expectancy effects tend to be debilitating (Gollum) effects rather than enhancing (Galatea) effects. Children viewing ability as stable should be more likely to be affected by these Gollum effects; messages from teachers that they are not doing well should be more debilitating for these children. Changes in the school and classroom environment that occur during the later elementary school years also may make expectancy effects more likely to happen then. As children move through school, formal evaluation practices increase (see Blumenfeld et al., 1982; Hill & Wigfield, 1984), and often there is a greater emphasis on social comparison and competition between students. Also, there is increased use of between-classroom ability grouping practices and whole-classroom instruction, and greater focus on discipline and control (see Eccles, Midgley, & Adler, 1984; Eccles & Midgley, 1989; Marshall & Weinstein, 1984; Stipek & Mac Iver, 1989).

Eccles, Midgley, and Adler (1984) and Eccles and Midgley (1989) argued persuasively that these systematic changes in school environments may be responsible for the negative changes in many children's ability perceptions, achievement values, and intrinsic motivation. Moreover, these changes in classroom environments can interact with changes in children's processing of evaluative information to influence their achievement beliefs (see Marshall & Weinstein, 1984). For instance, teachers who emphasize normative comparisons between students and use competitive grading practices will heighten the salience of social comparison between children, especially as children learn to use that information to evaluate their competence. Although many high-achieving children may maintain positive achievement beliefs when these practices are used, as their usage increases other children will become more pessimistic about their prospects for school success.

The combination of changes in the nature of children's perceptions of ability, the stronger relations between children's ability perceptions and actual performance, and the increased focus on competitive performance in school may make it most likely for teacher expectancy effects to occur in the middle to late elementary school years. Raudenbush's (1984) findings that expectancy effects were strongest in the early elementary grades could be explained by his inclusion only of studies in which expectancies were *induced* by experimenters giving false information to teachers; that information may have more of an impact when teachers have had less experience with children. Brophy (1983) noted that studies of induced expectancies show less consistent results than studies of teachers' "real" expectancies.

Having made this claim, we should address why many of the relations between teachers' beliefs and student self-perceptions in our study were relatively modest. Blumenfeld et al. (1982) discussed that in classroom settings the information children receive about their performance often is not very clear. Teachers give many different messages to children about their conduct, effort, and ability, and students must interpret that information. Sometimes these messages may conflict with one another, and often they are not very clear. The ambiguity and lack of clarity in teachers' messages, coupled with the developmental differences in children's understanding of ability and processing of feedback discussed earlier, are probable reasons why teachers' perceptions of children and children's own achievement self-perceptions relate only modestly. Another important reason is that teachers' beliefs are only one source of information for children; their own previous performance, the performance of their peers, and messages from their parents also will influence their developing achievement self-perceptions.

Issues for Future Research

Our data show how teachers view students in different areas and how teachers' and children's beliefs relate to each other. These data provide support for the models of teacher expectancy effects that include students' interpretations of teacher beliefs and behavior as one important part of the self-fulfilling prophecy process (Brophy & Good, 1970, 1974; Cooper & Good, 1983). What is needed next is research on the processes by which teachers' and students' beliefs become related. Social psychologists have been interested in how individuals interpret each others' behavior in social interaction sequences, such as teacher--student interactions. For instance, Darley and Fazio (1980) discussed how individuals (called "perceivers" by Darley and Fazio) actively construct and create their own perceptions of other (called "targets") based on the processes ongoing in interaction sequences as well as on other information individuals have about each other. They proposed that the target tries to determine why the perceiver acted as he or she did, which usually involves making a personal or situational attribution about the target's behavior. Using a classroom example to illustrate, was the teacher nice because he or she is a friendly person (a personal attribution), or because the situation called for friendly actions? In addition, Darley and Fazio proposed that the target will make similar personal or situational inferences about him or herself; did the perceiver treat me that way because of something about me (e.g., the teacher criticized me because I am a low achiever), or because of the situation we are in (e.g., my group was acting inappropriately)? The target's response then will be based on these different interpretations of the perceiver's action. If targets accept perceivers' beliefs, they often adjust their behavior to reflect perceivers' beliefs. Thus, the target would be acting in accord with the perceiver's beliefs, and so may help fulfill the perceiver's prophecy.

This work offers some important insights into how students (targets) interpret the behavior of teachers (perceivers). From a developmental perspective, however, an important question for future work is at what point do children begin to make the inferences about the reasons for teachers' behaviors and reasons for their own behavior that Darley and Fazio discuss, such as deciding that teachers' behavior occurs because of teacher's characteristics, or because of aspects of the particular situation. Our work and Weinstein and her colleagues' work (see Weinstein, 1985, 1989) suggest that relations between teacher beliefs and student self-perceptions exist quite early on in elementary school, but to date we know less about how students actually interpret the messages they receive from teachers.

Based on the brief review of the development of achievement perceptions presented earlier, we would argue that early in elementary school children are not very sophisticated in interpreting teachers' evaluations; for instance, in deciding whether the teachers' messages are due to personal or situational aspects of behavior. Also, teachers' messages may be interpreted broadly so that children's general self-esteem is influenced more than their specific self-perceptions. Children may not accurately judge messages from teachers as indications of success or failure, or relate those messages to previous messages or to their own previous interpretations of their performance (see Blumenfeld et al., 1982). As children experience more evaluative feedback teachers' beliefs about their performance in a given domain will begin to relate more closely to their own self-evaluations. By the middle elementary school years teachers' specific beliefs (e.g., about students' ability) in a given domain will begin to relate more strongly to children's beliefs about their ability in that domain. Additionally, if students interpret teachers' feedback as reflecting something about themselves (I am a high/low achiever) rather than something about the situation, these relations may be stronger. This proposed developmental sequence should be assessed.

EDUCATIONAL IMPLICATIONS

Because of the publicity Rosenthal and Jacobson's (1968) study has received and the subsequent debate concerning its results, many teachers are aware of how their beliefs may influence children's achievement. Most educational psychology textbooks have sections on teacher expectancy effects, and so teacher trainees learn how their beliefs about students can influence their treatment of those students. Other researchers in this area, notably Brophy (1983, 1985) and Brophy and Good (1974), made important recommendations for teachers about how to minimize Gollum expectancy effects. These suggestions include being aware of one's expectancies, keeping them current, and focusing on students' progress and mastery.

Although teachers may be aware that their expectancies can affect children's learning, it may be difficult for them to know exactly how they treat different students, primarily because teachers' interactions with students occur so frequently and quickly (see Jackson, 1968). Teachers may not be able to "process" those interactions and so may not realize the kinds of messages they provide to different students or how they treat students differently. Brophy (1983, 1985) has argued that teachers should not try to treat all students alike or have the same expectations for all students, since there are individual differences among students. Although we generally concur with this view, some differential treatment that could arise from teachers' beliefs is not appropriate. For instance, different studies show that boys often get more response opportunities in math classes than do girls, because boys tend to be more active but also because some teachers think boys do better in math (see Brophy & Good, 1974; Eccles et al., 1983). Having fewer response opportunities can inhibit girls' subsequent motivation to take further math courses (see Eccles, Midgley, & Adler, 1984; Jacobs & Wigfield, 1989), which could be thought of as a Gollum expectancy effect if the differential treatment was based on teachers' beliefs that girls cannot do math.

Other teachers may not even realize that they give differential response opportunities to different groups, such as boys and girls. Wheaton (1991) interviewed a group of teachers and found that most believed that they treated boys and girls similarly. She observed the teachers in their classrooms and found that the response opportunities they allowed and feedback they provided differed for boys and girls. When told of these results the teachers were quite shocked! Thus, along with being aware of the possibility of expectancy effects, perhaps teachers should observe one another teaching in order to gauge the kinds of differential treatment going on in classrooms, and discuss it among themselves. Such observations and discussions may provide some important insights to teachers about their behaviors and how those behaviors may reflect their beliefs about students.

Second, we would suggest that teachers need to be much more aware of the work on how children's achievement self-perceptions develop over the school years, and the kind of impact they can have on those beliefs. In discussing the results of our project with teachers they often have a general sense of which students are motivated or not in their classrooms, but little sense of children's beliefs about specific subjects. When given the results they find them fascinating, and generate many interesting explanations for them. The two aspects of the changes in children's self-perceptions that seem most useful for teachers to understand are the decline in children's achievement beliefs, and the change toward believing ability is more stable. Teachers' sensitivity to these changes may help some children maintain more positive ability perceptions.

However, from our earlier discussion of how classroom environments change across elementary school, it is apparent that children get evaluated more frequently on the basis of their abilities and in general more emphasis is placed on ability. This focus on ability may make teacher expectancy effects more likely to occur, and also make it more difficult for many children to maintain positive ability perceptions. To counter this trend, like Brophy (1983, 1985) we would suggest that student progress and mastery be the focus of evaluation, rather than competitive ability assessments. Ames (1990, this volume) and Brophy (1987) have developed interesting classroom-based programs to promote children's mastery orientation. Ames' program provides teachers with strategies for presenting tasks in more novel ways, involving students in decisions making, evaluating students privately rather than publicly, and evaluating students on mastery and improvement rather than on ability. A major goal of the program is to tie students' self-worth to effort and thus promote a mastery orientation. Because of this focus, this program should reduce the likelihood of Gollum expectancy effects occurring.

Teachers' own beliefs about ability influence how they treat different students. Work on teachers' understanding of the nature of ability (e.g., Swann & Snyder, 1980) and on teachers' sense of teaching efficacy, or their beliefs about how much they can influence each student's performance, are the critical constructs here. Teachers who believe they can effectively teach all students have been shown to have important positive influences on children's achievement outcomes and achievement self-perceptions, with the effects often stronger for low achievers (see Ashton, 1985; Ashton & Webb, 1986; Midgley, Feldlaufer, & Eccles, 1989; Woolfolk & Hoy, 1990). In our discussions with teachers, we have found that many believe children's abilities are rather stable, and that some children lack this stable ability; hence teachers' expectations for these students are not very high. Teachers holding such beliefs may be most prone to letting their beliefs act as self-fulfilling prophecies (see Brophy, 1983). Changing these views on the nature of ability and helping teachers promote a mastery orientation may be the best ways to improve teachers' own sense of efficacy, thus allowing them to reach more students.

ACKNOWLEDGMENT

We thank the principals, teachers, and students in the cooperating school districts for allowing us to work with them. We also acknowledge the contributions of our colleagues Jacquelynne Eccles, Phyllis Blumenfeld, Carol Freedman-Doan, and Kwang Suk Yoon to the project described in this chapter.

REFERENCES

Alexander, K., & Entwisle, D. (1988). Achievement in the first two years of school: Patterns and processes. *Monographs of the Society for Research in Child Development, 53* (2, Serial No. 218).

Ames, C. (1990, April). *Achievement goals and classroom structure: Developing a learning orientation in students.* Paper presented at the meeting of the American Educational Research Association, Boston.

Ashton, P. T. (1985). Motivation and the teachers' sense of efficacy. In C. Ames & R. Ames (Eds.), *Research on motivation in education* (Vol. 2, pp. 141–174). Orlando, FL: Academic Press.

Ashton, P. T., & Webb, R. B. (1986). *Making a difference: Teachers' sense of efficacy and student achievement.* New York: Longman.

Blumenfeld, P., Pintrich, P., Meece, J., & Wessels, K. (1982). The formation and role of self-perceptions of ability in elementary school classrooms. *Elementary School Journal, 82,* 401–420.

Brattesani, K A., Weinstein, R. S., & Marshall, H. H. (1984). Student perceptions of differential teacher treatments as moderators of teacher expectation effects. *Journal of Educational Psychology, 76,* 236–247.

Braun, C. (1976). Teacher expectation: Sociopsychological dynamics. *Review of Educational Research, 46,* 185–213.

Brophy, J. E. (1983). Research on the self-fulfilling prophecy and teacher expectations. *Journal of Educational Psychology, 75,* 631–661.

Brophy, J. E. (1985). Teacher-student interaction. In J. B. Dusek (Ed.), *Teacher expectancies* (pp. 303–328). Hillsdale, NJ: Lawrence Erlbaum Associates.

Brophy, J. E. (1987). Socializing students' motivation to learn. In M. Maehr & D. Kleiber (Eds.), *Advances in motivation and achievement* (Vol. 5, pp. 181–210). Greenwich, CT: JAI Press.

Brophy, J. E., & Good, T. (1970). Teachers' communication of differential expectations for children's classroom performance: Some behavioral data. *Journal of Educational Psychology, 61,* 365–374.

Brophy, J. E., & Good, T. (1974). *Teacher-student relationships: Causes and consequences.* New York: Holt, Rinehart & Winston.

Bruininks, R. H. (1977). Bruininks–Oseretsky Test of Motor Proficiency Skills manual. Circle Pines, MN: American Guidance Service.

Cooper, H. M. (1979). Pygmalion grows up: A model for teacher expectation communication and performance influence. *Review of Educational Research, 49,* 389–410.

Cooper, H. M. (1985). Models of teacher expectation communication. In J. B. Dusek (Ed.), *Teacher expectancies* (pp. 135–158). Hillsdale, NJ: Lawrence Erlbaum Associates.

Cooper, H. M., & Good, T. (1983). *Pygmalion grows up: Studies in the expectation communication process.* New York: Longman.

Darley, J. M., & Fazio, R. H. (1980). Expectancy confirmation processes arising in the social interaction sequence. *American Psychologist, 35,* 867–881.

Dusek, J. B. (1975). Do teachers bias children's learning? *Review of Educational Research, 45,* 661–684.

Dusek, J. B. (Ed.). (1985). *Teacher expectancies.* Hillsdale, NJ: Lawrence Erlbaum Associates.

Dweck, C. S., & Bempechat, J. (1983). Children's theories of intelligence. In S. Paris, G. Olsen, & H. W. Stevenson (Eds.), *Learning and motivation in the classroom* (pp. 239–256). Hillsdale, NJ: Lawrence Erlbaum Associates.

Dweck, C. S., & Elliott, E. S. (1983). Achievement motivation. In P. H. Mussen (Ed.), *Handbook of child psychology* (Vol. 4, pp. 643–691). New York: Wiley.

Eccles, J., Adler, T. F., Futterman, R., Goff, S. B., Kaczala, C. M., Meece, J., & Midgley, C. (1983). Expectancies, values and academic behaviors. In J. T. Spence (Ed.), *Achievement and achievement motives* (pp. 75–146). San Francisco: W. H. Freeman.

Eccles, J. S., Adler, T., & Meece, J. L. (1984). Sex differences in achievement: A test of alternate theories. *Journal of Personality and Social Psychology, 46,* 26–43.

Eccles, J. S., & Midgley, C. (1989). Stage–environment fit: Developmentally appropriate classrooms for young adolescents. In C. Ames & R. Ames (Eds.), *Research on motivation in education* (Vol. 3, pp. 139–186). San Diego: Academic Press.

Eccles (Parsons), J., Midgley, C., & Adler, T. (1984). Grade-related changes in the school environment: Effects on achievement motivation. In J. G. Nicholls (Ed.), *The development of achievement motivation* (pp. 283–331). Greenwich, CT: JAI Press.

Eccles, J. S., & Wigfield, A. (1985). Teacher expectancies and student motivation. In J. B. Dusek (Ed.), *Teacher expectancies* (pp. 185–226). Hillsdale, NJ: Lawrence Erlbaum Associates.

Eccles, J. S. & Wigfield, A. (1991). *In the mind of the achiever: The structure of adolescents' academic achievement related-beliefs and self-perceptions.* Manuscript submitted for publication.

Eccles, J. S., Wigfield, A., Flanagan, C., Miller, C., Reuman, D., & Yee, D. (1989). Self-concepts, domain values, and self-esteem: Relations and changes at early adolescence. *Journal of Personality, 57,* 283–310.

Eccles, J. S., Wigfield, A., Harold, R., & Blumenfeld, P. (1991). *Age and gender differences in children's achievement self-perceptions during the elementary school years.* Unpublished manuscript, University of Michigan Ann Arbor, MI.

Elashoff, J. D., & Snow, R. E. (1971). *Pygmalion reconsidered.* Worthington, OH: Jones.

Harold, R., Eccles, J. S., Jacobs, J., Wigfield, A., Blumenfeld, P., & Aberbach, A. (1989, March). *In the eye of the beholder: Teachers as perceivers.* Paper presented at the annual meeting of the American Educational Research Association, San Francisco.

Harter, S. (1981). A new self-report scale of intrinsic versus extrinsic orientation in the classroom: Motivational and informational components. *Developmental Psychology, 17,* 300–312.

Harter, S. (1982). The perceived competence scale for children. *Child Development, 53,* 87–97.

Harter, S. (1985). Competence as a dimension of self-evaluation: Toward a comprehensive model of self-worth. In R. Leahy (Ed.), *The development of the self* (pp. 55–121). New York: Academic Press.

Harter, S. (1986). Processes underlying the construction, maintenance and enhancement of the self-concept in children. In J. Suls & A.C. Greenwald (Eds.), *Psychological perspectives on the self* (pp. 137–181). Hillsdale, NJ: Lawrence Erlbaum Associates.

Hill, K. T., & Wigfield, A. (1984). Test anxiety: A major educational problem and what can be done about it. *Elementary School Journal, 85,* 105–126.

Jackson, P. (1968). *Life in classrooms.* New York: Holt, Rinehart & Winston.

Jacobs, J., & Wigfield, A. (1989). Sex equity in math and science education: Research-policy links. *Educational Psychology Review, 1,* 39–56.

Marsh, H. W. (1989). Age and sex effects in multiple dimensions of self-concept: Preadolescence to early adulthood. *Journal of Educational Psychology, 81,* 417–430.

Marsh, H. W., Barnes, J., Cairns, L., & Tidman, M. (1984). Self-Description Questionnaire: Age and sex effects in the structure and level of self-concept for preadolescent children. *Journal of Educational Psychology, 76,* 940–956.

Marshall, H. W., & Weinstein, R. S. (1984). Classroom factors affecting students' self-evaluations: An interactional model. *Review of Educational Research, 54,* 301–325.

Marshall, H. W., & Weinstein, R. S. (1986). Classroom context of student-perceived differential teacher treatment. *Journal of Educational Psychology, 78,* 441–453.

Marshall, H. W., Weinstein, R. S., Sharp, L., & Brattesani, K. A. (1982, March). *Students' descriptions of the ecology of the school environment for high and low achievers.* Paper presented at the meeting of the American Educational Research Association, New York.

Meece, J. L., Wigfield, A., & Eccles, J. S. (1990). Predictors of math anxiety and its consequences for young adolescents' course enrollment intentions and performances in mathematics. *Journal of Educational Psychology, 82,* 60–70.

Midgley, C., Feldlaufer, H., & Eccles, J. S. (1989). Change in teacher efficacy and student self- and task-related beliefs in mathematics during the transition to junior high school. *Journal of Educational Psychology, 81,* 247–258.

Nicholls, J. G. (1978). The development of the concepts of effort and ability, perceptions of academic attainment, and the understanding that difficult tasks require more ability. *Child Development, 49,* 800–814.

Nicholls, J. G. (1979). Development of perception of own attainment and causal attributions for success and failure in reading. *Journal of Educational Psychology, 71,* 94–99.

Nicholls, J. G. (1984). Achievement motivation: Conceptions of ability, subjective experience, task choice, and performance. *Psychological Review, 91,* 328–346.

Parsons, J. E. (1980). *Self-perceptions, task perceptions, and academic choice: Origins and change.* Washington, DC: National Institute of Education.

Parsons, J. E., Kaczala, C., & Meece, J. L. (1982). Socialization of achievement attitudes and beliefs: Classroom influences. *Child Development, 53,* 322–339.

Parsons, J. E., & Ruble, D. N. (1977). The development of achievement-related expectancies. *Child Development, 48,* 1075–1079.

Raudenbush, S. W. (1984). Magnitude of teacher expectancy effects on pupil IQ as a function of the credibility of expectancy induction: A synthesis of findings from 18 experiments. *Journal of Educational Psychology, 76,* 85–97.

Rosenthal, R. (1974). *On the social psychology of the self-fulfilling prophecy: Further evidence for Pygmalion effects and their mediating mechanisms.* New York: MSS Modular Publications.

Rosenthal, R. (1985). From unconscious experimenter bias to teacher expectancy effects. In J. B. Dusek (Ed.), *Teacher expectancies* (pp. 37–65). Hillsdale, NJ: Lawrence Erlbaum Associates.

Rosenthal, R., & Jacobson, L. (1968). *Pygmalion in the classroom: Teacher expectation and pupils' intellectual development.* New York: Holt, Rinehart & Winston.

Schunk, D. H. (1984). Self-efficacy perspective on achievement behavior. *Educational Psychologist, 19,* 48–58.

Schunk, D. H. (1990). Goal setting and self-efficacy during self-regulated learning. *Educational Psychologist, 25,* 71–86.

Stipek, D. J. (1984). Young children's performance expectations: Logical analysis or wishful thinking? In J. G. Nicholls (Ed.), *The development of achievement motivation* (pp. 33–56). Greenwich, CT: JAI Press.

Stipek, D. J., & Mac Iver, D. (1989). Developmental change in children's assessment of intellectual competence. *Child Development, 60,* 521–538.

Swann, W. B., & Snyder, M. (1980). On translating beliefs into actions: Theories of ability and their applications in an instructional setting. *Journal of Personality and Social Psychology, 38,* 879–888.

Thorndike, R. L. (1968). Review of *Pygmalion in the classroom. American Educational Research Journal, 5,* 708–711.

Weinstein, R. S. (1983). Student perceptions of schooling. *Elementary School Journal, 83,* 287–312.

Weinstein, R. S. (1985). Student mediation of classroom expectancy effects. In J. B. Dusek (Ed.), *Teacher expectancies* (pp. 329–350). Hillsdale, NJ: Lawrence Erlbaum Associates.

Weinstein, R. S. (1989). Perceptions of classroom processes and student motivation: Children's views of self-fulfilling prophecies. In C. Ames & R. Ames (Eds.), *Research on motivation in education* (Vol. 3, pp. 187–221). San Diego: Academic Press.

Weinstein, R. S., Marshall, H. H., Brattesani, K. A., & Middlestadt, S. E. (1982). Student perception of differential teacher treatment in open and traditional classrooms. *Journal of Educational Psychology, 75,* 678–692.

Weinstein, R. S., Marshall, H. H., Sharp, L., & Botkin, M. (1987). Pygmalion and the student: Age and classroom differences in children's awareness of teacher expectations. *Child Development, 58,* 1079–1093.

Weinstein, R. S., & Middlestadt, S. E. (1979). Student perceptions of teacher interactions with male high and low achievers. *Journal of Educational Psychology, 71,* 421–431.

West, C., & Anderson, T. (1976). The question of preponderant causation in teacher expectancy research. *Review of Educational Research, 46,* 613–630.

Wheaton, C. A. (1991). *Teachers' interactions with boys and girls in junior high school.* Unpublished manuscript, University of Maryland, College Park, MD.

Wigfield, A. (1984, April). *Relations between ability perceptions, other achievement-related beliefs, and school performance.* Paper presented at the annual meeting of the American Educational Research Association, New Orleans.

Wigfield, A., & Eccles, J. S. (1989). Test anxiety in elementary and secondary school students. *Educational Psychologist, 24,* 159–183.

Wigfield, A., & Eccles, J. S. (in press). The development of achievement task values: A theoretical analysis. *Development Review.*

Wigfield, A., Eccles, J. S., Mac Iver, D., Reuman, D., & Midgley, C. (1991). Transitions at early adolescence: Changes in children's domain-specific self-perceptions and general self-esteem across the transition to junior high school. *Developmental Psychology, 27,* 552–565.

Wigfield, A., Harold, R., Eccles, J. S., Aberbach, A., Freedman-Doan, K., & Yoon, K. S. (1990, April). *Children's ability perceptions and values during the elementary school years*. Paper presented at the meeting of the American Educational Research Association, Boston.

Wigfield, A., & Meece, J. (1988). Math anxiety in elementary and secondary school students. *Journal of Educational Psychology, 80*, 76–81.

Woolfolk, A. E., & Hoy, W. K. (1990). Prospective teachers' sense of efficacy and beliefs about control. *Journal of Educational Psychology, 82*, 81–91.

Student Perceptions and Academic Help-Seeking

RICHARD S. NEWMAN
MAHNA T. SCHWAGER
University of California, Riverside

Students' beliefs and interpretations of schooling can affect achievement in numerous ways. How students view themselves in the context of the classroom is associated with their level of interest, persistence, task engagement, and task performance. This chapter examines students' beliefs and interpretations of schooling in relation to a particular type of task engagement, namely, academic help-seeking. We examine why, and under what conditions, certain children feel confident and comfortable seeking assistance from teachers and classmates, whereas other children do not.

Traditionally, help-seeking has been viewed as a manifestation of dependency, immaturity, and even incompetence. More recently, however, it has been discussed in a very different way (Nelson-Le Gall, 1981, 1985; Newman, 1991). Seeking assistance from teachers and classmates can be considered a strategy of self-regulated learning (Paris & Newman, 1990; Zimmerman & Schunk, 1989). It is a type of task engagement often utilized by high achievers (Zimmerman & Martinez-Pons, 1986). The value of actively seeking out clarification of ambiguous assignments, explanation of misunderstood procedures, and confirmation of answers of which the child is uncertain seems clear. Yet for a good number of schoolchildren, in fact often those who are most in need of academic assistance, sitting passively in the classroom and not seeking help are the norm.

It is important to understand what it means to different children to seek help; to identify factors both within the child and the classroom environment that explain help-seeking behavior; and based on these understandings, to propose ways in which teachers might encourage children to take a more active role in their own learning by seeking assistance when needed. We address these goals here by adopting a cognitive-motivational approach. Such an approach is based on the premise that individuals' interpretations, thoughts, views, attitudes, and beliefs—in short, their perceptions—about themselves and their world are instrumental in defining their "reality" and in guiding their actions.

We rely on cognitive-motivational theories that focus on perceptions of the academic self, in particular self-perceptions of ability, perceived control, and motivational orientation (for reviews see Eccles, 1983; Harter, 1983). We also rely on theories of students' perceptions of classroom life. Students constantly construct interpretations of their teachers' behavior and expectations, classmates' abilities, and the nature and purpose of classroom activity (for review see Weinstein, 1983). Both sets of perceptions, about the self and the classroom, play an important role in whether or not students are likely to seek academic assistance.

The organization of the chapter consists of three parts. We discuss, first, why academic help-seeking can be considered a strategy of self-regulated learning; second, how students' self-perceptions are related to help-seeking behavior; and third, how students' interpretations of classroom events are related to help-seeking behavior.

HELP-SEEKING AS A MEDIATING STRATEGY OF STUDENT LEARNING

There are two different theoretical conceptions of children's help-seeking, and this is largely because of different conceptions of "independence" and "dependence" (Hartup, 1963). Some theorists consider independence and dependence at opposite poles on a single continuum; independence is simply a lack of dependence. Following this conception, seeking help has been perceived traditionally as one component, along with seeking physical contact, seeking proximity, seeking attention, and seeking recognition, of a general dependency drive (Beller, 1955). Although psychoanalytic accounts of object relations and social learning theory recognize that such manifestations of dependence on others can be quite normal and healthy, overdependence is another matter. Unfortunately—but not surprisingly because of Western emphasis on self-reliance and competitiveness—help-seeking among school-aged children and adults generally has been given a connotation of "overdependence." Accordingly, it has come to be perceived negatively, as an activity to be avoided. Help-seeking generally elicits perceptions of personal inadequacy and threats to the help-seeker's self-esteem (e.g., Nadler, 1983; Nelson-Le Gall, 1985; Rosen, 1983).

Other theorists consider independence as something more than a lack of dependence; it is characterized by an infrequent seeking of nurturance from others in addition to a manifestation of initiative and achievement-striving. Following this conception, seeking help is perceived not as a component of dependence but rather independence. An independence-based view of help-seeking characterizes the help-seeker as acting maturely and purposefully, alleviating a "real" difficulty, learning and mastering the task at hand, and in the end, achieving autonomy. Help-seeking recently has been acknowledged by a number of researchers as representing an important element of strategic school learning. Kuhl (1985), for example, discussed help-seeking as a way of achieving environmental control in the learning process, that is, as a volitional or coping strategy for dealing with difficulty and potential failure. Rohrkemper and Corno (1988) categorized skills and strategies according to their adaptive use. In order to adapt to challenging situations, children might modify the task, modify themselves, or modify the situation. One particular way of modifying the situation is by seeking assistance from teachers and classmates. Nelson-Le Gall (1981, 1985; Nelson-Le Gall, Gumerman, & Scott-Jones, 1983) and Ames (1983) emphasized academic help-seeking as an instrumental strategy for long-term success (i.e., learning and mastery), rather than simply a means for completing assignments and getting good grades.

Following along these same lines, Newman (1991) has discussed *adaptive help-seeking* as a strategy of self-regulated learning. Briefly, adaptive help-seeking is the strategic posing of direct, verbal questions for the purpose of obtaining information required for the successful completion of school tasks. Included are questions regarding academic matters such as solving problems, understanding class material, and completing assignments. To differentiate adaptive from dependency-based help-seeking, it is important to consider both the child's purpose in seeking help and the sequence of mental actions and decisions prior to, and during, the act of seeking help. Newman (1991) has proposed, first, that the goal or purpose of the adaptive help-seeker is to obtain information for learning or mastering some task. Mere expedient completion of an assignment would be excluded under this definition. Second, the adaptive help-seeker follows, in a particular way, a sequence of actions and decisions (cf. Nelson-Le Gall, 1985). That is, adaptive help-seeking:

1. follows the child's awareness of a need for help;
2. involves the child having considered all pertinent and available information (e.g., regarding task demands, personal resources, and costs and benefits) in making the following decisions:
   - *Necessity of the request:* Is it necessary that I ask for help (or should I take some other action, for example, persevering or giving up)?;
   - *Content of the request:* What should I ask (i.e., formulation of a particular question)?;
   - *Target of the request:* Whom should I ask?;
3. involves the child having expressed the request for help at a particular time and with a particular tone and attitude that is most suitable to the particular circumstance; and
4. involves the child having processed and considered the help that is received in such a way that the probability of success in subsequent help-seeking attempts is optimized.

Simply put, an adaptive request for help is necessary, well-planned, and well-processed. The child matches the content and target of the request with the specific needs of the task at hand. The reader is directed to Newman (1991) for a discussion of how self-regulated learners consider necessity, content, and target in their help-seeking requests.

Unfortunately, this description of adaptive help-seeking no doubt sounds foreign to many classroom teachers. Generally, students ask very few questions of any sort in class (Dillon, 1988), and of the questions they do ask, many would not be classified as instances of "adaptive help-seeking." The implicit rule perceived by elementary school students is that if one does not know an answer to a question, one keeps quiet or perhaps listens but definitely does not raise a hand to ask for help (Morine-Dershimer, 1985). As children progress through elementary, junior high, and high school, there may be an increase in individual differences, actually a divergence, in attitudes and behavior regarding help-seeking and questioning. High school students report putting less effort into getting academic help than they put into achieving any of 12 different classroom goals (Wentzel, 1989). Yet Zimmerman and Martinez-Pons (1986) and Karabenick and Knapp (1991) have shown that academic help-seeking is an important strategy in the repertoire of high achievers at the high school and college levels.

Over time, relatively successful students would seem to develop positive attitudes about help and freely engage in academic questioning, whereas relatively unsuccessful students develop negative attitudes and become increasingly inhibited from asking questions (Good, Slavings, Harel, & Emerson, 1987).

In this chapter, we examine developmental and individual differences in adaptive help-seeking behavior as a function of how children perceive themselves and how they perceive classroom life. Children with similar backgrounds and accomplishments often perceive themselves differently, and children within the same classroom often interpret events differently. It is individualized perceptions that we believe are critical in explaining help-seeking.

HELP-SEEKING AS A CONSEQUENCE OF STUDENTS' SELF-PERCEPTIONS

How children perceive themselves in terms of their academic competence, the degree of control they have over school outcomes, and their purposes, goals, and reasons for going to school are major components of their system of beliefs about themselves (see Eccles, 1983; Harter, 1983). Developmental and individual differences in these three particular components of the "self-system" are examined in relation to help-seeking.

Self-Perception of Ability

Children who perceive themselves as academically competent tend to display high levels of task engagement and have high achievement. There is consistent evidence supporting this relationship, whether researchers use measures of self-concept of ability, perceived academic competence, or beliefs of agency or capacity (Harter, 1982; Skinner, Wellborn, & Connell, 1990; Wylie, 1979). Students who perceive themselves as academically competent are likely then to view help-seeking as an instrumental strategy for classroom learning (Ames, 1983). The key to this relationship is the *necessity* of help. Generally, those with high self-perceptions of ability are high in achievement and/or domain-specific knowledge and do not need much help. However, if the need arises, they can be expected to seek assistance readily.

In a study of children at Grades 3, 5, and 7, Newman (1990) tested relationships among (a) three "background variables": children's perceived academic competence and two components of intrinsic orientation (i.e., preference for challenge and preference for independent mastery), (b) two "mediating variables": children's beliefs about costs (e.g., fear of looking dumb) and benefits (e.g., learning, feeling smart) of help, and (c) an "outcome variable": children's stated intentions of seeking help (i.e., self-reported likelihood of asking for help when not understanding directions or how to do problems in math class). Results showed that at all three grades, the greater children's perceived academic competence, the less strongly children felt there were personal costs associated with seeking help. We conclude that when children feel competent, they are not afraid of looking dumb by asking for help. Support for a connection between self-perceptions and beliefs about costs, on the one hand, and intentions to seek help, on the other, was strongest at Grade 7. When older children feel competent, they are not afraid of looking dumb, and furthermore, they say they intend to seek help.

Although future research needs to examine not just intentions but actual behavior, implications are that children who perceive themselves as competent students are relatively likely to seek assistance in the classroom, whereas children who perceive themselves as poor students are relatively likely not to seek assistance. From a developmental perspective, it will be interesting to examine further whether negative beliefs regarding help play an increasingly important mediating role over the elementary and middle school years, that is, whether children's decisions not to seek help may be increasingly attributed to their concern about costs such as potential embarrassment.

Perceived Control

A second factor we consider in relation to help-seeking is perceived control. We know from the Coleman Report (Coleman et al. 1966) that students' sense of a lack of environmental control is very important in explaining poor school achievement. Numerous studies utilizing constructs of locus of control (see Rotter, 1966) and causal attribution (see Weiner, 1986) have shown that children who believe that school outcomes are contingent on their own internal (i.e., personal) behavior such as the use of learning strategies or the expenditure of effort are motivated to learn, perform well on achievement tests, and get good grades (Findley & Cooper, 1983; Stipek & Weisz, 1981). Recent work by Skinner, Chapman, and Baltes (1988) and Skinner et al. (1990) has presented a conceptualization of perceived control that may be especially promising in terms of explaining academic help-seeking.

According to Skinner and her colleagues, there are three interrelated sets of beliefs that need to be taken into account in understanding student task engagement. *Strategy beliefs* are beliefs about "what it takes for me to do well in school" (e.g., effort, ability, powerful others, luck, and unknown factors); these are beliefs about means–goals connections. *Capacity beliefs* are expectations about whether "I have what it takes," where "it" refers to the specific means mentioned in the strategy beliefs (e.g., Can I exert effort? Am I smart? Liked by powerful others? Lucky?). *Control beliefs* are expectations about "whether or not I can do well in school;" these beliefs refer to the goal mentioned in the series of strategy beliefs (i.e., doing well in school), but without reference to any specific means. The Skinner conceptualization is integrative in the sense that control beliefs (i.e., I can do well in school) express a multiplicative relation between strategy beliefs (e.g., What it takes for me to do well in school is effort) and corresponding capacity beliefs (e.g., I can exert effort). Notice that it differentiates locus of control and self-perception of ability in the following ways: (a) strategy beliefs for effort and ability are analogous to expressions of internal locus of control; (b) strategy beliefs for powerful others, luck, and unknown factors are analogous to expressions of external locus of control; and (c) capacity beliefs for ability are analogous to self-perception of ability.

Skinner et al. (1990) have shown that elementary school children's task engagement is affected by control beliefs as well as specific patterns of strategy and capacity beliefs. Although findings do not deal with help-seeking per se, expectations are fairly clear. Task engagement is undermined when students have low control beliefs and when they have high strategy beliefs for ability, powerful others, luck, and unknown factors. Children who are high in the first three of these strategy beliefs and at the same time low in the corresponding capacity beliefs show especially low levels of task engagement. The highest levels of engagement are shown by students with high strategy and capacity beliefs for effort.

Implications are that the following children are relatively unlikely to seek help adaptively: (a) those who do not expect to do well, (b) those who are in the dark about what it takes to do well, and (c) those who believe that ability, powerful others, and luck are what it takes but believe that they themselves are *not* smart, *not* liked by the teacher, and *not* lucky. In other words, those who feel they do not have control over their own academic success—perhaps because they do not know what is important or because they perceive they do not have access to what is important—are expected to be disengaged in the classroom. Children who recognize the value of effort and who feel they themselves are self-efficacious (cf. Schunk, 1989), on the other hand, will engage in adaptive help-seeking. Given what we know about the importance in self-regulated learning of children's beliefs regarding the utility and control of strategies (e.g., Paris, Newman, & Jacobs, 1985), we expect future research will show that children who regard help-seeking as a useful and "do-able" strategy are, in fact, likely to seek needed assistance in school.

Motivational Orientation

Achievement-related goals have been shown to have positive effects on adults' and children's task performance, and so we expect that goals are important in explaining students' help-seeking behavior in the classroom. Goals have been discussed both as personal characteristics of the child, that is, individual difference variables, and as situational characteristics of the classroom (e.g., Meece, Blumenfeld, & Hoyle, 1988). We focus here on ways in which children have been characterized, for example, according to their focus on *learning* versus *performance* (Ames, this volume; Dweck, 1986; Wentzel, this volume), *task-involvement* versus *ego-involvement* (Jagacinski, this volume; Nicholls, 1979, this volume), and *intrinsic orientation* versus *extrinsic orientation* (Harter, 1981).

The individual difference measure of achievement goals that has been shown most clearly to be predictive of help-seeking in schoolchildren is intrinsic versus extrinsic orientation (Harter, 1981). Children with an intrinsic orientation to learning strive for independent mastery and competence, prefer academic challenge, and show curiosity and interest in their work. In contrast, children with an extrinsic orientation are overly dependent on others, prefer relatively easy assignments and subjects, and do their schoolwork in order to satisfy the teacher and get good grades.

Findings by Nelson-Le Gall and Jones (1990) support a positive relationship between help-seeking and intrinsic orientation. Third and fifth graders who were characterized as intrinsic, in particular in their striving for independent mastery (vs. being dependent on their teacher) were more likely to seek academic help of an indirect type (i.e., hints) than of a direct type (i.e., answers). Children characterized as extrinsic, on the other hand, showed no such preference. Interpretations of the findings are based on the assumption that requests for hints, more than answers, are indicative of an inquisitive, active, and instrumentally motivated type of learning.

Further evidence of a positive relationship between intrinsic orientation and help-seeking comes from Newman (1990). Findings showed an interesting differentiation between two dimensions of Harter's (1981) measure of intrinsic orientation, preference for challenge and striving for independent mastery. At Grades 3, 5, and 7, the greater children's preference for challenge, the greater was their likelihood of seeking help. Preference for independent mastery, however, was related to help-seeking in a more complex, age-related way. At the elementary grades, the greater children's *dependence* on the teacher, the greater was the likelihood of seeking help, whereas at the middle school grades, the greater children's preference for *independence* from the teacher, the greater the likelihood. Thus, for younger children, two seemingly divergent purposes (challenge and dependency) may be important in explaining help-seeking; for older children, on the other hand, two seemingly convergent purposes (challenge and independent mastery) may be important.

Findings remind us that asking for help can serve independent and even contradictory purposes. A given behavior, for example raising a hand and asking for help, can serve different purposes for different children or, for that matter, it can serve different purposes under different circumstances with the same child. There can be multiple influences—that are not always consonant with one another—that operate simultaneously in the same child and that have differing degrees of importance over the school years.

In summary, it is clear that the ways students perceive themselves in the classroom in terms of competence, beliefs about control, and goals play an important role in their academic help-seeking behavior. Certain children—those who have poor perceptions of competence, lack a sense of control in their academic world, and have an extrinsic orientation to learning—are relatively unlikely to seek help from a teacher or classmate when facing academic difficulty. Self-perceptions and motivational factors however provide only a partial understanding of children's help-seeking. Seeking assistance from knowledgeable others is a social-interactional strategy, involving teachers, classmates, and a host of factors embedded in the moment-to-moment dynamics of the classroom context. In order to understand more fully help-seeking attitudes and behavior, one must examine how students perceive classroom life.

HELP-SEEKING AS A CONSEQUENCE OF STUDENTS' PERCEPTIONS OF THE CLASSROOM

Students' perceptions of classroom life have been measured traditionally by constructs such as classroom climate (see Fraser, 1986; Moos,

1979). Although the usefulness of classroom climate for explaining specific classroom processes may be limited because of its global and aggregated (i.e., over individuals within a classroom) nature (Weinstein, 1983), focusing on specific components of climate is useful as a way of organizing our discussion of student perceptions of classroom life. Three components in particular—personal relationships, classroom goal orientation, and system maintenance—are important to consider in relation to help-seeking.

Personal Relationships in the Classroom

An important component of climate is the personal relationships that exist in the classroom, between children and their teacher and classmates. Perceptions of the teacher and classmates as potential helpers play an obviously important role in whether or not students feel comfortable seeking help when needed.

Choice of Helpers: Teachers and Classmates. Over the elementary school years, children increasingly become aware of numerous characteristics that distinguish effective from ineffective helpers (Barnett, Darcie, Holland, & Kobasigawa, 1982). Whereas kindergartners seem concerned with the "personal side" of help and helpers (e.g., choosing helpers whom they say are nice and kind), children in middle and upper grades seem more concerned with the "academic side" (e.g., choosing helpers whom they say are competent and willing to help). Similarly, Nelson-Le Gall and Gumerman (1984) have shown that, with age, elementary school children increasingly reason about helper selections by focusing on traditional academic and social roles (e.g., "I ask the teacher for help because that's the teacher's job"). For adolescents, rationales for choosing helpers become more complex. Decisions are based not only on the helper's competence, expected guidance, and familiarity, but also on degree of confidentiality and skill at communicating (Wintre, Hicks, McVey, & Fox, 1988). As children become more aware of such factors, the presence (or absence) of competent teachers and classmates who can gain the confidence of students and easily communicate with them no doubt becomes increasingly important in determining if students do in fact approach them for assistance.

Children as young as 8 years express an awareness of both personal costs and benefits of seeking help in class. According to van der Meij (1988) and Newman and Goldin (1990), elementary-aged children commonly report that teachers and classmates are unavailable or unwilling to help, they fear a negative reaction from the teacher (especially if there is an expectation that they should not require additional assistance), and they fear resulting embarrassment in the eyes of classmates. On a more positive note, however, children are also aware of benefits of seeking help. In fact, children at Grades 3, 5, and 7 rate benefits of seeking help in math class (e.g., "I think that asking questions helps me learn math," or "I feel smart when I ask a question during math") more strongly than they do costs (e.g., "I think the teacher might think I'm dumb when I ask a question," or "I feel like it's just too much of a bother to ask questions"; Newman, 1990).

Children have differing perceptions of teachers and classmates as helpers, and these perceptions are reflected in their choice of helpers. Newman and Goldin (1990) have shown, across Grades 2, 4, and 6, that children believe that asking for help from the teacher is more likely than asking for help from a classmate to result in learning, and that asking the teacher is less likely than asking a classmate to result in that person thinking they are dumb. In fact, children say they prefer to ask the teacher more than a classmate when they need help with an academic problem in math or reading (see also Nelson-Le Gall & Gumerman, 1984). Correlations among these various beliefs are revealing. At all three elementary grades, there were positive associations between the belief that asking questions of the teacher or peer helps in learning and the child's liking to ask that particular person. However, the expected negative associations between the belief that asking questions of either the teacher or peer results in perceptions of dumbness and the child's liking to ask that particular person were not significant. It appears that elementary school children's choices of whom to approach for help are motivated primarily by positive beliefs about potential benefits and not by negative beliefs about potential costs.

We can conclude then that one important element of personal relationships in the classroom, in terms of facilitation of help-seeking, is a sense among students that question-asking helps them learn. Next we turn to the person—the teacher—who often is perceived by students as the primary academic help-giver in the classroom.

Teacher Involvement. Past research has shown that perceived teacher involvement and feelings of relatedness, mutual liking, and lack of alienation in relation to the teacher are all associated with student engagement, grades, and achievement test scores (e.g., Moos & Moos, 1978; Skinner et al., 1990). To examine students' perceptions of teacher involvement in relation to help-seeking, with a particular interest in possible differences between elementary and middle school contexts, Newman (1990) and Schwager and Newman (1991) interviewed third, fifth, and seventh graders.

Findings from Newman (1990) showed that, at each grade, students' beliefs about the benefits of seeking help from the teacher (e.g., learning, feeling smart) had a positive, encouraging effect on intentions of asking questions; this is consistent with the findings at Grades 2, 4, and 6 of Newman and Goldin (1990). However, beliefs about potential costs (e.g., fear of looking dumb) had an additional effect on seventh-graders' intentions of asking questions; the effect was to inhibit question-asking. Although individual differences in attitudes about only the benefits of help-seeking are predictive of elementary school students' help-seeking intentions, attitudes about costs as well as benefits are predictive of intentions of middle school students. This is not to say that younger children do not express an awareness of potential costs; they do. With age, however, there may be increased complexity in how children's attitudes affect—in two opposing ways— help-seeking in the classroom. This increased effect of fear of looking dumb is consistent with the fact that older children tend to place greater emphasis on ability attributions and less on effort attributions (Nicholls, 1984) and have a greater need to protect their sense of self-worth from looking dumb than do younger children (Covington & Beery, 1976).

To pursue further how teachers are involved in establishing a facilitative climate for help-seeking, Schwager and Newman (1991) asked students about two somewhat independent roles played by teachers— the friend and the provider of task-related support. We tested whether there were grade differences in (a) students' perceived personal involvement with their teacher, (b) the extent to which students perceive that the teacher explicitly encourages question-asking in math class, and (c) the relative importance of these two factors in predicting children's intentions to seek help. Perceived personal involvement with the teacher was measured with items such as, "I like my teacher" and "My teacher likes me"; perceived encouragement of question-asking with items such as, "The teacher likes it when students ask questions" and "The teacher likes to answer students' questions;" and intention to seek help with items such as, "How likely are you to ask the teacher for help when you don't understand how to do the problem?"

Findings showed that third graders perceived more personal involvement with their teacher than did fifth or seventh graders. The older children however perceived their teacher as more encouraging of question-asking than did third graders. The relative importance of these two factors in predicting students' intentions of seeking help varied across grade level. At Grade 3, perceived personal involvement predicted help-seeking intentions; at Grade 5, perceptions of teacher encouragement predicted help-seeking intentions; and at Grade 7, both factors were important. So among young elementary school children there is an especially strong sense of mutual liking with the teacher, and this would seem to play a part in determining who does or does not seek help. Among both older elementary and middle school children there is an especially strong sense of encouragement for question-asking from their teacher. For the older elementary school students, this sense of task-related encouragement would seem to be important in determining who seeks help and who does not, whereas for the middle school students, perceptions of both personal relationship and encouragement appear to be important.

Our findings suggest that as children go through elementary school they increasingly emphasize the academic, versus the personal, role of effective helpers (cf. Barnett et al., 1982; Nelson-Le Gall & Gumerman, 1984). With age and transition to middle school, there may be increased complexity in the influences on help-seeking (cf. Wintre et al., 1988). At middle school, students' help-seeking intentions are influenced by attitudes and beliefs about costs as well as benefits and by perceptions representing multiple roles played by their teacher.

Classroom Goal Orientation

A second dimension of classroom climate, namely the underlying goal orientation in the classroom, is no doubt critical in determining students' attitudes and behavior regarding help-seeking. Researchers focusing on achievement goals, as a situational rather than a personal characteristic, have distinguished between *learning* and *performance* goals (Dweck, 1986; Wentzel, this volume), *mastery* and *performance* goals (Ames, this volume; Ames & Archer, 1988), and *task-involved* and *ego-involved* goals (Jagacinski, this volume; Nicholls, 1979, this volume). Different goals in the classroom have different outcomes in terms of children's achievement-related behavior such as attention, persistence, and employment of effort and task-relevant strategies (Ames & Archer, 1988; Locke, Saari, Shaw, & Latham, 1981). In classrooms that emphasize learning, children are socialized with the goal of long-term mastery; success is seen as dependent on effort; and performance feedback stresses each individual child's intellectual and social development. In classrooms that emphasize performance, children are socialized with the goal of getting good grades and being judged able; success is seen as dependent on ability; and performance feedback stresses social comparison with classmates.

Ames (1983) argued that these classroom goal orientations have associated with them distinctive student attitudes and behaviors regarding help-seeking. Classrooms emphasizing learning goals presumably encourage all children to deal with academic difficulty as a challenge—with positive affect, increased persistence, and seeking of assistance when needed. Classrooms emphasizing performance goals, on the other hand, presumably lead to a wide dispersion of help-seeking attitudes and responses within the classroom. This is because of the salience of public evaluation and social comparison that generally accompany performance goals. Although some children in such a classroom are likely to engage in adaptive help-seeking, others are likely to deal with academic difficulty by exhibiting negative affect, maladaptive self-attributions, and by giving up.

According to Eccles, Midgely, and Adler (1984), classroom environments and goal orientations evolve over the school years toward performance goals, changing most dramatically at the point of transition from elementary school to middle school or junior high. Classrooms tend to become more impersonal, formal, and competitive and more highly characterized by normative comparison. Following the argument of Ames (1983), classrooms would be expected then to show increased dispersion over the school years in students' help-seeking attitudes and behavior and a divergence between high- and low-achievers' patterns of classroom interaction (cf. Good et al., 1987).

One particularly salient feature of the upper elementary and middle school classroom that is expected to inhibit students' willingness to seek help is the degree of normative comparison in the class. A classroom environment that engenders normative comparison may well promote competitiveness and increase the opportunities for one to judge oneself negatively in comparison to another's better performance. Students' perceptions of interindividual competitiveness are related negatively to task engagement and achievement (Fraser, 1986; Moos & Moos, 1978; Slavin, 1983). Of course, under certain circumstances, normative comparison may also allow one to see that he or she is not alone in experiencing difficulty.

To examine students' thoughts about social comparison in relation to help-seeking, Schwager and Newman (1991) had children in Grades 3, 5, and 7 rate on a 5-point scale the likelihood of their asking for help in math class (a) "when you are having trouble and other kids are also having trouble," and (b) "when you are having trouble but nobody else is having trouble." Results indicate that children are more likely to report asking for assistance if they think that others also need assistance; conversely, they are less likely to report asking for assistance if they think they are alone. The contrast was especially strong at Grades

5 and 7. So although normative comparison might inhibit help-seeking if children come to perceive their need as being different from that of classmates, it can also encourage help-seeking if children come to perceive their need as being "normal." An inhibiting/encouraging effect is especially strong at upper grade levels presumably because older elementary and middle school children are especially concerned about social acceptance, peer-group belongingness, and maintaining their sense of self-worth (Covington & Beery, 1976; Kimmel & Weiner, 1985).

System Maintenance

A third dimension of climate, system maintenance, is expected to be related to students' help-seeking. As envisioned by Moos (1979), system maintenance represents the degree of structure, clarity, teacher control, and openness to innovation and change in the classroom. Two components that may be especially important in affecting help-seeking are: (a) the structure or organization in the classroom, and (b) the degree of teacher control.

Structure in the Classroom. The structure of the class activity is an important feature around which teachers organize rules of classroom communication, feedback, and student–teacher interaction. According to Berliner (1983), there are three major types of structure or organization of classroom activity. Each generally has associated with it a particular system of goals (Ames, 1984). Whole-class structure is characterized by a high level of teacher control in an activity such as presentation of a new lesson, class discussion, or question and answer period. Students compete with one another for some goal. Small-group structure is characterized by a nondirective, supervisory role of the teacher, with students engaged in activities such as small-group discussion or development of group projects. Students often cooperate with one another for a common goal. Individual structure is also characterized by a nondirective, supervisory role of the teacher, with students engaged in activities such as silent reading or completion of worksheets. Students work toward independent goals.

Differences in classroom structure clearly are related to students' choice of helper and to their help-seeking attitudes and behavior. In whole-class activity, there generally is less help-seeking than in either of the other two types of classroom activity (Nelson-Le Gall & Glor-Scheib, 1985). Students in small-group and individual activities, in comparison to students in whole-class activities, are relatively likely to seek help not just from other students but from the teacher as well (Meece, Blumenfeld, & Puro, 1989). Small-group structure is explicitly designed to promote children's interacting with one another in terms of both giving and receiving help (Cooper, Marquis, & Ayers-Lopez, 1982; Slavin, 1983; Webb, 1982). Students in small groups frequently seek help from one another, and these interactions are positively related to achievement (Webb, 1982).

Individual and small-group activity, with their accompanying goal orientations, may facilitate students' help-seeking for a number of reasons. Encouragement from the teacher and resulting positive affect and lack of anxiety among students are incorporated relatively easily into individual and small-group instruction. Small-group activity, especially if designed according to a plan of cooperative learning (see Slavin, 1983), may be facilitative of help-seeking because of additional effects of group reward structures, lack of interindividual competitiveness, and the accompanying sense that students have of control over their own academic outcomes.

Teacher Control. Although students' perception of control over their own learning may be a function of the structure of classroom activity, it may also be a function of teachers' expectations of the students, teachers' perception of control in the classroom, and the ways in which teachers interact with the students. Whatever the source of students' perception of control in the classroom, it is expected to affect the students' initiative and task engagement, in particular, their help-seeking behavior.

Teachers have different expectations of, and exhibit different behavior toward, high and low achievers (Cooper, 1979; Cooper, Hinkel, & Good, 1980; Eccles & Wigfield, 1985). Teachers call on students perceived to be low achievers less often, wait less time for them to respond, give them answers rather than guidance when they respond incorrectly, and rarely praise their successes. According to Cooper, teachers tend to manipulate interactions with students in order to enhance a sense of classroom control. Teachers view low achievers as less controllable than high achievers, and accordingly attempt to control the timing, duration, and initiation of interactions with them.

Importantly, elementary-aged students are perceptive of such within-classroom differences in teachers' expectations and control-related behavior (Weinstein & Middlestadt, 1979). These perceptions affect children's self-expectations and self-perceptions, achievement motivation, and we believe, help-seeking behavior. It is likely that the degree to which students exert control over their own learning, for example by initiating help-seeking attempts, is inversely related to the degree to which they perceive control to be in the hands of their teacher. Low achievers, who generally are given direction and help under the watchful eye of the teacher, perceive controlling behavior and learn not to volunteer questions and answers; instead they learn to be passive. High achievers, who generally are given autonomy and chances for self-direction, perceive an absence of teacher control and learn to initiate interactions with the teacher and classmates.

Implicit in the discussion of student perception of teacher control is the existence of individual differences among teachers. "Autonomy-oriented" (vs. "control-oriented") teachers have been characterized as providing choices and meaningful feedback to their students (Deci & Ryan, 1985). Similarly, certain teachers have an "origin" orientation, whereas others can be characterized with a "pawn" orientation (de-Charms, 1976). Originlike teachers encourage their students to take control of their own learning by fostering in the students self-confidence and by helping them set realistic goals and take responsibility for performance outcomes. Students of autonomy-oriented and originlike teachers perceive themselves in a more positive light than students of control-oriented and pawnlike teachers. They tend to show higher levels of intrinsic motivation, self-esteem, perceived competence, and academic outcome, and accordingly would be expected to be relatively likely to initiate help-seeking attempts.

In summary, students' perceptions of their classroom environment must play an important role in academic help-seeking behavior. Perceptions involving personal relationships, goal orientation, classroom organization, and the degree to which the teacher is willing to share control in the classroom affect help-seeking. Further research needs to clarify these relations. We feel that an especially important issue to be pursued is how teachers and students come to share control, in particular, how teachers help students develop a sense of task involvement and empowerment in the classroom.

CONCLUSIONS

Self-regulated learners control their own learning. They possess a repertoire of cognitive and metacognitive strategies and are aware of conditions under which each strategy has personal utility. Challenge and difficulty present to them an inducement not to give up but rather to persevere and try alternative strategies. This chapter has examined one particular strategy, adaptive help-seeking, that self-regulated learners commonly employ when facing academic difficulties. These children know when they need help with an assignment, take the initiative to seek assistance, and are able to formulate and express their requests in such a way that resulting help is likely to lead to task mastery.

Conceptualizing adaptive help-seeking as a strategy of self-regulated learning emphasizes the responsibility that students have in controlling their own learning. After all, children who raise their hand and request a clarification or explanation of something not understood give evidence of not only an active executive monitoring of their own cognitive processing but also an active attempt to alleviate their difficulty and ensure success. In contrast, those who are reluctant to seek needed assistance and who sit in class disengaged from the learning process would seem to have defaulted on their potential self-control.

The major point emerging from this chapter is that students' perceptions—self-perceptions and perceptions of classroom factors—influence help-seeking. The child constructs his or her own reality of self and environment, and the resulting self- and environmental-schema influence classroom behavior. We emphasize the influence of the *student's* rather than the *teacher's* perceptions, for children tend to view classrooms differently, in fact usually less positively, than their teachers do (Fraser, 1986). Students perceive themselves as receiving less teacher support and being less engaged than teachers perceive. In other words, it is quite possible that teachers may not realize that a problem—in the child's view—exists.

To some extent, the construction of children's perceptions and their influence on classroom behavior are delimited by developmental factors. Children's definition of *effective* helper changes—generally in the direction of increased complexity—as they get older and as they experience new classroom structures and social pressures at middle school. Perceptions of competence and control show developmental change. Children come to be more realistic in their assessments of their own competencies and more knowledgeable about factors that are responsible for school success. There is greater complexity in the way in which attitudes about costs and benefits affect help-seeking intentions (and presumably action). At middle school, students seem to be influenced by not only perceived benefits of learning but potential costs of social embarrassment as well. At the same time, we see different achievement-related goals affecting children's intentions to seek help. Middle school students seem to be influenced by preference for challenge and independent mastery, whereas younger students seem to be influenced by preference for challenge and dependence on the teacher.

Although there are general developmental trends in help-seeking attitudes and behavior, there also are clear individual differences. As a function of children's achievement level (and perhaps other factors such as culture, ethnicity, and gender that we have not addressed), children are perceived and treated differentially by teachers, and there develops over time a divergence in attitudes and behavior regarding help-seeking. Competition, goal orientation stressing performance, normative comparison of grades, and ability tracking take on special significance at the middle school, and these factors may at that time reinforce the reluctance of many children to seek assistance in class. Some children come to feel empowered and exercise that empowerment, whereas many others do not.

We have addressed the effect of environmental factors on help-seeking from the perspective of student perceptions of classroom life. Of course there is also a "reality" to the classroom. Implications of the research reviewed in the chapter are that definite actions can be taken by the teacher so as to affect student perceptions of the classroom and thereby facilitate children's seeking needed assistance. Several suggestions follow.

First, simple interpersonal actions of teacher involvement such as expression of personal warmth and explicit encouragement and reinforcement of question-asking can help children be engaged more fully. For young children, expression of personal warmth may be especially important; for older children, this in addition to explicit encouragement and reinforcement. Second, the underlying goal orientation in the classroom can be arranged to emphasize learning and task involvement rather than mere performance and ego involvement. The teacher can encourage students to set realistic goals of task mastery for themselves and help students evaluate their own progress rather than comparing them with classmates. The teacher can stress the importance of understanding, improving, trying new strategies, and the fact that making and correcting mistakes are a normal part of learning. Third, the content and means of presentation of academic lessons can promote help-seeking. Presentation of material that is interesting, novel, meaningful, and that elicits an intrinsic desire to know can be expected to induce students' question-asking (Hidi, 1990).

A final suggestion has as its aim "making thinking public," making students aware of alternative problem-solving strategies, and convincing students that question-asking has personal value. To achieve this aim, classroom activity can be organized in a small-group structure. Within such a structure, specific pedagogical strategies can decrease undue competition and normative comparison and increase the likelihood of students cooperating among themselves, in giving, seeking, and receiving help. Examples of such strategies are reciprocal teaching, where students and teacher interact in monitoring, summarizing, and questioning class material (Palinscar & Brown, 1984) and reciprocal peer-questioning, where students are guided in generating and responding to task-appropriate questions (King, 1990). Although it remains to be tested, our expectation is that students who learn to be active participants in such activities are likely to come to see the personal utility of, and their own capacity to engage in, help-seeking in general, even in situations that are not explicitly supportive of questioning.

Finally, we note that although the chapter has examined, in parallel, perceptions of the self and the classroom, the two sets of perceptions interact with one another in affecting help-seeking. For example, in addition to a direct effect on help-seeking, changes in environmental factors no doubt have a very important indirect effect because they help formulate over time children's goals, values, and beliefs about themselves as learners. Similarly, self-perceptions influence the way in which children interpret classroom life. We have discussed developmental and individual differences in children and have identified "types" of self-perceptions and perceptions of the classroom that can be expected to influence help-seeking. There is no doubt, however, a great degree of intraindividual difference, for example due to domain-specificity (e.g., according to academic subject matter) and person-specificity (e.g., according to one particular teacher or classmate vs. another), in how these perceptions are formed and how they influence help-seeking in the moment-to-moment dynamics of the classroom. We believe children's interactions with the teacher and classmates are determined partially by general "rules" and partially by context-specific variations of those rules. Sometimes an individual may seek help adaptively and other times he or she may not.

In conclusion, this chapter has examined an important strategy of self-regulated learning, namely help-seeking. Although we have focused on a specific strategy, we have used that particular focus to address broader issues of self-regulation and task engagement. Our hope is that linkages between student perceptions and help-seeking will be further researched and that resulting knowledge and change in classroom environments will lead to students becoming more actively engaged in their own learning.

REFERENCES

Ames, C. (1984). Competitive, cooperative, and individualistic goal structures: A cognitive-motivational analysis. In R. Ames & C. Ames (Eds.), *Research on motivation in education: Student motivation* (Vol. 1, pp. 177–207). New York: Academic Press.

Ames, C., & Archer, J. (1988). Achievement goals in the classroom: Students' learning strategies and motivation processes. *Journal of Educational Psychology, 80,* 260–267.

Ames, R. (1983). Help-seeking and achievement orientation: Perspectives from attribution theory. In B. M. DePaulo, A. Nadler, & J. D. Fisher (Eds.), *New directions in helping* (Vol. 2, pp. 165–186). New York: Academic Press.

Barnett, K., Darcie, G., Holland, C. J., & Kobasigawa, A. (1982). Children's cognitions about effective helping. *Developmental Psychology, 18,* 267–277.

Beller, E. K. (1955). Dependency and independence in young children. *Journal of Genetic Psychology, 87,* 23–25.

Berliner, D. C. (1983). Developing conceptions of classroom environments: Some light on the T in classroom studies of ATI. *Educational Psychologist, 18,* 1–13.

Coleman, J. S., Campbell, E. Q., Hobson, C. J., McPartland, J., Mood, A. A., Weinfeld, F. S., & York, R. L. (1966). *Equality of educational opportunity* (Report from the Office of Education). Washington, DC: U.S. Government Printing Office.

Cooper, C. R., Marquis, A., & Ayers-Lopez, S. (1982). Peer learning in the classroom: Tracing developmental patterns and consequences of children's spontaneous interactions. In L. C. Wilkinson (Ed.), *Communicating in the classroom* (pp. 69–84). New York: Academic Press.

Cooper, H. M. (1979). Pygmalion grows up: A model for teacher expectation communication and performance influence. *Review of Educational Research, 49*(3), 398–410.

Cooper, H. M., Hinkel, G. M., & Good, T. L. (1980). Teacher's beliefs about interactional control and their observed behavioral correlates. *Journal of Educational Psychology, 72,* 345–354.

Covington, M. V., & Beery, R. (1976). *Self-worth and school learning.* New York: Holt, Rinehart & Winston.

deCharms, R. (1976). *Enhancing motivation: Change in the classroom.* New York: Irvington Publishers.

Deci, E. L., & Ryan, R. M. (1985). *Intrinsic motivation and self-determination in human behavior.* New York: Plenum Press.

Dillon, J. T. (1988). The remedial status of student questioning. *Journal of Curriculum Studies, 20,* 197–210.

Dweck, C. (1986). Motivational processes affecting learning. *American Psychologist, 41,* 1040–1048.

Eccles, J. (1983). Expectancies, values, and academic behaviors. In J. T. Spence (Ed.), *Achievement and achievement motives: Psychological and sociological approaches* (pp. 75–146). San Francisco: Freeman.

Eccles, J., Midgley, C., & Adler, T. F. (1984). Grade-related changes in the school environment: Effects on achievement motivation. In J. Nicholls (Ed.), *Advances in motivation and achievement* (Vol. 3, pp. 283–331). Greenwich, CT: JAI Press.

Eccles, J., & Wigfield, A. (1985). Teacher expectations and student motivation. In J. Dusek (Ed.), *Teacher expectancies.* Hillsdale, NJ: Lawrence Erlbaum Associates.

Findley, M. J., & Cooper, H. M. (1983). Locus of control and academic achievement: A literature review. *Journal of Personality and Social Psychology, 44,* 419–427.

Fraser, B. J. (1986). *Classroom environment.* London, England: Croom Helm.

Good, T. L., Slavings, R. L., Harel, K. H., & Emerson, H. (1987). Student passivity: A study of question asking in K-12 classrooms. *Sociology of Education, 60,* 181–199.

Harter, S. (1981). A new self-report scale of intrinsic versus extrinsic orientation in the classroom: Motivational and informational components. *Developmental Psychology, 17,* 300–312.

Harter, S. (1982). The Perceived Competence Scale for Children. *Child Development, 53,* 87–97.

Harter, S. (1983). Developmental perspectives on the self-system. In P. Mussen (Ed.),

Handbook of child psychology: Socialization, personality and social development (Vol. 4, pp. 275–385). New York: Wiley.

Hartup, W. W. (1963). Dependence and independence. In H. W. Stevenson (Ed.), *Child psychology: The sixty-second yearbook of the National Society for the Study of Education* (pp. 333–363). Chicago: The University of Chicago Press.

Hidi, S. (1990). Interest and its contribution as a mental resource for learning. *Review of Educational Research, 60,* 549–571.

Karabenick, S. A., & Knapp, J. R. (1991). Relationship of academic help seeking to the use of learning strategies and other instrumental achievement behavior in college students. *Journal of Educational Psychology, 83,* 221–230.

Kimmel, D. C., & Weiner, I. B. (1985). *Adolescence: A developmental transition.* Hillsdale, NJ: Lawrence Erlbaum Associates.

King, A. (1990). Enhancing peer interaction and learning in the classroom through reciprocal questioning. *American Educational Research Journal, 27,* 664–687.

Kuhl, J. (1985). Volitional mediators of cognition-behavior consistency: Self-regulatory processes and action versus state orientation. In J. Kuhl & J. Beckmann (Eds.), *Action control: From cognition to behavior.* West Berlin: Springer-Verlag.

Locke, E. A., Saari, L. M., Shaw, K. N., & Latham, G. P. (1981). Goal setting and task performance: 1969–1980. *Psychological Bulletin, 90,* 125–152.

Meece, J. L., Blumenfeld, P. C., & Hoyle, R. H. (1988). Students' goal orientations and cognitive engagement in classroom activities. *Journal of Educational Psychology, 80,* 514–523.

Meece, J. L., Blumenfeld, P. C., & Puro, P. (1989). *A motivational analysis of elementary science learning environments.* Paper presented at the annual meeting of the American Association for the Advancement of Science, San Francisco, CA.

Moos, R. H. (1979). *Evaluating educational environments.* San Francisco: Jossey-Bass.

Moos, R. H., & Moos, B. S. (1978). Classroom social climate and student absences and grades. *Journal of Educational Psychology, 70,* 263–269.

Morine-Dershimer, G. (1985). *Talking, listening, and learning in elementary classrooms.* New York: Longman.

Nadler, A. (1983). Personal characteristics and help-seeking. In B. M. DePaulo, A. Nadler, & J. D. Fisher (Eds.), *New directions in helping: Help-seeking* (Vol. 2, pp. 303–340). New York: Academic Press.

Nelson-Le Gall, S. (1981). Help-seeking: An understudied problem-solving skill in children. *Developmental Review, 1,* 224–246.

Nelson-Le Gall, S. (1985). Help-seeking behavior in learning. In W. Gordon (Ed.), *Review of research in education* (Vol. 12, pp. 55–90). Washington, DC: American Educational Research Association.

Nelson-Le Gall, S., & Glor-Scheib, S. (1985). Help seeking in elementary classrooms: An observational study. *Contemporary Educational Psychology, 10,* 58–71.

Nelson-Le Gall, S., & Gumerman, R. A. (1984). Children's perceptions of helpers and helper motivation. *Journal of Applied Developmental Psychology, 5,* 1–12.

Nelson-Le Gall, S., Gumerman, R. A., & Scott-Jones, D. (1983). Instrumental help-seeking and everyday problem-solving: A developmental perspective. In B. M. De-Paulo, A. Nadler, & J. D. Fisher (Eds.), *New directions in helping: Help-seeking* (Vol. 2, pp. 265–283). New York: Academic Press.

Nelson-Le Gall, S. & Jones, E. (1990). Cognitive-motivational influences on the task-related help-seeking behavior of Black children. *Child Development, 61,* 581–589.

Newman, R. S. (1990). Children's help-seeking in the classroom: The role of motivational factors and attitudes. *Journal of Educational Psychology, 82,* 71–80.

Newman, R. S. (1991). Goals and self-regulated learning: What motivates children to seek academic help? In M. L. Maehr & P. R. Pintrich (Eds.), *Advances in motivation and achievement.* (Vol. 7, pp. 151–183). Greenwich, CT: JAI Press.

Newman, R. S., & Goldin, L. (1990). Children's reluctance to seek help with schoolwork. *Journal of Educational Psychology, 82,* 92–100.

Nicholls, J. G. (1979). Quality and equality in intellectual development: The role of motivation in education. *American Psychologist, 34,* 1071–1084.

Nicholls, J. G. (1984). Conceptions of ability and achievement motivation. In R. Ames & C. Ames (Eds.), *Research on motivation in education: Student motivation* (Vol. 1, pp. 39–73). New York: Academic Press.

Palinscar, A., & Brown, A. L. (1984). Reciprocal teaching of comprehension-fostering and comprehension-monitoring activities. *Cognition and Instruction, 1,* 117–175.

Paris, S. G., & Newman, R. S. (1990). Developmental aspects of self-regulated learning. *Educational Psychologist, 25,* 87–102.

Paris, S. G., Newman, R. S., & Jacobs, J. E. (1985). Social contexts and functions of children's remembering. In M. Pressley & C. J. Brainerd (Eds.), *Cognitive learning and memory in children.* New York: Springer-Verlag.

Rohrkemper, M., & Corno, L. (1988). Success and failure on classroom tasks: Adaptive learning and classroom teaching. *The Elementary School Journal, 88,* 297–312.

Rosen, S. (1983). Perceived inadequacy and help-seeking. In B. M. DePaulo, A. Nadler, & J. D. Fisher (Eds.), *New directions in helping: Help-seeking* (Vol. 2, pp. 73–107). New York: Academic Press.

Rotter, J. (1966). Generalized expectancies for internal versus external control of reinforcement. *Psychological Monographs, 1* (Whole No. 609).

Schunk, D. H. (1989). Self-efficacy and cognitive skill learning. In C. Ames & R. Ames (Eds.), *Research on motivation in education* (Vol. 3, pp. 13–44). New York: Academic Press.

Schwager, M. T., & Newman, R. S. (1991). *Children's perceptions of the classroom in relation to help-seeking.* Paper presented at the annual meeting of the American Educational Research Association, Chicago, IL.

Skinner, E. A., Chapman, M., & Baltes, P. B. (1988). Control, means-ends, and agency beliefs: A new conceptualization and its measurement during childhood. *Journal of Personality and Social Psychology, 54,* 117–133.

Skinner, E. A., Wellborn, J. G., & Connell, J. P. (1990). What it takes to do well in school and whether I've got it: A process model of perceived control and children's engagement and achievement in school. *Journal of Educational Psychology, 82,* 22–32.

Slavin, R. (1983). *Cooperative learning.* New York: Longman.

Stipek, D. J., & Weisz, J. R. (1981). Perceived personal control and academic achievement. *Review of Educational Research, 51,* 101–137.

van der Meij, H. (1988). Constraints on question asking in classrooms. *Journal of Educational Psychology, 80,* 401–405.

Webb, N. M. (1982). Student interaction and learning in small groups. *Review of Educational Research, 52,* 421–445.

Weiner, B. (1986). *An attributional theory of motivation and emotion.* New York: Springer-Verlag.

Weinstein, R. S. (1983). Student perceptions of schooling. *The Elementary School Journal, 83,* 287–312.

Weinstein, R. S., & Middlestadt, S. (1979). Student perceptions of teacher interactions with male high and low achievers. *Journal of Educational Psychology, 71,* 421–431.

Wentzel, K. R. (1989). Adolescent classroom goals, standards for performance, and academic achievement: An interactionist perspective. *Journal of Educational Psychology, 81,* 131–142.

Wintre, M. G., Hicks, R., McVey, G., & Fox, J. (1988). Age and sex differences in choice of consultant for various types of problems. *Child Development, 59,* 1046–1055.

Wylie, R. (1979). *The self-concept: Theory and research on selected topics* (Vol. 2). Lincoln: University of Nebraska Press.

Zimmerman, B. J., & Martinez-Pons, M. (1986). Development of a structured interview for assessing student use of self-regulated learning strategies. *American Educational Research Journal, 23,* 614–628.

Zimmerman, B. J., & Schunk, D. H. (Eds.). (1989). *Self-regulated learning and academic achievement: Theory, research, and practice.* New York: Springer-Verlag.

III

Ability-Related Perceptions

Students' Motivational Beliefs and Their Cognitive Engagement in Classroom Academic Tasks

PAUL R. PINTRICH
BARBARA SCHRAUBEN
The University of Michigan

Research on student cognition has demonstrated that students' prior knowledge as well as their use of a variety of cognitive strategies play a very important role in their actual learning from academic tasks (Alexander & Judy, 1988; Pintrich, Cross, Kozma, & McKeachie, 1986; Weinstein & Mayer, 1986). These cognitive models are very relevant and useful for conceptualizing student learning, but their reliance on a model of academic learning as "cold and isolated" cognition (Brown, Bransford, Ferrara, & Campione, 1983) presents some difficulties when it is applied to the classroom. In particular, cognition-only models have difficulty explaining why students who seem to have the requisite prior knowledge and relevant cognitive strategies do not activate them for many school tasks, not to mention out-of-school tasks. In addition, intervention studies that teach students to use specific cognitive strategies to improve their memory, comprehension, and learning often show that students fail to transfer their use of these strategies to other school tasks after the training (Brown et al., 1983; Schneider & Pressley, 1989).

The failure to activate or transfer appropriate knowledge and strategies can be attributed to purely cognitive factors (e.g., automatization, encoding processes, metacognitive and regulatory processes, see Schneider & Pressley, 1989), but it seems likely that motivational components also play a role. Cognition-only models of learning tend to ignore or avoid questions about individuals' intentions, purposes, goals, and expectations while engaged in an activity (Pintrich, 1990). This may be sufficient for investigating issues related to the general competence of compliant subjects in an experimental setting where they are provided with a relatively clearly defined problem or task, but the model is less useful when applied to students' actual performance in the classroom setting. Students must attend school, but becoming cognitively engaged in the academic tasks they confront is really a choice they make for themselves (Pintrich & De Groot, 1990a). The level of their cognitive engagement may vary as a function of their self-defined goals and purposes for the tasks as well as their beliefs about the tasks and themselves.

In addition, the tasks that are presented to students in the classroom are often not as structured conceptually or procedurally as in the laboratory setting (Blumenfeld, Mergendoller, & Swarthout, 1987; Blumenfeld, Pintrich, Meece, & Wessels, 1982). Given that classroom tasks are often not clearly defined, students must often define the tasks for themselves, providing their own goals and structure. For example, there is evidence to suggest that students do not perceive classroom tasks in the same way that teachers do and often do not understand what cognitive strategies are appropriate for different tasks (Newman, Griffin, & Cole, 1989; Winne & Marx, 1982). In everyday activities, including school, individuals often have to make choices about whether they have a problem, then make choices about the specification of what constitutes the problem, and finally decide how they will go about solving it (Lave, 1989). This seems to be the case for many types of classroom tasks and students' reactions to those tasks. Given that this is a choice individuals can make for themselves, there is a need for a theory of motivation about what motivates individuals to recognize a problem, define it, and attempt to solve it. Accordingly, we need to find ways to integrate cognitive constructs related to competence with motivational constructs related to actual performance.

Motivational constructs and theory can provide some insight into students' choice to become cognitively engaged in classroom academic tasks (Pintrich, 1990; Pintrich & De Groot, 1990a). Motivation theory has traditionally focused on three general aspects of individuals' motivated behavior: (a) what activities they choose to become involved in, (b) the level of intensity in which they engage in an activity, and (c) their persistence at the activity. Cognitive engagement in academic tasks is a good exemplar of these three aspects of motivated behavior. First, there seems to be an element of choice in students' use of cognitive strategies, given that many students have knowledge of appropriate strategies, but do not employ them in all situations. Second, students may become engaged in an academic task, but they may only apply relatively simple or "surface" processing strategies (i.e., rehearsal), in comparison to becoming more intensely involved through the use of "deeper" processing strategies (i.e., elaboration, Entwistle & Marton, 1984; Marton & Saljo, 1976a, 1976b; Pintrich & Garcia, 1991). Finally, students' willingness to persist in the face of a difficult academic task by monitoring their performance and, if needed, regulating their behavior by trying different problem solving or cognitive strategies to complete the task reflects both motivation and cognition (Corno, 1986; Corno & Mandinach, 1983). Given this description of cognitive engagement as motivated behavior, it is important to link the research on motivational constructs with the research on student cognition for academic tasks.

The purpose of this chapter is to sketch the nature of the relations between different motivational constructs and students' cognitive engagement in academic tasks. We draw most heavily on our own class-room research on junior high and college students but include findings from other studies in both classroom and laboratory settings. The first section of the chapter defines the relevant motivational and cognitive constructs and places them in a conceptual framework. The next section summarizes the empirical studies that have explored the relations between motivation and cognition. We conclude with recommendations for future research and implications for pedagogical practice.

A SOCIAL COGNITIVE MODEL OF STUDENT MOTIVATION

A general social cognitive model of student motivation guides our research program (Pintrich, 1988a, 1988b, 1989, 1990). In this model, students' beliefs (cognitions, perceptions) about themselves and the task or classroom environment act as mediators of their behavior, in line with the student mediating paradigm in research on teaching (Marx, 1983) and other general social cognitive models (Bandura, 1986; Dweck & Leggett, 1988; Weiner, 1986). Moreover, a social cognitive approach assumes that self-beliefs and self-regulatory processes (the self-system) are crucial in explicating how an individual negotiates and adapts to the social environment. The social aspect of the model implies that the self-system is embedded in a social context that includes the individual and the individual's interactions and relations with the "task" and with others in the situation. Accordingly, the model assumes that students' motivational beliefs and self-regulatory processes may be situation-specific rather than traits of the individual.

Figure 7.1 represents the general conceptual model for our research program. This chapter focuses on the relations between just two of the components in the model, the motivation and cognition components (in italics in Fig. 7.1). On the far right side of the model is the main outcome of student academic achievement. Given that this is our main concern, we have included constructs that we think are most relevant to this outcome. If other outcomes (e.g., social or personal development) were the focus, different constructs would have to be included in the model. Student involvement in learning represents the ideas that motivational and cognitive components are operating jointly when the student engages in classroom learning. We have included this component in our model to reflect our belief that both motivational and cognitive components are essential to describe students' actual learning in the classroom. It is important to note, however, that both motivation and cognition are influenced by the characteristics of the academic tasks that students confront in the classroom as well as the nature of the instructional process (Brown et al., 1983; Doyle, 1983; Pintrich, 1989). These environmental features provide the social context that partially shapes, defines, and activates relevant aspects of students' motivation and cognition. At the same time, however, the individual student brings certain "entry" characteristics to the situation (e.g., demographic characteristics, personal beliefs, motivational beliefs, prior knowledge, cognitive strategies, prior achievement levels) that help to shape their interactions with and personal construals of the academic tasks and instructional processes that they confront in different classroom situations.

As can be seen in Fig. 7.1, there are three general components of students' motivational beliefs—expectancy, value, and affect (Pintrich, 1988a, 1988b, 1989). We concentrate on the expectancy and value components in this chapter. Affective components include students' emotional reactions to the task and their performance (i.e., anxiety, pride, shame, Weiner, 1986) and their more emotional needs in terms of self-worth or self-esteem (Covington & Beery, 1976; Veroff & Veroff, 1980). These affective responses are more a consequence of performance and a reflection on task involvement rather than anticipatory affect. Affective components address the basic question: How does the task and my performance on it make me feel? Although these components are certainly important (Pintrich, 1989; Pintrich & De Groot, 1990a), the length and scope of this chapter does not permit us to address how affective components are linked to cognition.

Expectancy Components

Expectancy components concern students' beliefs or answers to the basic question: Can I do this task? Expectancy components include

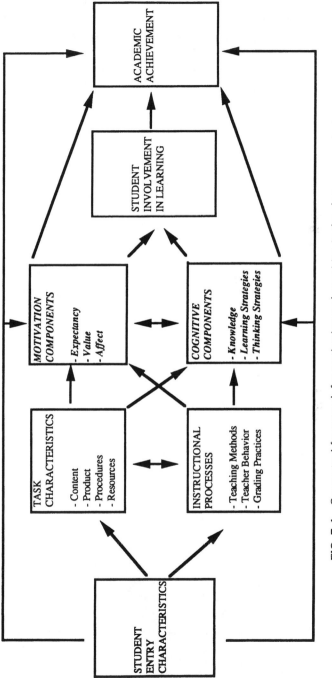

FIG. 7.1   Conceptual framework for motivation and cognition in the classroom context.

153

individuals' beliefs about their ability to perform a task, their judgments of self-efficacy and control, and their expectancy for success at
the task. The focus on being able to do a task has been operationalized
in terms of two types of motivational beliefs: self-efficacy and control
beliefs. In addition, these two expectancy components should be
related to cognitive engagement in terms of use of learning strategies.
Students who feel efficacious about learning and in control of their own
learning should be more willing to exert effort and become cognitively
engaged in the task.

Self-Efficacy Beliefs. *Self-efficacy* has been defined as individuals'
beliefs about their performance capabilities in a particular domain
(Bandura, 1982, 1986; Schunk, 1985). The construct of self-efficacy
includes individuals' judgments about their ability to accomplish certain goals or tasks through their own actions in specific situations
(Schunk, 1985). This approach implies a relatively situational or domain-
specific construct rather than a global personality trait. In an achievement context, it includes students' confidence in their cognitive skills
to perform an academic task. In our research program, we have
operationalized it as students' beliefs that they are able to learn and
understand the course material in order to do well in the class, given
our empirical findings that students' ratings of self-efficacy and expectancy for success are highly correlated (Pintrich & De Groot, 1990a;
Pintrich, Smith, Garcia, & McKeachie, 1991). Our measure of self-
efficacy, therefore, is somewhat broader than other measures of self-
efficacy (Schunk, 1985) and expectancy for success (Eccles, 1983).

Control Beliefs. Social cognitive theories of self-efficacy make a
distinction between perceptions of efficacy and students' beliefs about
outcome. As Schunk (1985) pointed out, outcome expectations refer
to individuals' beliefs concerning their ability to influence outcomes,
that is, their belief that the environment is responsive to their actions.
The idea that individuals' perceptions of control influence their behavior has a long history in motivational research (Lefcourt, 1976;
Rotter, 1966). Many of the theories built around perceptions of control
are based on organismic models of development and imply that
perceptions of control are relatively stable traits of the individual. For
example, Deci (1975) and de Charms (1968) discussed perceptions of
control in terms of students' belief in self-determination. de Charms
coined the terms "origins" and "pawns" to describe students who
believed they were able to control their actions and students who
believed others controlled their behavior.
    More recently, Connell (1985) has suggested that there are three

aspects of control beliefs: an internal source, an external source or powerful others, and an unknown source. Students who believe in internal sources of control are assumed to perform better than students who believe powerful others (e.g., teachers, parents) are responsible for their success or failure or those students who don't know who or what is responsible for the outcomes. We have operationalized our measure of control beliefs in terms of individuals' perception of internal control for learning. Our measure refers to students' beliefs that their own efforts to learn will result in positive outcomes, in particular, that outcomes in the course or the classroom are contingent on one's own effort (Pintrich et al., 1991). Accordingly, our measure of control beliefs is very similar to Connell's (1985) measure of internal control.

Value Components

Value components of our model incorporate individuals' goals for engaging in a task as well as their beliefs about the importance, utility, or interest of a task. Essentially, these components concern students' answer to the basic question: Why am I doing this task? These beliefs about the reasons for doing a specific task provide a "self-constructed" context in which students operate that can determine their activation and utilization of cognitive strategies (Dweck & Leggett, 1988). There seem to be two general aspects of value beliefs: goal orientation and task value.

Goal Orientation Beliefs. All motivational theories posit some type of goal, purpose, or intentionality to human behavior, although these goals may range from social cognitive proposals of relatively accessible and conscious goals to psychodynamic proposals of relatively inaccessible and unconscious goals (Zukier, 1986). In recent cognitive reformulations of achievement motivation theory, goals are assumed to be cognitive representations of the different purposes students may adopt in different achievement situations (Dweck & Elliott, 1983; Dweck & Leggett, 1988; Ford & Nichols, 1991). A number of researchers have discussed goal orientation (Ames, this volume; Ames & Ames, 1984; Covington & Beery, 1976; Dweck & Elliott, 1983; Jagacinski, this volume; Nicholls, 1984, this volume; Wentzel, this volume) using alternative terms and definitions, but one of the main distinctions that seems to be most crucial is between intrinsic and extrinsic goal orientation. Harter (1981) distinguished between students who offer intrinsic rationales such as mastery, challenge, learning, and curiosity from students who are more oriented to extrinsic considerations such as grades, rewards, and approval from others. These intrinsic and extrinsic orientations parallel to some extent Dweck and Elliott's (1983) distinction between learning and performance goals and Nicholls' (1984) task-involved versus ego-involved orientations. Covington and Beery (1976) also suggested that some students are not necessarily intrinsically motivated for challenge or mastery, but are motivated to increase, or at least protect, their self-worth and self-esteem. This self-worth motive is similar to Nicholls' concern with students who are ego-involved in a task (e.g., involved to show how smart they are rather than to learn the material).

In our research program we have distinguished between two general goal orientations: intrinsic and extrinsic. These two goal orientations reflect students' rationale or reasons for engaging in a task. Students operating with an intrinsic goal orientation are assumed to be approaching the task with a focus on learning and mastery. Students operating with an extrinsic goal orientation are assumed to be approaching the task with a focus on performance or grades or pleasing others. These two orientations might lead to different patterns of cognitive engagement. For example, Elliott and Dweck (1988) found that students who adopted a learning goal used more effective strategies to solve a laboratory concept learning task. A general information-processing resource allocation perspective (Kanfer & Ackerman, 1989; Kanfer & Kanfer, 1991) suggests that students with a learning goal may have more of their working memory devoted to the task and task-related cognitions, thereby resulting in more effective cognition. In comparison, students with a performance goal may be using more of their working memory in thoughts about their performance, their own ability, and what others will think of them (Dweck & Leggett, 1988). Given the limitations of working memory, these "self-peturbing ideations" (Bandura, 1986) will interfere with effective cognitive performance.

In the reality of the classroom there may be a cost–benefit mechanism operating that provides a rationale for the stronger link between an intrinsic orientation and strategy use. Students with an intrinsic orientation to learning and mastery of the course content might be more willing to invest cognitively in the task and use "deeper" processing strategies (e.g., summarizing, paraphrasing) that do have some costs associated with their use (e.g., more time needed to read the course material). In contrast, students with an extrinsic orientation focused on obtaining good grades may be less willing to make this kind of investment in learning and turn to the use of more "surface" processing strategies like rehearsal. The use of rehearsal strategies also may be very effective in terms of less time spent involved in the course, but with no or little cost in terms of lower grades. It appears that many tasks in classrooms, even college classrooms (Crooks, 1988; Pintrich, 1987, 1989), may be rather low level and focus on simple recall of information (Doyle, 1983). If this is the case, then students may not need to use deeper processing strategies to master the academic tasks and receive a good grade. Consequently, an extrinsic orientation leading to the use of surface processing strategies may actually be a relatively adaptive response to the nature of the task environment. This type of analysis highlights the interactions between actual classroom task characteristics, students' motivational beliefs, and their cognitive engagement (Fig. 7.1) and reflects some of the differences between our research and other researchers who have examined motivational and cognitive components only in the laboratory context or in relative isolation from one another.

The two different goal orientations are often thought to be extremes on a bipolar continuum from intrinsic to extrinsic (Harter, 1981). However, it seems likely that students can adopt multiple goals (Wentzel, 1991, this volume). We have argued that adults, including college students, can have multiple goals for a course. For example, a student might want to understand and master the course material due to an intrinsic rationale, but, at the same time, be concerned about grades in the class because of its implications for graduate school admission or career prospects (Pintrich & Garcia, 1991). In the same fashion, we assume that younger students, at least those in junior and senior high school, could have both intrinsic and extrinsic goal orientations operating at the same time. Nicholls and his colleagues also have found that ego and task orientations are relatively independent of one another for students ranging in age from second grade to college (Nicholls, Cheung, Lauer, & Patashnick, 1989; Nicholls, Patashnick, & Nolen, 1985). We would expect that adopting an intrinsic goal orientation would lead to deeper levels of cognitive engagement than an extrinsic orientation, but that there may be an interaction between intrinsic and extrinsic orientation where the most facilitative effect would be for students who are high in both intrinsic and extrinsic orientation.

Task Value Beliefs. Goal orientation refers to the students' general goals for their learning in a specific course or class. In our model, task value refers to students' perceptions of the course material in terms of their beliefs about the importance and interest of the content of the course. An individual's goal orientation may guide the general direction of behavior, whereas value may influence the strength or intensity of the behavior. Three components of task value have been proposed by Eccles (1983) as important in achievement dynamics: the individual's perception of the importance of the course material or task, the intrinsic interest in the course content or task, and the utility value of the material or task for future goals. Schiefele (in press) in his conceptualization of interest makes a distinction between feeling-related valences (feelings of interest and enjoyment) and value-related valences (assigning personal meaning, significance, or utility to a task) that parallel our three components of task value.

In our model, the importance component of task value refers to the individuals' perception of the task's importance, significance, or salience for them. Some courses or tasks might be seen as more important to the students' sense of self-worth or to their self-schema. For example, if a student defines him or herself as a psychologist in terms of one of his or her possible selves (Markus & Nurius, 1986; Markus & Wurf, 1987), then a psychology course may be perceived as more important to the student, regardless of his or her goal orientation to learning. In contrast, utility value refers to the instrumental motivation of the student (Eccles, 1983). Utility value is determined by the individual's perception of the usefulness of the task for him or her. Utility is a more "extrinsic" belief about how the material will help the student achieve some goal (e.g., getting into college or graduate school).

Student interest in the task is a more process and less instrumental aspect of task value. Interest is assumed to be individuals' general attitude or liking of the task. In an educational setting this includes the individual's interest in the course content and reactions to the other characteristics of the course such as the instructor (Wlodkowski, 1988). Interest in the task is partially a function of individuals' preferences as well as aspects of the task (Malone & Lepper, 1987). Schiefele (in press) noted that interest may be evoked by the situation only, what he terms situational interest, but that individual interest is a latent characteristic of the individual that is activated in certain situations. Our conception of interest is similar to this latter conception, in that it is a characteristic of the individual, but it is activated at different levels depending on the situational features of the course or task.

Although the distinctions between these three types of task value may be important, in our empirical work (see Pintrich, 1989; Pintrich & De Groot, 1990a; Pintrich et al., 1991), these three aspects of task value were not differentiated by college students. Moreover, for junior high school students, goal orientation and task value were not distinguished empirically. Students who endorsed intrinsic goals for a specific class also rated their interest and value high for that course (Pintrich & De Groot, 1990a). In our review, we distinguish between goal orientation and task value components, but the relations between these two value components and cognitive engagement may be very similar.

A GENERAL COGNITIVE MODEL FOR CONCEPTUALIZING COGNITIVE ENGAGEMENT

Most cognitive models of learning assume that there are at least two general cognitive components, broadly defined, that are important for performance: students' knowledge base and their strategic behavior (Alexander & Judy, 1988; Pintrich et al., 1986). In our general model (see Fig. 7.1) we have proposed three general cognitive components: knowledge, learning strategies, and thinking strategies. Knowledge refers to the quantity and quality (i.e., the organization and structure) of a students' knowledge base (Glaser, 1984). Learning strategies refer to students' use of different strategies for the selection, acquisition, and integration of new information with prior knowledge (Weinstein & Mayer, 1986). Thinking strategies include the students' use of different heuristics and strategies for problem solving, making inferences, and thinking critically (Nickerson, Perkins, & Smith, 1985; Pintrich, 1990).

Both knowledge and strategy use are obviously important for academic performance; however, there has been very little research on the links between motivation and knowledge or motivation and thinking strategies. Given our interest in exploring the theoretical and empirical relations between motivation and cognition and our research program, we have focused this chapter on motivation and learning strategy use. Following the work of Weinstein and Mayer (1986), we have identified rehearsal, elaboration, and organizational strategies as important cognitive strategies that are related to academic performance in the classroom (McKeachie, Pintrich, Lin, & Smith, 1986; Pintrich, 1989; Pintrich & De Groot, 1990a, 1990b). These strategies can be applied to simple memory tasks (recall of information, words, lists, etc.) or more complex tasks that require comprehension of the information (understanding a piece of text or a lecture), not just recall (Weinstein & Mayer, 1986). Besides these general cognitive strategies, there are a variety of metacognitive and self-regulatory strategies that students can use to plan, monitor, and regulate their learning (Pintrich, 1989; Weinstein & Mayer, 1986).

Cognitive Strategies and Performance

Students do confront classroom tasks that call for the memorization of facts, names of places, foreign words, and the like. There are a number of different strategies available that students might use for these basic memory tasks including rehearsal, clustering, imagery, and use of mnemonic techniques (see Schneider & Pressley, 1989; Weinstein & Mayer, 1986). Rehearsal strategies involve the reciting of items to be learned or the saying of words aloud as one reads a piece of text. Highlighting or underlining text in a rather passive and unreflective manner also can be more like a rehearsal strategy than an elaborative strategy. These rehearsal strategies are assumed to help the student attend to and select important information from lists or texts and keep this information active in working memory.

Rehearsal strategies are helpful for many classroom tasks when students are only asked to remember certain information. However, there are many classroom tasks that require more than just recall of information. In fact, it may be a more important educational goal that students come to understand the material they are learning at a relatively deep, conceptual level rather than just the surface level of recall. Research on strategy use and information processing suggest that students will gain a deeper level of comprehension when they use elaboration and organizational strategies in contrast to simple rehearsal strategies (Marton, Hounsell, & Entwistle, 1984). Rehearsal strategies do not seem to be very effective in helping the student incorporate the new information into existing schemas in long-term memory (McKeachie et al., 1986; Weinstein & Mayer, 1986). Cognitive strategies such as elaboration and organization seem to be much more useful for integrating and connecting new information with previous knowledge.

Elaborative strategies include paraphrasing or summarizing the material to be learned, creating analogies, generative note-taking (where the student actually reorganizes and connects ideas in their notes in contrast to passive, linear note-taking), explaining the ideas in the material to be learned to someone else, and question asking and answering (Weinstein & Mayer, 1986). The other general type of deeper processing strategy, organizational, includes behaviors such as selecting the main idea from text, outlining the text or material to be learned, and the use of a variety of specific techniques for selecting and organizing the ideas in the material (e.g., sketching a network or map of the important ideas, identifying the prose or expository structures of texts, see Weinstein & Mayer, 1986). All these strategies have been shown to result in a deeper understanding of the material to be learned in contrast to rehearsal strategies.

It should be noted that knowledge of these cognitive strategies may be different from actual use. Some students may know about these strategies but not use them at all, or when formally trained to use the strategies, fail to transfer them to domains outside the experimental training context. Knowledge of these different strategies is necessary for actual strategy use, but it may not be sufficient (Schneider & Pressley, 1989). Students may have to be motivated to actually use this knowledge. Accordingly, it may be that knowledge about cognitive strategies is not related to motivational components, but actual use of strategies is related to student motivation.

Metacognitive and Self-Regulatory Strategies

Besides these cognitive strategies, there are two general aspects of metacognition, knowledge about cognition and self-regulation of cognition, that can influence performance (Brown et al., 1983; Flavell, 1979). Metacognitive knowledge about strategy and task variables can influence level of involvement (e.g., if you don't know about elaboration strategies, then you may not use them to become more deeply engaged in learning), but this type of metacognitive knowledge probably does not influence choice, effort, or persistence directly. Self-regulation of cognition, however, does pertain to these issues of effort and persistence and, therefore, may be more closely linked to motivational beliefs than metacognitive knowledge. Most models of metacognitive control or self-regulation include three general types of strategies: planning, monitoring, and regulating (Corno, 1986; Zimmerman & Martinez-Pons, 1986, 1988) and our model is no different (see Pintrich, 1988a, 1988b; Pintrich, 1989; Pintrich & De Groot, 1990a, 1990b; Pintrich & Garcia, 1991; Pintrich et al., 1991). The focus of this chapter will be on these three self-regulatory strategies. Although these three types of strategies are highly related and, at least in our data (Pintrich, 1989; Pintrich et al., 1991), seem to be highly correlated empirically, they can be discussed separately.

Planning activities that have been investigated in various studies of students' learning include setting goals for studying, skimming a text before reading, generating questions before reading a text, and doing a task analysis of the problem. These activities seem to help the learners plan their use of cognitive strategies and also seem to activate or prime relevant aspects of prior knowledge, making the organization and comprehension of the material much easier. Learners who report using these types of planning activities seem to perform better on a variety of academic tasks in comparison to students who do not use these strategies (McKeachie et al., 1986; Pressley, 1986).

Monitoring of one's thinking and academic behavior seems to be an essential aspect of metacognition. Weinstein and Mayer (1986) see all metacognitive activities as partly the monitoring of comprehension. Monitoring activities include tracking of attention while reading a text or listening to a lecture, self-testing through the use of questions about the text material to check for understanding, monitoring comprehension of a lecture, and the use of test-taking strategies (i.e., monitoring speed and adjusting to time available) in an exam situation. These various monitoring strategies alert the learner to breakdowns in attention or comprehension that can then be subjected to repair through the use of regulating strategies.

Regulation strategies are closely tied to monitoring strategies. For example, as learners ask themselves questions as they read in order to monitor their comprehension, and then go back and reread a portion of the text, this rereading is a regulatory strategy. Another type of self-regulatory strategy for reading occurs when students slow the pace of their reading when confronted with more difficult or less familiar text. Of course, reviewing any aspect of course material (e.g., lecture notes, texts, lab material, previous exams and papers, etc.) that one does not remember or understand that well while studying for an exam reflects a general self-regulatory strategy. During a test, skipping questions and returning to them later is another strategy that students can use to regulate their behavior during an exam. All these strategies are assumed to improve learning by helping students correct their studying behavior and repair deficits in their understanding.

The final aspect in our model of learning and self-regulatory strategies, resource management strategies, concerns strategies that students use to manage their environment (their time, their study environment, and others including teachers and peers) and themselves (their own effort) as they attempt different academic tasks (Corno, 1986; Zimmerman & Martinez-Pons, 1986, 1988). In line with a general adaptive approach to learning, we assume that these resource management strategies help students adapt to their environment as well as change the environment to fit their goals and needs (Sternberg, 1985). The resource management strategies that we have focused on include time and study environment, effort management, and help-seeking.

Students' management of their time and the actual place they choose to study are not cognitive or metacognitive strategies that may have a direct influence on eventual learning, but they are general strategies that can help or hinder the students' efforts at completing the academic task. Effort management seems to be an important aspect of self-control in terms of persisting in the face of difficult or boring tasks (Corno, 1986; Kuhl, 1985). Students who are able to protect their intention to study in terms of arranging their time, their study place, and their actual behavior while studying to facilitate concentrated and deeper processing of the material should perform better than those students who are not able to manage their resources as effectively. In the same fashion, students who know when, how, and from whom to seek help (see Newman, 1991, this volume) should be more likely to be successful than those students who do not seek help appropriately.

In summary, our model of cognitive engagement includes three general components: knowledge (both prior knowledge about content and metacognitive knowledge), learning strategies, and thinking strategies. For the purpose of this chapter, we focus on the learning strategies component including students' use of cognitive and self-regulatory strategies for planning, monitoring, and regulating their environment, cognition, effort, and behavior. In the following section we review the empirical research on the relations between motivational beliefs and these learning strategies.

EMPIRICAL RELATIONS BETWEEN MOTIVATIONAL BELIEFS AND COGNITIVE ENGAGEMENT

Although there has not been a great deal of empirical research on how motivational beliefs are linked to cognitive engagement, there have been studies that have examined this issue. For example, in our research program here at Michigan we have been explicitly examining the relations between students' motivational beliefs and their use of cognitive and self-regulatory strategies for learning. The purpose of this section is to summarize our own research on how motivational beliefs are linked to cognitive engagement in terms of the use of cognitive and self-regulatory strategies. The findings from other studies that have examined the same relations are included, although the review is not exhaustive of all studies in this area.

Relations Between Self-Efficacy Beliefs and Cognitive Engagement

We have been involved in a series of studies that have examined the linkages between students' motivational beliefs and their cognitive engagement at the college and junior high school levels. The research has been classroom-based, focusing on students' beliefs and perceptions and their academic performance in actual courses and classrooms. Of course, given the emphasis on ecological validity, there has been some reduction in internal validity. The studies have been correlational and used self-report measures, both limitations of the data. Nevertheless, the consistency of the results across different waves of data collection and relatively large samples as well as the complementary nature of the findings to other experimental studies suggest that the conclusions we have drawn are applicable to cognitive engagement in classroom settings.

In a series of studies beginning in 1982 and continuing through the present (McKeachie, Pintrich, & Lin, 1985a, 1985b; Pintrich, 1985, 1986, 1987, 1989; Pintrich & Garcia, 1991), we asked college students to use a self-report instrument (The Motivated Strategies for Learning Questionnaire or MSLQ, see Pintrich et al., 1991) to report on their motivational beliefs and their cognitive engagement in a specific college course. We also collected data on their actual performance on different academic tasks throughout the term for this course. The data include studies where the MSLQ was given only once in the term as well as studies where the MSLQ was given at both the beginning and end of the term to allow for the examination of change over time. The samples have included students from a variety of liberal arts courses (e.g., English, biology, psychology, sociology, philosophy, chemistry, history) at a community college, a small liberal arts institution, a comprehensive university, and a research university in the Midwest. Most of the courses have been at the introductory level, resulting in samples comprised of mostly first and second year college students. The sample sizes have ranged from 80 to 758 in the different studies with over 3,000 college students across all the studies. The findings reported here are general summaries of the results combined across the different studies. It should be noted that some of the relations varied in different studies depending on the size of the sample, the measures used, and the classroom context.

The findings for self-efficacy showed positive relations between efficacy and cognitive engagement. Students who felt more efficacious about their ability to do well in the course were more likely to report using all three types of cognitive strategies (rehearsal, elaboration, and organizational strategies). Students high in self-efficacy were more likely to be cognitively involved in trying to learn the material in comparison to those low in efficacy, even if some of their strategies (i.e., rehearsal) were not deep level comprehension strategies. Self-efficacy also was positively related to self-regulatory strategies and effort management. Although weaker, the positive correlations between self-efficacy and management of study environment and time were significant also. Students high in efficacy were more likely to monitor and regulate their learning, persist in the face of difficult or boring tasks, and manage their time and study environment more effectively than students low in efficacy. Students did not differ in their help-seeking as a function of self-efficacy beliefs. Self-efficacy also was strongly related to academic performance including exams, lab reports, papers, and overall final grade.

In studies of junior high school students, Pintrich and De Groot (1988, 1990a, 1990b) found a similar pattern of results. Self-efficacy was positively related to cognitive strategy use and use of self-regulatory strategies. Self-efficacy also was related to academic performance including exams, papers or essays, seatwork, and grades at the beginning and at the end of the marking period. Analyses revealed that self-efficacy was not a significant predictor of academic performance when the cognitive strategy use and self-regulatory strategy variables were included as predictors. This suggested that self-efficacy had an indirect effect on performance through its relation with the cognitive engagement variables (Pintrich & De Groot, 1990a). A study of motivational beliefs and cognitive engagement across three domains of English, science, and social studies for 48 junior high school students (Pintrich & De Groot, 1990b) found similar results. Self-efficacy was correlated positively to use of cognitive strategies and self-regulatory strategies in all three domains. In addition, self-efficacy was positively correlated with students' grades in the three domains with only self-efficacy at the beginning of the term in science not being significantly associated with grades at the end of the term.

Although the self-report instrument (the MSLQ) used for these two studies was adapted to reflect the realities of student life in junior high as compared to college classrooms (see Appendix in Pintrich & De Groot, 1990a), it still had separate items reflecting the use of rehearsal, elaboration, and organizational strategies. In addition, we had items reflecting planning and comprehension monitoring as well as effort management. However, factor analyses of these items showed that junior high school students did not reliably differentiate between the use of different cognitive strategies. That is, if they tended to use rehearsal strategies, they also reported using elaboration or organizational strategies more often. The same was true for metacognition and effort management strategies (Pintrich & De Groot, 1990a). In general, in contrast to the college students who did show different patterns of cognitive engagement (see Pintrich, 1989), if junior high students reported being cognitively engaged, it reflected a general engagement in learning that included the use of a variety of cognitive and self-regulatory strategies.

In these junior high and college studies we have demonstrated that self-efficacy beliefs are related to cognitive engagement and actual academic achievement in the ecologically valid setting of the classroom. The pattern of these relations parallel findings from other experimental and correlational studies. Schunk, in his program of research on both the antecedents and consequences of self-efficacy in elementary and junior high classrooms, has found self-efficacy to be consistently related to cognitive engagement and academic performance (see reviews by Schunk, 1985, 1989, in press). Many of these studies involved experimental manipulations to change efficacy beliefs and cognitive skills. Other field-based, correlational studies have found similar relations. For example, Paris and Oka (1986) showed that elementary students' perceptions of competence were positively related to performance on a reading comprehension cloze task, metacognitive knowledge and awareness about reading, and actual reading achievement. Shell, Murphy, and Bruning (1989) found that college students' self-efficacy beliefs about their actual reading skills (e.g., decoding words, recognizing main ideas) and their writing skills (e.g., spelling correctly, using proper grammar, organizing their ideas) were related to students' performance on a reading comprehension cloze task as well as their performance on an essay writing task, respectively.

In summary, self-efficacy is positively related to various measures of cognitive engagement. In addition, self-efficacy can have both direct and indirect effects on actual academic performance depending on the outcome measure. In studies (i.e., Shell et al., 1989; many of Schunk's) that use very specific measures of cognitive skills (e.g., reading comprehension tasks, arithmetic tasks, writing tasks) there is a direct relation between self-efficacy and performance. In our studies where we have used more global measures of performance such as actual grades on academic coursework, self-efficacy does not seem to have a direct effect when cognitive engagement variables (cognitive strategy use, self-regulatory strategies) are included as predictors of academic performance. Nevertheless, self-efficacy beliefs seem to be important mediators of cognitive engagement and academic performance in classrooms.

Relations Between Control Beliefs and Cognitive Engagement

In our work here at Michigan, we have included an internal control beliefs scale on the MSLQ (see Pintrich et al., 1991). Pintrich (1989) found that internal control beliefs were positively related to all the cognitive and self-regulatory scales on the MSLQ except help-seeking. College students who believed that their behavior and effort influenced their performance in the course were more likely to use rehearsal strategies, elaboration strategies, organizational strategies, and self-regulatory strategies like comprehension monitoring. In addition, students who were high in internal control also reported that they were better managers of their study time, their study environment, and their actual effort in the face of boring or difficult tasks, but they did not differ in their reported help-seeking behavior from those low in internal control. Higher ratings of internal control also were strongly associated with higher performance on exams, lab reports, papers, and final grade in the course. In our work with junior high school students we have not constructed a separate control beliefs scale because of the high correlation with the self-efficacy scale items.

Other studies have generally found positive relations between internal control beliefs and cognitive engagement. For example, Fabricius and Hagen (1984) showed that internal attributions to ability were causally related to first and second graders' subsequent use of a memory sorting strategy more strongly than previous use of memory strategies. Kurtz and Borkowksi (1984) also found that first and third graders who attributed their memory performance to controllable factors after receiving strategy training used more memory strategies on the maintenance and generalization tasks than students who made attributions to uncontrollable factors. In other studies of upper elementary and junior high age students, attributional beliefs in the importance or utility of effort were positively related to metacognitive knowledge (i.e., metamemory, reading awareness) as well as strategy use and actual performance (Borkowski, Carr, Rellinger, & Pressley, 1990; Schneider, Borkowski, Kurtz, & Kerwin, 1986). In contrast, Schneider, Korkel, and Weinert (1987) only found positive relations between a combined attributions and self-concept measure and students' metamemory knowledge and actual memory performance for fifth graders, but not for third graders. More recently, other studies of second through sixth graders did not find positive relations between attributional beliefs and memory performance (Chapman, Skinner, & Baltes, 1990) and general engagement (Skinner, Wellborn, & Connell, 1990), although both these studies did find a strong relation between self-efficacy beliefs and engagement. Finally, Weed, Ryan, and Day (1990) found that attributional beliefs only played a role in memory performance when their fourth graders confronted a novel task. When a transfer task was tried, metacognitive knowledge and metacognitive monitoring were more strongly related to performance in comparison to attributional beliefs.

In summary, it appears that control beliefs can be positively related to aspects of cognitive engagement, including metacognitive knowledge and actual cognitive stratey use, paralleling the findings for control beliefs and overall academic performance (Findley & Cooper,

1983; Stipek & Weisz, 1981). However, the relations may vary depending on the age of the student, the definition of the construct, the type of measures employed, and the timing of the assessments of motivational beliefs. Future research is needed that clarifies the different aspects of control beliefs and their interactions with other motivational beliefs as well as how these beliefs operate in classroom settings longitudinally and developmentally (Chapman et al., 1990; Skinner et al., 1990).

Relations Between Goal Orientation and Cognitive Engagement

There seems to be a very consistent, positive relation between students' goal orientation and their cognitive engagement in learning. In our studies of college students we have asked them about their general goal orientation for the course. The MSLQ generates two separate scales for their endorsement of intrinsic goals such as learning, mastery, and challenge as well as extrinsic goals such as getting good grades or competing with others (see Pintrich et al., 1991). These studies have shown that college students who endorse an intrinsic goal orientation are more likely to be cognitively engaged than those students who rate themselves lower on intrinsic goals (Pintrich, 1985, 1986, 1987, 1989; Pintrich & Garcia, 1991). In general, students high in intrinsic orientation were more likely to use rehearsal strategies, elaboration and organizational strategies, and self-regulatory strategies. In addition, these students reported being better managers of their time and effort and were more likely to do well on the academic performance measures (i.e., exams, papers, and final course grade).

In another study of college students where we specifically addressed the interactions between intrinsic and extrinsic orientations (Pintrich & Garcia, 1991), we found that intrinsic orientation was significantly related to cognitive engagement. Students who endorsed intrinsic goals at a higher level were more likely to use elaboration and organizational strategies, self-regulatory strategies, and to be better managers of their time and study efforts, consistent with previous results. Extrinsic goal orientation was not significantly related to cognitive or self-regulatory strategy use directly. However, extrinsic goal orientation did moderate the effect of intrinsic goal orientation on use of elaboration/organizational strategies and self-regulatory strategies. Results with intrinsic and extrinsic goal orientation divided into three levels (high, average, and low) showed that different levels of intrinsic goal orientation had the predicted positive influence on cognitive engagement when extrinsic goal orientation was low. In contrast, at high levels of extrinsic goal orientation, students who differed in intrinsic goal orientation did not differ in cognitive engagement. We concluded from these results that it is better to be high in intrinsic orientation and low in extrinsic orientation as suggested by intrinsic motivation theory (e.g., Deci & Ryan, 1985). However, lacking an intrinsic orientation, it is at least better to care about grades and other extrinsic concerns than to be "alienated" from school, not endorsing either intrinsic or extrinsic goals (Pintrich & Garcia, 1991).

This study involved college students and the findings need to be replicated with younger students. However, it is interesting to speculate that if extrinsic goal orientation can provide some impetus to be cognitively involved in school work, then these results provide one potential psychological mechanism to explain why good classroom management and control may be important, contrary to the arguments of some intrinsic motivation theorists. That is, good classroom management may foster adoption of an extrinsic goal orientation and endorsement of classroom norms (e.g., Blumenfeld, Hamilton, Bossert, Wessels, & Meece, 1983; Blumenfeld, Pintrich, & Hamilton, 1987) that at least leads to some cognitive engagement. Intrinsic goals, of course, lead to deeper levels of cognitive engagement, but lacking an intrinsic goal, it is important to be motivated extrinsically, to participate in the classroom and not be alienated from it. Accordingly, good classroom management, mediated through its effects on student adoption of an extrinsic goal orientation, may be necessary for a modicum of cognitive engagement, but not sufficient for very high levels of cognitive engagement that would be fostered by individuals adopting intrinsic goals as a function of other classroom characteristics related to intrinsic motivation (cf. Deci & Ryan, 1985).

In studies of junior high school students, we have not measured extrinsic goal orientation separately, so we do not have data to support this argument at this time. However, the results show that junior high students who endorse intrinsic goals are more likely to use cognitive and self-regulatory strategies in general (Pintrich & De Groot, 1988, 1990a). In a study of the relations between intrinsic goal orientation and cognitive engagement across the three domains of English, science, and social studies classes for the same students, the results showed strong positive correlations between intrinsic goals and use of cognitive and self-regulatory strategies in all domains. In addition, it was interesting to note that the relations were stable across individuals and domains. That is, individuals who were intrinsically oriented in one domain also tended to be intrinsically oriented in the other two domains as well as being more likely to use cognitive and self-regulatory strategies in all three domains (Pintrich & De Groot, 1990b). This finding of strong individual differences needs to be replicated with larger samples and include the domain of school mathematics. The qualitative data in this study suggested that the junior high school students perceived mathematics quite differently from the other three domains, so that the same relations might not be found when mathematics courses are included in future research.

Intrinsic goal orientation also was related to classroom academic performance in the two junior high studies. However, paralleling the results for self-efficacy, intrinsic orientation did not have a direct influence on performance when the cognitive engagement variables were included as predictors. This suggests that both of the motivational variables of self-efficacy and intrinsic goal orientation have an indirect relation with classroom academic performance through their direct relation to the cognitive variables like cognitive strategy use and self-regulation.

Our findings for intrinsic goal orientation are similar to other experimental and field-based studies. For example, Nolen (1988), in a laboratory study of eighth graders' use of learning strategies for text comprehension, showed that students with higher levels of a task orientation (i.e., a focus on learning) were more likely to be cognitively engaged, including more frequent use of both deeper (i.e., elaboration) and surface processing strategies (i.e., rehearsal). An ego orientation (i.e., a focus on the extrinsic rationale of besting others) was positively related to the use of surface processing strategies. Most importantly, and paralleling our findings, these motivational orientations were not directly related to actual performance in comparison to cognitive strategy use, suggesting that motivational orientation only plays an indirect role in fostering academic performance through its link to the use of cognitive strategies. In a correlational classroom study of fifth and sixth graders, Meece, Blumenfeld, and Hoyle (1988) found that students' general intrinsic orientation to learning as well as task specific mastery goals (assessed for six different classroom tasks) predicted subsequent use of cognitive and metacognitive strategies for the different tasks.

In summary, an intrinsic goal orientation that focuses the student on learning and mastery seems to have a positive relation with a variety of cognitive engagement measures. There are several issues to keep in mind, however. First, the results may differ depending on whether a general measure or a more task specific measure is used (Meece et al., 1988; Nolen, 1988). Second, the idea that intrinsic and extrinsic goal orientations may be two separate dimensions rather than opposite endpoints on one continuum needs to be explored in more detail in future research. It seems likely that students can adopt both intrinsic and extrinsic goals at the same time and that there may be benefits for having both types of goals. Finally, goal orientation does not seem to be related directly to actual performance measures (grades, idea units recalled), but it is strongly linked to the use of cognitive and meta-cognitive strategies that then lead to better performance.

Relations Between Task Value and Cognitive Engagement

In our research program we have operationalized task value as students' perceptions of the importance, utility, and interest of the course material for them (see Pintrich et al., 1991). These beliefs are usually correlated with intrinsic goal orientation in college students (Pintrich & Garcia, 1991), but factor analyses show them to be separate factors (Pintrich et al., 1991). However, in junior high school students we have not found intrinsic goal orientation and task value beliefs to be separable empirically (Pintrich & De Groot, 1990a).

Task value beliefs of college students were correlated with cognitive strategy use including rehearsal, elaboration, and organizational strategy use. In addition, students who reported higher levels of interest and value were more likely to report that they were thinking critically about the course material and using more strategies to regulate their cognition and their effort. We also found that task value was correlated to performance, albeit these relations were not as strong as those for self-efficacy (Pintrich, 1989; Pintrich & Garcia, 1991; Pintrich et al., 1991).

These findings are similar to those of Shell et al. (1989) who found that college students' beliefs about the importance of reading skills for different outcomes in life (e.g., career success, family life, personal development) were related to reading comprehension performance, but not as strongly as self-efficacy beliefs. Schiefele (in press), using both experimental and correlational designs, has shown college students' interest to be related to the use of deeper processing strategies like elaboration, the seeking of information when confronted with a problem, their engagement in critical thinking, and self-reports of time and effort investment. In addition, interest was negatively related to the use of rehearsal strategies.

The effects of interest on cognitive engagement have not been limited to studies of college students. For example, Renninger and Wozniak (1985) have shown that, even for preschoolers, interest in different objects influences their attention, recognition, and recall. Pokay and Blumenfeld (1990), in a study of high school geometry students, found that students' perceptions of the value of math did not predict performance directly, but was positively related to the use of general cognitive strategies, specific geometry strategies, metacognitive strategies and management of effort. These findings for task value beliefs support the view that perceptions of the value of a task do not have a direct influence on academic performance, but they do relate to students' "choice" of becoming cognitively engaged in a task or course.

FUTURE DIRECTIONS FOR RESEARCH AND
IMPLICATIONS FOR INSTRUCTION

The consistency of the findings for the linkages between motivational beliefs and cognitive engagement represent an important contribution to our knowledge about the role of motivation and cognition in classroom contexts. The general finding is relatively easy to summarize. Students who have positive motivational beliefs, that is, those who believe that they can accomplish certain tasks, believe that learning is under their control, approach tasks with an orientation to learning and mastery, and are interested in and value the task content, will be more likely to become engaged in learning in a deeper, more self-regulating fashion than those students who do not have these beliefs. Moreover, having positive motivational beliefs may not lead directly to improved academic performance, but these beliefs can lead to increased cognitive engagement in the task which does have a direct influence on academic performance. That being said, however, still leaves many issues to be resolved in future research.

One important direction concerns the interactions between the different motivational beliefs and students' knowledge of and use of cognitive strategies. The discussion in this chapter has focused on the linear relations between single motivational variables and cognitive engagement variables. However, as noted in Fig. 7.1, student involvement in learning includes both motivation and cognition, operating together, not in isolation from one another. We have not found many two-way interactions between different levels of motivational variables (e.g., high and low levels of intrinsic orientation with high and low levels of self-efficacy) and cognitive engagement or performance, or between different levels of motivation and cognitive engagement on performance (Pintrich, 1989; Pintrich & De Groot, 1990a). This may be due to the limited range of students in the samples. At the same time, by examining how the motivational and cognitive variables are distributed within individuals, we have shown how different profiles of motivation and cognition may lead to similar outcomes. Pintrich (1989) found five clusters of college students, two who represented typically high and low achievers, while the other three clusters were all average achievers in terms of grades. The interesting finding was that these three average groups were differentiated in terms of their profiles of motivation and cognition. One of these groups was motivated (high in intrinsic orientation and efficacy) but not self-regulating. The second and third groups reported similar levels of self-regulated learning, but one group was low in intrinsic motivation, whereas the other group was low in self-efficacy. The fact that these three groups all showed similar levels of performance suggests that the motivational and cognitive variables can work in complementary ways to influence learning. This finding needs to be replicated with younger students and in different settings, but the general strategy of developing multivariate profiles of students' motivation and cognition seems to be a useful tool for understanding how motivation and cognition operate jointly in the classroom context.

This approach does not address the issue of causality between motivation and cognition, but in the classroom this issue may not be as important as determining how they work together. In a recent study (Garcia & Pintrich, 1991), we found that the motivational variables of intrinsic goal orientation and self-efficacy predicted levels of self-regulated learning, but the relation was not reciprocal. This finding parallels Borkowski et al.'s (1990) conclusion that motivational variables "power" self-regulated learning. Although these findings are helpful in explicating the relations between motivation and cognition, we think that future research should avoid pursuing a "definitive" answer to the causal predominance question (cf. the research on causality between self-concept and achievement, Wigfield & Karpathian, in press). It will be more productive to concentrate instead on understanding how different aspects of motivation and cognition operate together in a classroom setting to influence achievement.

At a more global level, a key issue in future research will be more theoretical and empirical work to clarify the domain-specificity of students' motivational beliefs. The issue of general traits or orientations and situational or domain specific beliefs needs to be clarified. There are many different levels of analysis and concomitant measurement differences in the studies reviewed here. Some of the measures have been very situation specific and dynamic (e.g., Schunk's work on self-efficacy judgments), others have been more global (e.g., measures of control beliefs) and others have tried to operationalize their constructs at an intermediate level between these extremes (e.g., our work with course or classroom level beliefs). It may be that self-efficacy and control beliefs are more domain or situation-specific, whereas goal orientations and task value beliefs are more global and "carried" by the person as they confront different tasks. If this is so, then measures of these beliefs will have to reflect these differences. Studies comparing general, global self-reports of motivational beliefs with "on-line" measures (i.e., think-alouds, stimulated recall) of students' statements about their efficacy, goals, or interest would help to clarify the measurement concerns as well as the relation between global beliefs and situation-specific beliefs.

A related issue concerns the theoretical nature of the self-system. It seems clear that there is a need for some "structural" model of how all these different beliefs about the self are organized and represented within the individual. It may be that students' motivational beliefs are not organized in any kind of system, that there are a multiplicity of beliefs available to the student, and they are simply activated as a function of different cues in the situation. However, there does seem to be some consistency and coherence in students' beliefs and behavior over time and situations, at least at a macrolevel. There needs to be some way to represent this consistency and coherence but maintain a dynamic view of the self and the different motivational beliefs that can be activated in different situations. This problem of how self-beliefs are stored or represented within the person is analogous to the problem of how knowledge is stored and represented in cognitive psychology. There are a variety of models in cognitive psychology for how knowledge is represented that could be applied to self-knowledge and self-beliefs (Cantor & Kihlstrom, 1987; Harter, 1985; Markus & Nurius, 1986; McCombs, 1989).

Another general issue concerns the nature of academic tasks and the links between these tasks and students' cognitive and self-regulatory strategies. The issue of the domain specificity or situational specificity of these strategies is an important issue in cognitive and instructional psychology paralleling the work in motivational and personality psychology on traits and states. It may be that certain types of strategies are tied closely to certain types of tasks (e.g., specific memory strategies and memory tasks) and these strategies are invoked almost automatically by the task demands. Laboratory research certainly suggests that this may be the case. However, more research on the nature of classroom tasks and their links to students, use of cognitive strategies may reveal somewhat different relations. We need to develop a taxonomy of classroom academic tasks that reflects not only an "expert" or teacher view of the tasks and its demands (Doyle, 1983), but also a taxonomy that reflects students' view of classroom academic tasks (Blumenfeld et al., 1987; Thorkildsen & Nicholls, in press).

The issue of how classroom tasks influence cognitive engagement is related to issues regarding the improvement of instruction. There seem to be two general categories of classroom life that may be amenable to change to facilitate student motivation and cognitive engagement: first, teacher talk and feedback and, second, structural characteristics of the classroom (tasks, reward structures, choice and control). In terms of teacher talk and feedback, it seems likely that certain patterns of feedback and the nature of the attributional statements teachers make can influence students' motivational beliefs (Brophy, 1981; Schunk, 1985; Skinner et al., 1990). However, attempts to raise students' self-efficacy or control beliefs through the use of contingent positive feedback will not necessarily result in performance increases directly. Knowledge of appropriate cognitive and self-regulatory strategies for the task is necessary, albeit it may not be sufficient if students are not motivated to use the strategies (Pintrich, 1989). It appears that positive motivational beliefs about efficacy and control can have the facilitative effect of rendering the student confident enough to activate previously acquired strategies. If the students do not have the appropriate knowledge or strategies, then it seems more important to teach or model the strategies than to work on simply changing their self-perceptions through positive feedback (Blumenfeld, Pintrich, Meece, & Wessels, 1982).

Besides teacher feedback, the nature of teachers' attributional statements may influence cognitive engagement given the success of attribution retraining interventions in facilitating future achievement (Foersterling, 1985). In the case of cognitive engagement, it appears that directing students' attention to the strategy aspects of a learning task, that is, the aspects that they can learn and bring under their control, especially at the beginning of a novel task (Weed et al., 1990) can have beneficial effects. Accordingly, teachers should take care when introducing new tasks to make appropriate attributional statements that communicate to students that the strategies required for the task are learnable and under their control (Clifford, 1986a, 1986b). At the same time, just making appropriate attributional statements without accompanying instruction in the strategies or knowledge necessary to accomplish the new task will be less useful than interventions that include both attributional and strategy training (Borkowski et al., 1990).

In terms of structural changes in the classroom, there are a variety of suggestions based on changing the task, goal, reward, and participation structures of classrooms (Ames, 1984; Ames & Archer, 1988; Deci & Ryan, 1987; Maehr & Midgley, in press). Most of these suggestions are based on changing students' beliefs about control and their goal orientation. So, for example, Deci and Ryan (1987) argued for contexts that allow individuals to feel autonomous and self-determining by providing them with some choice and control. Although there may be ways to make major changes in classroom structures to facilitate students' perceptions of control, we believe that existing classroom practices need be altered in only minor ways that might permit major changes in students' perceptions of control. For example, a math assignment consisting of "Solve the 25 problems on page 59." could be broadened to offer at least one alternative, such as "Solve only the first 20 problems on page 59 and compose five similar problems of your own." Another small adjustment could be allowing students the choice to work alone or with another peer, as long as the individuals are still held accountable for their own work.

Furthermore, because students' perception of control is of import here rather than actual control, educators might do well to bring to student attention opportunities for control that do occur during a typical school day (i.e., allowing choice in times to complete work) and to minimize attention to the aspects beyond the students' control. For example, an outline of course requirements emphasizes what's not controlled by the student by using the statement: "All students will complete four reports on topics from an approved list." The same requirement also could be set forth emphasizing student choice: "From a list of 50 topics, students will choose eight topics of highest personal interest for preliminary exploration, and will write a report on any four of these topics." More far-reaching changes, although difficult to implement, might result in greater changes in perceptions of control. For example, one local elementary school bases all assignments on individual student proposals, contracted for daily or weekly, that allow students some freedom in deciding the order in which they will accomplish certain tasks, while still maintaining teacher control over the actual content of the curriculum.

Given our review of the empirical research that suggests that goal orientation beliefs may be more strongly and directly linked to cognitive engagement and strategy use than control beliefs, it may be more important to concentrate on changing classrooms to help students adopt mastery and learning goals. Programs that attempt to change the goal and reward structures of classrooms (or schools) like the TARGET program (e.g., Ames, 1989, this volume; Maehr & Midgley, in press) do provide a number of specific suggestions that teachers can use in their classrooms. These involve changing the types of tasks students work on to make them more intrinsically valuable and interesting, changing the authority structure to allow some student choice, developing ways to recognize individual accomplishments, grouping students to work together not alone, developing evaluation methods that focus on improvement not social comparison, and improving the use of time in the classroom or school. These programs should result in changes in students' goals and encourage them to adopt a mastery or learning orientation to their school work.

It is difficult to separate out these different features of the classroom given that the instructional approach of the teacher interacts with teacher feedback and the structural characteristics of the classroom. Teachers who change the goal or task structure of the classroom without also changing the nature of their instruction to focus on meaningful learning and the intrinsic value of learning may not have students who are cognitively engaged (Meece, 1991). Our data suggest that just changing teacher feedback patterns or structural features of the classroom may not be sufficient for all students, especially students who lack the appropriate cognitive and self-regulatory strategies for learning. Changing the goals of the classroom may only facilitate the use of more memorization strategies for less effective students without direct instruction in more appropriate strategies for learning (Pintrich & De Groot, 1990b). At the same time, strategy intervention programs (Pressley, 1990) that attempt to teach students more appropriate strategies may be "undermined" by the traditional goal and task structures of the average classroom. If students aren't required by the type of classroom tasks and evaluation procedures or encouraged by the goal orientation in the classroom to use more sophisticated learning strategies, it seems unlikely that even the more effective students will use these strategies. Accordingly, programs will need to incorporate both motivational or "will" components as well as cognitive or "skill" components in their attempts to change classroom instruction in order to foster more self-regulated learning in students.

ACKNOWLEDGMENTS

Funding for the empirical research summarized in this chapter was provided by a Spencer Fellowship from the National Academy of Education to the first author and a grant awarded to the National Center for Research to Improve Postsecondary Teaching and Learning (NCRIPTAL) from the Office of Educational Research and Improvement/ Department of Education (Grant #OERI-86-0010). The opinions expressed in this chapter do not reflect the positions or policies of the Spencer Foundation, National Academy of Education, NCRIPTAL, or OERI/ED. Special thanks to our colleagues at Michigan, Teresa Garcia, Marty Maehr, and Bill McKeachie, as well as the editors of this volume, Dale Schunk and Judith Meece, for helpful comments on an earlier draft.

REFERENCES

Alexander, P., & Judy, J. (1988). The interaction of domain-specific and strategic knowledge in academic performance. *Review of Educational Research, 58,* 375–404.

Ames, C. (1984). Competitive, cooperative, and individualistic goals structures: A cognitive-motivational analysis. In R. Ames & C. Ames (Eds.), *Research on motivation in education: Vol. 1. Student motivation* (pp. 177–207). New York: Academic Press.

Ames, C. (1989). *School-home strategies to enhance motivation.* Unpublished manuscript, Department of Educational Psychology, University of Illinois, Urbana-Champaign.

Ames, C., & Ames, R. (1984). Systems of student and teacher motivation: Toward a qualitative definition. *Journal of Educational Psychology, 76,* 535–556.

Ames, C., & Archer, J. (1988). Achievement goals in the classroom: Student learning strategies and motivation processes. *Journal of Educational Psychology, 80,* 260–267.

Bandura, A. (1982). Self-efficacy mechanisms in human agency. *American Psychologist, 37,* 122–148.

Bandura, A. (1986). *Social foundations of thought and action: A social cognitive theory.* Englewood Cliffs, NJ: Prentice-Hall.

Blumenfeld. P., Hamilton, V. L., Bossert, S., Wessels, K., & Meece, J. (1983). Teacher talk and student thought: Socialization into the student role. In J. Levine & M. Wang (Eds.), *Teacher and student perceptions: Implications for learning* (pp. 143–192). Hillsdale, NJ: Lawrence Erlbaum Associates.

Blumenfeld, P., Mergendollar, J., & Swarthout, D. (1987). Task as a heuristic for understanding student learning and motivation. *Journal of Curriculum Studies, 19,* 135–148.

Blumenfeld, P., Pintrich, P. R., Hamilton, V. L. (1987). Teacher talk and students' reasoning about morals, conventions, and achievement. *Child Development, 58,* 1389–1401.

Blumenfeld, P., Pintrich, P. R., Meece, J., & Wessels, K. (1982). The formation and role of self-perceptions of ability in elementary classrooms. *Elementary School Journal, 82,* 401–420.

Borkowski, J., Carr, M., Rellinger, E., & Pressley, M. (1990). Self-regulated cognition: Interdependence of metacognition, attributions, and self-esteem. In B. Jones & L. Idol (Eds.), *Dimensions of thinking and cognitive instruction* (pp. 53–92). Hillsdale, NJ: Lawrence Erlbaum Associates.

Brophy, J. (1981). Teacher praise: A functional analysis. *Review of Educational Research, 51,* 5–32.

Brown, A., Bransford, J., Ferrara, R., & Campione, J. (1983). Learning, remembering, and understanding. In J. H. Flavell & E. M. Markman (Eds.), *Handbook of child psychology: Vol. 3. Cognitive development* (pp. 77–166). New York: Wiley.

Cantor, N., & Kihlstrom, J. (1987). *Personality and social intelligence.* Englewood Cliffs, NJ: Prentice-Hall.

Chapman, M., Skinner, E. A., & Baltes, P. B. (1990). Interpreting correlations between children's perceived control and cognitive performance: Control, agency, or means-ends beliefs? *Developmental Psychology, 26,* 246–253.

Clifford, M. (1986a). The comparative effects of strategy and effort attributions. *British Journal of Educational Psychology, 56,* 75–83.

Clifford, M. (1986b). The effects of ability, strategy, and effort attributions for educational, business, and athletic failure. *British Journal of Educational Psychology, 56,* 169–179.

Connell, J. P. (1985). A new multidimensional measure of children's perceptions of control. *Child Development, 56,* 1018–1041.

Corno, L. (1986). The metacognitive control components of self-regulated learning. *Contemporary Educational Psychology, 11,* 333–346.

Corno, L., & Mandinach, E. (1983). The role of cognitive engagement in classroom learning and motivation. *Educational Psychologist, 18,* 88–100.

Covington, M., & Beery, R. (1976). *Self-worth and school learning.* New York: Holt, Rinehart & Winston.

Crooks, T. (1988). The impact of classroom evaluation practices on students. *Review of Educational Research, 58,* 438–481.

de Charms, R. (1968). *Personal causation.* New York: Academic Press.

Deci, E. L. (1975). *Intrinsic motivation.* New York: Plenum.

Deci, E. L., & Ryan, R. (1985). *Intrinsic motivation and self-determination in human behavior.* New York: Plenum.

Deci, E. L., & Ryan, R. (1987). The support of autonomy and the control of behavior. *Journal of Personality and Social Psychology, 53,* 1024–1037.

Doyle, W. (1983). Academic work. *Review of Educational Research, 53,* 159–200.

Dweck, C. S., & Elliott, E. S. (1983). Achievement motivation. In E. M. Heatherington (Ed.), *Handbook of child psychology: Vol 4. Socialization, personality, and social development* (pp. 643–691). New York: Wiley.

Dweck, C. S., & Leggett, E. L. (1988). A social-cognitive approach to motivation and personality. *Psychological Review, 95*(2), 256–273.

Eccles, J. (1983). Expectancies, values and academic behaviors. In J. T. Spence (Ed.), *Achievement and achievement motives* (pp. 75–146). San Francisco: Freeman.

Elliott, E. S., & Dweck, C. S. (1988). Goals: An approach to motivation and achievement. *Journal of Personality and Social Psychology, 54,* 5–12.

Entwistle, N., & Marton, F. (1984). Changing conceptions of learning and research. In F. Marton, D. Hounsell, & N. Entwistle (Eds.), *The experience of learning* (pp. 211–236). Edinburgh, Scotland: Scottish Academic Press.

Fabricius, W. V., & Hagen, J. W. (1984). Use of causal attributions about recall performance to assess metamemory and predict strategic memory behavior in young children. *Developmental Psychology, 20,* 975–987.

Findley, M., & Cooper, H. (1983). Locus of control and academic achievement: A review of the literature. *Journal of Personality and Social Psychology, 44,* 419–427.

Flavell, J. (1979). Metacognition and cognitive monitoring: A new area of cognitive-developmental inquiry. *American Psychologist, 34,* 906–911.

Foersterling, F. (1985). Attributional retraining: A review. *Psychological Bulletin, 98,* 495–512.

Ford, M., & Nichols, C. (1991). Using goal assessments to identify motivational patterns and facilitate behavioral regulation and achievement. In M. Maehr & P. R. Pintrich (Eds.), *Advances in motivation and achievement: Vol. 7. Goals and self-regulatory processes* (pp. 51–84). Greenwich, CT: JAI.

Garcia, T., & Pintrich, P. R. (1991). *Student motivation and self-regulated learning: A LISREL model.* Paper presented at the American Educational Research Association convention, Chicago, IL.

Glaser, R. (1984). Education and thinking: The role of knowledge. *American Psychologist, 39,* 93–104.

Harter, S. (1981). A new self-report scale of intrinsic versus extrinsic orientation in the classroom: Motivational and informational components. *Developmental Psychology, 17,* 300–312.

Harter, S. (1985). Competence as a dimension of self-evaluation: Toward a comprehensive model of self-worth. In R. L. Leahy (Ed.), *The development of the self* (pp. 95–121). New York: Academic Press.

Kanfer, R., & Ackerman, P. (1989). Motivation and cognitive abilities: An integrative/aptitude-treatment interaction approach to skill acquisition. *Journal of Applied Psychology, 74,* 657–690.

Kanfer, R., & Kanfer, F. (1991). Goals and self-regulation: Applications of theory to work settings. In M. Maehr & P. R. Pintrich (Eds.), *Advances in motivation and achievement: Vol. 7. Goals and self-regulatory processes* (pp. 287–326). Greenwich, CT: JAI.

Kuhl, J. (1985). Volitional mediators of cognition-behavior consistency: Self-regulatory processes and action versus state orientation. In J. Kuhl & J. Beckmann (Eds.), *Action control: From cognition to behavior* (pp. 101–128). Berlin: Springer-Verlag.

Kurtz, B. E., & Borkowski, J. G. (1984). Children's metacognition: Exploring relations among knowledge, process, and motivational variables. *Journal of Experimental Child Psychology, 37,* 335–354.

Kurtz B., Schneider W., Carr M., Borkowski J., & Rellinger E. (1990). Strategy instruction and attributional beliefs in West Germany and the United States: Do teachers foster metacognitive development? *Contemporary Educational Psychology, 15,* 268–283.

Lave, J. (1989). *Cognition in practice: Mind and culture in everyday life.* Cambridge: Cambridge University Press.

Lefcourt, H. (1976). *Locus of control: Current trends in theory research.* Hillsdale, NJ: Lawrence Erlbaum Associates.

Maehr, M., & Midgely, C. (in press). Enhancing student motivation: A school-wide approach. *Educational Psychologist.*

Malone, T., & Lepper, M. (1987). Making learning fun: A taxonomy of intrinsic motivations for learning. In R. Snow & M. Farr (Eds.), *Aptitude, learning, and instruction: Vol. 3. Conative and affective process analyses* (pp. 223–253). Hillsdale, NJ: Lawrence Erlbaum Associates.

Markus, H., & Nurius, P. (1986). Possible selves. *American Psychologist, 41,* 954–969.

Markus, H., & Wurf, E. (1987). The dynamic self-concept: A social psychological perspective. *Annual review of psychology, 38,* 299–337.

Marton, F., Hounsell, D., & Entwistle, N. (1984). *The experience of learning.* Edinburgh, Scotland: Scottish Academic Press.

Marton, F., & Saljo, R. (1976a). On qualitative differences in learning: I. Outcomes and process. *British Journal of Educational Psychology, 46,* 4–11.

Marton, F., & Saljo, R. (1976b). On qualitative differences in learning: II. Outcome as a function of the learners' conceptions of the task. *British Journal of Educational Psychology, 46,* 115–127.

Marx, R. (1983). Student perceptions in classrooms. *Educational Psychologist, 18,* 145–164.

McCombs, B. (1989). Self-regulated learning and academic achievement: A phenomenological view. In B. Zimmerman & D. Schunk (Eds.), *Self-regulated learning and academic achievement: Theory, research, and practice* (pp. 51–82). New York: Springer-Verlag.

McKeachie, W. J., Pintrich, P. R., & Lin, Y. G. (1985a). Learning to learn. In G. d'Ydewalle (Ed.), *Cognition, information processing, and motivation* (pp. 601–618). Amsterdam: Elsevier Science.

McKeachie, W. J., Pintrich, P. R. & Lin, Y. G. (1985b). Teaching learning strategies. *Educational Psychologist, 20,* 153–160.

McKeachie, W. J., Pintrich, P. R., Lin, Y. G., & Smith, D. (1986). *Teaching and learning in the college classroom: A review of the research literature.* Ann Arbor, MI: National Center for Research to Improve Postsecondary Teaching and Learning, The University of Michigan.

Meece, J. (1991). The classroom context and students' motivational goals. In M. Maehr

& P. R. Pintrich (Eds.), *Advances in motivation and achievement: Vol. 7. Goals and self-regulatory processes* (pp. 261–286). Greenwich, CT: JAI.

Meece, J., Blumenfeld, P., & Hoyle, R. (1988). Students' goal orientations and cognitive engagement in classroom activities. *Journal of Educational Psychology, 80,* 514–523.

Newman, D., Griffin, P., & Cole, M. (1989). *The construction zone: Working for cognitive change in school.* Cambridge: Cambridge University Press.

Newman, R. (1991). Goals and self-regulated learning: What motivates children to seek academic help? In M. Maehr & P. R. Pintrich (Eds.), *Advances in motivation and achievement: Vol. 7. Goals and self-regulatory processes* (pp. 151–184). Greenwich, CT: JAI.

Nicholls, J. (1984). Achievement motivation: Conceptions of ability, subjective experience, task choice, and performance. *Psychological Review, 91(3),* 328–346.

Nicholls, J., Cheung, P., Lauer, J., & Patashnick, M. (1989). Individual differences in academic motivation: Perceived ability, goals, beliefs, and values. *Learning and Individual Differences, 1,* 63–84.

Nicholls, J., Patashnick, M., & Nolen, S. (1985). Adolescents' theories of education. *Journal of Educational Psychology, 77,* 683–692.

Nickerson, R., Perkins, D., & Smith, E. (1985). *The teaching of thinking.* Hillsdale, NJ: Lawrence Erlbaum Associates.

Nolen, S. (1988). Reasons for studying: Motivational orientations and study strategies. *Cognition and Instruction, 5,* 269–287.

Paris, S. G., & Oka, E. (1986). Children's reading strategies, metacognition, and motivation. *Developmental Review, 6,* 25–56.

Pintrich, P. R. (1985). *Motivation, strategy use, and student learning.* Paper presented at the American Psychological Association convention, Los Angeles, CA.

Pintrich, P. R. (1986). *Motivation and learning strategies interactions with achievement.* Paper presented at the American Educational Research Association convention, San Francisco, CA.

Pintrich, P. R. (1987). *College students' motivated strategies and learning.* Paper presented at the American Educational Research Association convention, Washington, DC.

Pintrich, P. R. (1988a). A process-oriented view of student motivation and cognition. In J. S. Stark & L. Mets (Eds.). *Improving teaching and learning through research. Vol. 57. New directions for institutional research* (pp. 55–70). San Francisco: Jossey-Bass.

Pintrich, P. R. (1988b). Student learning and college teaching. In R. E. Young & K. E. Eble (Eds.), *College teaching and learning: Preparing for new commitments. Vol. 33. New Directions for teaching and learning* (pp. 71–86). San Francisco: Jossey-Bass.

Pintrich, P. R. (1989). The dynamic interplay of student motivation and cognition in the college classroom. In C. Ames & M. Maehr (Eds.). *Advances in motivation and achievement: Vol. 6. Motivation enhancing environments* (pp. 117–160). Greenwich, CT: JAI.

Pintrich, P. R. (1990). Implications of the psychological research on student learning and college teaching for teacher education. In R. Houston (Ed.), *The handbook of research on teacher education* (pp. 826–857). New York: Macmillan.

Pintrich, P. R., Cross, D. R., Kozma R. B., & McKeachie, W. J. (1986). Instructional Psychology. *Annual Review of Psychology, 37,* 611–651.

Pintrich, P. R., & De Groot, E. (1988). *Motivation and metacognition in different academic settings.* Paper presented at the International Congress of Psychology, Sydney, Australia.

Pintrich, P. R., & De Groot, E. (1990a). Motivational and self-regulated learning components of classroom academic performance. *Journal of Educational Psychology, 82,* 33–40.

Pintrich, P. R., & De Groot, E. (1990b). *Quantitative and qualitative perspectives on student motivational beliefs and self-regulated learning.* Paper presented at the American Educational Research Association conference, Boston, MA.

Pintrich, P. R., & Garcia, T. (1991). Student goal orientation and self-regulation in the college classroom. In M. Maehr & P. R. Pintrich (Eds.), *Advances in motivation and achievement: Vol. 7. Goals and self-regulatory processes* (pp. 371–402). Greenwich, CT: JAI.

Pintrich, P. R., Smith, D., Garcia, T., McKeachie, W. (1991). *The motivated strategies for learning questionnaire (MSLQ).* Ann Arbor, MI: NCRIPTAL, The University of Michigan.

Pokay, P., & Blumenfeld, P. (1990). Predicting achievement early and late in the semester: The role of motivation and use of learning strategies. *Journal of Educational Psychology, 82,* 41–50.

Pressley, M. (1986). The relevance of the good strategy user model to the teaching of mathematics. *Educational Psychologist, 21,* 139–161.

Pressley, M. (1990). *Cognitive strategy instruction that really improves children's academic performance.* Cambridge, MA: Brookline Books.

Renninger, K. A. & Wozniak, R. H. (1985). Effect of interest on attentional shift, recognition, and recall in young children. *Developmental Psychology, 21,* 624–632.

Rotter, J. B. (1966). Generalized expectancies for internal versus external control reinforcement. *Psychological Monographs, 80,* 1–28.

Schiefele, U. (in press). Interest, learning, and experience. *Educational Psychologist.*

Schneider, W., Borkowski, J. G., Kurtz, B. E., & Kerwin, K. (1986). Metamemory and motivation: A comparison of strategy use and performance in German and American children. *Journal of Cross-Cultural Psychology, 17,* 315–336.

Schneider, W., Korkel, J., & Weinert, F. E. (1987). The effects of intelligence, self-concept, and attributional style on metamemory and memory behavior. *International Journal of Behavioral Development, 10,* 281–299.

Schneider, W., & Pressley, M. (1989). *Memory development between 2 and 20.* New York: Springer-Verlag.

Schunk, D. (1985). Self-efficacy and school learning. *Psychology in the Schools, 22,* 208–223.

Schunk, D. (1989). Social cognitive theory and self-regulated learning. In B. Zimmerman & D. Schunk (Eds.), *Self-regulated learning and academic achievement: Theory, research, and practice* (pp. 83–110). New York: Springer-Verlag.

Schunk, D. (in press). Self-efficacy and academic motivation. *Educational Psychologist.*

Shell, D., Murphy, C., & Bruning, R. (1989). Self-efficacy and outcome expectancy mechanisms in reading and writing achievement. *Journal of Educational Psychology, 81,* 91–100.

Skinner, E. A., Wellborn, J. G., & Connell, J. P. (1990). What it takes to do well in school and whether I've got it: A process model of perceived control and children's engagement and achievement in school. *Journal of Educational Psychology, 82,* 22–32.

Sternberg, R. (1985). *Beyond IQ: A triarchic theory of human intelligence.* New York: Cambridge University Press.

Stipek, D., & Weisz, J. (1981). Perceived personal control and academic achievement. *Review of Educational Research, 51,* 101–137.

Thorkildsen, T., & Nicholls, J. (in press). Student critiques as motivation. *Educational Psychologist.*

Veroff, J., & Veroff, J. B. (1980). *Social incentives: A life-span developmental approach.* New York: Academic Press.

Weed, K., Ryan, E., & Day, J. (1990). Metamemory and attributions as mediators of strategy use and recall. *Journal of Educational Psychology, 82,* 849–855.

Weiner, B. (1986). *An attributional theory of motivation and emotion.* New York: Springer-Verlag.

Weinstein, C. E., & Mayer, R. E. (1986). The teaching of learning strategies. In M. Wittrock (Ed.), *Handbook of research on teaching* (pp. 315–327). New York: Macmillan.

Wentzel, K. (1991). Social and academic goals at school: Motivation and achievement in context. In M. Maehr & P. R. Pintrich (Eds.), *Advances in motivation and achievement: Vol. 7. Goals and self-regulatory processes* (pp. 185–212). Greenwich, CT: JAI.

Wigfield, A., & Karpathian, M. (in press). Who am I and what I can do: Children's self-concepts and motivation in achievement situations. *Educational Psychologist.*

Winne, P., & Marx, R. (1982). Students' and teachers' views of thinking processes for classroom learning. *Elementary School Journal, 82,* 493–518.

Wlodkowski, R. (1988). *Enhancing adult motivation to learn.* San Francisco: Jossey-Bass.

Zimmerman, B., & Martinez-Pons, M. (1986). Development of a structured interview for assessing student use of self-regulated learning strategies. *American Educational Research Journal, 23,* 614–628.

Zimmerman, B., & Martinez-Pons, M. (1988). Construct validation of a strategy model of student self-regulated learning. *Journal of Educational Psychology, 80,* 284–290.

Zukier, H. (1986). The paradigmatic and narrative modes in goal-guided inference. In R. M. Sorrentino & E. T. Higgins (Eds.), *Handbook of motivation and cognition: Foundations of social behavior* (pp. 465–502). New York: Guilford Press.

Perceptions of Efficacy and Strategy Use in the Self-Regulation of Learning

BARRY J. ZIMMERMAN
MANUEL MARTINEZ-PONS
The City University of New York

At the turn of the century, a prominent English scientist and statesman offered this advice about the ultimate goal of education, "The important thing is not so much that every child should be taught, as that every child should be given the wish to learn" (Lubbock, 1897, p. 192). John Lubbock's concern about student passivity during instruction has proven prophetic. Although students in the United States today live in an age of information and attend schools having unsurpassed technical facilities to convey knowledge, substantial numbers of them display declining academic motivation and greater passivity with increased schooling, and many drop out at the earliest opportunity (Finn, 1989). Among the potential causes of their academic apathy, two have been discussed widely—the students' low perceptions of academic competence (Covington, 1985) and their lack of strategies to guide learning (Loper & Murphy, 1984).

Recently a number of researchers (e.g., Borkowski, Carr, Rellinger & Pressley, 1990; McCombs, 1989; Zimmerman, 1989a) have suggested that student efforts to initiate and self-regulate learning may depend on their perceptions of personal competence about their use of learning strategies—particularly in the face of difficulty such as competing activities or stress. *Learning strategies* are systematic plans that help learners encode information and perform a task (Weinstein, Goetz, & Alexander, 1988). However, over a decade of research has shown that merely teaching students learning strategies does not guarantee the motivation to use them (Schneider, 1985). Several additional processes appear to be instrumental in promoting self-regulated use of learning strategies such as metacognitive monitoring (Ghatala, 1986; Pressley & Ghatala, 1990) and strategy attributions (e.g., Anderson & Jennings, 1980). *Metacognitive monitoring* refers to self-observations of ongoing cognitive actions, and, *strategy attributions* refer to ascriptions of performance outcomes to the use of a particular strategy. Only recently have attempts been made to study the impact of these processes on student perceptions of academic competence (e.g., Borkowski et al., 1990). This chapter considers the hypothesis that student perceptions of efficacy play an important role in a strategic control system that is described here. As a measure of perceived competence, *self-efficacy* is distinctive in that it refers to beliefs of personal capabilities for different levels of attainment in a particular task domain according to mastery criteria (Bandura, 1977, 1986, 1989a). This construct has the advantage of regulating student motivation on a wide range of academic tasks (e.g., Schunk, 1984, 1989).

The first section of this chapter offers a formal description of the processes through which students self-regulate their academic learning and performance, focusing particular attention on how feedback from strategic efforts convey information about self-efficacy. *Academic self-regulation* refers to students' proactive efforts to regulate their own academic learning and performance metacognitively, motivationally, and behaviorally (Zimmerman, 1986). Examples of students' academic self-regulation are given. The second section summarizes research indicating the academic and self-efficacy benefits when students monitor and attribute outcomes to their use of strategies. The third section suggests several areas where additional research on strategy use and self-efficacy is needed, and the final section addresses the implications of research and theory on self-regulated learning processes for educational practice.

A SELF-REGULATED LEARNING STRATEGY SYSTEM

We are all familiar with examples of self-regulated learners: A boy busily recording notes in the margins of a medieval history book, oblivious to surrounding noises in the cafeteria; a girl staying after school to practice her speech at a lectern before an empty classroom; two pupils testing each other during the noon hour before a literature test. Each of these students approached their educational task with confidence, diligence, and strategic resourcefulness. Unlike their passive classmates, they proactively sought out opportunities to acquire information and to self-evaluate their academic skill. Obstacles such as distracting study conditions, lack of practice time, or the need for a test partner did not deter them.

Research has shown that self-regulated learners view acquisition of proficiency as a strategically controllable process and accept greater responsibility for their achievement outcomes (Zimmerman & Martinez-Pons, 1986, 1988, 1990). Although much research has focused on how strategies provide learners with a powerful means to improve their acquisition, performance, and memory (e.g., Schneider, 1985; Weinstein & Mayer, 1986), relatively little attention has been given to the impact of strategy use on self-perceptions of proficiency by learners. It is suggested that when use of learning strategies becomes associated with self-perceptions of agency, purpose, and instrumentality, academic self-regulation will occur (Zimmerman, 1986, 1990a). Although all learners use regulatory processes to some degree, self-regulated learners are distinguished *metacognitively* by their awareness of strategic relations between regulatory processes and learning outcomes and their use of specific strategies to achieve their academic goals. Thus, self-regulated learning involves the awareness and use of learning strategies, perceptions of *self-efficacy,* and a commitment to academic *goals.* It is assumed that *knowledge* of strategies is distinct from the capability for using them consistently and persistently (Pressley, Borkowski, & Schneider, 1987; Zimmerman, 1989a) and that *affect* such as anxiety or elation can impair or facilitate strategy use (Kuhl, 1985).

These elements have been linked in a triadic system of self-regulation (Zimmerman, 1990b). As depicted in Table 8.1, this system involves behavioral and environmental as well as personal determinants of self-regulated learning. Among personal influences, strategy awareness is a form of metacognition, and strategy knowledge is a type of knowledge. Students' *use* of strategies depends on two closely linked behavioral processes: monitoring the effectiveness of these strategies and attributing academic outcomes to them. Each of these three strategic processes is subsumed within a more general behavioral category of self-regulation: Strategy monitoring is a form of self-observation, strategy attribution is a type of self-judgment, and strategy use is an important self-reaction (Bandura, 1986).

The role of these three behavioral forms of self-regulation have been the subject of discussion and research (Bandura, 1989a; Schunk, 1989; Zimmerman, 1989a). *Self-observation* refers to efforts to monitor specific aspects of overt behavior, covert functioning, and situational factors such as pages of completed homework, off-task thoughts, and

Table 8.1
Triadic Influences in a Self-Regulated Learning Strategy System

Personal Influences	Behavioral Influences	Environmental Influences
1. Goals	Self-observation *Strategy Monitoring	Academic outcomes
2. Self-efficacy	Self-judgment *Strategy Attribution	
3. Metacognition *Strategy Awareness	Self-reaction *Strategy use	
4. Knowledge *Strategy Knowledge		
5. Affect		

*Strategy components in academic self-regulation.

distractions (Thoresen & Mahoney, 1974). Social cognitive researchers distinguish *self-judgment* from self-observation because learners may attribute or interpret their performance outcomes according to various factors, standards, or goals. Indeed, the selection or setting of appropriate goals for oneself may be one of the most distinguishing characteristics of self-regulated individuals. In the 1940s, Sears (1940) reported that children who had a history of academic success set their goals at a realistic level (slightly above their current level), whereas students who were prone to failure set their goals too high or too low.

Self-reaction refers to a wide range of responses ranging from self-praise to self-criticism, from further strategy persistence to strategy change, and from greater goal commitment to goal adjustment. According to a social cognitive perspective (Zimmerman, 1989a), three classes of self-reaction can be distinguished: (a) behavioral self-reactions, which are overt responses that students use to optimize their learning outcomes; (b) environmental self-reactions, which involve students' selection, adaptation, or creation of physical settings where learning can occur readily; and (c) personal self-reactions, which seek to enhance covert cognitive and affective processes involved in learning. For example, students plagued by anxiety about writing: (a) behaviorally, might keep a record of words they have written; (b) environmentally, might select a quiet area free from intrusions during writing; and (c) personally, might practice covert relaxation techniques whenever fears of a writing block occur.

Student *academic outcomes* such as grades, social esteem, or postgraduate opportunities fall within the last triadic category, environmental influences. According to social cognitive theory (Bandura, 1986, 1989a), each of the three major triadic sources can influence the other two reciprocally. In addition, the various subtypes of influences are reciprocally interdependent. For example, self-efficacy beliefs can be both a proactive determinant of academic achievement as well as a reactive outcome of them. However, it is important to note that reciprocal causation emerges sequentially over time: That is, earlier student self-efficacy beliefs can affect later academic achievement, or conversely, earlier academic achievement outcomes can influence later perceptions of efficacy.

This triadic approach to self-regulated learning contrasts with traditional willpower views and with noncognitive behavioral views. Willpower approaches treat motivation as a personal struggle between one's inner will and opposing external forces. Advocates of this perspective often rely on "pep talks" or preaching as a way to improve a person's resistence to temptation: "The flesh is weak but the will can be made strong!" Unfortunately, a depressing result of this dialectical view of self-regulation is that momentary transgressions or relapses, such as a student's failure to concentrate when studying for a test, are viewed often as further evidence of personal inadequacy. According to Thoresen and Mahoney (1974), willpower approaches can be criticized for treating self-regulation as the triumph of an undefined inner will over a weak body or resistant environment rather than as three potentially compatible sources of influence—personal, behavioral, and environmental.

Noncognitive behavioral approaches rely on overt methods of self-regulation such as self-recording and self-reinforcement. These overt stimulus and response control methods, although often effective, do not tap the power of cognitive learning strategies such as goal-setting, mental imagery, or covert rehearsal. This limitation can be substantial, for example when the inappropriate covert setting of goals too high or too low undermines the effectiveness of overt response outcomes (see Bandura & Cervone, 1983, 1986). Thus, noncognitive approaches provide only a limited perspective on self-regulatory processes.

Historically, self-regulation systems have been discussed by information-processing theorists (e.g., Carver & Scheier, 1981) in terms of negative feedback loops. According to this cybernetic view, learners compare feedback continuously from their performance against their learning goals. If the feedback indicates substandard performance (i.e., is negative), they try to improve. For example, students who are trying to learn the poem "Casey at the Bat" might compare their last attempt to recite it against a goal of perfect recall. They would continue rehearsing the poem until it could be recited without prompting (even by residents of Mudville)! Information-processing theorists assume that reductions in amount of negative feedback are motivating and that once a person's goal is achieved, his or her motivation on the task ceases. The latter "closed" feature of negative feedback loops can be viewed as a significant liability in explaining students' continuing motivation (e.g., Bandura, 1989b).

In contrast, social cognitive theorists (Bandura, 1989b, 1991; Zimmerman, 1990b) have argued that self-regulatory systems are open: Student's *goals* as well as their proactive attempts to reach them are subject to change on the basis of performance feedback. Goal accomplishment can lead subjects to *raise* their goals (Bandura & Cervone, 1986) rather than desist from learning. For example, an ambitious student who reached his or her goal of typing at 30 words per minute might try to reach 50 words per minute rather than discontinuing typing practice. Or, as a Girl Scout leader once commented about her most successful cookie salesperson, "Today she's closing in on the neighborhood market, tomorrow she'll go for the whole city!"

Social cognitive researchers have found that teaching students to set goals appropriately can have important academic benefits for students who have deficits in self-regulation. A good example of this research involves proximal goal-setting. Bandura and Schunk (1981) found that when elementary school children were given daily goals regarding a mathematics unit, they perceived greater personal efficacy and displayed greater motivation than youngsters who were given only distal goals (for an entire 7-day unit). Interestingly, youngsters given distal goals did no better than students who did not set goals for themselves. Thus, teaching students a goal-setting strategy helped them sustain their motivation and increase their acquisition.

The Role of Learning Strategies in Self-Regulated Learning

Paris, Newman, and McVey (1982) have suggested that one of the most important accomplishments during children's cognitive development is the acquisition of learning strategies. These strategies enable youngsters to improve their use of study time, their communication with others, and their self-monitoring skills. "A common thread among these diverse strategies for tackling and solving problems is the self-management of cognitive resources" (p. 490).

There is widespread agreement that students' selection of learning strategies varies on the basis of their specific academic purpose or goal. Weinstein and Mayer (1986) have identified two major classes of academic goals: (a) goals concerning the *products* of learning such as basic or complex task outcomes, and (b) goals concerning the *processes* of learning such as monitoring or controlling affect. With regard to academic task products, strategies for recalling basic facts such as forming a mental image differ substantially from strategies for extracting complex information from prose such as summarizing. Of particular interest are strategies for optimizing learning processes: These strategies are by definition self-directed and thus have particular self-regulatory implication.

In similar fashion, Pressley et al. (1987) distinguish goal-specific, *cognitive* strategies designed to improve memory, comprehension, and problem solving from monitoring and higher order sequencing strategies designed to regulate goal-specific strategies. Flavell (1979) has labeled monitoring and higher order strategies as *metacognitive* and has described their explicit role in older children's self-regulation of learning.

Pintrich and De Groot (1990) have also differentiated cognitive or academic task-related strategies from metacognitive or self-regulation strategies for planning, modifying, and monitoring cognition. However, they found evidence of a substantial correlation between these two types of strategies and placed them together within a generic category of *self-regulated learning strategies.* Thus, although cognitive and metacognitive strategies are widely distinguished, it appears that both are involved when students self-regulate their academic performance (see Pintrich & Schrauben, this volume).

Initial training research on learning strategies focused on issues of acquisition and transfer rather than on motivation. For example, students were trained to use strategies such as verbal elaboration (Rohwer, 1973), imaginal elaboration (Pressley, 1976), semantic organization (Moely, 1977), and study time apportionment (Brown & Campione, 1977). However, students often failed to continue to use of these strategies (Cavanaugh & Perlmutter, 1982). This limitation in strategy training effectiveness led to a search for additional variables that could explain student motivation to self-regulate learning (Pressley et al., 1987).

The Role of Strategy Attributions in Self-Regulated Learning

As noted in Table 8.1, strategy attributions are a vital self-judgmental process linking strategy monitoring and use. In an early study, Diener and Dweck (1978) investigated the effects of using learning strategies and outcome attributions on fifth-grade students' motivation to learn. Children classified as helpless verbally attributed their failures to a lack of ability, however, children classified as mastery-oriented made surprisingly few verbal attributions. Instead, these students were found to employ two key self-regulation strategies: self-monitoring and self-instruction. Perhaps as a result of their improved monitoring, they also

made more effective alterations in their strategies when they encountered failure. Mastery-oriented students displayed superior motivation—persisting longer, displaying sustained concentration, and reflecting more positive affect. Clearly, mastery-oriented children were
not only differentiated from helpless youngsters by their superior
motivation but also by their apparent awareness of the effectiveness of
their self-regulated learning strategies. However, the students' strategy
attributions were not measured directly in this investigation.

Subsequently, Anderson and Jennings (1980) sought to compare
experimentally the motivational effects of strategy attributions with
ability attributions. They found that individuals who were taught to
attribute failure to ineffective strategies demonstrated higher expectations for success than subjects who were taught to attribute failure to
an uncontrollable personal factor, their ability. It was interesting that
subjects who attributed task outcomes to their strategies monitored
the effectiveness of their strategies and modified their strategies more
frequently. In contrast, subjects who attributed task outcomes to their
abilities failed to attend to strategic outcomes and believed they could
not improve their performance.

The influence of strategy attributions on students' motivation to
learn was verified in a descriptive study by Clifford (1986). She sought
to compare the effects of strategy attributions with attributions to
another personally controllable factor—effort. According to Anderson
and Jennings (1980), strategy attributions will sustain student motivation in the face of negative results better than effort attributions
because strategies enable changes in the *direction* of learning attempts,
whereas effort attributions produce only changes in the *intensity* of
learning attempts. If a student is exerting high levels of effort already,
external exhortations to try harder are less credible than suggestions to
try another strategy. Even if effort exhortations are viewed as credible,
they have another ultimate disadvantage: They convey a message of
limited capacity to a student. That is, maximal effort without success
implies fixed ability.

Clifford (1986) gave a self-rating form containing items that attributed course outcomes to ability, effort, and strategy use, to female
college students and asked them to rate their expectancy regarding
future course performance. These students responded differently to
strategy and effort attributions: Strategy attributions for academic
failures were associated with more positive self-judgments and greater
expectations for future success than effort or ability attributions.
Clifford's findings indicate that strategy attributions preserve students'
expectations of eventual success. It should be noted, however, that the
success of strategy attributions depends on the size of the student's

repertoire of strategies: A small number of strategies would limit the amount of negative feedback that a student could tolerate before being compelled to make fixed ability attributions.

These descriptive data imply that *strategy attribution training* may be necessary to convey a sense of personal agency in addition to strategy training, particularly for students with adverse learning histories. Borkowski, Weyhing, and Carr (1988) examined the effects of attribution training, in combination with strategy training on learning disabled students' reading comprehension. Learning disabled children who were given training in a summarization strategy plus attribution showed reliable gains in summarization skills from pretesting to posttesting. These subjects also performed significantly better than controls on the inferential subtest of the Stanford reading test. Thus, attribution training did augment strategy training for both acquisition and generalization of reading skills by learning disabled youngsters.

Recently Borkowski et al. (1990) sought to determine whether at-risk students differ from regular achieving students in their attributional processes. They hypothesized that underachievers possess knowledge of learning strategies but do not attribute learning outcomes to strategic efforts. These researchers studied reading awareness (a strategy measure), attributions, and self-esteem processes of elementary school underachievers and achievers. Underachievers were identified using a measure of the disparity between their achievement and intelligence. Borkowski and colleagues found that students who achieved at or above their intelligence level displayed greater reading strategy awareness, greater belief in the value of effort in applying the strategy, and higher self-esteem, academic performance, and intrinsic motivation than students who achieved below their intelligence level. The underachievers were distinguished from achievers by the absence of a causal link between their measured ability and their use of attributional processes, whereas achievers displayed a clear linkage. Borkowski and colleagues concluded that, unlike achievers, underachievers did not credit themselves for their prior performance. This implies that training underachievers to appropriately attribute learning outcomes to their use of strategies could augment development and coordination of other components in their self-regulative system.

This was the purpose of a second experimental study. Strategy training conveyed reading comprehension strategies to elementary school students and attribution training prompted them to attribute strategic outcomes to effort. Strategy plus attribution training promoted not only students' acquisition of reading strategies, but also generalization of these strategies to the classroom. Students who received only strategy training, although more metacognitively knowledgeable, failed to translate their advantage into improved reading performance. Borkowski and his associates concluded that attribution training bridged the gap between strategy knowledge and actual reading performance. Finally, they reported that student perceptions of self-esteem linked students' attributions to their awareness of reading strategies. This evidence of improved self-esteem when attributions and strategy use are linked is concordant with a self-regulated learning control system hypothesis (Zimmerman, 1989a, 1990b). It should be noted, parenthetically, that persuasory self-attributions have their greatest effects on people who feel confident about their capabilities (Chambliss & Murray, 1979a, 1979b).

The Role of Strategy Monitoring in Self-Regulated Learning

Closely linked to the role of strategy attributions in Table 8.1 is students' strategy monitoring. *Strategy monitoring* refers to the on-line evaluation of strategic processes and their outcomes. It is assumed that students' self-regulated use of a learning strategy depends on their awareness of the benefits produced by the strategy (e.g., Pressley & Ghatala, 1990). If students fail to monitor the outcomes of their strategic learning efforts (and there is considerable evidence this is often the case, e.g., Markman, 1977, 1979), their motivation to continue to use the strategy will be diminished. However, a learner must not only monitor the outcomes of strategy use accurately, he or she must attribute them to the appropriate strategy. It has been noted already that subjects who attribute task outcomes to learning strategies monitor the effectiveness of their strategies more closely than subjects who do not make strategy attributions (Anderson & Jennings, 1980).

There is evidence that students' monitoring of their strategy outcomes is related to their motivation. Hunter-Blanks, Ghatala, Pressley, and Levin (1988) examined adults' monitoring their learning of two types of factual sentences that appeared to be alike semantically but actually varied in their cognitive difficulty level. As expected, they found that virtually none of the students were aware of the differential difficulty of the two types of sentences before studying them, however, approximately 75% of the students became aware of the differences during the study. Only those subjects who perceived their recall accurately after taking the test were aware of the greater difficulty of one cognitive type of sentence. It appears that accurate strategy judgments depended on the students' skill in monitoring their learning outcomes.

In a subsequent series of experiments, Ghatala, Levin, Foorman, and Pressley (1989) investigated students' monitoring learning during reading and their self-regulation of study time. The students were given a passage to study and told to continue until they achieved 100% mastery on a multiple-choice posttest. It was found that unless the students were given external feedback, they greatly overestimated their acquisition and understudied the passage. Ghatala and colleagues continued to believe that accurate self-monitoring could occur in the absence of external feedback if the criteria for learning are unambiguous. Specifically, they hypothesized that the students' overestimations of their test results were due to the effectiveness of distractors in the multiple-choice test items, not to their inability to monitor accurately. To test this hypothesis, children in a second study took a short completion test after each study cycle. As predicted, these youngsters were accurate in monitoring their learning, and they continued to study the material until it was mastered.

These studies by Ghatala, Pressley, Levin, and colleagues reveal that monitoring strategic outcomes plays a major role in the self-regulation of learning. Other research by Ghatala, Levin, Pressley, and Goodwin (1986) has shown that training students to attribute effects to strategies led to greater monitoring. It appears that strategy monitoring and attribution are interdependent as is depicted in Table 8.1. According to a social cognitive model of self-regulated learning, student motivation to use self-regulated learning strategies depends on a linkage between self-observation and self-judgment processes and a third learning process, self-reaction. One key student self-reaction associated with strategy attributions has already been noted—perceptions of academic self-esteem (Borkowski et al., 1990).

Perceptions of Efficacy in Self-Regulated Learning

There is a growing body of evidence that self-perceptions of academic efficacy, competence, and control are critical in motivating students to self-regulate their learning (e.g., Pokay & Blumenfeld, 1990; Skinner, Wellborn, & Connell, 1990). According to McCombs (1986, 1989), a learner's self-system affects his or her degree of self-regulation by influencing the processing, transformation, and encoding of information as well as motivation. Youngsters with positive self-concepts (along with a number of other key system constructs) are more likely to process, store, and use newly acquired information than children with negative self-concepts. Thus, the self-system is key to motivating self-regulated efforts to learn.

Social cognitive theorists have devoted considerable study to the self-system variable of academic self-efficacy (Bandura, 1977, 1986; Schunk, 1984, 1989; Zimmerman, 1989b, 1990b). According to a strategic control system hypothesis, academic learning becomes self-regulated when students view acquisition as a strategic process and when they accept responsibility for their achievement outcomes. Self-efficacy has proven to be a reliable measure of students' acceptance of personal responsibility.

Training Studies.   There is evidence that instruction in learning strategies improves student perceptions of efficacy. Zimmerman and Ringle (1981) examined the importance of self-efficacy perceptions in students' motivation to persist on difficult learning tasks. They compared the effectiveness of an adult model who verbalized optimism with one who expressed pessimism when using a strategy to solve a wire puzzle with young elementary school children. Compared to a no-model control group of children, pupils exposed to an optimistic model remained self-efficacious about obtaining a solution even after failing in their initial effort to solve the puzzle. In contrast, pupils exposed to a pessimistic model displayed a significant decline in efficacy and a significantly briefer problem-solving effort. These self-efficacy and persistence differences were evident on an embedded word puzzle transfer task as well. It appears that young children's perceptions of efficacy played a vital role in motivating them to persist at a problem-solving task and to transfer their motivation to a unfamiliar transfer task.

Students' perceptions of self-efficacy are expected to be greatly enhanced by the use of self-regulated learning strategies such as self-recording. Schunk (1983) conducted a study that examined the role of two dimensions of self-judgment when self-recording—the difficulty of the goal (a high or low number of problems) and the students' justification for success (personal or social). A personal justification informed the students they personally should be able to attain the problems goal, and a social justification informed them that socially comparable students can achieve the goal. Elementary school children who were deficient in mathematical division were asked to self-record the number of problems solved during two learning sessions. Students given high personal goals and a personal justification achieved the highest mathematical achievement and displayed the highest level of self-efficacy. Providing social comparative information was significantly less effective in enhancing the students' perceptions of personal efficacy. This study revealed that student variations in self-judgmental criteria influenced their efficacy reactions to self-recording, which is a form of self-observation. This pattern of causation is concordant with the three behavioral influences identified in Table 8.1.

The Zimmerman and Ringle (1981) study indicated that self-verbalizations by a model may increase students' awareness of the importance of learning strategies. Verbalizing, whether by others or by oneself, is an important strategy for self-regulating attention, encoding or retrieval, and academic task performance (Meichenbaum & Beimiller, 1990; Schunk, 1990). Researchers who have trained students to use a self-verbalization strategy have reported significant increases in perceived self-efficacy.

For example, Schunk and Rice (1984) examined the effects of strategy verbalization on the self-efficacy perceptions and listening skills of elementary school children who were deficient in their listening. In general, self-verbalization of a listening strategy for choosing a pictorial referent to a story led to higher perceptions of efficacy and greater listening accuracy than nonverbalized use of the strategy. Schunk and Rice also reported that strategy verbalization accounted for 25% of the variation in posttest self-efficacy. Schunk and Rice (1985) reported similar results in a subsequent study that taught elementary school children to use a reading comprehension strategy. All students received strategy training involving steps to follow such as "Read the questions" or "Look for key words" before reading several passages. Compared to students in a control group, subjects given self-verbalization training reported higher self-efficacy and displayed greater reading comprehension. As in their earlier study, Schunk and Rice found that strategy verbalization training enhanced students' perceptions of efficacy as well as their academic performance.

There is thus considerable evidence that training students to use self-regulated learning strategies such as proximal goal-setting (Bandura & Schunk, 1981), self-judging (Schunk, 1983), and self-verbalization (Schunk & Rice, 1984, 1985) improves their perceptions of efficacy, motivation, and learning.

Descriptive Studies. A number of correlational studies indicate that students' reported use of self-regulated learning strategies not only enhances their academic learning but also their perceptions of self-efficacy. Zimmerman and Martinez-Pons (1986) have developed a structured interview procedure that prompts students to describe their response to a number of contexts or problems that are commonly encountered during either studying or class such as preparing for tests, doing mathematics homework, and even motivating themselves. An example of these contexts is: "Some students find it easier if they can arrange the place where they study. Do you have a particular method for arranging the place where you study?"

Students' answer to these contexts are classified into a system of self-regulated learning strategies. Some strategies, such as goal-setting and planning, organizing and transforming, and rehearsing and memorizing, focus primarily on enhancing personal influences (see Table 8.1). Other strategies, such as record keeping and monitoring, self-evaluation, and giving self-consequences, are designed mainly to optimize behavioral influences. A third group of strategies, such as environmental structuring, seeking social assistance (from peers, teachers, and other adults), seeking information, and reviewing (notes, books, or tests), are intended primarily to improve students' immediate learning environment. However, each of these strategies also have indirect effects on the other two triadic classes of self-regulation. For example, when students set their academic goal as an A in a writing course, they are prompted to self-monitor and self-evaluate their papers more closely, and these strategies could, in turn, prompt them to seek social assistance in the form of critical comments on their papers from classmates. Therefore, when viewed as a system, self-regulated learning strategies capitalize on triadic resources for achieving academic outcomes.

In an initial study, Zimmerman and Martinez-Pons (1986) examined high school students' reported use of these strategies according to their placement in an achievement track in school. Placement of students in a track was based on a variety of academic criteria including prior standardized test scores, course grades, and teacher recommendations. Compared with students in regular achievement tracks, youngsters in the high track reported greater use of all strategies, although the magnitude of one strategy difference, self-evaluation, did not reach statistical significance. Discriminant function analyses revealed that these students' achievement track placement could be predicted with 93% accuracy on the basis of their weighted strategy totals. These data indicated that student use of self-regulated learning strategies was related highly to their achievement in school.

An unexpected finding with self-efficacy implications emerged from this study: Students in regular achievement tracks not only gave more nonstrategic answers than students in high achievement track, they also gave more passive–dependent answers. For example, the response "If I am having difficulty motivating myself to complete my homework, I just work harder" indicates reliance on effort rather than a specific motivation strategy such as setting self-consequences for goal attainment. In terms of their perceived dependency, these students also reported a greater frequency of statements such as "I just do what my teacher tells me" than students in the high achievement track. It appeared that students who were nonstrategic also were more passive and dependent.

A second study (Zimmerman & Martinez-Pons, 1988) was undertaken to determine whether students reporting extensive use of self-regulated learning strategies would demonstrate greater actual use of these strategies, more initiative in class, and more intrinsic motivation to learn than students reporting little strategy use. Teachers were asked to rate their students' use of learning strategies such as (a) soliciting information about tests, grading criteria, or assignments; (b) seeking social assistance when experiencing difficulty with school work; and (c) displaying self-evaluativeness about their test results. The teachers also rated the students' for class preparation, timely completion of assignments, asking unusual questions, and unique opinions. Finally, the teachers rated students' for intrinsic motivation such as expressions of interest in course matter, volunteering for out-of-class academic activities, and as contributing information in class that had not been assigned.

Analyses revealed a large academic self-regulation factor that emerged from these teacher ratings and that was separate from, but correlated with, student achievement. The latter results indicated students' use of self-regulated learning strategies played a distinctive role (apart from other factors such as content knowledge) in their academic achievement. As was hypothesized, a student self-regulation factor derived from the teacher ratings correlated substantially (+ .70) with student self-reports of strategy use. These results indicated a close association between students' reported use of self-regulated learning strategies and their teachers' judgments of their strategy use, initiative, and their intrinsic motivation. This investigation set the stage for a direct examination of the role of student perceptions of efficacy in self-regulated learning.

To test this hypothesis, Zimmerman and Martinez-Pons (1990) selected students enrolled in a school for the gifted as well as students enrolled in regular classes. Thirty gifted and 30 regular students from the Grades 5, 8, and 11 were tested using the structured interview measure of strategy use. In addition, the students' perceptions of mathematical and verbal efficacy were assessed using a series of math and word definition problems that graduated in difficulty. Gifted children were of particular interest because they exhibit not only high intellectual ability, but also two characteristics closely associated with self-efficacy: "persistence of motive and effort," and "confidence in their abilities" (Cox, 1976, p. 23).

Gifted students not only displayed greater use of self-regulated learning strategies, but they also reported significantly greater verbal and mathematical efficacy than regular students. There was a significant increase in strategy use from Grade 5 to Grade 11, and there was also a significant increase in both types of efficacy with grade level. Student giftedness was positively associated with academic efficacy (+.59); Gifted students displayed much greater self-efficacy regarding their verbal skill than regular students. These data indicated that individual differences in learning strategy use and in perceptions of academic efficacy covaried on the basis of the students' giftedness and grade level in school. Once again, there appeared to be a close students' association between learning strategy use and perceptions of self-efficacy.

Other researchers have examined the relationship between perceptions of efficacy and student use of learning strategies. Pintrich and De Groot (1990) investigated relationships between measures of self-efficacy, intrinsic value, text anxiety, self-regulation, and cognitive strategies on seventh-grade students' classroom performance (grades, seatwork, exams, reports, and essays). Cognitive strategy measures assessed students' rehearsing, elaborating, and organizing class material, whereas self-regulation measures assessed strategies used to control metacognitive and effort management activities. Self-efficacy items pertained to perceived competence and confidence about classwork, and intrinsic motivation measures dealt with students' interest in and the perceived importance of school work.

Pintrich and De Groot found that students high in self-efficacy were significantly more likely to report use of cognitive strategies, self-regulation strategies, and to persist at all five academic tasks than students low in self-efficacy. Interestingly, self-efficacy was not related significantly to performance on seatwork, exams, or essays when the cognitive strategy variable was included in the analyses. These researchers interpreted this finding as indicating that cognitive strategies may be more important for improving performance on academic tasks but that self-efficacy perceptions may be more important in motivating students to use these strategies. Perceived intrinsic value was also correlated with student perceptions of self-efficacy. Although use of self-regulation and cognitive strategies were highly correlated (+.83), the former measure predicted the students' academic performance much better. Pintrich and De Groot concluded the two types of strategies were conceptually distinct because there was evidence that cognitive strategy use without self-regulation was not conducive for academic performance. Apparently, students require more than task-oriented strategies, they need learning strategies that focus on self-regulative processes. Although these findings are complex, they are consistent with a self-regulated strategy control system hypothesis (Zimmerman, 1990b). Student perceptions of self-efficacy served as a determinant of their motivation to use self-regulation strategies that, in turn, triggered specific learning responses (see Pintrich & Schrauben, this volume).

FUTURE RESEARCH ON SELF-EFFICACY AND STRATEGY USE

To date, most studies of the relationship between student perceptions of efficacy and their use of learning strategies have been summary in focus. Descriptive studies have relied almost exclusively on generalized measures of student use of strategies, generalized measures of academic efficacy, and summary measures of academic performance. Although training studies have employed more focused measures of self-efficacy and learning outcomes, the frequency and sequencing of these assessments during various learning activities have been limited. In order to understand the interactive role of self-regulative processes in greater detail, researchers need to undertake microanalyses of the role of self-efficacy at numerous points before, during, and after various strategic efforts to learn. This task-specific, outcome-dependent approach should reveal whether reciprocal causation exists between students' perceptions of efficacy and their efforts to self-regulate their academic learning.

A second issue in need of further investigation involves the *accuracy* of students' efficacy perceptions during self-regulated learning. There is evidence that young children often have inflated perceptions of competence regarding their school achievement (e.g., Eccles, Midgely, & Adler, 1984), however, these judgments generally become more accurate with age. Several hypotheses have been advanced for these optimistic self-assessments such as young children's limited cognitive skills for assessing their ability (Parsons & Ruble, 1977), their "wishful thinking" (Stipek, 1984), or their reliance on non-normative criteria for self-assessment (Butler, 1990). Even older students have displayed inflated self-efficacy such as on pretest measures (Schunk, 1990), which may be due to their lack of skills or knowledge of the task at hand. Bandura (in press) has argued that overly optimistic self-appraisals can be *motivationally* beneficial because they sustain persistence in the face of difficulty or negative feedback. However, there are some downsides regarding inaccurate self-appraisals for student *learning.* For example, Ghatala et al. (1989) found that student failures to monitor their performance accurately led to significant understudying of learning materials. The predictive importance of the *accuracy* of self-efficacy measures needs to be investigated with regard to learning strategy use as well as the *level* of these measures. Evidence has been reported that students' reports of using learning strategies were related significantly their awareness of their test results before actual grading (Zimmerman & Martinez-Pons, 1988). As depicted in Table 8.1, self-regulated learners are ultimately more successful in reaching their academic achievement goals than passive learners because they monitor their performance closely and attribute causation appropriately to strategy use. Such students should also be more accurate in their self-efficacy assessments.

IMPLICATIONS FOR EDUCATIONAL PRACTICE

The research discussed in this chapter indicates that teachers cannot expect to produce lasting improvements in students' self-regulated capability to learn by merely showing them a cognitive learning strategy such as summarizing a text passage or elaborating mediators for a list of words. Students will judge the effectiveness of learning strategies against their own personal goals, their own level of skill, and their own study conditions. This typically requires direct task enactment to ensure personal adoption and continued use of a strategy. Thus, teachers must find ways to prompt inefficacious students to try learning strategies for themselves.

To encourage recalcitrant students to use learning strategies, social cognitive researchers (e.g., Bandura, 1986; Schunk, 1990; Zimmerman, 1989a) recommend the use of peer coping models who gradually overcome their fears and self-doubts. These models not only display strategy use but also self-observation, self-judgment, and self-correction of errors in applying the strategy. Social cognitive researchers have warned that initial attempts to use a cognitive learning strategy by students who lack self-efficacy may not prove effective. Often these youngsters have trouble screening out distractions (Corno, 1989), implementing the strategy properly (Schunk & Rice, 1985), and monitoring and attributing outcomes appropriately (Pressley & Ghatala, 1990). Training in the use of self-regulative processes such self-verbalization, outcome monitoring, and strategy attribution may be required for the adoption and adaptive use of a strategy.

From a social cognitive perspective, efforts to teach self-regulation of learning processes to students should be triadic in form. That is, in addition to providing cognitive and affective *personal supports* such as strategy self-verbalization training, teachers should employ *social en-*

vironment supports and *behavioral supports* as well. For example, a high school boy who is plagued by speech anxiety might be assisted by watching a series of videotapes of another anxious student gradually overcome his dysfluencies (um, er, ah, etc.). Fluent speech could be facilitated by using an insertion strategy in which 3-second pauses are made between sentences. After watching successive videotapes of the coping model, the anxious orator would try to give his own speech in the protected environment of a speech laboratory using the pause insertion strategy. Each enactive effort would be videotaped, and afterward, the boy would review the tape—self-recording his pauses and dysfluencies. His teacher should help him review these records and attribute his decreases in dysfluencies to the use of the pausing strategy. Over time, charts of increasing pauses and decreasing dysfluencies would enhance the boy's perceptions of self-efficacy for speaking.

CONCLUSION

John Lubbock's concern about the importance of stimulating a student's active involvement in learning may be addressed by educators now from the vantage of research on self-regulated learning. When students' perceptions of efficacy are linked to a sequence of self-regulative responses, namely, strategy monitoring (self-observation), strategy attributions (self-judgment) and strategy use (self-reaction), their learning is no longer passive but becomes self-motivated (Bandura, in press). It is especially encouraging that self-regulation training has proven to be effective with students who are at risk academically and who often display passivity or learned helplessness. Given the prevalence of these characteristics among students who drop out of school, it is time to consider the effectiveness of training these youngsters in the use of self-regulated learning strategies.

ACKNOWLEDGMENTS

Preparation of this chapter was supported in part by grant number 2-RO1 HL 28907 from the Lung Division, National Heart, Lung, and Blood Institute, and a gift from the Spunk fund.

We would like to express our appreciation to Albert Bandura, Dale H. Schunk, and Judith Meece for their helpful comments on this manuscript.

REFERENCES

Anderson, C. A., & Jennings, D. L. (1980). When experiences of failure promote expectations of success: The impact of attributing failure to ineffective strategies. *Journal of Personality, 48,* 393–405.

Bandura, A. (1977). Self-efficacy: Toward a unifying theory of behavioral change. *Psychological Review, 84,* 191–215.

Bandura, A. (1986). *Social foundations of thought and action: A social cognitive theory.* Englewood Cliffs, NJ: Prentice-Hall.

Bandura, A. (1989a). Human agency in social cognitive theory. *American Psychologist, 37,* 122–147.

Bandura, A. (1989b). Self-regulation of motivation and action through internal standards and goal systems. In L. A. Pervin (Ed.), *Goal concepts in personality and social psychology* (pp. 19–85). Hillsdale, NJ: Lawrence Erlbaum Associates.

Bandura, A. (in press). Social cognitive theory of self-regulation. *Organizational Behavior and Human Performance.*

Bandura, A. (1991). The changing icons in personality psychology. In J. H. Cantor (Ed.), *Psychology at Iowa: Centennial essays* (pp. 117–139). Hillsdale, NJ: Lawrence Erlbaum Associates.

Bandura, A., & Cervone, D. (1983). Self-evaluative and self-efficacy mechanisms governing the motivational effects of goal systems. *Journal of Personality and Social Psychology, 45,* 1017–1028.

Bandura, A., & Cervone, D. (1986). Differential engagement of self-reactive influences in cognitive motivation. *Organizational Behavior and Human Decision Processes, 38,* 92–113.

Bandura, A., & Schunk, D. H. (1981). Cultivating competence, self-efficacy, and intrinsic interest through proximal self-motivation. *Journal of Personality and Social Psychology, 41,* 586–598.

Borkowski, J. G., Carr, M., Rellinger, E., & Pressley, M. (1990). Self-regulated cognition: Interdependence of metacognition, attributions, and self-esteem. In B. F. Jones & L. Idol (Eds.), *Dimensions of thinking and cognitive instruction* (pp. 53–92). Hillsdale, NJ: Lawrence Erlbaum Associates.

Borkowski, J. G., Weyhing, R. S., & Carr, M. (1988). Effects of attributional retraining on strategy-based reading comprehension in learning disabled students. *Journal of Educational Psychology, 80,* 46–53.

Brown, A. L., & Campione, J. C. (1977). Training strategic study time apportionment in educable retarded children. *Intelligence, 1,* 94–107.

Butler, R. (1990). The effects of mastery and competitive conditions on self-assessment at different ages. *Child Development, 61,* 201–210.

Carver, C. S., & Scheier, M. F. (1981). *Attention and self-regulation: A control theory approach to human behavior.* New York: Springer-Verlag.

Cavanaugh, J. C., & Perlmutter, M. (1982). Metamemory: A critical examination. *Child Development, 53,* 11–23.

Chambliss, C., & Murray, E. J. (1979a). Cognitive procedures for smoking reduction: Symptom attribution versus efficacy attribution. *Cognitive Therapy and Research, 3,* 91–95.

Chambliss, C., & Murray, E. J. (1979b). Efficacy attribution, locus of control, and weight loss. *Cognitive Therapy and Research, 3,* 349–353.

Clifford, M. (1986). Comparative effects of strategy and effort attributions. *British Journal of Educational Psychology, 56,* 75–83.

Corno, L. (1989). Self-regulated learning: A volitional analysis. In B. J. Zimmerman & D.

H. Schunk (Eds.), *Self-regulated learning and academic achievement: Theory, research, and practice* (pp. 111–141). New York: Springer-Verlag.

Covington, M. (1985). The motive for self-worth. In C. Ames & R. Ames (Eds.), *Research on motivation in education: The classroom milieu* (pp. 77–113). New York: Academic Press.

Cox, C. M. (1976). The early traits of three hundred geniuses. In W. Dennis & M. W. Dennis (Eds.), *The intellectually gifted* (pp. 17–24). New York: Grune & Stratton.

Diener, C. I., & Dweck, C. S. (1978). An analysis of learned helplessness: Continuous changes in performance, strategy, and achievement cognitions following failure. *Journal of Personality and Social Psychology, 97*, 161–168.

Eccles, J. E., Midgely, C., & Adler, T. (1984). Age-related changes in the school environment: Effects on achievement motivation. In J. G. Nicholls (Ed.), *The development of achievement motivation* (pp. 283–331). Greenwich, CT: JAI Press.

Finn, J. (1989). Withdrawing from school. *Review of Educational Research, 59*, 117–142.

Flavell, J. (1979). Metacognition and cognitive monitoring: A new area of cognitive-developmental inquiry. *American Psychologist, 34*, 906–911.

Ghatala, E. S. (1986). Strategy-monitoring training enables young learners to select effective strategies. *Educational Psychologist, 21*, 43–54.

Ghatala, E. S., Levin, J. R., Foorman, B. R., & Pressley, M. (1989). Improving children's regulation of their reading PREP time. *Contemporary Educational Psychology, 14*, 49–66.

Ghatala, E. S., Levin, J. R., Pressley, M., & Goodwin, D. (1986). A componential analysis of the effects of derived and supplied strategy-utility information on children's strategy selections. *Journal of Experimental Child Psychology, 22*, 199–216.

Hunter-Blanks, P., Ghatala, E. S., Pressley, M., & Levin, J. R. (1988). Comparison of monitoring during study and during testing on a sentence-learning task. *Journal of Educational Psychology, 80*, 279–283.

Kuhl, J. (1985). Volitional mediators of cognitive-behavioral consistency: Self-regulatory processes and action versus state orientation. In J. Kuhl & J. Beckman (Eds.), *Action control* (pp. 101–128). New York: Springer.

Loper, A. B., & Murphy, D. M. (1984). Cognitive self-regulatory training for underachieving children. In D. L. Forrest-Pressley, G. E. MacKinnon, & T. G. Waller (Eds.), *Metacognition, cognition and human performance* (Vol. 1, pp. 223–265). Orlando, FL: Academic Press.

Lubbock, J. (1897). *Pleasures of life.* London: Macmillian.

Markman, E. M. (1977). Realizing that you don't understand: A preliminary investigation. *Child Development, 48*, 986–992.

Markman, E. M. (1979). Realizing you don't understand: Elementary school children's awareness of inconsistencies. *Child Development, 50*, 643–655.

McCombs, B. (1986). The role of the self-system in self-regulated learning. *Contemporary Educational Psychology, 11*, 314–332.

McCombs, B. (1989). Self-regulated learning and academic achievement: A phenomenological view. In B. J. Zimmerman & D. H. Schunk (Eds.), *Self-regulated learning and academic achievement: Theory, research, and practice* (pp. 51–82). New York: Springer-Verlag.

Meichenbaum, D., & Biemiller, A. (1990). *In search of student expertise in the classroom: A metacognitive analysis.* Paper presented at the Conference on Cognitive Research for Instructional Innovation, University of Maryland, College Park, MD.

Moely, B. E. (1977). Organizational factors in the development of memory. In R. V. Keil & J. W. Hagen (Eds.), *Perspectives on the development of memory and cognition* (pp. 203–236). Hillsdale, NJ: Lawrence Erlbaum Associates.

Paris, S. C., Newman, R. S., & McVey, K. A. (1982). Learning the functional significance of mnemonic actions: A microgenic study of strategy acquisition. *Journal of Experimental Child Psychology, 34,* 490–509.

Parsons, J., & Ruble, D. N. (1977). The development of achievement-related expectancies. *Child Development, 48,* 1975–1979.

Pintrich, P. R., & De Groot. E. V. (1990). Motivational and self-regulated learning components of classroom academic performance. *Journal of Educational Psychology, 82,* 33–40.

Pokay, P., & Blumenfeld, P. C. (1990). Predicting achievement early and late in the semester: The role of motivation and use of learning strategies. *Journal of Educational Psychology, 82,* 41–50.

Pressley, M. (1976). Mental imagery helps eight-year-olds remember what they read. *Journal of Educational Psychology, 61,* 355–359.

Pressley, M., Borkowski, J. G., & Schneider, W. (1987). Cognitive strategies: Good strategy users coordinate metacognition and knowledge. *Annals of Child Development, 4,* 89–129.

Pressley, M., & Ghatala, E. S. (1990). Self-regulated learning: Monitoring learning from text. *Educational Psychologist, 25,* 19–33.

Rohwer, W. D., Jr. (1973). Elaboration and learning in childhood and adolescence. In H. W. Reese (Ed.), *Advances in child development and behavior* (Vol. 8, pp. 2–57). New York: Academic Press.

Schneider, W. (1985). Developmental trends in the metamemory-memory behavior relationship: An integrative review. In D. L. Forrest-Pressley, G. E. MacKinnon, & T. Gary Waller (Eds.), *Metacognition, cognition and human performance* (Vol. 1, pp. 57–109). Orlando, FL: Academic Press.

Schunk, D. H. (1983). Goal difficulty and attainment information: Effects on children's achievement behaviors. *Human Learning, 2,* 107–117.

Schunk, D. H. (1984). The self-efficacy perspective on achievement behavior. *Educational Psychologist, 19,* 119–218.

Schunk, D. H. (1989). Social cognitive theory and self-regulated learning. In B. J. Zimmerman & D. H. Schunk (Eds.), *Self-regulated learning and academic achievement: Theory, research, and practice* (pp. 83–110). New York: Springer-Verlag.

Schunk, D. H. (1990). Self-concept and school achievement. In C. Rogers & P. Kutnick (Eds.), *The social psychology of the primary school* (pp. 70–91). London: Routledge.

Schunk, D. H., & Rice, J. M. (1984). Strategy self-verbalization during remedial listening comprehension instruction. *Journal of Experimental Education, 53,* 49–54.

Schunk, D. H., & Rice, J. M. (1985). Verbalization of comprehension strategies: Effects on children's achievement outcomes. *Human Learning, 4,* 1–10.

Sears, P. S. (1940). Levels of aspiration in academically successful and unsuccessful children. *Journal of Abnormal and Social Psychology, 35,* 498–536.

Skinner, E. A., Wellborn, J. G., & Connell, J. P. (1990). What it takes to do well in school and whether I've got it: A process model of perceived control and children's engagement and achievement in school. *Journal of Educational Psychology, 82,* 22–32.

Stipek, D. (1984). Young children's performance expectations: Logical analysis or wishful thinking? In J. G. Nicholls (Ed.), *Advances in motivation and achievement: Vol. 3. The development of achievement motivation* (pp. 33–56). Greenwich, CT: JAI.

Thoresen, C. E., & Mahoney, M. (1974). *Behavioral self-control.* New York: Holt, Rinehart & Winston.

Weinstein, C. E., Goetz, E. T., & Alexander, P. A. (1988). *Learning and study strategies: Issues in assessment instruction and evaluation.* San Diego, CA: Academic Press.

Weinstein, C. E., & Mayer, R. E. (1986). The teaching of learning strategies. In M. C. Wittrock (Ed.), *Handbook of research on teaching* (3rd ed., pp. 315–327). New York: Macmillan.

Zimmerman, B. J. (1986). Development of self-regulated learning: Which are the key subprocesses? *Contemporary Educational Psychology, 16,* 307–313.

Zimmerman, B. J. (1989a). A social cognitive view of self-regulated learning. *Journal of Educational Psychology, 81,* 329–339.

Zimmerman, B. J. (1989b). Models of self-regulated learning. In B. J. Zimmerman & D. H. Schunk (Eds.), *Self-regulated learning and academic achievement: Theory, research, and practice* (pp. 1–25). New York: Springer-Verlag.

Zimmerman, B. J. (1990a). Self-regulated learning and academic achievement: An overview. *Educational Psychologist, 25,* 3–17.

Zimmerman, B. J. (1990b). Self-regulating academic learning and achievement: The emergence of a social cognitive perspective. *Educational Psychology Review, 2,* 173–201.

Zimmerman, B. J., & Martinez-Pons, M. (1986). Development of a structured interview for assessing student use of self-regulated learning strategies. *American Educational Research Journal, 23,* 614–628.

Zimmerman, B. J., & Martinez-Pons, M. (1988). Construct validation of a strategy model of student self-regulated learning. *Journal of Educational Psychology, 80,* 284–290.

Zimmerman, B. J., & Martinez-Pons, M. (1990). Student differences in self-regulated learning: Relating grade, sex, and giftedness to self-efficacy and strategy use. *Journal of Educational Psychology, 82,* 51–59.

Zimmerman, B. J., & Ringle, J. (1981). Effects of model persistence and statements of confidence on children's efficacy and problem solving. *Journal of Educational Psychology, 73,* 485–493.

9

Gender Differences in Students' Perceptions: Consequences for Achievement-Related Choices

JUDITH L. MEECE
University of North Carolina at Chapel Hill

DARIA PAUL COURTNEY
North Carolina Central University

For many years, researchers have examined the motivational variables that contribute to the differential academic and vocational achievement of men and women. Aspects of this research have focused on gender differences in achievement-related perceptions. Early studies emphasized factors that can increase women's avoidance motivation such as their low need for achievement, low expectations for success, fear of success, and debilitating causal attributions (Dweck, 1986; Sutherland & Veroff, 1985). According to Eccles (1987), this research focus has perpetuated a distorted view of women's achievement motivation. It provides more information about what inhibits rather than what sustains the achievement striving of girls and women.

In the early 1980s, Eccles and her colleagues developed a model of academic choice to explain gender differences in students' achievement patterns (Eccles [Parsons], 1984; Eccles et al., 1983; Meece, Parsons, Kaczala, Goff, & Futterman, 1982). The model assumes that achievement behavior involves an element of choice, although socialization experiences and cultural norms also have a role in determining those choices. Whether intentionally or not, individuals make choices concerning which activities to try, how much effort to expend, the types of problem-solving strategies to use, how long to persist, and so forth. The academic choice model thus focuses on the motivational and sociocultural variables that influence children and adults to choose, persist, and excel at different achievement activities.

This chapter reviews gender-difference research based on the academic choice model. Much of this research has examined students' decisions concerning whether or not to continue taking mathematics. The model proposes that gender differences in these achievement choices are linked to students' expectancy and value perceptions. The chapter begins with a brief description of the model. The next section reviews recent empirical research on the academic choice model along with findings from several related studies. The chapter concludes with suggestions for future research and educational practice.

ACADEMIC CHOICE MODEL

Initial research on the academic choice model was supported by the former National Institute of Education (NIE). Policymakers at NIE wanted to know why so few girls enrolled in advanced mathematics courses in high school. The lack of a strong background in mathematics prevents many capable women from entering math- and science-related college majors and traditionally male-dominated occupations. Research also suggests that the differential course-taking behavior of high school students explains some, but not all, of the gender-related differences in standardized tests of mathematics achievement (SAT-M) during late adolescence and young adulthood (Armstrong, 1981; Fennema & Sherman, 1977; Kimball, 1989; Pallas & Alexander, 1983).

Previous efforts to explain gender differences in mathematics course enrollment and achievement patterns have examined the influence of numerous variables, which range from aptitude differences to the sex-typing of mathematics as a male domain (Meece et al., 1982). This research suggested that differential enrollment patterns could not be explained by aptitude differences alone. The sex stratification found in advanced high school mathematics courses appears to be self-selected. That is, many academically capable girls choose to discontinue their mathematical studies early in high school when this option becomes available. Here was an opportunity to test a motivational model of academic choice.

The motivation model developed by Eccles and her colleagues is based in part on expectancy-value theories of behavioral choice (Atkinson, 1964). The model thus links achievement behavior to students' perceptions of their ability to successfully perform a task (expectations for success) and to the value they attach to the task (subjective task value). Consistent with attribution, self-efficacy, and other cognitive theories of motivation, the model emphasizes the important influence of cognitive and inferential processes. It assumes that students' ability and task perceptions have a more important influence on behavior than objective evidence of their achievement. The model also assumes that early achievement experiences, gender-role socialization, and the cultural milieu each plays a role in determining how students construe, interpret, and respond to their achievement experiences.

The academic choice model includes two major components. One focuses on psychological variables that directly influence achievement behavior, and the other specifies the developmental origins of individual differences in those variables. A full description of the model is beyond the scope of this chapter. The research reviewed here focuses only on the psychological component, namely students' expectancy- and value-related perceptions. Readers interested in a description of the full model are referred to Eccles (Parsons) (1984), Eccles et al. (1983), and Meece et al. (1982).

Expectancy-Related Perceptions. Achievement expectancies are defined as the subjective probability of success on a task (Atkinson, 1964). Expectancy judgments are conceptually related to estimates of self-confidence and self-efficacy in achievement situations. For example, measures of self-confidence in mathematics typically assess individuals' confidence in their abilities to learn math (Fennema & Sherman, 1977; Kloosterman, 1988), whereas measures of mathematics self-efficacy assess individuals' perceptions of their abilities to obtain a certain level of performance on a mathematics task (Norwich, 1987; Schunk & Lilly, 1984) or to obtain passing grades in math-related courses (Betz & Hackett, 1983; Hackett & Betz, this volume). Expectancy judgments are also related to self-concepts of ability. However, the latter entails a global assessment of the individual's capabilities, and these assessments tend to be less predictive of achievement outcomes than domain- or task-specific measures (Assor & Connell, this volume; Schunk, 1987).

Research based on expectancy-value and self-efficacy theories of motivation has shown that the expectations individuals hold for their performance influence a wide range of achievement behaviors including task choice, task persistence, and performance measures (Bandura, 1986; Feather, 1982; Hackett & Betz, this volume; Pintrich & Schrauben, this volume). Individuals who are confident of their abilities and expect to succeed demonstrate high levels of persistence and performance on achievement tasks. They also are likely to choose challenging tasks when given the opportunity.

Because women in our society are typically stereotyped as less competent than men, these sex-typed beliefs, if incorporated into the self-perceptions of girls, can lead girls to have less confidence than boys in their intellectual abilities. Although findings are inconsistent across studies, girls generally report lower estimates of their academic abilities and lower achievement expectations, even if they perform as well as or better than boys (Eccles et al., 1983; Licht & Dweck, 1984; Meece et al., 1982). The causal attributions of girls in achievement situations also reflect a low expectancy pattern. Girls are more likely than boys to attribute their learning difficulties to low ability, and when they perform well, girls are less likely than boys to attribute their success to high ability (Dweck, Goetz, & Strauss, 1980; Nicholls, 1975). Gender differences in both achievement expectations and causal attributions are especially marked for tasks presented or perceived as appropriate for their gender (Lenny, 1977; McHugh, Fisher, & Frieze, 1982) and for novel or ambiguous tasks (Kimball, 1989; McHugh, Frieze, & Hanusa, 1982).

Evidence suggests that math is sex-typed as a male domain (Fennema & Sherman, 1977), and boys have higher performance expectancies in mathematics than do girls (Betz & Hackett, 1983; Entwisle & Baker, 1983; Fennema & Sherman, 1977; Hackett & Betz, this volume; Heller & Parsons, 1981; Stevenson & Newman, 1986). The expected pattern of gender differences in causal attributions also appears for mathematics performance (Wolleat, Pedro, Becker, & Fennema, 1980). However, gender differences in expectancy-related perceptions do not emerge with any consistency until adolescence when students begin to consider future educational and occupational plans. According to the academic choice model, students' achievement expectations exert a strong influence on those plans.

Value-Related Perceptions. Expectancy-value theorists propose that the incentive value of an achievement task or activity is another important determinant of achievement behavior (Atkinson, 1964; Eccles et al., 1983; Feather, 1982). Individuals tend to engage in, and to persist at, tasks they positively value. As first conceptualized by Atkinson (1964), the value of engaging in a task was thought to be directly related to the degree of difficulty or challenge it was assumed to have. Success at harder tasks was assumed to have greater value than success at easier tasks.

Eccles et al. (1983) conceptualized task value in terms of four dimensions: attainment value, intrinsic value or interest, utility value, and perceived cost. *Attainment value* represents the importance of doing well on a task. *Intrinsic* or *interest value* is the inherent enjoyment or pleasure the individual derives from engaging in an activity. *Utility value* is the valence a task acquires because it is instrumental in reaching short- or long-range objectives. *Perceived cost* refers to the individual's perception of what is lost, given up, or suffered as a consequence of engaging in a particular activity. This component can be influenced by negative emotional states (e.g., performance anxiety, fear of failure, fear of success) or by the anticipated amount of effort needed to succeed.

The academic choice model identifies several sources of gender differences in students' achievement values based on previous research (Eccles et al., 1983; Meece et al., 1982). Individuals with strong gender-role identities are likely to value achievement activities and careers they perceive as appropriate for their gender. Other evidence suggests that socialization practices can influence children's value orientations (Parsons, Adler, & Kaczala, 1982). If, for example, parents or teachers provide boys and girls with different information about the appropriateness or importance of various academic or careers options, then children are likely to develop gender-differentiated value perceptions.

Previous research indicates that male and female students may not value mathematics achievement in the same way. Studies of junior high school students have found that boys are more likely than girls to perceive mathematics as important to future career goals (Brush, 1980; Fennema & Sherman, 1977). High school boys also place greater importance on their grades in mathematics than do girls (Eccles et al., 1983). In addition, most studies indicate that female students are more math anxious than are male students (Brush, 1980; Meece, 1981; Wigfield & Meece, 1988). This research has further shown that math anxiety relates negatively to the perceived value of math.

Summary. The academic choice model is particularly useful for analyzing gender differences in achievement patterns. Gender differences in students' expectancy and value perceptions have been well documented. The academic choice model proposes that students' expectancy and value perceptions jointly influence achievement behavior. Students are most likely to continue taking courses in a particular subject area and to perform well, when they expect to do well and they want to do well. Students' achievement expectancies are likely to have less of an influence when value perceptions are low and vice versa.

Next, we review empirical research on the academic choice model and related studies. To demonstrate support for expectancy-value theories of motivation, the evidence should reveal (a) significant sex differences in students' expectancy and value perceptions, and (b) direct links between these perceptions and achievement outcomes.

EMPIRICAL RESEARCH 1980–1990

Research on the Academic Choice Model

The first test of the academic choice model involved 668 students in Grades 5–12 from a Midwestern university community (Eccles [Parsons], 1984; Eccles et al., 1983; Eccles, Adler, & Meece, 1984). The study used a longitudinal design in which students' self-perceptions and achievement outcomes were assessed over a 2-year period. Students completed group-administered questionnaires in the spring of each year to assess their expectancies for success, perceived values, perceived ability, math anxiety, and course enrollment intentions, along with the sociocultural influences included in the model. Math grades, standardized test scores, and course enrollment information were collected from school records.

This first study found significant gender differences in most, but not all, of the major motivational constructs of the model, including future course performance expectations, perceptions of the utility value of mathematics, math anxiety, and causal attribution patterns (Eccles [Parsons], 1984; Eccles et al., 1983). In general, the gender differences favored boys, but relative to grade-level effects, gender had only a small effect on students' achievement-related perceptions. There were no significant gender differences in students' math grades and course enrollment intentions, but a greater number of boys than girls were enrolled in mathematics at Grade 12.

Additional analyses revealed that gender differences in students' value perceptions were subject matter specific (Eccles et al., 1984). Compared to boys, girls rated math as less important and English as more important. Also, girls rated English as more important than math, whereas boys showed the reverse pattern. Students' expectancy-related perceptions did not show the same pattern. All students rated their English abilities higher than their math abilities, even though their actual performance (semester grades) in these courses did not significantly differ.

The results also provided support for the relations among variables in the academic choice model. Expectancy and value perceptions related positively to these outcomes. Sex and ability level each had an indirect effect on achievement outcomes through their influence on students' expectancy, value, and anxiety ratings.

The predictive value of expectancy and value perceptions differed depending on the achievement outcome under investigation (Eccles et al., 1984). The perceived value of mathematics had the strongest influence on students' course enrollment plans, and it was a stronger predictor than were objective measures of achievement (grades and standardized test scores). However, math grades and value perceptions were the strongest predictors of students' enrollment in mathematics at Grade 12. A different pattern of relations appeared when course performance was the outcome measure. Students' subsequent grades in both math and English were predicted by their expectancy-related perceptions (self-concepts of ability) and by their prior grades in these courses.

The second study involved 250 students in Grades 7–9 (Meece, Wigfield, & Eccles, 1990). This study was part of a larger investigation involving approximately 860 students in Grades 5–12 from two predominantly middle- and upper middle-class communities (Eccles, Wigfield, Meece, Kaczala, & Jayarante, 1986). The research design and data-collection procedures were comparable to the first study. The findings discussed here focus on the junior high school students and their mathematics achievement.

The pattern of gender differences in students' self-perceptions and achievement variables differed from the first set of studies, possibly due to the socioeconomic diversity of the new sample. Compared with girls, boys reported higher performance expectancies, higher perceptions of their math abilities, and stronger intentions to continue taking mathematics. Girls reported higher levels of math anxiety than did boys. There were no gender differences in the importance students attached to doing well in math or in their course performance for either year of the study. As before, the magnitude of the gender differences was small.

The findings also indicated that students' course enrollment decisions related most directly to the subjective value of mathematics, whereas their course performance related most directly to their expectancy perceptions and prior performance in mathematics. Students' self-reports of math anxiety did not directly relate to either course enrollment plans or performance in mathematics even though girls reported more math anxiety than did boys. This finding suggests that although math anxiety correlates moderately with expectancy and value perceptions, it does not add significantly to the prediction of achievement outcomes beyond those variables. It appears that expectancy and value perceptions can compensate or override the effects of math anxiety on course performance and enrollment plans, but these findings need further investigation (Meece et al., 1990).

The findings of the Meece et al. study also suggested that the pattern of relations among variables was consistent across male and female samples. Previous research indicated that affective and attitudinal measures differentially influence the achievement patterns of male and female students (Meyer & Fennema, 1986; Sherman, 1979). We tested this hypothesis and found no evidence that prior performance or math anxiety differentially predicted the course performance and enrollment plans of male and female students in mathematics. Thus, gender differences in achievement outcomes are due more to the magnitude of differences in boys' and girls' achievement-related perceptions than to the differential influence of one or more variables.

Related Research

Feather (1988) examined the influence of expectancy and value constructs on college students' decisions to enroll in humanities, social science, or science courses. He found gender differences in the subjective value of mathematics and English, but no difference in self-concepts of math and English abilities. Male students assigned more value to mathematics courses than did female students, whereas female students assigned higher value to English courses. Overall, students assigned more value to English than to mathematics courses and rated their English abilities higher than their math abilities. Also, students' expectancy and value perceptions in each domain were positively related. Self-concepts of English abilities did not predict students' enrollment in social science and humanities courses; the subjective value of English was the most significant predictor. In contrast, enrollment patterns in science were influenced more by self-concepts of math ability than by the subjective value of math.

Berndt and Miller (1990) examined the relative contribution of expectancies and values to the academic achievement of seventh-grade students. They reported sex differences for value perceptions, but no differences for expectancy perceptions. Girls had more positive value perceptions than did boys. Students' expectancy and value perceptions were positively correlated, and both constructs contributed significantly to the prediction of overall academic achievement. When math and English grades were analyzed separately, expectancies had a stronger influence than values on achievement, but each had a significant influence.

Meece, Courtney, and Blumenfeld (1987) examined the effects of gender on elementary school students' expectancy and value perceptions, achievement goal orientations, and cognitive engagement patterns in science. Previous research indicates that boys have more positive perceptions of their science abilities than do girls (Licht, Strader, & Swenson, 1989; Steinkamp & Maehr, 1983). Several theorists have also hypothesized that sex differences in students' ability perceptions and expectations for success result in different achievement orientations in mathematics or science (Dweck, 1986; Maehr, 1983; Steinkamp, 1984). Because some girls are less certain of their abilities, their achievement orientation may reflect a concern with evaluation and teacher approval. The achievement orientation of boys appears to be more mastery-oriented. They express confidence in their abilities, seek to independently master activities, and persist when challenged.

Research has further shown that students' goal orientations relate to their selection and use of different learning strategies (see Pintrich & Schrauben, this volume). For example, Meece, Blumenfeld, and Hoyle (1988) showed that children with mastery-oriented goals report high cognitive engagement in learning activities (i.e., high reported use of self-regulated learning strategies). By contrast, students primarily concerned with the evaluation of others (ego-oriented) or with doing as little work as possible (work-avoidant) report low levels of cognitive engagement. Therefore, if boys and girls differ in their ability and value perceptions, these differences may have important consequences for students' goal and achievement patterns in science.

The results of Meece et al.'s (1987) study provided very little support for previous research findings. The results revealed a gender effect for only three variables. Boys rated their science abilities, but not their general academic competence, higher than girls. Although girls reported less confidence in their science abilities, they did not report a greater concern with evaluation in science than boys. Boys were more oriented toward work-avoidant goals, and they reported greater use of effort-minimizing strategies.

Significant gender-by-ability effects also appeared in students' ratings of their general academic competence, intrinsic motivation to learn, and mastery goals. Girls with achievement test scores above the 60th percentile (sample median) had a more positive motivational profile than their male counterparts. The opposite pattern appeared for low-achieving students. There were no gender-by-ability differences in students' task-specific expectancies or reported use of self-regulated learning strategies.

SUMMARY AND CONCLUSIONS

The studies reviewed in this chapter demonstrate the utility of expectancy-value models of motivation for explaining gender differences in students' achievement. The general pattern of findings suggests that gender alone does not adequately explain differences in students' achievement patterns. Similarly, students' achievement-related behavior is not based solely on objective measures of ability such as prior course grades or standardized test scores. Rather, the data support cognitive mediation models of motivation that focus on students' perceptions and interpretations of their achievement experiences. Findings across studies indicate that students' choice-related behavior relates most directly to expectancy and value perceptions, which vary as a function of gender and ability.

Most of the studies discussed here examined the relative influence of expectancy and value perceptions on achievement outcomes. Findings on this issue are mixed. Elementary school children's selection of learning strategies are more strongly linked to the value of learning goals than to ability perceptions and task expectancies (Meece et al., 1988). Among junior high school students, expectancy-related perceptions have the strongest influence on course performance (Berndt & Miller, 1990; Eccles et al., 1984; Meece et al., 1990), whereas value perceptions have the strongest influence on future course enrollment plans (Eccles et al., 1984; Meece et al., 1990). These patterns are not replicated in older students. Feather (1988) showed that college students' enrollment patterns in science majors related more strongly to expectancies than to values. Hackett and Betz (this volume) also reported that self-efficacy expectations are strong predictors of students' college major choices.

These inconsistent findings suggest that the relative influence of expectancy and value perceptions on students' achievement patterns depends on the age and ability levels of the students as well as the measures used. Furthermore, the studies reviewed here indicate that expectancy and value perceptions are positively related. Therefore, even though one of the variables is not directly related to a given achievement outcome, it may have an indirect effect through its influence on the variable that is directly related.

What conclusions can be drawn about gender differences in students' expectancy and value perceptions? First, the data indicate that the nature and magnitude of the gender difference reported depends on the academic domain, the specificity of the measure, and the students' ages. Researchers have argued that stereotypes regarding the gender appropriateness of an achievement domain can influence students' achievement-related perceptions (Eccles et al., 1983; Hackett & Betz, this volume; Marsh, 1989; McHugh, Fisher, & Frieze, 1982; Meece et al., 1982). The data reported here suggest that a sex-typing bias appears only for elementary and secondary students in mathematics and science, favors boys, and occurs when boys and girls are performing equally well. The fact that gender differences appear in some domain-specific but not general measures of ability and value perceptions lends further support to this hypothesis.

The absence of a significant gender difference in task-specific measures of performance expectancies is consistent with research on the familiarity versus novelty hypotheses (Kimball, 1989; Lenny, 1977; McHugh, Frieze, & Hanusa, 1982). Performance expectancies in the Meece et al. (1987) study were assessed in relation to science activities of varying difficulty that students performed on a regular basis. Girls generally expect to do as well as boys when achievement tasks are familiar and when they receive clear feedback about their performance (Parsons, Meece, Adler, & Kaczala, 1982). Collectively, the findings support recent theories that gender differences in attitudes and behavior represent situational effects rather than enduring dispositions (Deaux & Major, 1987; Lenny, 1977; McHugh et al., 1982).

Second, gender differences in students' achievement-related perceptions are not as large as previous research would indicate. Gender differences reported in the studies we reviewed, although predictive of achievement outcomes, are quite small in magnitude. The findings are consistent with a recent review by Hyde, Fennema, Ryan, Frost, and Hopp (1990) who analyzed data from 70 empirical studies. They reported gender effects of .15 of a standard deviation or less on several of the Fennema–Sherman measures of mathematics attitudes and affect, including confidence, anxiety, and usefulness. The exception to this pattern was the stereotyping of mathematics scale, which had a fairly large effect size favoring boys.

Finally, it is important to recognize that the findings presented in this chapter are based on a select group of students. A majority of the studies involved academically capable students. None of the studies we reviewed reported gender differences in students' course grades or academic abilities. Prior research suggests that gender differences in ability-related perceptions are strongest among high-achieving students (Licht & Dweck, 1984). The data provide some support for this suggestion, although there are conflicting findings. For instance, some research indicates that the traditional pattern of gender differences is more evident in low- than high-achieving students (Meece et al., 1987). Similar findings are reported by Parsons, Meece et al. (1982) with regard to students' causal attributions and task-specific expectancies. Additional research is needed to determine the nature and magnitude of gender differences in students' perceptions across ability levels.

FUTURE RESEARCH DIRECTIONS

There are several directions for future research suggested by the studies reviewed in this chapter. Most of the studies have focused on gender differences in adolescents' and young adults' achievement-related perceptions. Although there are discrepant findings (Stevenson & Newman, 1986), a few studies indicate that gender differences in expectancy perceptions (Alexander & Entwisle, 1988) and ability perceptions (Wigfield, Eccles, Harold-Goldsmith, Blumenfeld, & Yoon, 1989) emerge as early as the first grade and reliably predict academic performance by the end of the second grade (Alexander & Entwisle, 1988). Consistent with research on older samples, the gender effect favors boys. However, gender differences in students' perceptions of their reading abilities are not consistently found in the early grades. In addition, elementary school girls rate both their math and reading abilities as significantly more important to them than do boys (Wigfield et al., 1989).

Developmental research on children's achievement-related perceptions raises some interesting questions for future research. For example, why is there more gender differentiation in children's ability perceptions in math than in reading? Sex-typing influences presumably operate in both areas. The gender differences in children's math-related value perceptions favors girls in the early school years, but then favors boys by adolescence. Is this developmental pattern due to the intensification of sex-role socialization during the early adolescent years, as some theorists suggest (Hill & Lynch, 1983)? Also, how are children's ability and value perceptions related over time? Do children come to value those activities they are good at? If so, then the lack of confidence young girls express in their math abilities could lead them to lower the value of science or mathematics, especially as they enter adolescence and the perceived difficulty of these courses increase (Eccles et al., 1983). The answers to these questions require longitudinal research designs that permit the tracking of developmental changes in children's achievement-related perceptions and behavior over time.

Another area in need of further study is the developmental origins of gender differences in students' achievement-related perceptions. Because gender differences are evident at the start of elementary school, and perhaps before, the home environment is likely to play an important role in shaping children's expectancy and value perceptions. Research suggests that parents hold sex-typed beliefs regarding their sons' and daughters' academic abilities. Parsons, Adler, and Kaczala's (1982) research on adolescents indicates that parents of sons rate their children's math abilities higher than do parents of daughters, even after school performance levels are statistically controlled. The opposite pattern appears when parents rate their children's English abilities. Entwisle and Baker (1983) reported similar differences in mothers' expectations for their sons' or daughters' performances in math and reading during the early elementary years. Both studies demonstrate that parents' beliefs can have a stronger influence on children's perceptions of their abilities than any objective measures of academic performance (see also Phillips, 1987).

Several issues in the parent literature need further examination. It is not clear why some children are particularly susceptible to parental evaluations. For example, parental evaluations are more closely linked to girls' than to boys' academic self-perceptions (Eccles et al., 1983). Parental expectations have only a weak influence on both boys' and girls' achievement expectations in low-income, racially integrated schools (Alexander & Entwisle, 1988; Entwisle & Baker, 1983). In addition, it is not clear where parents derive information about gender differences in children's academic abilities. Some researchers (Eccles & Jacobs, 1986; Parsons, Adler, & Kaczala, 1982) have argued that gender stereotypes have a strong influence on parental expectations. Other evidence suggests that gender differences in parents' expectations are a function of their children's early performance in school (Alexander & Entwisle, 1988; Entwisle & Baker, 1983).

The school environment is considered to be another potential source of gender differences in children's achievement attitudes and behavior (Meece, 1987). Research has shown that teachers do not necessarily have lower achievement expectations for girls than for boys (Dusek & Joseph, 1983; Wigfield & Harold, this volume). There is, however, a high degree of gender differentiation in classroom interaction patterns. Boys tend to have more classroom interactions of the type that would lead them to form higher expectations for their performance than girls (Brophy, 1985; Eccles & Blumenfeld, 1985; Meece et al., 1982). Some studies also show that gender differences in classroom interactions vary as a function of the student's ability level (Brophy, 1985; Eccles & Blumenfeld, 1985; Parsons, Kaczala, & Meece, 1982). High-ability boys have the most favorable interactions, whereas high-ability girls have the least number of interactions of any type with their teachers.

Additional research is needed to clarify the influence of classroom interaction variables on students' perceptions and achievement (see also Wigfield & Harold, this volume). One study showed no relation between the differential treatment of boys and girls in high school algebra classes and their algebra achievement, even though boys received more favorable treatment (Koehler, 1990). Parsons, Kazcala, and Meece (1982) found that only a few classroom interaction variables relate to students' self-concepts of math ability, and the relations differed for boys and girls. Studies also indicate that gender differences in students' ability perceptions and achievement expectancies are largely context specific because gender effects are not observed in all classroom settings (Brophy, 1985; Eccles & Blumenfeld, 1985; Parsons, Kaczala, & Meece, 1982). This research suggests that certain characteristics of the classroom environment (ability grouping, public teacher styles, competition, etc.) mediate gender effects.

Most studies of gender differences in classroom interaction patterns were conducted prior to 1985. In a recent study of high school mathematics classes, Leder (1988) reported patterns of interactions that are inconsistent with previous findings. This study raises the possibility that within the last few years some teachers may have become sensitive to the differential treatment of girls in traditionally male subject areas.

Only a limited number of studies have examined cultural differences in gender effects. Evidence suggests that the characteristic gender differences in achievement expectations are not evident in African-American children, at least during the early school years (Alexander & Entwisle, 1988). Because a high percentage of African-American women are single heads of households and are employed outside the home, African-American parents may have more egalitarian gender-role conceptions (Scott-Jones & Nelson-LeGall, 1986). Future research should examine how variations in gender-role expectations and socialization experiences influence motivation and achievement patterns in ethnically diverse samples (Courtney, 1990).

EDUCATIONAL IMPLICATIONS

The research discussed in this chapter has important implications for teachers. Developmental studies indicate that children form gender-differentiated perceptions of their academic abilities and interests well before they enter school. Teachers will need to do much more than simply treat boys and girls equitably in the classroom, if they wish to overcome the heavy dose of gender-role socialization students receive outside the classroom (Eccles, 1989). Reducing gender differences in achievement behavior will involve using curriculum materials and teaching methods that enhance students' ability and value perceptions.

Students can derive a sense of competence or self-efficacy from their direct experience with an activity (Bandura, 1986). Several classroom studies have noted the strong emphasis on rote-level learning and memorization and the relative neglect of higher order reasoning processes in many mathematics and science classes, even at the upper grade levels (Eccles & Midgley, 1989). Teachers can enhance students ability-related perceptions by providing learning activities that challenge and stretch students' existing skills and knowledge. Activities in which information or problems become more progressively difficult also enhance ability perceptions because they allow students to observe that their skills are improving (Schunk, 1984).

For students with unrealistically low expectancy perceptions or skill deficits, direct intervention may be necessary. Teachers can enhance the ability perceptions and achievement of these students through strategy instruction and feedback practices. Schunk (1984) has shown that as students improve their skills, they develop a greater sense of self-efficacy, which leads to increased persistence, higher levels of performance, and more intrinsic interest in the subject matter. Teachers also need to convey the functional value of learning strategies for different types of tasks because low-achieving students often lack knowledge concerning when and why to apply certain strategies. In addition, research demonstrates that teacher feedback that links skill improvement to the use of specific strategies (e.g., "You're getting a lot correct because you are using the borrowing rules") or to their increased ability (e.g., "You're getting really good at subtraction") can result in higher self-efficacy and achievement (Schunk & Gunn, 1986).

These strategies are likely to have limited success unless teachers create an intellectually and socially supportive classroom environment. Kahle (1984) and Eccles (1987) have analyzed the characteristics of "girl-friendly" classrooms that have a positive influence on girls' motivation and achievement in nontraditional subjects. These classrooms are characterized by low competition and social comparison among students, high levels of individualized and cooperative learning, high teacher support, and equitable treatment of male and female students. Teachers in the girl-friendly classes also use a number of strategies to increase the general value of mathematics and science. Examples include making the subject matter personally relevant and meaningful, providing active encouragement, explicitly communicating the importance of math or science, and providing career information or counseling.

Meece (1991) described how elementary school teachers can create a classroom environment that promotes a mastery-orientation in science (see also Ames, this volume). The results indicate that teachers can enhance students' ability and value perceptions in science by using instructional methods that emphasize conceptual understanding, promoting meaningful learning, and actively involving students in the learning process. Teachers in the mastery-oriented classes provided opportunities for students to work collaboratively and to engage in self-directed learning. They also actively modeled problem-solving strategies and provided the type of assistance students need to become independent learners. Most importantly, these teachers emphasized the intrinsic value of learning by adapting lessons to students' personal interests, pointing out the importance of science for their lives outside school, and posing interesting questions and problems so that students could experience firsthand the value of learning material. Grades and evaluation were not salient features of mastery-oriented classes.

Much more attention needs to be focused on changing the masculine image of mathematics and science. Recent studies indicate that these subject areas continue to be strongly sex-typed, especially by boys, as a male domain (Hyde et al., 1990). Teachers can help reduce sex-typing by using nonsexist learning materials and language, providing information about women scientists and mathematicians, and exposing students to successful female role models. Several curriculum projects have been developed to reduce sex-typing in mathematics (Project Equals, University of California at Berkeley; Project Multiplying Options and Subtracting Bias, University of Wisconsin). Available evidence suggests that curriculum interventions of this type are effective in reducing sex bias in students' achievement attitudes and behavior (Klein, 1985).

In conclusion, the more successful educational programs have used multiple strategies to increase girls' and women's participation and achievement in nontraditional fields. Gender differences in students' achievement behavior in school settings are primarily due to well-established gender-role conceptions rather than to teacher bias or systematic discrimination (Eccles & Blumenfeld, 1985; Meece, 1987). If teachers are to be faulted, it is because they do very little to actively change or reduce gender differences in achievement-related perceptions and behavior.

ACKNOWLEDGMENTS

We would like to acknowledge the special contributions of Terry Adler, Phyllis Blumenfeld, Jacquelynne Eccles, Caroline Kaczala, Carol Midgley, and Allan Wigfield to the research described in this chapter. We also wish to thank Paula Krist and Dale Schunk for their helpful comments on an earlier version of this draft and Blanche Arons for her assistance with the preparation of this manuscript.

REFERENCES

Alexander, K., & Entwisle, B. (1988). Achievement in the first 2 years of school: Patterns and processes. *Monographs of the Society for Research in Child Development, 53* (2, Serial No. 218).

Armstrong, J. (1981). Achievement and participation of women in mathematics: Results of two national surveys. *Journal of Research in Mathematics Education, 12,* 356–372.

Atkinson, J. W. (1964). *An introduction to motivation.* Princeton, NJ: Van Nostrand.

Bandura, A. (1986). *Social foundations of thought and action: A social cognitive theory.* Englewoods Cliffs, NJ: Prentice-Hall.

Berndt, T. J., & Miller, K. E. (1990). Expectancies, values, and achievement in junior high school. *Journal of Educational Psychology, 82,* 319–326.

Betz, N. E., & Hackett, G. (1983). The relationship of mathematics self-efficacy expectations to the selection of science-based college majors. *Journal of Vocational Behavior, 23,* 329–345.

Brophy, J. (1985). Interactions of male and female students with male and female teachers. In L. C. Wilkinson & C. B. Marrett (Eds.), *Gender influences in classroom interaction* (pp. 115–142). New York: Academic Press.

Brush, L. (1980). *Encouraging girls in math.* Cambridge, MA: Abt Books.

Courtney, D. P. (1990). *The relations between ego development and motivational orientations in African-American adolescents.* Unpublished doctoral dissertation, University of North Carolina at Chapel Hill.

Deaux, K., & Major, B. (1987). Putting gender into context: An interactive model of gender-related behavior. *Psychological Review, 94,* 369–389.

Dusek, J., & Joseph, G. (1983). The bases of teacher expectations: A meta-analysis. *Journal of Educational Psychology, 75,* 327–346.

Dweck, C. S. (1986). Motivational processes affecting learning. *American Psychologist, 41,* 1040–1048.

Dweck, C. S., Goetz, T. E., & Strauss, N. L. (1980). Sex differences in learned helplessness: IV. An experimental and naturalistic study of failure generalization and its mediators. *Journal of Personality and Social Psychology, 38,* 441–452.

Eccles (Parsons), J. S. (1984). Sex differences in mathematics participation. In M. Steinkamp & M. Maehr (Eds.), *Advances in motivation and achievement: Women in science* (Vol. 2, pp. 93–137). Greenwich, CT: JAI.

Eccles, J. S. (1987). Gender roles and women's achievement-related decisions. *Psychology of Women Quarterly, 11,* 135–172.

Eccles, J. S. (1989, January). *Bringing young women into math and science.* Paper presented at the annual meeting of the American Association for the Advancement of Science, San Francisco.

Eccles (Parsons), J. S., Adler, T., Futterman, R., Goff, S., Kaczala, C., Meece, J., Midgley, C. (1983). Expectancies, values, and academic behavior. In J. Spence (Ed.), *Achievement and achievement motives* (pp. 75–146). San Francisco: Freeman.

Eccles (Parsons), J. S., Adler, T., & Meece, J. (1984). Sex differences in achievement: A test of alternative theories. *Journal of Personality and Social Psychology, 46,* 26–43.

Eccles, J. S., & Blumenfeld, P. C. (1985). Classroom experiences and student gender: Are there differences and do they matter? In L. C. Wilkinson & C. Marrett (Eds.), *Gender influences in classroom interaction* (pp. 79–114). Hillsdale, NJ: Lawrence Erlbaum Associates.

Eccles, J. S., & Jacobs, J. (1986). Social forces shape math participation. *Signs, 11,* 367–380.

Eccles, J. S., & Midgley, C. M. (1989). Changes in academic motivation and self-perception during early adolescence. In R. Montemayor, G. Adams, T. Gullotta (Eds.), *From childhood to adolescence: A transition period? (Advances in Adolescent Development)* (Vol. 2, pp. 134–155). CA: Sage.

Eccles, J. S., Wigfield, A., Meece, J., Kaczala, C., & Jayarante, T. (1986). *Sex differences in attitudes and performance in math.* Unpublished manuscript, University of Michigan, Ann Arbor.

Entwisle, D., & Baker, D. (1983). Gender and young children's expectations for performance in arithmetic. *Developmental Psychology, 19,* 200–209.

Feather, N. T. (Ed.). (1982). *Expectations and actions: Expectancy value models in
psychology.* Hillsdale, NJ: Lawrence Erlbaum Associates.

Feather, N. T. (1988) Values, valences, and course enrollment: Testing the role of
personal values within an expectancy-valence framework. *Journal of Educational
Psychology, 80,* 381–391.

Fennema, E., & Sherman, J. (1977). Sex-related differences in mathematics achievement, spatial visualization, and affective factors. *American Educational Research
Journal, 14,* 51–71.

Heller, K. A., & Parsons, J. E. (1981). Sex differences in teachers' evaluative feedback
and students' expectancies for success in mathematics. *Child Development, 52,*
1015–1019.

Hill, J., & Lynch, M. E. (1983). The intensification of gender-related role expectations
during early adolescence. In A. Peterson & J. Brooks-Gunn (Eds.), *Girls at puberty* (pp.
201–228). New York: Plenum Press.

Hyde, J. S., Fennema, E., Ryan, M., Frost, L. A., & Hopp, C. (1990). Gender comparisons
of mathematics attitudes and affect. *Psychology of Women Quarterly, 14,* 299–324.

Kahle, J. (1984, January). *Girl-friendly science.* Paper presented at the meeting of the
American Association for the Advancement of Science, New York.

Kimball, M., (1989). A new perspective on women's math achievement. *Psychological
Bulletin, 105,* 198–214.

Klein, S. (1985). *Handbook for achieving sex equity through education.* Baltimore, MD:
Johns Hopkins University Press.

Kloosterman, P. (1988). Self-confidence and motivation in mathematics. *Journal of
Educational Psychology, 80,* 345–351.

Koehler, M. S. (1990). Classrooms, teachers, and gender differences in mathematics. In
E. Fennema & G. Leder (Eds.), *Mathematics and gender* (pp. 10–25). New York:
Teachers College.

Leder, G. C. (1988). Do teachers favor high achievers? *Gifted Child Quarterly, 32,*
315–320.

Lenny, E. (1977). Women's self-confidence in achievement settings. *Psychological Bulletin, 84,* 1–13.

Licht, B. B., & Dweck, C. S. (1984). Determinants of academic achievement: The
interactions of children's achievement orientations and skill area. *Developmental
Psychology, 20,* 628–636.

Licht, B. G., Strader, S., Swenson, C. (1989). Children's achievement-related beliefs:
Effects of academic area, sex, and achievement level. *Journal of Educational Research,
82,* 253–260.

Marsh, H. W. (1989). Age and sex effects in multiple dimensions of self-concept:
Preadolescence to early adulthood. *Journal of Educational Psychology, 81,* 417–430.

Maehr, M. (1983). On doing well in science: Why Johnny on longer escels; why Sarah
never did. In S. Paris, G. Olson, & H. W. Stevenson (Eds.), *Learning and motivation in
the classroom* (pp. 179–210). Hillsdale, NJ: Lawrence Erlbaum Associates.

McHugh, M., Fisher, J., Frieze, I. (1982). Effect of situational factors on the self-
attributions of females and males. *Sex Roles, 8,* 389–398.

McHugh, M., Frieze, I. H., & Hanusa, B. H. (1982). Attributions and sex differences in
achievement: Problems and new perspectives. *Sex Roles, 8,* 467–479.

Meece, J. (1981). *Individual differences in the affective reactions of middle and high school
students in mathematics: A social cognitive perspective.* Unpublished doctoral dissertation, University of Michigan Ann Arbor.

Meece, J. (1987). The influence of school experiences on the development of gender schemata. In L. S. Liben & M. L. Signorella (Eds.), *Children's gender schemata (New Directions for Child Development,* no. 38, pp. 57–73). San Francisco, CA: Jossey-Bass.

Meece, J. (1991). Students' motivational goals and the classroom context. In M. Maehr & P. Pintrich (Eds.), *Advances in motivation and achievement: Goals and self-regulatory processes* (Vol. 7, pp. 261–285). Greenwich, CT: JAI.

Meece, J. L., Blumenfeld, P. C., & Hoyle, R. (1988). Students' goal orientations and cognitive engagement in classroom activities. *Journal of Educational Psychology, 80,* 514–523.

Meece, J. L., Courtney, D. P., Blumenfeld, P. C. (1987, June). *Sex differences in children's motivational orientations and involvement in elementary science activities.* Paper presented at Fourth Annual International Conference of Girls, Science, & Technology, Ann Arbor, MI.

Meece, J. L., Parsons, J. E., Kaczala, C. M., Goff, S. B., & Futterman, R. (1982). Sex differences in math achievement: Towards a model of academic choice. *Psychological Bulletin, 91,* 324–348.

Meece, J. L., Wigfield, A., Eccles, J. S. (1990). Predictors of math anxiety and its influence on young adolescents' course enrollment intentions and performance in mathematics. *Journal of Educational Psychology, 82,* 60–70.

Meyer, M., & Fennema, E. (1986, April). *Gender differences in relationships between affective variables and mathematics achievement.* Paper presented at the annual meeting of the American Educational Research Association, San Francisco, CA.

Nicholls, J. G. (1975). Causal attributions and other achievement related cognitions: Effects of task outcome, attainment value, and sex. *Journal of Personality and Social Psychology, 10,* 306–315.

Norwich, B. (1987). Self-efficacy and mathematics achievement: A study of their relationship. *Journal of Educational Psychology, 79,* 384–387.

Pallas, A. M., & Alexander, K. L. (1983). Sex differences in quantitative SAT performance: New evidence on the differential coursework hypothesis. *American Educational Research Journal, 20,* 165–182.

Parsons, J. E., Adler, T. F., & Kaczala, C. M. (1982). Socialization of achievement attitudes and beliefs: Parental influences. *Child Development, 53,* 310–321.

Parsons, J. E., Kaczala, C. M., & Meece, J. L. (1982). Socialization of achievement attitudes and beliefs: Classroom influences. *Child Development, 53,* 322–339.

Parsons, J. E., Meece, J. L., Adler, T. F., & Kaczala, C. M. (1982). Sex differences in attributions and learned helplessness. *Sex Roles, 8,* 421–432.

Phillips, D. (1987). Socialization of perceived academic competence among highly competent children. *Child Development, 58,* 1308–1320.

Schunk, D. (1984). Self-efficacy perspective on achievement behavior. *Educational Psychologist, 19,* 45–58.

Schunk, D. (1987). *Domain-specific measurements of students' self-regulated processes.* Paper presented at the annual meeting of the American Educational Research Association, Washington, DC.

Schunk, D., & Gunn, T. P. (1986). Self-efficacy and skill development: Influence of task strategies and attributions. *Journal of Educational Research, 79,* 238–244.

Schunk, D. H., & Lilly, M. (1984). Sex differences in self-efficacy and attributions: Influence of performance feedback. *Journal of Early Adolescence, 4,* 203–213.

Scott-Jones, D., & Nelson-LeGall, S. (1986). Defining black families: Past and present. In E. Seidman & J. Rappaport (Eds.), *Redefining social problems* (pp. 83–100). New York: Plenum Press.

Sherman, J. (1979). Predicting mathematics performance in high school girls and boys. *Journal of Educational Psychology, 71,* 242–249.

Steinkamp, M. (1984). Motivational style as a mediator of adult achievement in science. In M. Steinkamp & M. Maehr (Eds.), *Recent advances in motivation and achievement: Women in science* (Vol. 2, pp. 281–316). Greenwich, CT: JAI.

Steinkamp, M., & Maehr, M. (1983). Affect, ability, and science achievement: A quantitative synthesis of correlational research. *Review of Educational Research, 53,* 369–396.

Stevenson, H., & Newman, R. (1986). Long-term prediction of achievement attitudes in mathematics and reading. *Child Development, 57,* 646–659.

Sutherland, E., & Veroff, J. (1985). Achievement motivation and sex roles. In V. E. O'Leary, R. K. Unger, & B. S. Wallston (Eds.), *Women, gender, and social psychology* (pp. 101–128). Hillsdale, NJ: Lawrence Erlbaum Associates.

Wigfield, A., Eccles, J., Harold-Goldsmith, R., Blumenfeld, P. C., Yoon, K. S., & Freedman-Doan, C. (1989, April). *Gender and age differences in children's achievement self-perceptions during elementary school.* Paper presented at the biennial meeting of the Society for Research in Child Development, Kansas City, KS.

Wigfield, A., & Meece, J. L. (1988). Math anxiety in elementary and secondary school students. *Journal of Educational Psychology, 80,* 210–216.

Wolleat, P. L., Pedro, J. D., Becker, A. D., & Fennema, E. (1980). Sex differences in high school students' causal attributions of performance in mathematics. *Journal for Research in Mathematics Education, 11,* 356–366.

10

Self-Efficacy Perceptions and the Career-Related Choices of College Students

GAIL HACKETT
Arizona State University

NANCY E. BETZ
Ohio State University

In any discussion of educational outcomes, attention must eventually turn to career choice and development. By *career development* we do not mean job training, but the aspect of general human development that encompasses work-related behavior throughout the life span (Super, 1990). This chapter provides an overview of the research linking self-perceptions of capabilities, influenced by educational experiences, to career decision making, career choice, and career development. Historically the topic of career development has been central to the field of counseling psychology and the following discussion draws heavily from the counseling tradition.

Theoretical perspectives on career development vary along important dimensions, but all of the major theories address, at least to some extent, personality factors and self-perceptions connecting personal experiences to career decision making (Osipow, 1990). Developmental approaches, for example, ascribe a major role to the self-concept and other personal constructs (Super, 1990). In the developmental view, career decision making takes place over time and essentially involves translating the self-concept into a vocational self-concept. Developmental theories such as Super's (1990) describe the major developmental tasks that individuals must accomplish in order to negotiate the successive stages of career decision making. For example, for the elementary-age student a major developmental task involves developing a realistic self-concept; for adolescents, exploration and crystallization of preferences are important; whereas in later adolescence and early adulthood specification and implementation of choices are the major tasks confronted. Person–environment fit models emphasize perceptions of congruence between oneself and occupational environments. Holland (1985), for example, has identified six personality types corresponding to six occupational environments. Effective and satisfying career choices are, in this view, a result of a good match between one's personality and the corresponding occupational environment.

It has been the social learning perspectives on career development, however, that have most concretely detailed the mechanisms whereby learning experiences influence individuals' perceptions of their interests, capabilities, and values, and consequently importantly affect perceptions of potential occupational avenues (Krumboltz, Mitchell, & Jones, 1976). In the past decade the social learning theory of career decision making has been expanded to include Bandura's (1977) construct of self-efficacy as a crucial determinant of career choice and adjustment (Hackett & Betz, 1981).

In the following sections we provide an overview of self-efficacy theory and its applications to career-development processes, review the literature addressing career-related self-efficacy, and, based on theory and research, provide recommendations for educators for enhancing students' career self-efficacy expectations. Most of the empirical work on the career self-efficacy construct has been conducted with college students, so this comprises the bulk of the literature review.

SELF-EFFICACY THEORY

Bandura's Construct

Bandura introduced self-efficacy theory in the late 1970s (Bandura, 1977) and has since refined and extended the construct, according it a central place within his broader social cognitive theory (Bandura, 1986, 1989). Most simply defined as one's beliefs about one's capabilities to perform a given behavior, perceived efficacy involves judgments about one' ability to "organize and execute courses of action" (Bandura, 1986, p. 131). Bandura (1989) has also elaborated on the mechanisms by which self-efficacy expectations interact complexly with affective, motivational, personal goal setting, and other cognitive processes to influence a wide range of human behavior. Self-efficacy expectations then, affect not only what behaviors or tasks an individual will attempt but also the motivational and decisional processes that govern persistence and ultimate success in performance attempts (Bandura, 1986). Basically, stronger efficacy judgments produce more perseverance, especially in the face of obstacles. Bandura (1986) distinguished between self-efficacy expectations, or one's judgments about one's performance, and outcome expectations, or the perceived consequences of successful performance.

Four sources of information importantly influence perceived efficacy: enactive attainment or past performance accomplishments; vicarious experience, or the influence of modeling and other forms of observational learning; verbal persuasion, including support, encouragement, and discouragement; and physiological state, especially the debilitating effects of anxiety (Bandura, 1986). In other words, strong and positive efficacy judgments derive from experience, but perceived efficacy is not synonymous with ability or skills, but rather reflects the complex and mutually interactive experiences, cognitive evaluations, and emotional reactions that surround given performance situations. Bandura's construct explains variations in performance given similar achievement and ability levels.

Career Self-Efficacy

We (Hackett & Betz, 1981) first proposed that self-efficacy theory could enhance existing theories of career development and suggested some of the ways in which self-perceptions of ability might influence choice behavior. We were particularly interested in understanding women's career development. The problem of the underutilization of women's talents and abilities in career pursuits and the underrepresentation of women in higher status, higher paying male-dominated occupations has long been a concern of vocational theorists and researchers (Betz & Fitzgerald, 1987).

Drawing from self-efficacy theory, we hypothesized that early learning experiences, particularly sex-role socialization, might negatively affect women's career-related self-efficacy expectations. Specifically, we hypothesized that traditionally feminine sex-typed experiences in childhood often limit girls' exposure to the sources of information necessary for the development of strong perceptions of efficacy in many occupational areas. Lowered perceived efficacy along important career-related dimensions could, in turn, affect the range of occupational alternatives considered, the types of occupations considered (e.g., traditionally male- or female-dominated), and performance and persistence in the pursuit of occupational alternatives. Thus, self-efficacy theory explains the cognitive and affective consequences of women's sex-role socialization experiences and the resulting gender differences in career choice patterns observable in the work force.

Despite our initial emphasis on applications of self-efficacy theory to women's career development, research on career self-efficacy quickly moved to general applications for both men and women (Betz & Hackett, 1986; Lent & Hackett, 1987). Our original statements and early research (Betz & Hackett, 1981; Hackett & Betz, 1981) focused on efficacy judgments concerning specific occupations, termed *occupational self-efficacy*. However, because the scope of the research has broadened considerably since the early 1980s, subsequent writings often employ the term *career self-efficacy* to indicate self-efficacy in relation to the wide variety of vocationally relevant tasks, decisions, behaviors, and adjustment processes that are influential in determining career development (Betz & Hackett, 1986; Lent & Hackett, 1987). We follow established practice in using *career self-efficacy* as an umbrella term and employ more specific terms as they apply to topics under discussion.

EMPIRICAL BASE

Two aspects of the career choice process have typically been addressed in the career literature: (a) the *content* of career choices, that is, *what* the individual considers or chooses; and (b) the *process* of choosing, or *how* the individual goes about making career-related choices. Reflecting this distinction in the general literature, the sections that follow review research exploring both the content of career choice and the process of career decision making. The bulk of the research that has appeared has addressed the content issue, but some investigations have explored the relations between self-efficacy and interests, academic achievement, persistence in college major programs, and career indecision.

Self-Efficacy and Choice Behavior

Occupational Self-Efficacy. In our first empirical test of the usefulness of self-efficacy theory in understanding career development (Betz & Hackett, 1981), we examined gender differences in perceived efficacy and the relationship of occupational self-efficacy to vocational interests and the range of career options college students considered. Our early attempts at measuring occupational self-efficacy involved requesting college students to rate their confidence in their ability to successfully complete the educational requirements and perform the job duties of 20 occupations (10 "nontraditional for women" or male-dominated and 10 "traditional for women" or female-dominated, across six major career fields).

The results of this first investigation indicated no overall gender differences in occupational self-efficacy (Betz & Hackett, 1981). However, an interesting pattern of gender differences did emerge when the nontraditional and traditional occupations were examined separately. College men's occupational self-efficacy was equivalent across occupations, but women's occupational self-efficacy was significantly lower than men's for nontraditional (male-dominated) occupations, and significantly *higher* for traditionally female dominated occupations. Occupational self-efficacy, in combination with gender and vocational interests, was predictive of the range of occupations students had considered as viable options. Measured ability was not predictive of the range of occupational alternatives students considered.

Several studies that subsequently appeared closely replicated our first investigation with college students and the results were largely supportive (e.g., Layton, 1984). Post-Kammer and Smith (1985) studied a younger population and reported findings supportive of our major hypotheses concerning gender differences in occupational self-efficacy. However, with younger students (eighth and ninth graders) fewer gender differences emerged and vocational interests were found to be a stronger predictor of occupational consideration than self-efficacy. With a sample of disadvantaged precollege students Post-Kammer and Smith (1986) found gender differences in occupational self-efficacy for math/science careers, but not for non-math careers. Cross-cultural replications (e.g., Matsui, Ikeda, & Ohnishi, 1989; Wheeler, 1983) of the Betz and Hackett (1981) study have yielded supportive findings with the exception of an investigation by Clement (1987). Clement's data revealed that occupational self-efficacy was predictive of women's consideration of some occupations, but overall, interests were the most important predictor for women and men.

Several researchers have attempted to understand the interrelationships between career self-efficacy and vocational interests. Rotberg, Brown, and Ware (1987), for example, examined the occupational self-efficacy, vocational interests, gender, ethnicity, and socioeconomic status (SES) of community college students. They reported that career self-efficacy was predictive of range of occupations considered, and occupational self-efficacy and interests were interrelated. Gender alone was not predictive of the range of occupational alternatives considered, sex-role was predictive of career self-efficacy, and ethnicity and SES were not predictive of either self-efficacy or range of occupations considered.

Lapan, Boggs, and Morrill (1989) took a closer look at the self-efficacy/interest relationship by examining the possible role of self-efficacy in influencing gender differences in vocational interests. Lapan et al.'s (1989) analyses revealed gender differences in two career fields typically nontraditional for women and strong relationships between level of interest and occupational self-efficacy. Their data suggest a causal model whereby past performance accomplishments (e.g., years of high school math courses and mathematics scores on the ACT) influence career self-efficacy that in turn predicts occupational interests. Lent, Larkin, and Brown (1989) also reported results suggesting that, for college engineering majors, self-efficacy is a stronger predictor than interests of academic achievement (i.e., grades) and persistence in one's college major. Lent et al. found no gender differences in their sample of students who had already been accepted into an engineering program.

Several other studies have been generally supportive of the usefulness of the career self-efficacy construct but have failed to uncover gender differences in occupational self-efficacy (e.g., Bores-Rangel, Church, Szendre, & Reeves, 1990; Hannah & Kahn, 1989). And finally, numerous conceptual articles and reports have examined various aspects of self-efficacy in nonstudent populations (Hackett, Lent, & Greenhaus, 1991).

Self-Efficacy and College Major Choices.   Occupational choices are less relevant to college students than choices with regard to educational programs. Thus, some research has focused on the more immediate concerns of college students, namely, choice of academic majors. Because of the continuing problem of the underrepresentation of women in scientific and technical career fields, we (Betz & Hackett, 1983) decided to investigate gender differences in math self-efficacy and the choice of math/science college majors. Hypothesizing that women's lower overall math self-efficacy might explain gender differences in academic choice behavior, which might then influence gender differences in the choices of math/scientific careers, we examined gender, past performance, attitudes toward mathematics, math self-efficacy, and math-related college major choice. We developed a measure of mathematics self-efficacy with regard to three mathematical domains, namely, everyday math tasks, math/science-related college courses, and math problems. Gender differences in math self-efficacy were reported, and these differences in math self-efficacy were found to be strongly related to gender differences in math-relatedness of college major choices. We also found that math self-efficacy was correlated with attitudes toward mathematics (e.g., math anxiety and perceptions of math as a male domain); however, math self-efficacy was a much stronger predictor of college major choice than the other attitudes toward mathematics.

Hackett (1985) followed up this line of research to determine the possible ordering of predictors of math-related college major choices. Her results supported the central role of math self-efficacy in the prediction of college major choices. That is, her data fit a self-efficacy model wherein gender influences selection of high school math courses, which in turn influences math achievement and math self-efficacy; math self-efficacy is then the immediate predictor of choice of math/science college majors. In a follow-up study, we (Hackett & Betz, 1989) reported further evidence that math self-efficacy is of greater importance than ability or past experience in predicting career-related choice behavior. In this later study we did not, however, find evidence that women's lower math self-efficacy expectations were *unrealistically* low. That is, comparisons between efficacy ratings on the math problems subscale of the math self-efficacy measure and a corresponding math problems performance scale revealed a high degree of correspondence between perceived math ability and actual math performance for college men and women.

Lent, Lopez, and Bieschke (in press) likewise explored the relationships between gender, sources of efficacy information, past achievement in mathematics, and math self-efficacy. In their study, gender and past performance accomplishments were the strongest predictors of math self-efficacy. These findings are congruent with Bandura's (1986) hypotheses that performance accomplishments have the most powerful influence on perceived efficacy.

Self-Efficacy, Grades, and Persistence in College Majors

Although the studies just reviewed investigated general hypotheses about gender differences in self-efficacy and career-related choices, another line of research has examined connections between self-efficacy and academic achievement and persistence. Lent, Brown, and Larkin (1984, 1986) studied the relationship between scientific/technical self-efficacy and achievement and persistence in scientific/technical college majors. In their first study, Lent et al. (1984) assessed occupational self-efficacy for scientific/technical careers. With their sample of college students who had declared engineering majors, Lent et al. found that students with higher levels of scientific/technical self-efficacy achieved higher grades and persisted longer in their majors. Although scientific/technical self-efficacy was related to mathematics aptitude and high school achievement, no gender differences in self-efficacy were found.

In a subsequent study, Lent et al. (1986) added another measure of self-efficacy, that is, self-efficacy for "academic milestones," referring to confidence in one's ability to negotiate major hurdles in an engineering program (e.g., "complete the mathematics requirements for most engineering majors"). Engineering self-efficacy was significantly correlated with scientific/technical interests, but academic milestones self-efficacy was not. Academic milestones self-efficacy, on the other hand, was correlated with high school performance. Both self-efficacy measures were significantly predictive of consideration of scientific/technical occupations, but self-efficacy for academic milestones was somewhat more predictive of academic achievement and persistence. No gender differences were observed. Hackett, Casas, Betz, and Rocha-Singh (1987) replicated and extended the Lent et al. (1986) study, reporting supportive results; their findings also revealed some additional predictive utility obtained by the inclusion of measures of perceived faculty support, faculty discouragement, and measures of stress and strain.

An investigation revealing the complexity of the self-efficacy/achievement relationship was conducted by Brown, Lent, and Larkin (1989). Academic milestones self-efficacy was found to be strongly predictive of grade-point average and persistence in college major regardless of aptitude. However, occupational self-efficacy moderated the relationship between aptitude and academic achievement and persistence; that is, occupational self-efficacy was not predictive of the achievement and persistence of high-ability students, but had a facilitative effect on students of more moderate aptitude levels.

Finally, Lent, Brown, and Larkin (1987) compared a self-efficacy model with two alternate theoretical models predicting career and academic behavior. Self-efficacy was found to be more predictive than interests of academic achievement and persistence, although both interests and self-efficacy were significantly predictive of range of career options. Lent et al.'s (1987) results, in combination with the other studies reviewed thus far, strongly suggest that, although perceived career efficacy is important in predicting certain aspects of career-related and academic behavior, particularly choice and persistence, occupational self-efficacy may not be as useful in the prediction of other career-related behaviors (e.g., indecision and exploratory behavior). This actually is in keeping with the situation-specific nature of the self-efficacy construct. If self-efficacy is defined as cognitive judgments of one's capabilities with regard to specific tasks, problems, or activities, then assessments of efficacy judgments for occupations should be predictive of the *content* of choices but would not be expected to predict career choice *process* variables (Lent & Hackett, 1987). In the next section we turn to attempts to develop measures of self-efficacy specific to important career-related processes.

Self-Efficacy and Career Decision-Making Processes

Career decision making and career indecision have received a great deal of attention in the career literature over the years (Hackett et al., 1991). Several behavioral components of effective career decision making have been identified and include goal selection, obtaining relevant and accurate occupational information, problem-solving capabilities, planning skills, and realistic self-appraisal skills (Crites, 1981). Taylor and Betz (1983) developed the Career Decision Making Self-Efficacy (CDMSE) scale to assess perceptions of efficacy with regard to these five dimensions of career decision making. A major assumption guiding their research was that effective career decision making involves not only the development of skills, but also confidence in one's decision-making abilities along these specific behavioral dimensions. In fact, Taylor and Betz (1983) hypothesized that low decision-making self-efficacy could impede exploratory behavior and the development of decision-making skills, and thus may be predictive of career indecision. Their findings supported the usefulness of the CDMSE in predicting career indecision, especially the aspects of indecision relating to lack of structure and lack of confidence with regard to career decisions. Taylor and Betz (1983) did not find gender differences in CDMSE, and their results supported a generalized factor reflecting lack of confidence in career decision-making abilities rather than self-efficacy with regard to the individual components of career decision making.

Taylor and Popma (1990) extended this research by investigating the interrelationships between CDMSE and career indecision, occupational self-efficacy, and other variables relevant to career choice. No gender differences on CDMSE were found, and CDMSE was only moderately related to occupational self-efficacy. However, Taylor and Popma's results were again supportive of the utility of CDMSE in predicting career indecision; of the variables examined, only CDMSE was significantly (and negatively) predictive of career indecision. Several other studies have explored the relationships between CDMSE, gender, and sex role (e.g., Arnold & Bye, 1989). More generally, investigations of self-efficacy with regard to various other career-choice process variables have been published and the research litera-ture is slowly moving beyond consideration of initial career choices to encompass adult adjustment processes (e.g., Betz & Hackett, 1987).

Causal Research on Career Self-Efficacy

One of the main advantages of the career self-efficacy construct, according to Hackett and Betz (1981), is that it is suggestive of ways in which unrealistic or detrimental self-perceptions may be modified, and the primary avenue of intervention is hypothesized to be performance accomplishments. Results of the research cited thus far have con-firmed the connection between past performance experiences and self-efficacy expectations. However, the causal relationship between performance and self-efficacy has received less attention. Hackett and Campbell (1987) examined the effects of success and failure experi-ences on task self-efficacy and task interest, finding that for a gender-neutral task (involving verbal anagrams), performance influenced both self-efficacy and task interest, albeit to different degrees. Campbell and Hackett (1986), in a companion study, found a similar pattern of results using a gender-stereotypical task (i.e., math problems). In both studies, task success (i.e., successful completion of math or verbal problems) produced enhanced task self-efficacy and, to a lesser extent, increased task interest, whereas task failure resulted in lowered self-efficacy and task interest. These researchers also found gender differ-ences on the gender-stereotypical (math) task but not on the gender neutral (verbal) task, and found gender differences in attributions, or how students perceived the cause of their performance. College women tended to ascribe task success externally (i.e., women who succeeded ascribed that successful performance to luck) and task failure internally (perceiving failure as due to their own lack of ability). College men exhibited the opposite attributional pattern, with suc-cessful performance attributed to ability (internal attribution) and unsuccessful performance attributed to task difficulty (external attri-bution).

Hackett, Betz, O'Halloran, and Romac (1990) partially replicated and extended this line of research with similar results. Their findings demonstrated that task performance in one domain generalized to some extent to self-efficacy in unrelated domains, but not to overall academic self-efficacy.

SUMMARY AND IMPLICATIONS

Several conclusions can be drawn from the empirical investigations of career self-efficacy, many of which have implications for educators. First we summarize the status of career self-efficacy and identify promising avenues for future research, then we suggest some specific recommendations for educational practice.

Summary/Implications for Research

It seems clear from the research literature that self-efficacy judgments are a central mediator of past experience in the prediction of educational and occupational choices (see Meece & Courtney, this volume). Past performance accomplishments are importantly related to the development of strong career self-efficacy expectations, and occupational self-efficacy is a powerful predictor of choice behavior (Hackett & Lent, in press). In predicting more distant and more complex choice behavior, career self-efficacy is probably the superior predictor in that it encompasses information about past performance, as well as affective and motivational information. However, there is some evidence that past performance alone may be a stronger predictor than self-efficacy of future performance under certain conditions (Hackett & Betz, 1989). Research attention is necessary to clarify conditions under which self-efficacy expectations are of primary importance and where past performance and achievement are most strongly predictive of choice behavior.

Occupational self-efficacy is also related to other important predictors of career choice, especially vocational interests. Much more work needs to be done in teasing out the self-efficacy/interest interrelationships. Although the data reported thus far are supportive of a social cognitive model wherein experience influences both the development of interests and self-efficacy, further investigation is necessary to confirm or disconfirm current conclusions that vocational interests are not likely to blossom in areas where self-efficacy expectations are weak (Lent et al., 1987). Career self-efficacy and interests have consistently been found to be moderately related and may be differentially predictive of aspects of career choice and development (Hackett & Lent, in press); this hypothesis, too, warrants further empirical scrutiny.

Important work has been done to identify variables that moderate the self-efficacy/achievement correspondence. For example, development of strong self-efficacy expectations seems to be more important for students of moderate ability levels than for higher ability students (Brown et al., 1989), and attributions of the causes of performance appear to moderate the effects of past performance on self-efficacy (Hackett et al., 1990); however, research teasing out these complex interrelationships has just begun.

Occupational self-efficacy is predictive of academic achievement and persistence to some degree, but assessment of self-efficacy with respect to more academically relevant variables such as math self-efficacy or self-efficacy for academic milestones seems to yield more predictive utility (Betz & Hackett, 1983; Lent et al., 1986). Likewise, occupational self-efficacy is not predictive of important components of the process of career decision making, but self-efficacy assessments that are directly relevant to decision-making processes are helpful in understanding potential problems in career development such as indecision (Taylor & Betz, 1983; Taylor & Popma, 1990). Once again, the empirical examinations of self-efficacy for career decision making have just begun and must be pursued and expanded in order to more fully understand the role of self-efficacy in career decision making and indecision.

Gender differences in career self-efficacy are not pervasive; rather, gender differences in academic and career self-efficacy seem to be associated with perceptions of gender-relatedness of tasks, activities, or occupations (Betz & Hackett, 1983; Hackett et al., 1990; Meece & Courtney, this volume). The more stereotypically an activity or occupation is perceived, the more likely it is that gender differences in self-efficacy will appear; gender differences in self-efficacy seem to be strongly related to the differential socialization experiences of women and men (Hackett & Betz, 1989). Studies involving younger students have demonstrated fewer gender differences than research investigating the occupational self-efficacy of college students and adults (Post-Kammer & Smith, 1985); and studies involving students who have already chosen their college major reveal few if any gender differences (Lent et al., 1986). Although these findings appear robust, researchers have only sampled a small number of the potential groups of students, college majors, and career fields. Expanding the research base, particularly by including younger students and using developmental designs, will assist us in understanding the process more fully.

Research on the sources of efficacy information has yielded mixed results. Clearly, successful performance accomplishments are vital to the development of a strong sense of personal effectiveness. However, the evidence is at least suggestive of the importance of other sources of efficacy information such as modeling and encouragement and lowered anxiety and arousal. Research is required to determine whether our hypothesis that sources of efficacy information other than past performance may bring individuals to attempt performance in occupationally related areas, after which performance becomes the most powerful source of efficacy information. And finally, in addition to the experimental studies required to clarify the performance/self-efficacy interrelationship, there is a compelling need for investigations exploring efficacy-based interventions to determine the usefulness of self-efficacy theory in enhancing career development and broadening career choices.

Implications for Educational Practice

First and foremost, career self-efficacy research underscores the importance of *self-perceptions* of ability. Thus, teachers and other educators must be sensitive to students' judgments of their own aptitudes and abilities. Difficulties in both the academic and career arenas involve unrealistic judgments about personal capabilities; self-perceptions and objective indices of capabilities are not always congruent. Our goal as educators should be to enhance the development of strong perceived efficacy in our students. Unrealistically low career self-efficacy expectations have discouraged many students from the pursuit of realistic objectives, whereas grandiose self-estimates may set students up for debilitating failure experiences. Bandura (1989), however, pointed out that success is often facilitated by somewhat unrealistic *positive* self-efficacy judgments, so it is probably wise to focus primarily on the development of strong positive self-efficacy rather than be unduly concerned about overestimates of ability.

Second, the research covered in this chapter reinforces the interconnections among academic performance, self-efficacy, and career pursuits. Although educators must be most concerned about classroom performance, they must not lose sight of or ignore the relationships between education and work. As we have seen from the preceeding review of research, not only does academic performance enhance career-related self-efficacy, but strong career self-efficacy beliefs subsequently facilitate academic achievement and persistence. More generally, work will occupy a significant portion of the lives of the overwhelming majority of current students, male and female (Osipow, 1986). Therefore, some attention to the interplay of academics and career development is in the best interest of our students.

Third, girls' self-efficacy in nontraditional areas warrants special concern. Educators need to pay particular attention to the possibility of unrealistically low perceived efficacy in their female students in gender-stereotypical subject areas such as mathematics and science.

More specifically, the career self-efficacy research suggests that educators *assess* students' estimates of and confidence in their abilities, and attempt to intervene where self-efficacy judgments are low and/or weak. Performance-based experiences are clearly the most powerful avenue of intervention, so effective teaching may, in many cases, achieve the desired results. Yet pre-existing low levels of self-efficacy may interfere with students' achievement in various ways, and drawing on the other three sources of efficacy information may therefore be crucial to enhancing educational attainment. Although an extended discussion of the educational implications of career self-efficacy theory and research is beyond the scope of this chapter, we use the case of enhancing girls' math and science self-efficacy to illustrate some of the implications of self-efficacy theory for educational interventions that should enhance career choice and development. Although the following discussion specifically targets girls and women, the same general types of processes are applicable to boys and men.

A pivotal issue in women's career development, as mentioned earlier in this chapter, is circumscription of choice. Women are still seriously underrepresented in many occupational fields, particularly at the higher levels within nontraditional (i.e., traditionally male-dominated) careers; the nontraditional career fields where women are most severely underrepresented, and that also, ironically, offer the greatest potential for higher paying and higher status employment, are in the science and technical fields. Early in the career development process girls tend to begin avoiding math and science courses, thereby effectively and prematurely closing off potentially viable career options (Betz & Fitzgerald, 1987).

A number of factors have been identified as discouraging of girls' pursuit of and achievement in nontraditional fields, including attitudes toward mathematics and the sciences (e.g., perceptions of math as a male domain), math anxiety, negative peer pressure, and the different subjective value attached to mathematics and science by many girls as compared to boys (Betz & Hackett, 1983; Eccles, 1987; Meece & Courtney, this volume). All of these factors may impede performance accomplishments in science and mathematics, or forestall the development of strong math and science self-efficacy even in the context of successful school performance. Math anxiety, for example, can weaken self-efficacy expectations and interfere with successful performance in math courses. Girls' perceptions that mathematics and science are male domains may cause reduced motivation to perform, thereby limiting opportunities for success experiences.

In order to develop career self-efficacy, teachers must concentrate on self-efficacy with regard to academic endeavors, but must also assist students in seeing the applicability of school subjects to the world of work. Theory suggests that drawing on all four sources of efficacy information may be the most useful approach in attempting to strengthen perceptions of both academic and career self-efficacy. Extracurricular school activities, paid work, and volunteer experience can, of course, provide important learning opportunities and enhance career exploration. But these experiences can also be drawn on by teachers to establish connections for students between academic subject matter and work activities. Exposing female students to female models who are pursuing math/science careers may assist in overcoming biased assumptions about the gender-inappropriateness of science and mathematics. Role models can also provide information for all students about specific job activities and assist students in seeing the relevance of what they are learning in different subject areas to the world of work, thus further broadening educational and career options.

More immediately, ensuring that problems and examples used in math and science courses employ a range of male and female models, and that science experiments and math problems include content reflecting traditional female experiences can be helpful. For example, Betz and Hackett (1983) found gender differences in favor of women on only 3 of 52 items on their math self-efficacy scale. However all three items reflected stereotypically female socialization experiences, for example, "estimate your grocery bill in your head as you pick up items." The math required to successfully complete these three items was similar to that required by other items where gender differences favored men. In a similar vein, Eccles (1987) discussed the creation of "girl-friendly" classroom environments; her recommendations for enhancing the value that girls attach to math and science are congruent with enhancing self-efficacy through vicarious experiences and modeling.

Attention to the potentially debilitating effects of math anxiety and, in other content domains, test anxiety, is likely to enhance self-efficacy (Smith, Arnkoff, & Wright, 1990). Bandura (1986) proposed that anxiety is a consequence of low and/or weak self-efficacy, but can further exacerbate the downward spiral of performance. Thus, teachers who attempt to decrease negative emotional reactions such as math anxiety are likely to experience more success in enhancing student performance. In cases where anxiety is severe, obtaining the assistance of support personnel such as school counselors, if they are knowledgeable about anxiety intervention strategies, may be a useful adjunct to classroom interventions.

And finally, the role of encouragement and support (verbal persuasion, in Bandura's model) cannot be underemphasized. Hackett et al. (1987) found that faculty support was predictive of college students' occupational self-efficacy, and that both perceived support *and* discouragement from university faculty were predictive of academic performance and persistence. Betz (1989) emphasized the negative effects of an absence of support, termed the *null environment*, on women's academic pursuits. Basically, where support is not forthcoming, that lack of support may actually have discouraging effects, particularly on female students.

In conclusion, self-efficacy theory can serve as an organizing framework for guiding interventions to enhance student performance. Research on career self-efficacy suggests some promising avenues for academic and career-related interventions that may ultimately serve to enhance both academic achievement and career development. Although there are a number of issues that must be explored to ascertain the status of some of the specifics of self-efficacy theory applications in the career area, the research is generally supportive and promising implications for educational practice can be derived.

REFERENCES

Arnold, J., & Bye, H. (1989). Sex and sex role self-concept as correlates of career decision-making self-efficacy. *British Journal of Guidance and Counselling, 17,* 201–206.

Bandura, A. (1977). Self-efficacy: Toward a unifying theory of behavioral change. *Psychological Review, 84,* 191–214.

Bandura, A. (1986). *Social foundations of thought and action: A social cognitive theory.* Englewood Cliffs, NJ: Prentice-Hall.

Bandura, A. (1989). Human agency in social cognitive theory. *American Psychologist, 44,* 1175–1184.

Betz, N. E. (1989). Implications of the null environment hypothesis for women's career development and for Counseling Psychology. *The Counseling Psychologist, 17,* 136–144.

Betz, N. E., & Fitzgerald, L. F. (1987). *The career psychology of women.* San Diego: Academic Press.

Betz, N. E., & Hackett, G. (1981). The relationship of career-related self-efficacy expectations to perceived career options in college women and men. *Journal of Counseling Psychology, 28,* 399–410.

Betz, N. E., & Hackett, G. (1983). The relationship of mathematics self-efficacy expectations to the selection of science-based college majors. *Journal of Vocational Behavior, 23,* 329–345.

Betz, N. E., & Hackett, G. (1986). Applications of self-efficacy theory to understanding career choice behavior. *Journal of Social and Clinical Psychology, 4,* 279–289.

Betz, N. E., & Hackett, G. (1987). The concept of agency in educational and career development. *Journal of Counseling Psychology, 34,* 299–308.

Bores-Rangel, E., Church, T. A., Szendre, D., & Reeves, C. (1990). Self-efficacy in relation to occupational consideration and academic performance in high school equivalency students. *Journal of Counseling Psychology, 37,* 407–418.

Brown, S. D., Lent, R. W., & Larkin, K. C. (1989). Self-efficacy as a moderator of scholastic aptitude-academic performance relationships. *Journal of Vocational Behavior, 35,* 64–75.

Campbell, N. K., & Hackett, G. (1986). The effects of mathematics task performance on math self-efficacy and task interest. *Journal of Vocational Behavior, 28,* 149–162.

Clement, S. (1987). The self-efficacy expectations and occupational preferences of females and males. *Journal of Occupational Psychology, 60,* 257–265.

Crites, J. O. (1981). *Career counseling: Methods, models and materials.* New York: McGraw-Hill.

Eccles, J. S. (1987). Gender roles and women's achievement-related decisions. *Psychology of Women Quarterly, 11,* 135–172.

Hackett, G. (1985). The role of mathematics self-efficacy in the choice of math-related majors of college women and men: A path analysis. *Journal of Counseling Psychology, 32,* 47–56.

Hackett, G., & Betz, N. E. (1981). A self-efficacy approach to the career development of women. *Journal of Vocational Behavior, 18,* 326–339.

Hackett, G., & Betz, N. E. (1989). An exploration of the mathematics self-efficacy/mathematics performance correspondence. *Journal for Research in Mathematics Education, 20,* 261–273.

Hackett, G., Betz, N. E., O'Halloran, M. S., & Romac, D. S. (1990). Effects of verbal and mathematics task performance on task and career self-efficacy and interest. *Journal of Counseling Psychology, 37,* 169–177.

Hackett, G., & Campbell, N. K. (1987). Task self-efficacy and task interest as a function of performance on a gender-neutral task. *Journal of Vocational Behavior, 30,* 203–215.

Hackett, G., Casas, J. M., Betz, N. E., & Rocha-Singh, I. (1987, August). *Self-efficacy, gender and race: Relationships to progress in engineering majors.* Paper presented at the meeting of the American Psychological Association, New York.

Hackett, G., & Lent, R. W. (in press). Theoretical advances and current inquiry in career psychology. In S. D. Brown & R. W. Lent (Eds.), *Handbook of counseling psychology* (2nd ed.). New York: Wiley.

Hackett, G., Lent, R. W., & Greenhaus, J. H. (1991). Advances in vocational theory and research: A 20-year retrospective. *Journal of Vocational Behavior, 38,* 3–38.

Hannah, J. S., & Kahn, S. E. (1989). The relationship of socioeconomic status and gender to the occupational choices of grade 12 students. *Journal of Vocational Behavior, 34,* 161–178.

Holland, J. L. (1985). *Making vocational choices* (2nd ed.). Englewood Cliffs, NJ: Prentice-Hall.

Krumboltz, J. D., Mitchell, A. M., & Jones, G. B. (1976). A social learning theory of career selection. *The Counseling Psychologist, 6,* 71–81.

Lapan, R. T., Boggs, K. R., & Morrill, W. H. (1989). Self-efficacy as a mediator of Investigative and Realistic General Occupational Themes on the Strong-Campbell Interest Inventory. *Journal of Counseling Psychology, 36,* 176–182.

Layton, P. L. (1984). *Self-efficacy, locus of control, career salience, and women's career development.* Unpublished doctoral dissertation, University of Minnesota, Minneapolis.

Lent, R. W., Brown, S. D., & Larkin, K. C. (1984). Relation of self-efficacy expectations to academic achievement and persistence. *Journal of Counseling Psychology, 31,* 356–362.

Lent, R. W., Brown, S. D., & Larkin, K. C. (1986). Self-efficacy in the prediction of academic performance and perceived career options. *Journal of Counseling Psychology, 33,* 165–169.

Lent, R. W., Brown, S. D., & Larkin, K. C. (1987). Comparison of three theoretically derived variables in predicting career and academic behavior: Self-efficacy, interest congruence, and consequence thinking. *Journal of Counseling Psychology, 34,* 293–298.

Lent, R. W., & Hackett, G. (1987). Career self-efficacy: Empirical status and future directions [Monograph]. *Journal of Vocational Behavior, 30,* 347–382.

Lent, R. W., Larkin, K. C., & Brown, S. D. (1989). Relation of self-efficacy to inventoried vocational interests. *Journal of Vocational Behavior, 34,* 279–288.

Lent, R. W., Lopez, F. G., & Bieschke, K. J. (in press). Mathematics self-efficacy: Sources and relation to science-based career choice. *Journal of Counseling Psychology.*

Matsui, T., Ikeda, H., & Ohnishi, R. (1989). Relations of sex-typed socializations to career self-efficacy expectations of college students. *Journal of Vocational Behavior, 35,* 1–16.

Osipow, S. H. (1986). Career issues through the life span. In M. S. Pallak & R. O. Perloff (Eds.), *Psychology and work: Productivity, change, and employment* (pp. 141–168). Washington, DC: American Psychological Association.

Osipow, S. H. (1990). Convergence in theories of career choice and development: Review and prospect. *Journal of Vocational Behavior, 36,* 122–131.

Post-Kammer, P., & Smith, P. L. (1985). Sex differences in career self-efficacy, consideration, and interests of eighth and ninth graders. *Journal of Counseling Psychology, 32,* 551–559.

Post-Kammer, P. & Smith, P. L. (1986). Sex differences in math and science career self-efficacy among disadvantaged students. *Journal of Vocational Behavior, 29,* 89–101.

Rotberg, H. L., Brown, D., & Ware, W. B. (1987). Career self-efficacy expectations and perceived range of career options in community college students. *Journal of Counseling Psychology, 34,* 164–170.

Smith, R. J., Arnkoff, D. B., & Wright, T. L. (1990). Test anxiety and academic competence: A comparison of alternative models. *Journal of Counseling Psychology, 37,* 313–321.

Super, D. E. (1990). A life-span, life-space approach to career development. In D. Brown, L. Brooks, and Associates (Eds.), *Career choice and development* (pp. 197–261). San Francisco: Jossey-Bass.

Taylor, K. M., & Betz, N. E. (1983). Applications of self-efficacy theory to the understanding and treatment of career indecision. *Journal of Vocational Behavior, 22,* 63–81.

Taylor, K. M., & Popma, J. (1990). An examination of the relationships among career decision-making self-efficacy, career salience, locus of control, and vocational indecision. *Journal of Vocational Behavior, 37,* 17–31.

Wheeler, K. G. (1983). Comparisons of self-efficacy and expectancy models of occupational preferences for college males and females. *Journal of Occupational Psychology, 56,* 73–78.

11

The Achievement-Related Perceptions of Children With Learning Problems: A Developmental Analysis

BARBARA G. LICHT
Florida State University

The achievement-related perceptions of children with learning problems have received considerable attention over the past decade. Several theorists (e.g., Licht, 1983; Thomas, 1979) have proposed that when children experience repeated failures during the early school years, they will develop the perception that they do not have the ability to master their schoolwork. This perception will lead to low levels of effort and persistence, particularly on difficult tasks. Consistent with this, children with learning problems often show high rates of off-task behavior (Bryan, 1974; McKinney & Feagans, 1984). High rates of off-task behavior will, in turn, contribute to further academic difficulties (Hoge & Luce, 1979), which will reinforce the children's perceptions that they are incapable of succeeding in school. Although it may be realistic for children with learning problems to doubt their abilities, this self-perception can lead them to perform more poorly than one would predict on the basis of their original learning problems.[1]

---

[1] Research on the achievement-related perceptions of children with learning problems has come from several theoretical perspectives, including self-efficacy, locus of control, attributional, learned helplessness, and perceived competence/self-concept of ability. These perspectives differ in the theoretical assumptions, constructs, and measurement operations employed, but all perspectives share one common assumption—namely, that for children to persist in the face of difficulty, they must perceive their efforts as useful in reaching their goal. Thus, distinctions between these perspectives are not made in this chapter.

Evidence to support this conceptualization has accumulated over the years. For example, children with learning problems are more likely than their normally achieving peers to attribute their difficulties to low ability; and children with learning problems are less likely to see their efforts as useful in overcoming academic difficulties (Licht, Kistner, Ozkaragoz, Shapiro, & Clausen, 1985; Pearl, Bryan, & Donahue, 1980). This conceptualization also is supported by a large body of research showing that children's achievement-related perceptions have an impact on their achievement efforts. (For reviews, see Dweck & Elliott, 1983; Meece & Courtney, this volume; Pintrich & Schrauben, this volume.) For example, the perception that one's difficulties are due to low ability contributes to poor persistence on difficult tasks and to poor academic gains over the years. Further, this finding holds for children with learning problems (Kistner, Osborne, & LeVerrier, 1988) as well as normal children.

Despite empirical support for this conceptualization, a body of *developmental* research raises a dilemma. This developmental research suggests that young children are relatively robust to the debilitating effects of failure. In kindergarten and first grade, most children show an overly optimistic perception of their abilities. It is not until children are 7 years old (second grade) that their self-ratings of ability begin to lower and begin to show a significant relationship with more objective ratings (Stipek, 1981). In addition, the tendency for children who doubt their abilities to show poor persistence in the face of difficulty does not emerge clearly until children are about 10 years old (Nicholls & Miller, 1984). In light of these developmental data, it becomes difficult to argue that early school failures contribute to the off-task behavior that children with learning problems show in the early school years. The purpose of this chapter is to resolve this dilemma. '

First, I review developmental research suggesting that in the first couple years of school, children are relatively invulnerable to the negative motivational consequences of failure. I then argue that these data may be underestimating the vulnerability of young children. Specifically, I describe some recent research to show that under certain circumstances, children as young as preschool and kindergarten will lower their self-evaluations of ability in response to failure, and some will even show a maladaptive pattern of low persistence and negative affect that was not considered possible until children were 10 years old. Next, I review research on the achievement-related perceptions of children who have experienced learning problems. This research suggests that although children with learning problems are likely to develop the perception that their abilities are low, this is not true for all children who experience serious learning problems. I examine some of the variables that appear to mediate these individual differences. In the final section of this chapter I examine some teacher interventions for enhancing students' achievement-related perceptions and behavior. I focus on interventions that have been shown to be effective when administered by real teachers in real classroom settings.

Although a variety of achievement-related perceptions (e.g., achievement standards, values) influence and are influenced by children's academic achievements, this chapter focuses primarily on children's *ability-related* perceptions (e.g., self-evaluations of ability).

DEVELOPMENTAL DIFFERENCES IN CHILDREN'S ABILITY-RELATED PERCEPTIONS

Studies of children in kindergarten and first grade typically find that these children give unrealistically high self-evaluations of their academic achievements and abilities. In fact, the majority of children this age give themselves the highest possible rating (Miller, 1987; Stipek, 1981). Consequently, there is virtually no relationship between these children's actual abilities and their perceptions of their own abilities. It is not until children are at least 7 years old (typically second grade) that low achievers give themselves lower ratings than do high achievers. Even then, significant differences in self-evaluations are found only when children at the top of the class are compared to children at the bottom (Stipek, 1981). There seldom is a significant correlation (across all children) between children's self-evaluations and more objective evaluations (e.g., teacher ratings, achievement scores) until at least third grade (Nicholls, 1978, 1979).

These developmental changes appear to be due, in large part, to developmental changes in children's understanding of what academic ability means. Specifically, it is not until about second grade that most children understand the "normative conception" of ability (Butler, 1989; Miller, 1987; Nicholls, 1978). This means that children understand that their ability is judged on the basis of how they perform relative to their peers. The implication of this understanding is that to feel smart, a child needs to perform better than his or her peers. Before children understand the normative conception, they define ability in terms of task mastery and/or effort, which enables young children to feel smart as long as they are mastering tasks or making progress (Nicholls & Miller, 1984).

Consequently, children who are progressing much more slowly than their classmates could still maintain the highest possible self-evaluation until they understand the normative conception. Ironically, because children with learning problems are slower to develop this understanding (Miller, 1987), there may be a period of time when low achievers actually show more positive self-evaluations than do high achievers. Miller (1987) found this trend among first graders, but not second graders. Presumably by second grade, the low achievers had begun to understand the normative conception of ability.

Developmental differences in children's understanding of what ability means are not due entirely to *general* cognitive development. For example, it appears that young children do not understand the normative conception, in part, because kindergarten and first-grade teachers generally do not emphasize normatively based evaluations (Stipek & Daniels, 1988).

Another important development in children's understanding of ability is the "differentiation of effort from ability." Research shows that when most children are about 10 years old, they understand the notion of a "compensatory" or *negative* relationship between effort and ability (Nicholls, 1978; Nicholls & Miller, 1984). For example, a child who is low in ability must compensate for this with higher effort. Thus, if two children achieve the same outcome (e.g., both get 90% correct on a test), but one tried harder than the other, the one who tried harder will be judged as less intelligent. In contrast, children younger than 10 generally see effort and ability as *positively* related. Thus, if two children achieve the same outcome, the one who tried harder will be judged as smarter.

Consistent with the tendency to see effort and ability as positively related, children younger than 10 generally view ability as modifiable. That is, increased effort should lead to increased success and ability. In contrast, older children and adults are more likely to view ability as a relatively stable capacity (Nicholls & Miller, 1984).

Theoretically, the differentiation of effort and ability has important implications for how children respond to their academic difficulties. Although children between the ages of 7 and 9 should lower their self-evaluations of ability when they experience frequent difficulties, their low self-evaluations should not lead to low persistence. If children believe their abilities are modifiable through their efforts, continued effort in the face of difficulty should be seen as the road to success and enhanced ability. Children who view ability as a relatively stable capacity should be less optimistic.[2]

---

[2] *Understanding* the notion of ability as a stable capacity does not insure that children (or adults) will *believe* this notion is true (Dweck & Leggett, 1988). Further, believing in

Two studies provide support for the prediction that children who have not yet differentiated ability and effort will not show reductions of effort and performance in the face of failure. Rholes, Blackwell, Jordan, and Walters (1980) compared children in kindergarten, first, third, and fifth grades in terms of whether they lowered their efforts after confronting failure. Within each grade, half the children (determined randomly) experienced success on a series of hidden picture puzzles, and half the children were presented with unsolvable puzzles (failure). Persistence was assessed on a subsequent hidden picture puzzle, which was the same for all children. As predicted, it was only the fifth graders (mean age 10.9 years) who showed less persistence after failure than after success. Miller (1985) manipulated success and failure on a Matching Familiar Figures task, and he assessed performance on a subsequent task (anagrams) that was of moderate difficulty for all children. There was a significant tendency for sixth graders, but not second graders, to perform more poorly on the anagrams after failure than after success.

Understanding the compensatory relationship also affects how children make inferences about ability on the basis of a teacher's praise, rewards, or criticism (Barker & Graham, 1987; Meyer, 1982; Miller, Hom, McDowell, & Gionfriddo, 1989). Because teachers generally give praise or tangible rewards when they believe children are trying hard, children of *all ages* infer higher effort on the part of children who were praised or rewarded than on the part of children who performed equally well, but who were not praised or rewarded. When children understand the compensatory relationship (i.e., they infer that the child who tried harder was less intelligent), they will infer less ability on the part of children who were praised or rewarded. In a similar vein, children of *all ages* infer less effort on the part of children who receive criticism (i.e., indications of displeasure that go beyond corrective feedback). Thus, "mature" reasoners will attribute higher ability to the children who are criticized.

One implication of these data is that when children understand the compensatory relationship, teachers may be unable to raise the confidence of low achievers by praising or rewarding them for small accomplishments. In contrast, for very young children, praise and rewards should have more positive consequences because inferences of high

---

the "mature" conception of ability does not insure that one will *employ* it in all situations (Nicholls & Miller, 1984). Most probably, it is believing and employing the mature conception (rather than understanding alone) that increases one's vulnerability to failure. Nonetheless, individuals who are ten years and older should be more likely than younger children to believe and employ it as a result of their greater understanding.

effort should lead to inferences of high ability (Barker & Graham, 1987). Again, we see reason to expect less vulnerability on the part of young children.

Have We Underestimated the Vulnerability of Young Children?

The research described in the previous section leaves the impression that young children are relatively invulnerable to the debilitating effects of failure. However, some very recent research shows that under certain circumstances, even children as young as 5 years will make low self-evaluations and will show reduced persistence following failure.

Butler (1990) found that when 5-year-olds were asked to evaluate their performances against a tangible criterion of mastery (i.e., they evaluated how closely they copied a drawing that was placed in front of them), they were surprisingly accurate. These 5-year-olds did not show inflated self-evaluations. Indeed, the correlation between their self-evaluations and "objective" evaluations made by adults was moderately strong, and was not significantly different from the correlations found for 7- and 10-year-olds in this condition. In contrast, more typical developmental trends emerged when children were asked to evaluate their performances against a less tangible, normatively based criterion (i.e., whether they made the "best" copy). Five-year-olds gave inflated self-evaluations, and their self-evaluations were not significantly correlated with the adults' evaluations. The correlations for 7- and 10-year-olds in this condition were moderate and high, respectively. Thus, very young children are able to recognize when they have performed poorly when the criterion of success is very objective and tangible.

A naturalistic experiment by Stipek and Daniels (1988) showed that under certain circumstances, kindergartners can lower their self-evaluations of ability, even when these self-evaluations are in normative comparison terms. This study compared kindergartners and fourth graders from two types of classrooms. In one type, referred to as *high salience*, normative comparisons were salient, and teacher evaluations were frequent. For example, on most written assignments, fourth graders received letter grades and kindergartners received happy and sad faces. In the *low salience* classrooms, normative evaluations were de-emphasized, and the curriculum was highly individualized. Although the self-evaluations of fourth graders did not vary across classrooms, kindergartners from high salience classrooms gave significantly lower assessments of how smart they thought they were relative to their peers than did kindergartners from low salience classrooms. Importantly, kindergartners from the high salience classrooms did not rate their abilities more positively than did the fourth graders. Thus, even the normatively based self-evaluations of kindergartners can deflate if they are exposed to frequent and salient normative feedback. However, consistent with earlier research, kindergartners showed more optimism about the future. When asked to rate how well they thought they would perform in the next grade, kindergartners from both types of classrooms gave significantly higher estimates than did both groups of fourth graders.

Recent work by Dweck and colleagues (Dweck, in press) provides evidence that the persistence of young children can be adversely affected by failure. In a series of studies, preschoolers, kindergartners, and first graders worked on jigsaw puzzles. The first three puzzles were unsolvable. That is, children only could place half the pieces in the alloted time. The fourth was solvable. Afterward, children were shown the same four puzzles and were given a choice of which one they would like to try again. To insure that children correctly recalled their performances, the four puzzles were presented exactly as they were when the child stopped working on them. Children were classified as *persisters* if they chose one of the uncompleted puzzles, and they were classified as *nonpersisters* if they chose to rework the one puzzle they already completed. Across three separate studies (Cain & Dweck; Hebert & Dweck; Smiley & Dweck, as reported in Dweck, in press), 35%–40% of the children were classified as nonpersisters.

The nonpersisters showed a maladaptive pattern of self-perceptions and affect that was previously found only among older children. When asked if they thought they could finish any of the uncompleted puzzles if they had lots of time, nonpersisters were more likely than persisters to say they could not. Nonpersisters even expressed more pessimism about their future success on new puzzles. Further, nonpersisters tended to explain their choice of puzzles with "challenge-avoidant" reasons (e.g., the puzzle was easy), whereas persisters were more likely to give "challenge-seeking" reasons (e.g., wanting to figure it out). Finally, nonpersisters were more likely than persisters to show a deterioration in their mood over the course of the three unsolvable puzzles.

In conclusion, the developmental literature shows that young children are considerably less vulnerable than are older children to the debilitating effects of failure. However, this does not imply that children are invulnerable to the failures that occur during the very early school years. The vulnerability of young children seems most likely to emerge when failures are tangible, salient, and frequent.

THE ABILITY-RELATED PERCEPTIONS OF CHILDREN
WITH LEARNING PROBLEMS

In light of research showing that even preschoolers and kindergartners can be adversely affected by failure, it is important to examine the ability-related perceptions of children who experience repeated failures in the early school years. Accordingly, a number of researchers have examined the perceptions of children with learning disabilities (LD).

In theory, children with LD are average or above average in general intelligence, but have a deficit in one or more specific cognitive process (e.g., processes involved in understanding language). Approximately 5% of public school children in the United States have been diagnosed as learning disabled; and the principle academic areas in which they experience difficulty are reading, spelling, and/or math. Although there is considerable controversy over the definition of LD and over the methods used to diagnose children (Torgesen, 1991), there is no debating the fact that these children all experience frequent academic failures that begin when they are very young.

Until recently, virtually all research on the achievement-related perceptions of children with LD was conducted on children who were in third grade and older. These studies generally show that learning-disabled children rate their cognitive/academic abilities significantly lower than do their peers (Grolnick & Ryan, 1990; Kistner, Haskett, White, & Robbins, 1987), and they are less optimistic about their future attainment (Rogers & Saklofske, 1985). Children with LD are more likely than normally achieving children to attribute their difficulties to insufficient ability, and they are less likely to attribute their difficulties to insufficient effort (Licht et al., 1985; Pearl, 1982). (For reviews, see Licht, in press; Licht & Kistner, 1986.)

Children who have been diagnosed by their schools as having LD are not the only poor achievers who doubt their abilities. Similar findings have been reported for children who have received neither the label nor remedial services, but who would meet the diagnostic criteria for LD (Chapman, 1988; Pearl et al., 1980). In addition, children identified solely on the basis of low achievement show more negative self-evaluations than do average and high achievers (Licht, Stader, & Swenson, 1989; Marsh, Smith, Barnes, & Butler, 1983).

With respect to the self-perceptions that children with LD are likely to show *before* third grade, research reviewed earlier suggests two seemingly opposite predictions. The frequent and salient failures that these children experience should lead them to perceive their abilities less favorably than would their normally achieving peers. However, because children with LD should be slower to understand the normative conception of ability, one would predict that very young children with LD would be more likely to overestimate their abilities than would their peers.

A study of Israeli first and second graders suggests that both predictions can be true at the same time. Consistent with the first prediction, Priel and Leshem (1990) found that children with LD gave significantly lower self-ratings of cognitive ability than did their normally achieving peers. However, children with LD did not rate themselves nearly as low as their teachers rated them. Thus, when children's self-ratings were compared to the teachers' ratings, children with LD showed significantly more overestimation than did their peers.

Vaughn, Haager, Hogan, and Kouzekanani (1991) also examined the self-ratings of cognitive ability made by very young children with LD. This study followed the same children from kindergarten (prior to being diagnosed) through fourth grade. The self-ratings of these learning-disabled children were not significantly different from those of their peers at any point during this study. As discussed next, there are numerous reasons why some children who experience years of academic problems do not lower their self-evaluations.

Individual Differences Among Children With Learning Problems

Although children who perform poorly in school tend to develop negative perceptions of their abilities, considerable individual differences exist. As suggested, some children who frequently experience failure maintain confidence in their ability to master their schoolwork, and they persist toward this end (Kistner et al., 1988; Licht & Kistner, 1986). (It also is of note that there are a number of highly successful students who perceive their abilities as low; Phillips, 1987.) It is necessary to understand the variables that contribute to these individual differences if we are to fully understand how failure influences children's ability-related perceptions.

As suggested earlier, some children (perhaps as many as 35%–40%) may be vulnerable to the debilitating effects of failure even before they begin formal schooling. Although speculative, Dweck (in press) presented data to suggest that these vulnerable children may come from highly evaluative and/or punitive home environments. When asked to role-play how they thought adult evaluators (e.g., mother, father) would respond to their puzzle performance, nonpersisters were significantly more likely than persisters to role-play punishment. One also might speculate that the parents of nonpersisters were more likely to stress meeting specific criteria (e.g., being "right") rather than stressing the process of trying hard to learn (Ames & Archer, 1987).

Research by Grolnick and Ryan (1989) suggests that children may be less vulnerable to failure if their parents encourage "autonomy," for example, by giving the child choices and including the child in decision making. Encouragement of autonomy is one way parents can convey to the child that he or she has the ability to solve problems. Consistent with this, some studies suggest that children's perceptions of their abilities may be influenced more by parental appraisals of their children's abilities than by grades or test scores (Entwisle & Baker, 1983; Parsons, Adler, & Kaczala, 1982; Phillips, 1987).

Research on classroom grouping suggests another factor that may contribute to individual differences. When children are mature enough to use normative comparisons in assessing their abilities, their self-assessments should be influenced by the ability level of their classmates. Reuman (1989) found that children in low-ability classrooms (between-classroom grouping) rated their ability higher than did children in low-ability groups within heterogenous classrooms (within-classroom grouping). Presumably, this is because the most immediate social comparisons (i.e., classmates) for children in low ability classrooms are other low ability children. Thus, they will compare more favorably than if their classmates also included average and high-ability children. This same process can explain why children in high-ability classrooms rated their abilities lower than did children in high-ability groups within heterogenous classrooms. In a similar vein, students who attend low-achieving schools rate their academic abilities higher than do equally able students who attend high-achieving schools (Marsh, 1987).

Interestingly, teachers' evaluations of their students seem to be influenced by the same social comparison process. Reuman (1989) found that teachers gave higher grades to children in low ability classrooms than to children in low ability groups within heterogenous classrooms; and they gave lower grades to children in high ability classrooms than to those in high ability groups within heterogenous classrooms. This pattern of grades undoubtedly is part of the reason why children's self-perceptions vary as a function of their classroom grouping practices (Marsh, 1987).

Most children diagnosed as having LD receive "resource room" instruction for 1 or 2 hours daily. Theoretically, spending time in the resource room could enhance children's self-perceptions by increasing the chances that they will use other children with LD for social comparisons. Although receiving resource room instruction some-times results in higher self-evaluations (e.g., Battle & Blowers, 1982), frequently it does not (e.g., Rogers & Saklofski, 1985; Vaughn et al., 1991). This may be because most children with LD spend the majority of their day in a regular classroom. Thus, they are most likely to use regular classroom children for social comparisons (Renick & Harter, 1989).

Another variable that may contribute to individual differences is the degree to which teachers emphasize normative evaluations. Because children with learning problems are, by definition, performing more poorly than their peers, making normative evaluations salient should decrease their ability perceptions. Research shows that the salience of normative evaluations can influence students of all ages (Ames & Ames, 1984; Butler, 1990), although younger children can sometimes be more strongly effected than older ones (Stipek & Daniels, 1988).

The degree to which children manifest behavior problems is another contributor to individual differences. Among children with LD, the ones with the lowest self-evaluations of their academic abilities are the ones with "externalizing" behavior problems (e.g., hyperactivity, inat-tention, acting out) (Durrant, Cunningham, & Voelker, 1990). Most probably, this is because behavior problem children (with or without learning problems) receive the most negative teacher feedback (Bro-phy, 1985; Brophy & Rohrkemper, 1981). Although much of this negative feedback is directed at the children's disruptive behavior rather than at their intellectual abilities, the distinction between bad behavior and low ability may not be apparent to young children (Dweck, in press). For example, when first graders were asked what it meant to be intelligent or smart, many of them included characteristics such as being "polite" and being "nice" (Yussen & Kane, 1985).

Consistent with the finding that learning-disabled children with behavior problems have the most negative perceptions of their abili-ties, these children also show the worst long-term academic prognosis. McKinney and Speece (1986) found that learning-disabled children with attention deficits and/or conduct problems (approximately 54% of children with LD) were less likely to make progress in reading comprehension over a 3-year period than were learning-disabled chil-dren who were relatively free of maladaptive classroom behaviors (approximately 35%) or learning-disabled children who were exces-sively withdrawn and dependent (approximately 11%).

Although most disruptive classroom behavior should elicit negative teacher feedback, different *types* of disruptive behavior may elicit different types of feedback. For example, teachers are more likely to use highly punitive techniques for defiance and aggression, and they are more likely to attempt "self-control" training for inattention and overactivity (Brophy, 1985; Brophy & Rohrkemper, 1981).

Although feedback for defiance and aggression is more negative, it may also convey to children that they have the ability to control their behavior. In contrast, the feedback given for inattention and overactivity may convey that the children are not capable of controlling themselves. Thus, inattention and overactivity may be more likely to result in low self-evaluations of ability.

Hartsfield, Licht, Swenson, and Thiele (1989) provided data consistent with the prediction just given. Regular classroom children in Grades 3–5 rated their academic competence, behavioral conduct, social competence, physical appearance, athletic skill, and global self-worth. In addition, teachers rated each child in terms of his or her aggressiveness and overactivity/inattention. High ratings of overactivity/inattention predicted low self-ratings of academic competence, behavioral conduct, and global self-worth. These relationships held even when controlling for children's academic achievement and degree of aggressiveness. In contrast, after controlling for children's overactivity/inattention, aggressiveness did not predict low self-ratings on any of the scales.

In conclusion, the research reviewed suggests a wide range of factors that can contribute to individual differences in how children interpret and respond to their failures. These include parental encouragement and feedback, the ability level of children's classmates, the degree to which normative evaluations are emphasized in the classroom, and the degree to which children show certain types of behavior problems.

IMPLICATIONS FOR TREATMENT IN THE CLASSROOM

This chapter has suggested several classroom practices that could influence children's perceptions of their abilities. However, changing some of these practices may have negative consequences as well as positive ones. For example, although between-classroom grouping may enhance the self-evaluations of low-ability students, it is likely to *lower* the self-evaluations of high-ability students. Thus, although the research reviewed in this chapter helps us understand why children of equal ability often have different achievement-related perceptions, not all this research translates into practical recommendations for teachers. In this section, I focus on those treatment strategies that have been successfully implemented by teachers in actual classrooms.

Providing certain types of written comments on homework assignments and exams can enhance students' perceptions of their abilities and their actual achievements. Elawar and Corno (1985) trained sixth-grade teachers to write comments on their students' math homework assignments. These comments provided specific information about what the student did well and what he or she needed to do differently (e.g., "You know how to get percent but the computation is wrong in this instance . . ." [teacher underlined errors]). These comments are referred to as "subject-matter-oriented" comments (Krampen, 1987). Treatment students received these comments on math assignments three times each week for 10 weeks. At the end of this period, treatment students had significantly higher scores than control students in math achievement, liking of math, and self-esteem.

Krampen (1987) also evaluated the use of "subject-matter" comments by real mathematics teachers. However, these comments were written on the students' (6th–10th graders) exams. "Individually oriented" comments also were evaluated. These stressed how the student's current performance compared to his or her previous exam performance (e.g., "In comparison with your prior performance, you have improved a lot . . ."). Subject-matter comments significantly enhanced students' exam performance, report card grades, and expectancies for improvement in math. However, these effects were not as strong as the effects of individually oriented comments, which were particularly helpful for low achievers. Further, the magnitude of improvement from subject-matter comments was not as strong as that reported by Elawar and Corno (1985).

The fact that Elawar and Corno's teachers gave subject-matter comments on the students' homework and Krampen's teachers gave these comments on *exams* may account for the difference in the magnitude of their results. Comments that focus on what to do differently should be more beneficial when children are still mastering the material (i.e., on homework) than when the unit is over (i.e., on the exam). It also is possible that subject-matter comments were more effective in the Elawar and Corno study because the students received them more frequently.

It should be noted that most of the beneficial effects of written comments were not maintained after the teachers discontinued the comments (Krampen, 1987). This highlights the importance of developing interventions that teachers can *permanently* incorporate into their teaching regimes. Written teacher comments appear to have this potential.

Future research needs to evaluate these teacher comments with younger children. Because young children tend to feel smart when they show improvements, individually oriented comments should be effective. In addition, even kindergartners can effectively utilize concrete information about how to master a task (Butler, 1989, 1990). Thus, subject-matter comments also should be beneficial. For children too young to read, it may be possible to represent this feedback pictorially so it could be given on worksheets.

Another strategy that is often recommended for enhancing children's ability-related perceptions is attribution retraining (AR). Children are typically taught to attribute their failures to insufficient effort and/or improper strategies; and they are taught to attribute their successes to their efforts and/or their abilities. For example, when a child fails to complete some problems, the trainer might say, "You did not finish the problems. You need to try harder." The trainer might also demonstrate how an effortful application of a particular strategy might have been used to solve the problems. When children perform well, the trainer might say, "You have done well because you put a lot of effort into it."

AR has received considerable attention (for reviews, see Licht & Kistner, 1986; Licht, in press), and it can have impressive effects, especially when combined with training in specific task strategies (Borkowski, Weyhing, & Carr, 1988). However, the effectiveness of AR as a *teacher-administered* treatment has not been clearly demonstrated. Further, a study by Craven, Marsh, and Debus (1991) suggests that it may be difficult for teachers to implement AR in the classroom. Craven et al. trained teachers to give attributional feedback to children in Grades 3–6. Teachers gave these comments verbally in the context of their normal teaching routines. Results showed virtually no beneficial effects of this teacher-administered intervention, even though a similar treatment administered by experimenters enhanced students' perceptions of their academic abilities.

The ineffectiveness of the teacher-administered AR may have been due to the difficulty of making these comments frequently enough in the context of an ongoing lesson. In addition, AR is most likely to be effective when the trainer demonstrates in a *tangible* way that the child's efforts are important (see Licht, in press, for discussion). This may be best accomplished individually or in very small groups.

A number of additional strategies have been shown to enhance the achievement-related perceptions of children with learning problems. These include teaching children to set specific, proximal goals and a variety of modeling interventions (Schunk, 1989). Although teachers should be able to implement some of these strategies in the classroom, these strategies have not been systematically investigated in this context.

CONCLUSIONS

Developmental research on children's achievement-related perceptions initially led us to be optimistic about children with learning problems. This research suggested that at least for the first couple years of school, children are invulnerable to the negative motivational effects of failure. More recent research has tempered our optimism by showing that children as young as preschool can be adversely effected by failures that are tangible and salient.

Nonetheless, the negative motivational impact of repeated failure is not inevitable. Research on individual differences suggests that the degree to which children with learning problems will lower their self-evaluations and persistence depends on their home environment, the ability level of their classmates, the degree to which normative comparisons are salient in the classroom, and the degree to which children have certain types of behavior problems. Further, there are specific interventions (e.g., written comments) that teachers can implement to enhance children's self-evaluations. Thus, it is possible for children with learning problems to maintain the belief that they have the ability to overcome their difficulties, and this belief is likely to have a positive impact on their persistence and academic progress. Future research is expected to find additional ways to foster this belief.

ACKNOWLEDGMENT

I wish to thank Carol Dweck and the editors for their helpful comments on an earlier draft and Scott Saunders for his help with the library work.

REFERENCES

Ames, C., & Ames, R. (1984). Systems of student and teacher motivation: Toward a qualitative definition. *Journal of Educational Psychology, 76,* 535–556.

Ames, C., & Archer, J. (1987). Mothers' beliefs about the role of ability and effort in school learning. *Journal of Educational Psychology, 79,* 409–414.

Barker, G. P., & Graham, S. (1987). Developmental study of praise and blame as attributional cues. *Journal of Educational Psychology, 79,* 62–66.

Battle, J. & Blowers, T. (1982). A longitudinal comparative study of the self-esteem of students in regular and special education classes. *Journal of Learning Disabilities, 15,* 100–105.

Borkowski, J. G., Weyhing, R. S., & Carr, M. (1988). Effects of attributional retraining on strategy-based reading comprehension in learning-disabled students. *Journal of Educational Psychology, 80,* 46–53.

Brophy, J. (1985). Teachers' expectations, motives, and goals for working with problem students. In C. Ames & R. Ames (Eds.), *Research on motivation in education, Vol. 2: The classroom milieu* (pp. 175–214). Orlando, FL: Academic Press.

Brophy, J. E., & Rohrkemper, M. M. (1981). The influence of problem ownership on teachers' perceptions of and strategies for coping with problem students. *Journal of Educational Psychology, 73,* 295–311.

Bryan, T. S. (1974). Observational analysis of classroom behaviors of children with learning disabilities. *Journal of Learning Disabilities, 7,* 26–34.

Butler, R. (1989). Mastery versus ability appraisal: A developmental study of children's observations of peers' work. *Child Development, 60,* 1350–1361.

Butler, R. (1990). The effects of mastery and competitive conditions on self-assessment at different ages. *Child Development, 61,* 201–210.

Chapman, J. W. (1988). Cognitive-motivational characteristics and academic achievement of learning disabled children: A longitudinal study. *Journal of Educational Psychology, 80,* 357–365.

Craven, R. G., Marsh, H. W., & Debus, R. L. (1991). Effects of internally focused feedback and attributional feedback on enhancement of academic self-concept. *Journal of Educational Psychology, 83,* 17–27.

Durrant, J. E., Cunningham, C. E., & Voelker, S. (1990). Academic, social, and general self-concepts of behavioral subgroups of learning disabled children. *Journal of Educational Psychology, 82,* 657–663.

Dweck, C. S. (in press). Self-theories and goals: Their role in motivation, personality and development. In R. Dienstbier (Ed.), *Nebraska Symposium on Motivation (1990).* Lincoln: University of Nebraska Press.

Dweck, C. S., & Elliott, E. S. (1983). Achievement motivation. In E. M. Hetherington (Ed.), *Handbook of child psychology* (Vol 4, pp. 643–691). New York: Wiley.

Dweck, C. S., & Leggett, E. L. (1988). A social-cognitive approach to motivation and personality. *Psychological Review, 95,* 256–273.

Elawar, M. C., & Corno, L. (1985). A factorial experiment in teachers' written feedback on student homework: Changing teacher behavior a little rather than a lot. *Journal of Educational Psychology, 77,* 162–173.

Entwisle, D. R., & Baker, D. P. (1983). Gender and young children's expectations for performance in arithmetic. *Developmental Psychology, 19,* 200–209.

Grolnick, W. S., & Ryan, R. M. (1989). Parent styles associated with children's self-regulation and competence in school. *Journal of Educational Psychology, 81,* 143–154.

Grolnick, W. S., & Ryan, R. M. (1990). Self-perceptions, motivation, and adjustment in children with learning disabilities: A multiple group comparison study. *Journal of Learning Disabilities, 23,* 177–184.

Hartsfield, F., Licht, B., Swenson, C., & Thiele, C. (1989, August). *Control beliefs and behavior problems of elementary school children.* Paper presented at the meeting of the American Psychological Association, New Orleans, LA.

Hoge, R. D., & Luce, S. (1979). Predicting academic achievement from classroom behavior. *Review of Educational Research, 49,* 479–496.

Kistner, J., Haskett, M., White, K., & Robbins, F. (1987). Perceived competence and self-worth of LD and normally achieving students. *Learning Disability Quarterly, 10,* 37–44.

Kistner, J. A., Osborne, M., & LeVerrier, L. (1988). Causal attributions of learning-disabled children: Developmental patterns and relation to academic progress. *Journal of Educational Psychology, 80,* 82–89.

Krampen, G. (1987). Differential effects of teacher comments. *Journal of Educational Psychology, 79,* 137–146.

Licht, B. G. (1983). Cognitive-motivational factors that contribute to the achievement of learning-disabled children. *Journal of Learning Disabilities, 16,* 483–490.

Licht, B. G. (in press). Learning disabled children's achievement-related beliefs: Impact on their motivation and strategic learning. In L. Meltzer (Ed.), *Strategy assessment and instruction for students with learning disabilities: From theory to practice.* Austin, TX: ProEd.

Licht, B. G., & Kistner, J. A. (1986). Motivational problems of learning-disabled children: Individual differences and their implications for treatment. In J. K. Torgesen & B. Y. L. Wong (Eds.), *Psychological and educational perspectives on learning disabilities* (pp. 225–255). Orlando, FL: Academic Press.

Licht, B. G., Kistner, J. A., Ozkaragoz, T., Shapiro, S., & Clausen, L. (1985). Causal attributions of learning disabled children: Individual differences and their implications for persistence. *Journal of Educational Psychology, 77,* 208–216.

Licht, B. G., Stader, S. R., & Swenson, C. C. (1989). Children's achievement-related beliefs: Effects of academic area, sex, and achievement level. *Journal of Educational Research, 82,* 253–260.

Marsh, H. W. (1987). The big-fish-little-pond effect on academic self-concept. *Journal of Educational Psychology, 79,* 280–295.

Marsh, H. W., Smith, I. D., Barnes, J., & Butler, S. (1983). Self-concept: Reliability, stability, dimensionality, validity, and the measurement of change. *Journal of Educational Psychology, 75,* 772–790.

McKinney, J. D., & Feagans, L. (1984). Academic and behavioral characteristics of learning disabled children and average achievers: Longitudinal studies. *Learning Disability Quarterly, 7,* 251–264.

McKinney, J. D., & Speece, D. L. (1986). Academic consequences and longitudinal stability of behavioral subtypes of learning disabled children. *Journal of Educational Psychology, 78,* 365–372.

Meyer, W-U. (1982). Indirect communications about perceived ability estimates. *Journal of Educational Psychology, 74,* 888–897.

Miller, A. (1985). A developmental study of the cognitive basis of performance impairment after failure. *Journal of Personality and Social Psychology, 49,* 529–538.

Miller, A. (1987). Changes in academic self concept in early school years: The role of conceptions of ability. *Journal of Social Behavior and Personality, 2,* 551–558.

Miller, A., Hom, Jr., H. L., McDowell, J. W., & Gionfriddo, S. (1989). *Influence of developmental conceptions of ability, praise, blame and material rewards on judgments of ability and identification.* Paper presented at the meeting of the Society for Research in Child Development, Kansas City.

Nicholls, J. G. (1978). The development of the concepts of effort and ability, perception of academic attainment, and the understanding that difficult tasks require more ability. *Child Development, 49,* 800–814.

Nicholls, J. G. (1979). Development of perception of own attainment and causal attributions for success and failure in reading. *Journal of Educational Psychology, 71,* 94–99.

Nicholls, J. G. & Miller, A. (1984). Development and its discontents: The differentiation of the concept of ability. In J. G. Nicholls (Ed.), *The development of achievement motivation* (pp. 185–218). Greenwich, CT: JAI.

Parsons, J. E., Adler, T. F., & Kaczala, C. M. (1982). Socialization of achievement attitudes and beliefs: Parental influences. *Child Development, 53,* 310–321.

Pearl, R. A. (1982). LD children's attributions for success and failure: A replication with a labeled learning disabled sample. *Learning Disability Quarterly, 5,* 173–176.

Pearl, R. A., Bryan, T., & Donahue, M. (1980). Learning disabled children's attributions for success and failure. *Learning Disability Quarterly, 3,* 3–9.

Phillips, D. A. (1987). Socialization of perceived academic competence among highly competent children. *Child Development, 58,* 1308–1320.

Priel, B., & Leshem, T. (1990). Self-perceptions of first- and second-grade children with learning disabilities. *Journal of Learning Disabilities, 23,* 637–642.

Renick, M. J., & Harter, S. (1989). Impact of social comparisons on the developing self-perceptions of learning disabled students. *Journal of Educational Psychology, 81,* 631–638.

Reuman, D. A. (1989). How social comparison mediates the relation between ability-grouping practices and students' achievement expectancies in mathematics. *Journal of Educational Psychology, 81,* 178–189.

Rholes, W. S., Blackwell, J., Jordan, C., & Walters, C. (1980). A developmental study of learned helplessness. *Developmental Psychology, 16,* 616–624.

Rogers, H., & Saklofske, D. H. (1985). Self-concepts, locus of control and performance expectations of learning disabled children. *Journal of Learning Disabilities, 18,* 273–278.

Schunk, D. H. (1989). Self-efficacy and cognitive achievement: Implications for students with learning problems. *Journal of Learning Disabilities, 22,* 14–22.

Stipek, D. J. (1981). Children's perceptions of their own and their classmates' ability. *Journal of Educational Psychology, 73,* 404–410.

Stipek, D. J., & Daniels, D. H. (1988). Declining perceptions of competence: A consequence of changes in the child or in the educational environment. *Journal of Educational Psychology, 80,* 352–356.

Thomas, A. (1979). Learned helplessness and expectancy factors: Implications for research in learning disabilities. *Review of Educational Research, 49,* 208–221.

Torgesen, J. K. (1991). Learning disabilities: Historical and conceptual issues. In B.Y.L. Wong (Ed.) *Learning about learning disabilities.* San Diego, CA: Academic Press.

Vaughn, S., Haager, D., Hogan, A., & Kouzekanani, K. (1991, April). *Self-Concept and Peer Acceptance in Students with Learning Disabilities: A Four to Five Year Prospective Study.* Paper presented at the AERA annual meeting, Chicago, IL.

Yussen, S. R., & Kane, P. T. (1985). Children's conception of intelligence. In S. R. Yussen (Ed.), *The growth of reflection in children* (pp. 207–241). Orlando, FL: Academic Press.

IV

Goal Perceptions

Students as Educational Theorists

JOHN G. NICHOLLS
University of Illinois at Chicago

In this chapter I present a postmodern perspective wherein scientific and lay theories are seen as bound up with the values of the people doing the theorizing. Next I present evidence that children's theories about success in school accord with this postmodern view. Two broad theories of success are distinguished: one involving the desire for superior ability (ego orientation) and one the desire to comprehend (task orientation). Then I discuss less generic forms of task-oriented theories: theories about specific types of academic subjects. Finally, I illustrate the sort of discussion that can occur when teachers take seriously the idea that students are educational theorists. These discussions hint at a democratic approach to the enhancement of academic motivation wherein negotiation of the curriculum is an integral part of classroom life.

INTRODUCTION

At the beginning of his classic volume, *Pragmatism: A New Name for Some Old Ways of Thinking,* William James (1907) quoted Chesterton:

> There are some people—and I am one of them—who think that the most practical and important thing about a man is still his view of the universe. We think that for a landlady considering a lodger it is important to know

his income, but still more important to know his philosophy. We think that for a general about to fight an enemy it is important to know the enemy's numbers, but still more important to know the enemy's philosophy. We think the question is not whether the theory of the cosmos affects matters, but whether in the long run anything else affects them. (p. 3)

"I think," wrote James, "with Mr. Chesterton in this matter." For William James, scientific theories resembled lay individuals' "views of the universe." James saw differences among scientific theories as involving differences in the purposes of those who construct the theories. People with different priorities ask different questions and tell different stories about the world. Scientific theory is, in this view, very much a personal, social, human affair. This is the perspective—more postmodern than modern—proposed here for the study of students' theories of education.

This view of theory and, more generally, of scientific thought contrasts with that of attribution theory. Attribution theory has effectively employed scientific reasoning as a metaphor for lay individual's interpretations of everyday events (Kelley, 1973; Weiner, 1979). But attribution theory presents a modern rather than a postmodern view. Kelley and Weiner represent scientific, rational thought as distinct from personal, self-interested reasoning. Weiner (1979), for example, proposed that

the search for understanding is the (or a) basic "spring of action." This does not imply that humans are not pleasure seekers, or that they never bias information in the pursuit of hedonistic goals. Rather, information seeking and veridical processing are believed to be normative, [and] may be manifested in spite of a conflicting pleasure principle. (p. 3)

In this passage, Weiner created a dichotomy between the motive to understand and hedonistic motives; between veridical (accurate, truthful) and personal interpretations of events. He described information seeking and veridical processing as in conflict with the seeking of pleasure. Information seeking and veridical processing are not seen as pleasurable or in an individual's personal interests. This dichotomy, popular in psychology (e.g., Covington, 1984), is in keeping with modern perspectives on scientific thought. These perspectives are generally seen as originating about the time of Galileo who is seen as having helped "modernize" society by persuading people that the only true language of science is cold and impersonal like that of mathematics.

In postmodern views, the dichotomy of personal versus scientific is challenged (Barnes, 1977; James, 1907; Rorty, 1983; Toulmin, 1990). In these views, science is always a product of humans and reflects particular human concerns. The history of science, for example, is seen as involving change in what scientists see as important questions—not merely as linear progress toward a more veridical analysis of the world (Kuhn, 1970). As Kuhn implied, only those with a similar paradigm or world view can have simple disputes about facts. Many scientific disputes are about what questions to ask. When appearing to disagree about facts, scientists commonly disagree about what is important— about how to frame their inquiries.

According to James (1907), "ideas become . . . true just insofar as they help us to get into satisfactory relations with other parts of our experience" (p. 58). And,

> No theory is absolutely a transcript of reality, but . . . any one of them may from some point of view be useful . . . They are only a man-made language, a conceptual shorthand . . . in which we write our reports of nature; and languages, as is well known, tolerate much choice of expression and many dialects. Thus human arbitrariness has driven divine necessity from scientific logic. (p. 57)

Rather than speaking of mere accuracy or logic as the mark of good theory or interpretation, we might speak of the usefulness or adaptiveness of scientific interpretations. As for any given lay interpretation, usefulness cannot be judged from any abstract, absolute position because there is no such position. Rather, the value or adaptiveness of any scientific or lay interpretation depends on one's purposes or, as James put it, one's point of view. Students, like scientists, approach their work with different purposes. The concepts they employ, the data they collect and the way they interpret it can be understood in terms of these purposes. That is to say, students' interpretations of the different aspects of school are closely bound up, in a rational fashion, with their goals or concerns.

This is the logic of the ecological approach to social perception (McArthur & Baron, 1983) and the intentional approach to thought and action (Dennett, 1978; Nicholls, 1989). In these views, thought and action are seen as rational expressions of an individual's goals. What can appear irrational to an observer will, if considered in the light of the individual's purposes or intentions, appear rational.

The intentional stance is sometimes taken to be an extreme form of relativism: a claim that any lay or scientific theory will do as well as any other. This claim hardly merits a second glance (Rorty, 1985). The claim that one has to get the right sort of theory for one's purpose is not a claim that any old theory will do for any purpose. One has to get a relevant theory and one has to "use" it competently.

An important implication of the intentional perspective is that when people claim to have an ideal theory or the best theory, it will be a theory that serves their purposes but might not serve ours. This applies to students' theories about school as well as perspectives on motivation such as mine and others presented in this book. This does not mean we can never legitimately point to facts about academic motivation. What it means is that we should recognize that dialogue or argument about "the way things are" will also be argument about what is important. An example of such a dialogue about school is given in the last section of this chapter.

In the view I am presenting, students' theories about education could not be purely cognitive. They must involve students' concerns or purposes. We should, therefore, find beliefs about the nature of schooling to be related to personal goals or concerns in a rational, meaningful fashion (Nicholls, 1989). As William James implied, knowledge of a person's theories is useful because it is knowledge of their priorities as well as of their cognitive maps of the parts of the world that are important to them.

VARIETIES OF STUDENTS' THEORIES:
INDIVIDUAL DIFFERENCES

In this section, I describe two major dimensions of students' theories about academic success. These theories are orientations in the sense of predispositions to seek certain types of experience and they are theories in the sense that they are beliefs about success that generalize across different fields. They are, in other words, dispositions of individuals. (In this chapter, I do not deal with situational variation, which of course does occur.)

Task-Oriented and Ego-Oriented Theories

The idea that it might be useful to think of individual differences in achievement motivation in terms of separate dimensions of task orientation and ego orientation has been around for some time (Asch, 1952; Ausubel, Novak, & Hanesian, 1978; Crutchfield, 1962). Measurement efforts, however, have been more recent (Maehr & Braskamp, 1986; Meece, Blumenfeld, & Hoyle, 1988; Nicholls, Cheung Lauer, &

Patashnick, 1989; Nicholls, Cobb, Wood, Yackel, & Patashnick, 1989; Nicholls, Patashnick, & Nolen, 1985; Spence & Helmreich, 1983).

Ego orientation implies that one's purpose is the egotistical one of establishing one's superiority over others: One feels successful when establishing that one's ability is superior. Task orientation involves the purpose of gaining knowledge or performing one's best: One feels successful if one figures something out or thoroughly stretches one's skills. (The goal of "goofing off" or avoiding work also emerges as a separate dimension in most studies e.g., Nicholls et al., 1985 and Table 12.1.)

The questions used to assess motivational orientation are of the form, "What makes you feel really successful in school?" For younger students, the questions are of the form, "What makes you feel really pleased when you are doing schoolwork?" We find that success is not the same everywhere. One person's success or desired outcome is often not another's. Task orientation is indicated if students say that the experience of understanding occasions the feeling of success. Ego orientation is indicated if students feel successful when they show they are more able than their peers.

In task orientation and ego orientation, success requires some sort of performance, insight, or attainment. In the case of task orientation, the performance or insight is judged a success when the individual senses a gain in performance or insight. In the case of ego orientation, a gain is not, in itself, enough to signal success. For ego-oriented people, a gain in performance or insight must indicate that they are more competent than others if they are to feel successful. In general, the type of experience that occasions feelings of success identifies the person's goal orientation. Table 12.1 shows examples of scale items from a study of second-grade students' orientations to mathematics (Nicholls, Cobb, Yackel, Wood, & Wheatley, 1990).

Task- and ego-orientation scales are generally not appreciably correlated (Maehr & Braskamp, 1986; Meece et al., 1988; Nicholls et al., 1985; Nicholls et al., 1990; Thorkildsen, 1988). When they are, the associations are usually positive. There is no single (bipolar) dimension of task versus ego orientation (which implies a strong negative correlation) as suggested by the measures used by Ames and Archer (1987) to assess a mastery versus performance dimension, by Dweck and Leggett (1988) to assess a learning versus performance dimension, or by Vealey (1986) to assess a performance versus competitive dimension. In other words, in most samples, people are about as likely to be high on ego *and* task orientation as they are to be high on ego orientation and low on task orientation, or vice versa.

Goals are not beliefs about how the world works and the motivational

Table 12.1

Sample Items Assessing Motivational Orientations and Beliefs about the Causes of Success

Orientations	Beliefs
(The stem for every item was, "I feel really pleased in math when . . .") Task Orientation I: Effort	(Each item had the stem, "Students will do well in math if . . .") Success Requires Interest and Effort
. . . I solve a problem by working hard. . . . what the teacher says makes me think. . . . I keep busy. Task Orientation II: Insight and Collaboration	. . . they work really hard. . . . they are interested in learning. Success Requires Collaboration and Attempts to Understand
. . . I find a new way to solve a problem. . . . something I figure out really makes sense. . . . we help each other figure things out. . . . other students understand my ideas. Ego Orientation	. . . they try to understand each others ideas about math. . . . they try to understand instead of just get answers to problems. Success Requires Competitiveness
. . . I know more than the others. . . . I get more answers right than my friends. Work Avoidance	. . . they try to do more work than their friends. . . . they are smarter than the others. Success Requires Conformity
. . . it is easy to get the answers right. . . . the teacher doesn't ask hard questions.	. . . they solve the problems the way the teacher shows them and don't think up their own ways. Success Reflects Extrinsic Factors
	. . . they are just lucky. . . . they are quiet in class.

orientation scales do not assess such beliefs. Separate scales were constructed to assess beliefs about "what works" or what leads to success in school. Selected items from scales measuring such beliefs with reference to second-grade math are shown on the right side of Table 12.1. These questions refer to general beliefs about how students do well in mathematics or what must be done to attain success. These questions are about the reality of the classroom and not, as in the orientation scales, with personal goals or personal criteria of success.

The idea that task and ego orientations define or are an integral aspect of theories about schoolwork was tested by examining the associations among the scales measuring these orientations and scales measuring beliefs about the causes of success in school. There is considerable convergence between personal goals and beliefs about the causes of academic success. (Nicholls, Cheung et al., 1989; Nicholls, Cobb et al., 1989; Thorkildsen, 1988). There is a clear task-orientation dimension that includes the goals of accomplishing things by working hard, making sense of things, and collaborative work. It also includes the beliefs that success in mathematics requires interest, effort, collaboration, and attempts to understand. That is to say, students whose personal goal is to make sense of math also tend to value collaboration, believe that success requires collaboration, interest, and attempts to comprehend. There is also an ego-orientation dimension wherein the goals of being superior and of avoiding work are associated with the belief that students will do well if they are more able than others and set out to beat them.

The idea that these dimensions might be called theories (rather than merely specific beliefs) is further indicated by the results with a measure of beliefs about the long-term effects of studying mathematics: Students who were high on task orientation were also inclined to believe that studying mathematics makes one an independent thinker (Nicholls et al., 1990). Thus, the task-oriented theory is a rather encompassing view of academic and intellectual life.

The finding that peoples' theories about what is necessary for success are associated with their goals has interesting implications for casual and formal discussions of how to succeed. It raises the possibility that students who assert that the way to do well in graduate school is to avoid revealing to others what they are learning and to develop strategies of gaining superiority are probably also revealing their goals. For them, success probably means establishing their superiority. Students who claim that the way to do well is to figure out what professors want are probably revealing the priority of their concern to please the professors. All these students, I hope, might also believe that attempting to understand their topic will make some contribution to success. If students discuss such conflicting theories about how to succeed, our data indicate they will also be discussing how success *should* be defined. They will not just be discussing *how* to reach a predefined criterion of success. Such discussions could be an integral part of education long before graduate school.

Concepts Versus Theories. Concepts of ability change with age in ways that are complex and misunderstood by many writers (e.g., Dweck & Leggett, 1988; Stipek & MacIver, 1989) who confuse them with ability attributions and with concepts of intelligence (Nicholls, 1989, in press). I emphasize that I have not been discussing students' *concepts* of ability, intelligence, or learning in this chapter. Concepts are parts of theories, but the two should be distinguished.

From Grade 2 and up (and probably before then), it is possible to identify ego-oriented students who, more than those low in ego orientation, see high ability (as they construe it) as necessary for academic success. At any developmental level, the important individual differences in theories about schoolwork are differences in *use* of concepts such as ability, not in the *nature* of the concepts students have available. At all ages, ego-oriented students give their concepts of ability a major role in their interpretations of academic outcomes, whereas task-oriented students rely more on concepts like collaboration and understanding.

This argument is similar to that of Cole and Scribner (1974). Namely, that cultural differences are more often manifest in the ways concepts or cognitive processes are employed than in those concepts or processes themselves. This is not to say that developmental changes in conceptions of ability (and, more specifically, intelligence) are unimportant. These changes have important motivational consequences, but they are beyond the scope of this chapter.

Theories Across Domains. It is a common belief that motivation varies considerably across different domains. Yet, if students' theories about success are to deserve the term *theories,* they must have some generality of application—they need to be more than beliefs about isolated events. Duda and Nicholls (1991) examined this generality question by assessing the task- and ego-orientation dimensions of high school students for sport and schoolwork. The theories cut across schoolwork and sport: Students' orientations and their beliefs about the causes of success in schoolwork were highly predictive of their orientations and beliefs in sport. Correlations across the two domains were of the order of .60. Analysis of these data did not show separate sport or school factors. Instead the task and ego dimensions showed up just as if only one sphere of achievement had been involved. In short, students' theories about sport predict quite well their theories about other activities.

Theories Versus Motivational States. It does not follow from the previous findings that peoples' involvements are similar across domains like school and sport or even math and writing. The orientation scales ask what sort of satisfaction a person seeks. It is one thing to define success in terms of gains in performance or of demonstration of superiority over others in both school and sport. It is another thing altogether to actually seek these goals or even to think it is possible to achieve them equally in different types of situation.

The generality that is found for theories of success is rather specific to them: Perceived ability and intrinsic satisfaction or task involvement did not cut across the domains in the same way (Duda & Nicholls, 1991). Perceived ability in schoolwork was only slightly related to perceived ability in sport, and task involvement with schoolwork gave virtually no hint of how intrinsically involved students would be in sport. The task- and ego-oriented theories have the sort of generality one expects of a "view of the universe." The same cannot be said for perceived ability or task involvement. How then does task orientation relate to task involvement: the actual commitment (for endogenous reasons) to improving one's performance or insight in specific contexts?

Because a task-oriented student's goal is to make sense or improve performance, she or he should become task involved when work offers the opportunity to do these things. At least this should be so when situations are not ego-involving or dominated by exogenous incentives. Indeed, when situations are not explicitly ego-involving, task-oriented students are more likely than others to be task involved—to be trying to make sense or to improve their performance (Meece et al., 1988; Nolen, 1988). This trend is more marked for schoolwork than for sport. In schoolwork, task orientation is a good predictor of intrinsic task involvement. In sport, however, high perceived ability is a better predictor of intrinsic involvement than is task orientation (Duda & Nicholls, 1991). This appears to reflect the competitive nature of sport that can undermine task involvement, especially in those who doubt their competence. Consistent with this suggestion is other evidence that, in intellectual performance situations, the association between task orientation and intrinsic involvement declines and the association with perceived ability increases as situations become more test-like (Nicholls, Cheung et al., 1989; Sansone, 1986). Situational influences, including classroom effects, on motivational states and theories are discussed elsewhere (Ames, this volume; Dweck & Leggett, 1988; Jagacinski, this volume; Nicholls, 1989; Nicholls et al., 1990).

Correlates of Theories.   As the previous findings suggest, theories might not have simple relationships with other variables. Nevertheless, they seem to represent important individual differences and have a variety of important correlates. For example, task orientation (but not ego orientation or perceived ability) predicts (over 4–6 weeks) use of deep processing strategies for reading (Nolen, 1988). Task orientation and the associated beliefs, but not ego orientation, is correlated with higher order mathematical knowledge (Nicholls et al., 1990). Task orientation more than ego orientation is also associated with task preferences that would lead to learning (Nicholls, Cheung et al., 1989). In sport, task orientation was associated with endorsement of constructive, "sporting" conduct and with rejection of strategies such as allowing ineligible players to participate and faking injury to stop the clock (Duda, Olson, & Templin, 1991).

Task and ego orientation are also differentially related to wider beliefs about the purposes of education. Ego orientation is moderately associated with the view that school should help enhance one's wealth and socioeconomic status. Task orientation, on the other hand, is moderately associated with the views that school should prepare one for socially useful work and to understand the world (Nicholls, 1989; Nicholls, Cheung et al., 1989; Thorkildsen, 1988). In summary, these dimensions seem to reflect something of considerable importance about people.

CONCEPTIONS OF KNOWLEDGE AND THEORIES ABOUT SPECIFIC SUBJECTS

The picture of the task-oriented theory of academic success given here is rather vague. To say, for example, that task-oriented students see success as involving gaining understanding or that learning is an end in itself is not as enlightening as it might be. The concepts of understanding, intrinsic motivation, task involvement, or activity as an end in itself are rather generic.

Consider this from Lina Basquette, who acted in early silent movies. " 'I never married anyone or had an affair for an ulterior motive. I never did it for money or career . . . I'm a reformed nymphomaniac,' she likes to say, and gives her silent laugh—shaking all over and flashing her brilliant smile and batting her lashes" (Paris, 1989, p. 73).

The point of this example is that the intrinsic satisfactions she referred to are not those that can be gained from the academic disciplines. Similarly, the nature of knowledge and, correspondingly, the possible forms of endogenous satisfaction varies across disciplines and even across topics within any discipline. For this reason, I want to go beyond abstract and general formulations about task involvement like those outlined previously: beyond theories that are so general as to apply equally to sport and education (Nicholls, in press). This is of some importance as mortal teachers do not teach, and students do not learn all things at once. They always address specific forms of knowledge. In this section I examine students' conceptions of different forms of knowledge as well as their associated theories about how these forms are best acquired.

Intellectual Conventions Versus Matters of Substance

Even within any discipline, there are different types of knowledge that serve different purposes and offer different types of satisfaction. One such distinction that cuts across disciplines is inspired by the work of Nucci (1982), Smetana (1981), Turiel (1983), and others on social cognition. They find that even young children see matters of convention, such as how one addresses a teacher, as changeable if sanctioned by social consensus or the relevant authority. Such matters are seen as different from acts such as murder, which children do not believe can be made legitimate by social consensus or by authorities—even God (Nucci, 1985).

In the intellectual-academic sphere, students distinguish intellectual conventions (such as what symbols stand for, how a word is spelled, how a letter is formed, or how a geometry proof is presented) from matters of substance. Intellectual conventions are seen as alterable by social consensus, whereas matters of substance are not. And, among matters of substance they distinguish those involving logic (e.g., $1+1=2$) and laws of nature (rocks will fall when dropped) from potentially changeable facts about the world that do not directly reflect laws of nature (e.g., bikes are smaller than cars). The matters of empirical fact are, for example, seen as more likely than matters of logic or natural law to change (Miller, 1986; Nicholls & Thorkildsen, 1988).

Students endorse teaching standard positions on matters of logic, laws of nature, empirical fact, and intellectual convention (Nicholls & Thorkildsen, 1988). The weight students accord to conventions relative to matters of substance when both are involved in an intellectual activity (e.g., spelling and punctuation must be considered when communicating in writing) is, however, another question. The average tendency is to see conventions as less important (Nicholls & Thorkildsen, 1989).

Our two interview studies (Nicholls & Thorkildsen, 1988, 1989) also suggest there might be reliable individual differences in readiness to accept variation in intellectual conventions and in the importance attributed to them relative to matters of substance. Classroom observations also quickly reveal some young students who enjoy writing without regard to spelling and, sitting right beside them, others who want to spell each word correctly before they proceed to the next one (Nicholls & Hazzard, in preparation). The nature, source, and meaning of such differences is unclear but interesting.

Such differences exist among adults too. This was evident when a school allowed invented spelling in the compositions of kindergarten and first-grade children. Some parents raised a storm that was reported in the *Chicago Tribune* (Zorn, 1987). One parent said, "This really lit my fuse . . . When you learn math, they tell you 2 and 2 is 4. They never let you say 2 and 2 is 5." Said another, "My daughter is being told what is wrong is right. It's a bunch of crap." These parents' emphasis on the importance of conventions over the substance of the children's writing is probably out of keeping with their children's sense of what is reasonable. Most students' theories on this matter would suggest, as other writers propose (e.g., Schoenfeld, 1988), that when a teacher emphasizes conventions over matters of substance, children's motivation might suffer. In other words, most children might not see these parents' position as sensible.

Staying with this overly simple (see Nicholls, in press) but useful categorization of knowledge into conventions and substance, we find that students see exploration as highly appropriate for learning matters of substance such as the logic of addition but see didactic teaching as more likely to be valuable for teaching conventions (Nicholls & Thork-ildsen, 1989). Classrooms might, therefore, be seen as varying in the extent to which instruction is responsive to students' theories about the relative importance and the best methods of acquiring these different forms of knowledge.

Specific Academic Subjects

The evidence just presented on conventions versus matters of substance hardly touches the likely complexity of students' conceptions of different forms of knowledge and their theories about how best to acquire these different forms. If we focus on matters of substance, we will surely find that different disciplines are seen as offering different types of satisfactions—just as they are "designed" for different purposes (Perkins, 1986). Furthermore, any single discipline offers a diversity of possible purposes or sources of satisfaction.

Consider the business of being an academic philosopher. According to Alan Gewirth (1989), professor at the University of Chicago, philosophy evokes "an almost reverential feeling" because it "inquires into the first, the most basic principles . . . that apply to all things, although perhaps in different ways" (p. B 5). In some secular heaven, John Dewey is probably shaking his head and thinking he was right to leave Chicago. He argued that the quest for certainty, exemplified in a search for basic or universal principles, was counterproductive. There are, then, different theories about the purpose of philosophy and associated beliefs about how one can best succeed as a philosopher. It is also possible that these different theories would involve different degrees of intrinsic satisfaction with one's work in philosophy.

Similar questions could be asked for any discipline. Silva and Nicholls (1991) examined the dimensions of theories about writing among students in undergraduate composition courses. We found three dimensions of goals (purposes) and beliefs about how to succeed in writing. The first represented writing as an expressive and aesthetic activity. This factor included the goals of achieving a poetic form of expression and clarifying and enhancing one's personal values. Associated beliefs were that to write well one must be sensitive to poetic considerations, honestly express personal feelings and values, and be imaginative.

The second dimension involved the goals of improving one's logical reasoning ability and one's knowledge of subject matter and the belief that success in writing depends on flexibility of strategies for writing (writing to learn). The third dimension involved the goal of being methodical and correct in surface-level conventions (e.g., punctuation and spelling) and the beliefs that successful writing requires a focus on correctness of surface conventions.

In attempting to predict which of these dimensions would be most associated with commitment to writing as an end in itself, we found little to guide us in current perspectives on motivation. We turned instead to the Deweyian (1916) notion that the more an activity contributes to the broadening or total development of the person, the more educative the activity and the more whole-hearted the student's engagement. In this light, we expected the expressionistic cluster of goals and beliefs about the causes of success in writing to be most strongly related to commitment to writing as an end in itself. This proved to be the case. Furthermore, the more purely intellectual cluster of goals and beliefs (writing to learn) were less related to commitment. Still less (and not significantly) related to commitment were the goals and beliefs assuming the importance of surface conventions. In summary, the goals and beliefs that were less inclusive of larger personal concerns were less associated with the experience of writing as inherently valuable.

These different dimensions are roughly parallel to different academic perspectives on writing instruction. Our results could, therefore, have some relevance for the teaching of writing. If teachers seek to promote intrinsic satisfaction with writing, they would presumably be inclined toward approaches that emphasize expressive writing. However, students who have more immediately applied goals in writing might find instruction more satisfying if it dealt with topics of relevance to their vocations. A variety of further research questions might also be raised. For example, what are the determinants of different theories of writing and how do they affect the quality of writing?

There is ample scope for the study of students' theories about a variety of disciplines (Sosniak & Perlman, 1990). It is interesting, for example, that the reasons given by committed art students for art work indicate that self-construction or self-expression are primary purposes (Getzels & Csikszentmihalyi, 1976). Would the same apply to history or mathematics students? Which theories of these subjects are more likely to be linked to intrinsic satisfaction and the growth of insight?

THEORIES IN PRACTICE

If students were seen as active theorists, their theories might be given more attention in school. Rather than attempting to manipulate students' theories, teachers and researchers might treat them the way scientists should treat other scientists with divergent theories: by engaging in dialogue where it is uncertain whether one perspective will prevail or a new one will emerge. This might sound strange in the context of motivation theory. Researchers generally seek ways to get students to raise their expectations or to change their attributions or goals without promoting open dialogue. But young children are capable of spirited discussion of the nature and point of what they learn in school and can see such discussion as a valuable way of figuring out what matters in school and how to learn. This can be illustrated with excerpts from a year-long ethnographic study I conducted in collaboration with a second-grade teacher. As the year progressed, the teacher, Sue Hazzard, increasingly engaged the students in the negotiation of classroom practices and curriculum decisions (Nicholls & Hazzard, in preparation).

Egotism and Feelings of Inferiority

Consider the question of the effects of tests on feelings of self-worth. Here are some second-grade students in a discussion provoked by a speeded math test. Sue Hazzard has asked how they felt about having to work fast.

"I like doing it at my own speed," says Joan.

"You said you want a challenge," argues Jacob who stands out in the class as highly task oriented *and* ego oriented. "You could challenge yourself to get more than someone else."

"But maybe a person is trying all they can and can't get up higher," says Joan. "Everyone learns things," counters Jacob. "But," Joan insists, "They might have done best as they can and can't get up more . . ." "You can just keep on trying," responds Jacob. "If they just say they can't do it and quit, in a few years they'll say I don't have any money and they'll sit round saying, 'What'll I do?' "They can just do their best," suggests Alan. "It's hard," Matt notes. "When other people get done and say, 'I'm done.' " "There are other people that are much better than me. There's lots of people in other classes that can do all sorts of things I can't," Jacob replies.

In this discussion, Joan recognizes that not everyone can be top and keeps confronting the idea that people often want to be the "best" and thus make themselves miserable. Jacob's first answer is to advocate competing. He then suggests focusing on the ever-present possibility of learning new things. Yet, at times he draws the attention of his classmates to the fact that he learns faster than them. He wants to learn, but it is often an egotistical goal of learning more than others. His peers recognize this and their discussion then turns to the ethics of egotism.

"I feel unhappy 'cause Jacob is always bragging," says Tricia.

"How is he bragging?" asks Sue.

"He is saying like he's got his math book done." "But he's better than he was at the beginning of the year," declares Matt.

Jacob is spluttering so Sue asks, "So you don't feel like you're bragging?"

"No!" "But you do it!" says Joan. "I don't brag. In that way I'm better," says Jean. "Well my brother is smart and brags," says Matt. "But I don't brag. I say to him, 'that's good.' "

Because Jacob is taking the discussion as a personal attack, Sue asks the class, "What if you were the one who got everything right fast?"

"I'd hate it, 'cause if I'm the best in my family, when I ask my mother or dad things they don't know and I can't find out," says Nicky. "It's good to make mistakes 'cause if you knew everything, you wouldn't need a mother or dad or brothers or sisters." Nicky is a task-involved student. He values collaboration as much as learning.

"Sometimes you want to do everything and sometimes you don't," says Alan. "I think some people worry about themselves too much," says Matt, who has recently recovered from a serious bout of just such worry. "I don't want to be the best at things. I just want to be a normal kid." There is none of the smug moral superiority of the reformed smoker, but conviction nevertheless.

"Would you like to do *your* best?" asks Sue.

"But not if it was different from everyone else. I wouldn't want to show it."

These snatches of discussion indicate that young children can grapple meaningfully with the complexity of the question of egotism. Should not a democratic education help them decide where they stand on such matters? There is reason to think that if their views were listened to and stimulated more, schools might be more collaborative places with less ego-involvement (Nicholls & Hazzard, in preparation; Thorkildsen, 1989; Thorkildsen & Nicholls, 1991).

Subject Matter and Method

It seems strange that researchers on motivation have generally sought to improve student motivation without asking students what sorts of subject matter and what associated teaching methods make sense to them. For those teachers who do not need to be persuaded to avoid competition and extrinsic rewards, these are the important and challenging questions about motivation. Furthermore, even young children have theories about the nature and value of different topics and of how they should be learned. These theories can be the focus of classroom discussions wherein students participate in the formation of the purposes that guide their learning (Dewey, 1916). This might help develop them as educational philosophers and eventually make public debate on education a lot more illuminating than it is at present. Might not the subject of education itself be included in a child's education? A hint of what can transpire when this happens can be gained from the following selections from our ethnographic study.

"What's the best way to learn about science?" asks Sue (the teacher).

"Have a scientist instructor." "Science projects." "I like to see pictures," declares Matt. "Not just people telling. And it is neat how people can share ideas. Like, some of my friends have weird ideas. Ulp! I don't mean they're stupid. I think they are silly but then I think about it and it makes sense."

"Read books," suggests another student. "Have a scientist here." (. . .) "We could have an hour or 30 minutes and *do* things about science. Then we can write about it and tell it," says Jacob, developing Matt's ideas. "I think we should have experiments in the room," says Matt.

"How would you do it?" asks Sue.

"Use measuring things." "Take time bombs and see what would happen." says James.

"How would you do experiments?" Sue repeats. "Would you want me to do them?"

"I want us to do it. Like on our desks," says Matt. "We could have a center and probably make a book about it." "We could get paper and everyone can make a picture of what happens." "We could send notes home asking for help to get materials," says Ruth. "I'd like to do them safely," urges Nicky, thinking of the time bomb proposal. (. . .)

"Should I teach science like reading?" asks Sue, to provoke further clarification. A chorus of no's indicates the inappropriateness of the idea, not a dislike of reading.

Jacob leaps to rule out workbook-type tasks. "We should really do it in life. We get tired of answering lots of questions. Scientists aren't inside doing worksheets. They are in the world finding things."

"Jacob, do scientists write things?" asks Sue. In such discussions, she vigorously challenges her students.

"They write after their experiments," says Jacob.

"So you want to write afterwards?" asks Sue.

"We could write lists of what we want to do and then do them and then write it or maybe type it and then tell it," suggests Matt, who a couple of weeks earlier had been resisting any form of writing.

"Sometimes writing things down means you don't forget," says Sue hopefully.

"And you could keep those ideas and that would tell you what children think about." Matt, with his "reading problem" and propensity to be a troublemaker recognizes this as an issue for educators. This is not an isolated occasion. He takes the teacher's perspective quite often.

Jill proposes the learning of different sections of a book by different students who would then teach one another.

"You know what Jacob said!" bursts Matt. "We don't want to read [about science] all the time. We want to do real things."

These snippets hint at the possibilities that might emerge if we take students conceptions of knowledge and their theories of education more seriously. Jacob and Matt are clearly potential behavior problems. They are intellectually active and critical. Their critique of workbooks, only hinted at here, echoes that of many adult critics of school. When they are asked to do things that make no sense to them, they become bored and "create trouble." This class, with Jacob and Matt playing active roles, went on negotiating their ideas about science, coming to see it as an exciting exploration of mazes without end.

The negotiation of subject-matter-specific theories like these could be an important part of the work of schools (Nicholls & Hazzard, in preparation). The study of such theories and of classrooms that are devoted to the negotiation and implementation of such theories offers exciting prospects—more exciting than the sort of work I described in the first half of this chapter. That's my current theory anyhow.

ACKNOWLEDGMENT

This chapter was improved by the suggestions of Terri Thorkildsen.

REFERENCES

Ames, C., & Archer, J. (1987). Mothers' beliefs about the role of ability and effort in school learning. *Journal of Educational Psychology, 79,* 409–414.

Asch, S. E. (1952). *Social psychology.* Englewood Cliffs, NJ: Prentice-Hall.

Ausubel, D. P., Novak, J. D., & Hanesian, H. (1978). *Educational psychology: A cognitive view* (2nd ed.). New York: Holt, Rinehart & Winston.

Barnes, B. (1977). *Interests and the growth of knowledge.* London: Routledge & Kegan Paul.

Cole, M., & Scribner, S. (1974). *Culture and thought: A psychological introduction.* New York: Wiley.

Covington, M. V. (1984). The motive for self-worth. In R. E. Ames & C. Ames (Eds.), *Research on motivation in education: Student motivation* (Vol. 1, pp. 77–113). New York: Academic Press.

Crutchfield, R. S. (1962). Conformity and creative thinking. In H. E. Gruber, G. Terrell, & M. Wertheimer, (Eds.), *Contemporary approaches to creative thinking* (pp. 120–140). New York: Prentice-Hall.

Dennett, D. C. (1978). *Brainstorms: Philosophical essays on mind and psychology.* Montgomery, VT: Bradford.

Dewey, J. (1916). *Democracy and education.* New York: The Free Press.

Dweck, C. S. & Leggett, E. L. (1988). A social-cognitive approach to motivation and personality. *Psychological Review, 95,* 265–273.

Duda, J., & Nicholls, J. G. (1991). *Academic and athletic motivation.* Manuscript submitted for publication.

Duda, J., Olson, L. K., & Templin, T. J. (1991). The relationship of task and ego orientation to sportsmanship attitudes and the perceived legitimacy of injurious acts. *Research Quarterly for Exercise and Sport, 62,* 79–87.

Getzels, J. W., & Csikszentmihalyi, M. (1976). *The creative vision.* New York: Wiley.

Gewirth, A. (1989, February 15). *The Chronicle of Higher Education,* p. B5.

James, W. (1907). *Pragmatism: A new name for some old ways of thinking.* New York: Longmans, Green.

Kelley, H. H. (1973). The process of causal attribution. *American Psychologist, 28,* 107–128.

Kuhn, T. S. (1970). *The structure of scientific revolutions* (2nd ed.). Chicago: University of Chicago Press.

Maehr, M. L., & Braskamp, L. A. (1986). *The motivation factor: A theory of personal investment.* Lexington, MA: Lexington Books.

McArthur, L. Z., & Baron, R. M. (1983). Toward an ecological theory of social perception. *Psychological Review, 90*, 215–238.

Meece, J. L., Blumenfeld, P. C., & Doyle, R. H. (1988). Students' goal orientations and cognitive engagement in classroom activities. *Journal of Educational Psychology, 80*, 514–523.

Miller, S. A. (1986). Certainty and necessity in the understanding of Piagetian concepts. *Developmental Psychology, 22*, 3–18.

Nicholls, J. G. (1989). *The competitive ethos and democratic education.* Cambridge, MA: Harvard University Press.

Nicholls, J. G. (in press). The general and the specific in the development and expression of achievement motivation. In G. Roberts (Ed.), *Motivation in sport and exercise.* Champaign, IL: Human Kinetics.

Nicholls, J. G., Cheung, P. C., Lauer, J., & Patashnick, M. (1989). Individual differences in academic motivation: Perceived ability, goals, beliefs, and values. *Learning and Individual Differences, 1*, 63–84.

Nicholls, J. G., Cobb, P., Wood, T., Yackel, E., & Patashnick, M. (1989). Dimensions of success in mathematics: Individual and classroom differences. *Journal for Research in Mathematics Education, 21*, 109–122.

Nicholls, J. G., Cobb, P., Yackel, E., Wood, T., & Wheatley, G. (1990). Students' theories about mathematics and their mathematical knowledge: Multiple dimensions of assessment. In G. Kulm (Ed.), *Assessing higher order thinking in mathematics* (pp. 137–154). Washington, DC: American Association for the Advancement of Science.

Nicholls, J. G., & Hazzard, S. (in preparation). *Education as adventure: Lessons from the second grade.*

Nicholls, J. G., Patashnick, M., & Nolen, S. B. (1985). Adolescents' theories of education. *Journal of Educational Psychology, 77*, 683–692.

Nicholls, J. G., & Thorkildsen, T. A. (1988). Children's distinctions among matters of intellectual convention, logic, fact and personal preference. *Child Development, 59*, 939–949.

Nicholls, J. G., & Thorkildsen, T. A. (1989). Intellectual conventions versus matters of substance: Elementary school students as curriculum theorists. *American Educational Research Journal, 26*, 533–544.

Nolen, S. B. (1988). Reasons for studying: Motivational orientations and study strategies. *Cognition and Instruction, 5*, 269–278.

Nucci, L. P. (1982). Conceptual development in the moral and conventional domains: Implications for values education. *Review of Educational Research, 52*, 93–122.

Nucci, L. P. (1985). Children's conceptions of morality, societal convention, and religious prescription. In C. Harding (Ed.), *Moral dilemmas: Philosophical and psychological issues in the development of moral reasoning* (pp. 137–174). Chicago: Precedent.

Paris, B. (1989, February 13). The godless girl. *New Yorker,* pp. 54–73.

Perkins, D. N. (1986). *Knowledge as design.* Hillsdale, NJ: Lawrence Erlbaum Associates.

Rorty, R. (1983). Method and morality. In N. Haan, R. N. Bellah, P. Rabinow, & W. M. Sullivan (Eds.), *Social science as moral enquiry* (pp. 155–176). New York: Columbia University Press.

Rorty, R. (1985). Solidarity or objectivity. In J. Rajchman & C. West (Eds.), *Post-analytic philosophy* (pp. 3–19). New York: Columbia University Press.

Sansone, C. (1986). A question of competence: The effects of competence and task feedback on intrinsic motivation. *Journal of Personality and Social Psychology, 51*, 918–931.

Schoenfeld, A. H. (1988). When good teaching leads to bad results: The disasters of "well-taught" mathematics courses. *Educational Psychologist, 23*, 145–166.

Silva, T., & Nicholls, J. G. (1991). *Students as writing theorists*. Unpublished manuscript, University of Illinois–Chicago, Chicago.

Smetana, J. G. (1981). Preschool children's conceptions of moral and social rules. *Child Development, 52,* 1333–1336.

Sosniak, L. A., & Perlman, C. L. (1990). Secondary education by the book. *Journal of Curriculum Studies, 22,* 427–442.

Spence, J. T., & Helmreich, R. L. (1983). Achievement related motives and behaviors. In J. T. Spence (Ed.), *Achievement and achievement motives: Psychological and sociological perspectives* (pp. 7–74). San Francisco: Freeman.

Stipek, D., & MacIver, D. (1989). Developmental change in children's assessment of intellectual competence. *Child Development, 60,* 521–538.

Thorkildsen, T. A. (1988). Theories of education among academically able adolescents. *Contemporary Educational Psychology, 13,* 323–330.

Thorkildsen, T. A. (1989). Justice in the classroom: The student's view. *Child Development, 60,* 323–334.

Thorkildsen, T. A., & Nicholls, J. G. (1991). Students' critiques as motivation. *Educational Psychologist, 26,* 347–368.

Toulmin, S. (1990). *Cosmopolis: The hidden agenda of modernity*. New York: The Free Press.

Turiel, E. (1983). *The development of social knowledge: Morality and convention*. Cambridge, England: Cambridge University Press.

Vealey, R. (1986). Conceptualization of sport-confidence and competitive orientation: Preliminary investigation and instrument development. *Journal of Sport Psychology, 8,* 221–246.

Weiner, B. (1979). A theory of motivation for some classroom experiences. *Journal of Educational Psychology, 71,* 3–25.

Zorn, E. (1987, October 11). Peoples in Aperville are going through a rough spell. *The Chicago Tribune,* pp. 1, 8.

Motivation and Achievement in Adolescence: A Multiple Goals Perspective

KATHRYN R. WENTZEL
University of Maryland

Personal goals are of central theoretical importance for explaining motivational patterns of behavior (see Pervin, 1982). In this regard, goals have been described with respect to their content (Ford & Nichols, 1987), orientation (Dweck & Leggett, 1988; Jagacinski, this volume; Nicholls, 1984, this volume), levels of challenge, proximity, and specificity (Bandura, 1986), and their relations with each other (Emmons, 1989; Powers, 1978). Central to all of these descriptions is the notion that people do set goals for themselves and that these goals can be powerful motivators of behavior.

Research has also identified a wide range of "self-"processes that interact with and regulate goal pursuit. For example, beliefs concerning one's ability to achieve goals (e.g., Bandura, 1986), beliefs concerning standards for evaluating goal attainment (Ames & Ames, 1984; Nicholls, 1984), and theories about how to achieve goals (e.g., Dweck & Leggett, 1988), all appear to influence the degree to which goals are pursued and actually achieved. Similarly, specific skills and metacognitive strategies such as the ability to protect goals from distractions, to monitor progress, and to adjust behavior in light of feedback increase the likelihood of successful goal attainment (Kuhl, 1985).

The complex nature of these interactive processes underscores the importance of clearly defining what is meant when we discuss goals and the precise contribution of goals to the achievement process. In this chapter, *goals* are defined as cognitive representations of what individuals are trying to achieve, and their function is to direct behavior toward attaining these outcomes (see Emmons, 1989; Ford, in press). Thus, goals are part of a network of cognitive representations of the self in which goals specify *what* an individual is trying to accomplish and other "self-"processes regulate the degree to which that goal is pursued and ultimately achieved.

Traditionally, the study of achievement goals has focused on students' desires to increase or demonstrate levels of competence or ability (Dweck & Leggett, 1988; Nicholls, 1984, this volume). In contrast, a focus on goal content draws attention to the fact that classrooms afford students the opportunity to pursue many goals, both social and academic (Wentzel, 1989). Indeed, an examination of students' goals might reveal desires to achieve academically relevant objectives such as to learn or to be evaluated positively for academic accomplishments, but also social objectives such as to make friends, have fun, be cooperative and helpful, or to comply to social rules and norms. A consideration of these multiple classroom goals in relation to academic accomplishments raises somewhat different questions from those typically asked in research on achievement goals. In particular, a focus on goal content suggests that to understand academic achievement, we need to examine the degree to which both social and academic goals are rewarded and valued within the context of the classroom and the extent to which social and academic goals interact to influence academic outcomes.

In this chapter, a multiple goals perspective for understanding links between academic achievement and the goals that students try to accomplish is proposed. Research based on this perspective is then described. This research focuses on the social and academic goals that students try to achieve, how these goals are related to both intellectual and social competence at school, and how these goals are related to the behavior they are presumably designed to produce. Finally, implications of a multiple goals perspective for future research and classroom practice are discussed.

MULTIPLE GOALS AT SCHOOL

Central to theories of motivation and achievement is the notion that personal goals can be powerful motivators of behavior. With respect to learning and academic performance, empirical evidence suggests that patterns of single goals and self-regulatory processes are related to qualitatively distinct responses to success and failure (e.g., Dweck &

Leggett, 1988; Lepper & Hodell, 1989; Nicholls, 1984). In light of these findings, it has often been suggested that certain types of goals are more conducive to academic achievements than others.

In the following section it is argued that goals can either facilitate or constrain the learning process to the extent they reflect the social and intellectual objectives of the schooling process. Whereas it is acknowledged that successful goal pursuit is dependent on other self-regulatory processes, it is suggested that the unique contribution of goals to academic achievement is reflected in the behavioral outcomes and consequences they represent. Based on this perspective, it is proposed that how students coordinate the goals they try to achieve at school can also have a significant impact on their academic accomplishments.

Multiple Classroom Goals

Academic Goals. Students' goals most often associated with academic outcomes are described as concerns with either increasing one's ability, as reflected in task mastery and learning, or proving the adequacy of ability, as reflected in evaluations of performance (Ames, this volume; Ames & Ames, 1984; Dweck & Leggett, 1988; Nicholls, 1984, this volume). Briefly, learning goals represent outcomes derived from the actual process of learning, such as feelings of satisfaction and competence or actual intellectual development. With respect to academic motivation, Dweck and Leggett (1988) suggested that these goals are associated with beliefs that intellectual ability can be developed with effort and persistence over time. Whereas learning goals involve the development of skills, performance goals reflect one of two outcomes: obtaining positive judgments or avoiding negative judgments of one's ability. Performance goals are typically associated with beliefs that intellectual ability is a fixed, unchanging, and uncontrollable aspect of the self (Dweck & Leggett, 1988).

Others have defined achievement goals along similar dimensions, but have related goals to specific standards for evaluating ability (Ames & Ames, 1984; Jagacinski, this volume; Nicholls, 1984). In these models, learning goals are related to beliefs that ability is judged relative to past performance (evaluations based on self-set standards), whereas performance (or ego-involved) goals reflect beliefs that ability is judged with respect to normative, group-referenced standards of ability.

Nonacademic Goals. Several authors have suggested that socially integrative goals such as those to achieve social approval, conformity with group goals, or close interpersonal relationships are not only important for achieving social competence (Ford & Nicholls, 1987), but can be primary motivators of learning behavior as well (Ames & Ames, 1984; Entwistle & Kozeki, 1985; Maehr, 1983; Veroff, 1969). Although not extensively studied, goals to be dependable and responsible (Wentzel, 1989), to be cooperative (Ames, 1984), to gain social approval (Maehr, 1983), and to be conforming and compliant (Kozeki & Entwistle, 1984) represent a more general category of social responsibility goals that are related significantly to academic outcomes.

A consideration of social goals in relation to academic achievement is particularly important given the social nature of academic instruction. Indeed, the activities of instruction and learning occur within a larger social context defined by social rules and expectations for behavior that regulate the day-to-day activities of the classroom. For instance, rules reflecting cooperation, respect for others, and positive forms of group participation govern social interaction in the classroom. In addition, students are expected to work hard, pay attention, participate in classroom activities, do their assignments, and study lessons. Not all of these activities are social in nature. However, they reflect rules of social conduct designed to guide the learning process.

Relations Between Goals and Academic Outcomes

The importance of making a distinction between *what* it is that students are trying to achieve and other "self"-processes that regulate goal pursuit becomes especially important when trying to relate students' goals to their academic accomplishments. On the one hand, academic goals have been related consistently to distinct patterns of learning and problem-solving behavior, especially when initial attempts to learn result in failure. The pursuit of learning goals has been associated with high levels of effort, persistence at finding solutions to problems, and finding new or alternative learning strategies when difficulties arise. Conversely, performance goal orientations have been associated with helplessness, withdrawal from tasks, and negative emotional states that appear to place children at risk for academic failure (Ames, this volume; Dweck & Leggett, 1988; Nicholls, 1984, this volume).

Research linking social goals to learning behavior has been less frequent, although work by Kozeki and Entwistle (1984; Entwistle & Kozeki, 1985; Kozeki, 1985) suggests that the pursuit of goals to be compliant and responsible is associated with maladaptive outcomes typical of performance goal orientations. However, other research linking these social goals to academic outcomes suggests positive relations depending on the age of students (Crandall, 1966; Veroff, 1969), and whether these goals were pursued in conjunction with or in opposition to more academically relevant goals (Atkinson, 1974; Nakamura & Finck, 1980; Wentzel, 1989).

On the other hand, it is not clear whether students' goals—either to increase ability or to prove ability—are determining these outcomes or whether other self-regulatory processes are mediating the effects of these goals on subsequent performance. For instance, learning goals are typically associated with beliefs that ability is malleable and judged with respect to past performance. Such beliefs promote continued effort to increase one's ability when failure or negative evaluations are experienced.

In contrast, performance goals are linked to beliefs that ability is fixed and judged with respect to normative criteria. These beliefs do not promote continued effort in light of failure and, as such, they tend to place students at risk for academic failure or at least motivational deficits (e.g., Dweck & Leggett, 1988). Moreover, work by Elliot and Dweck (1988) suggests that children with performance goals typically display maladaptive responses to failure when they also lack the self-confidence necessary to obtain positive judgments of the self. Thus, it is possible that performance goals are related to behavior that can undermine the learning process, but only when they are also associated with self-referent belief systems that can influence the degree to which these goals are pursued and ultimately achieved.

Given that maladaptive learning behavior is most often associated with performance goal orientations, it has been suggested frequently that educators actively promote the development of learning goals and discourage goals or reward structures that focus on outcomes extrinsic to learning. However, because performance goals have rarely been studied independently of belief systems that are likely to constrain rather than facilitate goal pursuit, the potentially positive contributions of performance goals to classroom learning are not well understood. As with learning and performance goals, it is not clear whether outcomes associated with social goals reflect what it is that students are trying to achieve (the content of their goals) or the belief systems that regulate goal pursuit. Indeed, the tradition of comparing and contrasting the differential effects of goals on academic behavior, has led us to ignore the fact that students must achieve multiple goals if they are to succeed at school.

The pursuit of multiple goals can have a positive effect on students' academic achievements in at least two ways. First, it is likely that high levels of achievement cannot be sustained without the joint pursuit of social, performance, and learning goals. For instance, goals to obtain positive judgments of the self such as praise or high grades (one aspect of performance goals) are inextricably linked to learning goals in that it is impossible to obtain positive evaluations of the self without first achieving some level of task mastery (see e.g., Dweck & Leggett, 1988). In fact, these goals can be complementary in that learning goals focus a student's attention on producing actions necessary for skill development (strategic planning and monitoring), whereas performance goals remind them of the long-term consequences of those actions (positive feedback, achieving a standard of excellence). As with performance goals, active pursuit of social goals can also promote achievement in that goals to be cooperative and compliant are likely to direct attention to the instructional process and thus, support the pursuit of mastery and learning goals.

The positive motivational effects of performance and social responsibility goals, and obtaining extrinsic rewards in particular, can be especially salient when a learning task is not particularly interesting in the first place (e.g., memorizing multiplication tables) but nevertheless essential for subsequent learning. Performance on tests, which often requires demonstrations of skills that are presumably well-learned and therefore no longer challenging, might also be enhanced if a reward such as a high grade is expected. (See Lepper & Hodell, 1989, for a discussion of the positive as well as negative effects of extrinsic rewards on learning and performance.)

Multiple goals can also have a positive effect on academic achievement in that each goal directs effort toward the achievement of a socially desired outcome: Goals to improve ability lead to mastery-oriented behavior, goals to earn positive evaluations result in performance-oriented behavior, and goals to be socially responsible lead to classroom-appropriate forms of behavior. Once achieved, each of these outcomes is likely to be valued by teachers and other students and responded to in positive ways. On the one hand, mastery and performance-oriented behavior (learning and obtaining positive evaluations of work) are clearly important for achieving academic success at school. On the other hand, an implicit goal of educational institutions has always been to socialize children into adult society by teaching work- and responsibility-oriented values such as dependability, punctuality, and obedience in conjunction with the learning process (Wentzel, 1991a).

Summary

A multiple goals perspective focuses on the relations between the content of students' goals and classroom competence. A focus on goals as desired outcomes that are being actively pursued suggests that one important contribution of goals to academic achievement might be reflected in their content. That is, the extent to which students' goals match the multiple social and intellectual objectives of the schooling process might be an important factor in either facilitating or constraining academic accomplishments. Based on this perspective it has been suggested that a clear distinction between students' goals and processes that regulate goal pursuit is especially important when trying to relate students' goals to their academic accomplishments (see Fig. 13.1). It has been argued that efforts to achieve multiple goals, in particular, to improve ability, to obtain positive judgments of the self, and to be socially responsible, can contribute to academic accomplishments in positive ways because each of these outcomes is valued by teachers and students alike (see Fig. 13.1a). This is in contrast to other perspectives on motivation that describe the psychological processes that lead to efforts to achieve goals in the first place (see Fig. 13.1b).

A multiple goals perspective extends the work on motivation and achievement in several new directions. First, it considers the possibility that students can and often do pursue more than one goal while at school. Second, this perspective acknowledges the fact that academic accomplishments depend in part on the joint and interactive effects of goals and other self-regulatory processes on subsequent behavior. However, assuming that goals eventually lead to the behavior they are designed to produce, a multiple goals perspective also suggests that both social and academic goals can make positive contributions to achievement if the content of students' goals matches the behavioral requirements of the classroom.

In the next section, research on multiple classroom goals is described. This research suggests that unique sets of goals predict academic achievement more precisely than single goals and that

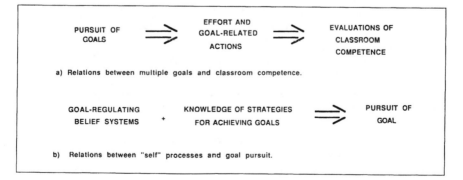

a) Relations between multiple goals and classroom competence.

b) Relations between "self" processes and goal pursuit.

FIG. 13.1   Alternate perspectives for studying goals.

classroom behavior might be an important mediator between goals and positive evaluations of classroom competence. This research also demonstrates that efforts to achieve both social and academic goals are related positively to both intellectual and social competence. In line with other research on achievement goals, performance and social responsibility goals are shown to be associated with less than optimal academic outcomes when associated with certain other self-regulatory processes.

RESEARCH ON MULTIPLE GOALS

Research that focuses on multiple goals in relation to academic achievement has not been widespread. One reason for this lack of research has been an interest in identifying psychological processes and distinct patterns of behavior associated with mastery and performance goals. Although it has been acknowledged that these goals may have joint effects on academic outcomes (e.g., Dweck & Leggett, 1988), methodological practices often preclude analyses that examine the interactive role of multiple goals on learning (cf. Ames & Archer, 1988; Meece & Holt, 1991). For instance, conclusions concerning the relative benefits of mastery versus performance goals reflect methodologies that place these goals on a continuum and assign goal orientations to children in trait-like terms (e.g., mastery- versus performance-oriented children; Dweck & Leggett, 1988), or experimental conditions that, by necessity, reflect qualitatively different reward structures (Ames & Ames, 1984). These methodological practices make it difficult to study the joint effects of different types of goals on academic outcomes.

Perhaps more importantly, students are rarely asked directly about the goals they are trying to achieve. Rather, students' goals are assessed either indirectly or manipulated experimentally rather than as "self-processes" that represent what students think they are trying to accomplish. Finally, we know much about relations between goal orientations and students' responses to failure at problem-solving tasks. However, goals are rarely studied under conditions of success and in direct relation to the outcomes they represent.

In response to these issues, the research described here was designed to examine the multiple goals that students report trying to achieve at school and their relations with each other, with classroom behavior, and with academic performance. In a first study, students' goals and academic achievement were examined in a group of 203 adolescents from a suburban high school in the San Francisco Bay area. Students represented a broad range of achievement levels; 71% of the students were Caucasian and 29% represented various ethnic minority groups.

A second study was conducted on 423 middle school students and their teachers in a predominantly working-class, midwestern community. Participating students constituted 76% of the school's Grade 6–7 population; the sample was equally representative of males and females, with 68% of the sample being Caucasian, 23% Black, and 5% Hispanic. In this research, multiple goals were examined in relation to four outcomes: students' grades, social status among peers, teachers' preferences for students, and classroom behavior. To help explain negative relations between academic achievement and performance and social responsibility goals often reported in the literature, beliefs about how to achieve goals were also examined.

Simultaneous Goal Pursuit

Multiple Goals and Academic Outcomes.   Relations between academic performance and goals to achieve social as well as academic outcomes were first investigated in a study of 9th- through 12th-grade students (Wentzel, 1989). This research focused on relations between students' grade-point averages (GPAs) and how often students reported trying to achieve a set of 12 goals while they were in class. Correlational results suggested that effort to achieve six of these goals was related significantly and positively to student GPAs: to be a successful student, be dependable and responsible, learn new things, understand things, do your best, and get things done on time. Trying to have fun was related negatively to students' grades.

Of particular interest, however, was whether relations between academic performance and student effort could be explained more precisely by examining the *sets* of goals that students tried to achieve at school. To examine this possibility, goal profiles were compared across three achievement groups: high GPA students (cumulative GPAs greater than or equal to an A-), medium GPA students (cumulative GPAs equivalent to a C+), and low GPA students (cumulative GPAs of a D+ or less).

The sets of goals students always tried and rarely tried to pursue were relatively homogeneous within the three achievement groups. In particular, analyses revealed that 84% of the high GPA students reported always trying to achieve at least three goals: be a successful student, be dependable and responsible, and get things done on time. Only 13% of the low GPA students said they always try to achieve these three goals.

Of additional interest is that although the high GPA students reported frequent pursuit of academic goals (i.e., to learn new things, to understand things), less frequent pursuit of these goals did not distinguish low-achieving from average students. Rather, the low GPA students were unlike other students in that they reported rarely trying to earn approval from others or to be dependable and responsible. Thus, these results suggested that an increase in motivation to learn may improve the academic performance of both average and low achievers. However, an unwillingness to try to conform to the social and normative standards of the classroom uniquely characterized the low-achieving students.

Based on the results of this research, relations between students' goals and academic outcomes were examined in a sample of middle school students (Wentzel, 1991b, 1991c, 1991d). In this second study, self-report measures were developed to assess academic and social responsibility goals. Two academic goals reflected efforts to master new and challenging things (mastery goals) and to earn positive evaluations (performance goals). Sample items for the mastery and performance goals, respectively, are: "How often do you try to learn things because its a challenge?"; "How often do you try to show your teachers how smart you are?"

Two social responsibility goals reflected efforts to be prosocial (helpful to others, cooperative and sharing) and compliant (following rules, keeping promises and commitments). Sample items for prosocial and compliance goals, respectively, are: "How often do you try to help other kids when they have a problem?"; "How often do you try to do what your teacher asks you to?" Students responded on 6-point scales (1 = rarely, 6 = almost always).

As in the first study, goal pursuit differed as a function of student academic achievement when the goals of high, medium, and low achievement groups were compared. Results indicated that the high GPA students reported trying to achieve the two academic goals and the two social responsibility goals significantly more often than did the medium and low GPA groups. The goal patterns of the medium and low GPA groups did not differ significantly from one another.

As in the first study, student achievement also differed significantly as a function of the sets of goals students reported trying to achieve. In this case, 59% of the high GPA students reported high levels (top tertile) of effort for *both* mastery and performance goals, as compared to 42% and 30% of the medium and low GPA students, respectively. In contrast, only 17% of the high GPA students reported low levels of effort (bottom tertile) for both mastery and performance goals, whereas 45% of both the medium and low GPA groups reported low levels of effort for both goals. Students who reported high levels of effort to achieve both goals also had higher GPAs than students who reported high levels of effort for only one of the goals. Thus, pursuing both mastery and performance goals was related to the most optimal academic outcome.

Composite scores representing average academic (mastery and performance) and social responsibility (prosocial and compliance) goal scores were also computed to compare combinations of academic and social goal pursuit across levels of student achievement. Once again, findings indicated a significant relation between combinations of goal pursuit and academic achievement: 59% of the high GPA students reported trying to achieve high levels (top tertile) of both social responsibility and academic goals in contrast with 38% of the medium and 34% of the low GPA students.

As in the first study, these results suggest that students actively pursue more than one type of goal at school and that academic achievement can be explained more precisely by accounting for the sets of goals that students pursue rather than just single goals. In short, mastery and performance goals, and at a more general level, academic and social responsibility goals, appear to have an additive and positive effect on academic outcomes.

These findings are in contrast to those reported in other research on multiple goals. For instance, in research by Ames and Archer (1988), performance goals did not seem to make an independent contribution to learning outcomes over and above mastery goals. Similarly, Meece and Holt (1991) reported that mastery-oriented students earned the highest grades in comparison to children reporting combined goal orientations. However, the Ames and Archer sample was restricted to high-achieving students and goals were measured with respect to perceived classroom reward structures. In the Meece and Holt study, cluster analyses were used to identify goal patterns rather than identifying children with the highest and lowest levels of multiple goal pursuit as was done in the present research. Studies using similar samples and methods are clearly needed to clarify these discrepancies.

Multiple Goals and Social Competence. Analyses were also conducted to examine relations between students' goals and their social acceptance by classmates and teachers. Indeed, documenting the social value of goals is necessary before conclusions about relations between goal pursuit and classroom competence can be drawn.

Social acceptance among classmates was measured using sociometric techniques designed to identify popular, rejected, neglected, controversial, and average status children (Coie, Dodge, & Coppotelli,

1982). These techniques classify children according to how many times they are nominated by classmates as a "best friend" and how often classmates like to do things with them at school. Popular children are those with many friends and who are disliked by few of their classmates, rejected children have few friends and are disliked by many, neglected children have few friends but are not disliked, and controversial children are those with many friends but who are also disliked by many of their peers. (See Wentzel, 1991c, for a more detailed description of this procedure.) To assess teachers' preferences for students, teachers were asked to rate how much they would like to have each of their students in their class again next year.

As with academic outcomes, patterns of goal pursuit uniquely characterized the sociometric status groups. For instance, when compared with average status children, popular children reported trying to achieve prosocial goals significantly more often, neglected children reported trying to achieve both prosocial and compliance goals significantly more often, and controversial children reported trying to achieve compliance goals significantly less often. Of interest is that goals related to academic competence (the two social responsibility goals) were also related positively to acceptance by peers.

In the case of teacher preferences, students reporting high levels of effort to achieve performance and compliance goals were preferred by teachers significantly more than other students (Wentzel, 1991d). What is intriguing is that the goals related to teachers' preference for students comprise only a subset of the goals related to high levels of academic achievement—the pursuit of mastery and prosocial goals was not related significantly to teachers' preference for students. Thus, the students most preferred by teachers were not necessarily those with the highest grades, but those who reported trying to comply to social rules and norms and who reported concern with obtaining positive evaluations of their work. In conjunction with the peer data, these results suggest that the pursuit of social responsibility goals may be a necessary (albeit insufficient) requirement for achievement in both social and academic domains of functioning.

Summary. The results of this research confirm the potential of a multiple goals perspective for understanding links between motivation and competence at school. However, although these data suggest that both academic and social responsibility goals are related significantly and positively to academic outcomes, they tell us little about the processes that link these self-perceived efforts to tangible results. Clearly, having good intentions is important, but students must also be able to accomplish what they set out to achieve. In the next two sections, research on processes that explain links between goal pursuit and classroom competence is described.

Relations Between Goals and Classroom Behavior

To examine relations between goals and classroom behavior, students participating in Study 2 were also assessed with respect to socially responsible, mastery-oriented, and evaluation-oriented behavior at school. Socially responsible behavior was measured by asking students to nominate classmates who display prosocial and compliant behavior (Wentzel, 1991c). "Mastery-oriented" behavior was assessed by asking teachers how often students show an interest in their schoolwork; "evaluation-oriented" behavior was measured by having teachers rate how often students show concern with getting good grades or being praised for their work (5-point scales; 1 = never, 5 = always).

Two sets of findings suggest that students' classroom behavior is indeed an important link between student goals and academic outcomes (Wentzel, 1991e). First, displays of socially responsible, mastery, and evaluation-oriented classroom behavior are significant, positive, and independent predictors of students' GPAs. In fact, the three types of behavior account for 18% of the variance in GPA after controlling for the potentially confounding effects of students' IQ, school attendance, gender, and teachers' preference for students. Thus, the behavioral counterparts of goal pursuit appear to be related significantly and meaningfully to academic performance.

Interestingly, goal pursuit was related significantly to classroom behavior but not in linear fashion. Students perceived by their classmates as displaying high levels of socially responsible behavior reported trying to be responsible significantly more often than students displaying low levels of responsible behavior but not significantly more often than students showing moderate amounts of responsible behavior. Relations between behavior and the two academic goals were also nonlinear. In this case, students perceived as displaying high levels of either mastery or evaluation-related behavior reported trying to achieve corresponding goals significantly more often than students displaying either moderate or low levels of such behavior. For both mastery and performance goals, self-reported effort did not distinguish students who displayed either moderate or low levels of mastery or evaluation-oriented behavior.

These findings suggest at least two ways in which students' goals may be related to their behavior at school. First, effort may contribute to outcomes in varying degrees, after which other factors such as planning, monitoring, and problem-solving skills play a role in producing competent behavior. Thus, highly irresponsible students may be distinguished from others by motivational deficits, whereas students displaying high levels of mastery and evaluation-related behavior may be distinguished by particularly high levels of effort and persistence.

A second explanation is that criteria used for judging behavior may reflect perceived effort and intentions to varying degrees. For instance, students who are consistently irresponsible at school may be clearly distinguishable from other students and their behavior easily attributed to a lack of good intentions, whereas other students may be judged on other criteria that are more salient than effort. If true, this second explanation suggests that we need to study social cognitive processes and competence criteria used by "behavioral evaluators" as well as motivational and skill levels of the individuals they evaluate to fully understand relations between goals and the behavior they are designed to produce.

Goals, Means–End Beliefs, and Academic Outcomes

As described earlier, it is possible for the pursuit of performance and social responsibility goals to place students at risk for academic failure if other self-regulatory processes constrain goal pursuit. It was suggested that one such process reflects beliefs about how to achieve goals. Although many causal connections between academic success and personal goals are possible, one potentially critical belief system concerns academic success as a means to achieve personal goals. In this case, students might perceive academic success as a way to increase academic abilities (to achieve mastery goals), as a means to prove the adequacy of ability (to achieve performance goals), or as a way to demonstrate social competencies (to achieve social responsibility goals).

To explore the role of these beliefs in mediating relations between goals and academic success, the students in Study 2 were also asked to indicate *why* they try to get good grades at school. Their choices were: "because you like to see how smart you are" (performance-oriented beliefs), "because that's what you're supposed to do at school" (social responsibility-oriented beliefs), and "because learning is fun and exciting" (mastery-oriented beliefs) (Wentzel, 1991b). Thus, students were presented with belief systems in which earning grades is perceived as a means to achieve mastery, performance, or social responsibility goals.

Eighty-five percent of students reported trying to get good grades in order to achieve social responsibility goals or performance goals, whereas only 15% of the students reported linking academic achievement with mastery goals. This finding is important in its suggestion that social responsibility goals are primary motivators of academic behavior. Perhaps more importantly, however, is that students who associated earning grades with mastery goals had significantly higher grades than students who associated earning grades with either performance or social responsibility goals. Moreover, these students reported pursuing multiple classroom goals—mastery, performance, and social responsibility—significantly more often than other students.

In short, these results suggest that belief systems and the pursuit of classroom goals interact in complex ways to influence academic performance. In doing so, however, these results also underscore the importance of making a distinction between the interactive effects of goals and belief systems on academic outcomes on the one hand, and relations between active goal pursuit and achievement on the other. In the first case, students seem to believe that earning grades can lead to quite different outcomes. In turn, these beliefs about how to achieve goals can influence academic performance in qualitatively different ways. In the case of performance and responsibility-oriented students, theories about means–ends relations would appear to place students at risk for less than optimal achievement outcomes. A reasonable explanation is that if grades do not lead to the desired outcome, academic success is abandoned as a means to achieve the goal and other, non-academic strategies are adopted.

In contrast, research reported in previous sections also suggests that a consideration of goals as outcomes, regardless of the means that are used to achieve them, can contribute significantly to our understanding of positive links between a wide range of goals and academic performance. In this case, goals and their behavioral counterparts can make positive, joint contributions to a students' success at school.

IMPLICATIONS FOR FUTURE RESEARCH AND EDUCATIONAL PRACTICE

In the classroom, students are expected to achieve multiple goals that reflect socially prescribed objectives as well as those to develop intellectual and academic competencies. The findings reported in this chapter suggest that adolescents' efforts to achieve these multiple goals are related to academic outcomes in significant and meaningful

ways. Adolescence is a particularly interesting period of development
for studying multiple goals in that children at this age become increasingly challenged to coordinate and achieve diverse social and academic outcomes in positive and complementary ways (Havighurst,
1972). In general, however, we know very little about how goals
develop over the course of the school years or the relative contribution
of schooling and socialization processes to individual differences in
children's goals. Thus, these findings raise further questions concerning the development of goal priorities and the ability to coordinate
multiple goals in adaptive ways.

One approach to understanding the development of students' goals
is to examine other psychological processes that either facilitate or
constrain goal pursuit. In this regard, we are beginning to understand
how goal pursuit is influenced by other self-regulatory processes such
as perceptions of ability and theories about how to achieve goals.
Given the social nature of learning and instruction, several other types
of information may also have a significant influence on student motivation and subsequent performance. For instance, social cognitions in
the form of perceived opportunities to pursue goals and perceived
adult and peer expectations for behavior have been linked with effort to
achieve both social and academic goals at school (Wentzel, 1989). The
importance of studying social cognitive functioning in relation to
motivation and achievement is especially important with respect to
children from minority cultures who are expected to adapt to normative expectations for behavior that are inconsistent with those espoused by their families and community.

A more precise understanding of teachers' social cognitive functioning is also important for understanding the content of students'
goals and how goals are related to evaluations of classroom performance. For instance, much research suggests that teacher expectations for and perceptions of students' abilities and behavior are related
to the quality of teacher–student interactions as well as students'
academic performance (Wigfield & Harold, this volume). Research that
examines how these factors influence the goals that students ultimately choose to pursue may also significantly enhance our understanding of students' classroom behavior and performance. In the
research described in this chapter, teachers tended to prefer students
who tried to be compliant and earn good grades, but not necessarily
those who tried to learn new things. Ultimately, we need to help
teachers become aware of the types of student behavior they value and
reward and how these values might subsequently contribute to or
detract from students' goals and corresponding efforts to learn.

Other social demands or pressures might also have an influence on the development of children's classroom-related goals. For instance, social responsibility is clearly valued and actively promoted by teachers, especially during the middle school years (Wentzel, 1991a). Although speculative, declines in intrinsic interest in schooling as children reach high school (Harter, 1981) might reflect this increase in demands to achieve social responsibility goals from adults. Increased demands from peers can also focus students' attention on other intrinsically interesting (albeit social) tasks such as forming new friendships. In both cases, pressure to comply to social norms and values can influence the goals that students try to achieve at school.

The degree to which goals espoused by adults and peers are conflicting or complementary can have an especially strong impact on students' classroom behavior. One way to coordinate adult and peer expectations for behavior is to use cooperative learning methods in which rewards are based on the achievement of group goals (Slavin, 1984). Not only does cooperative learning provide students with opportunities to learn with friends, but it can also promote socially responsible forms of behavior such as helping and sharing (Ames, 1984). Thus, in these learning contexts, students will perceive *both* peers and adults to expect positive social interaction with peers along with socially responsible and academically relevant behavior. Moreover, they will learn to coordinate goals to achieve these outcomes in socially acceptable ways.

Changing the social organization of classroom instruction may be one effective strategy for influencing the goals that students pursue and how efficiently they pursue them. It is also possible that students can be taught specific strategies that will help them organize and coordinate multiple goals (Wentzel, 1991d). One such strategy is to organize tasks in terms of hierarchically related goals. For instance, the achievement of learning goals might be facilitated by having children divide difficult tasks into sets of smaller and easier tasks. At the same time, goals to obtain positive judgments of ability could be achieved by focusing children's attention on the progress they make over time. Bandura and Schunk (1981) suggest that setting explicit proximal subgoals in the service of larger but future goals helps students coordinate goals and ensures greater persistence, enhanced perceptions of self-efficacy for learning, and increased intrinsic interest in the task at hand.

In summary, personal goals have the potential to have a powerful influence on students' classroom behavior and academic accomplishments. Much research on goals and achievement suggests that relations between single classroom goals and academic performance are jointly regulated by other "self" and metacognitive processes that can either increase or decrease the likelihood of successful goal attainment. The multiple goals perspective and research described in this chapter extends this work by suggesting that an examination of multiple goals and in particular, unique sets of goals, might provide us with a more precise explanation of students' performance at school.

First, a consideration of multiple goals suggests that learning to coordinate competing and seemingly incompatible goals may be an additional self-regulatory process that can influence levels of motivation and subsequent performance. Designing cooperative learning environments and teaching students to set proximal and distal goals when trying to accomplish academic tasks may be effective ways to promote successful coordination of classroom goals.

In addition, a multiple goals perspective suggests that the content of students' goals is worthy of study in and of itself. Indeed, social goals in the form of cooperation and compliance as well as academic goals in the form of task mastery and earning positive evaluations of the self, are related significantly to academic achievement, teachers' preferences for students, and the quality of relationships with peers. Thus, in conjunction with psychological processes that regulate the pursuit of these goals, understanding *what* it is that children believe they are trying to accomplish may provide important insights into how and why children succeed at school.

REFERENCES

Ames, C. (1984). Competitive, cooperative, and individualistic goal structures: A cognitive-motivational analysis. In R. Ames & C. Ames (Eds.), *Research on motivation in education* (Vol. 1, pp. 177–208). New York: Academic Press.

Ames, C., & Ames, R. (1984). Systems of student and teacher motivation: Toward a qualitative definition. *Journal of Educational Psychology, 76,* 535–556.

Ames, C., & Archer, J. (1988). Achievement goals in the classroom: Student learning strategies and motivational processes. *Journal of Educational Psychology, 80,* 260–267.

Atkinson, J. W. (1974). Strength of motivation and efficiency of performance. In J. W. Atkinson & J. O. Raynor (Eds.), *Motivation and achievement* (pp. 193–218). New York: Wiley.

Bandura, A. (1986). *Social foundations of thought and action: A social cognitive theory.* Englewood Cliffs, NJ: Prentice-Hall.

Bandura, A., & Schunk, D. (1981). Cultivating competence, self-efficacy and intrinsic interest through proximal self-motivation. *Journal of Personality and Social Psychology, 41,* 586–598.

Coie, J. D., Dodge, K. A., & Coppotelli, H. (1982). Dimensions and types of status: A cross-age perspective. *Developmental Psychology, 18,* 557–570.

Crandall, V. C. (1966). Personality characteristics and social and achievement behaviors associated with children's social desirability response tendencies. *Journal of Personality and Social Psychology, 4,* 477–486.

Dweck, C. S., & Leggett, E. L. (1988). A social-cognitive approach to motivation and personality. *Psychological Review, 95,* 256–272.

Elliot, E. S., & Dweck, C. S. (1988). Goals: An approach to motivation and achievement. *Journal of Personality and Social Psychology, 54,* 5–12.

Emmons, R. A. (1989). The personal striving approach to personality. In L. A. Pervin (Ed.), *Goal concepts in personality and social psychology* (pp. 87–126). Hillsdale, NJ: Lawrence Erlbaum Associates.

Entwistle, N. J., & Kozeki, B. (1985). Relationships between school motivation, approaches to studying, and attainment, among British and Hungarian adolescents. *British Journal of Educational Psychology, 55,* 124–137.

Ford, M. E. (in press). *Human motivation: Goals, emotions, and personal agency beliefs.* Newbury Park, CA: Sage.

Ford, M. E., & Nichols, C. W. (1987). A taxonomy of human goals and some possible applications. In M. E. Ford & D. H. Ford (Eds.), *Humans as self-constructing living systems: Putting the framework to work* (pp. 289–312). Hillsdale, NJ: Lawrence Erlbaum Associates.

Harter, S. (1981). A new self-report scale of intrinsic versus extrinsic orientation in the classroom: Motivational and informational components. *Developmental Psychology, 17,* 300–312.

Havighurst, R. (1972). *Developmental tasks and education.* New York: David McKay.

Kozeki, B. (1985). Motives and motivational style in education. In N. Entwistle (Ed.), *New directions in educational psychology: 1. Learning and teaching* (pp. 189–199). Philadelphia: Falmer Press.

Kozeki, B., & Entwistle, N. J. (1984). Identifying dimensions of school motivation in Britain and Hungary. *British Journal of Educational Psychology, 54,* 306–319.

Kuhl, J. (1985). Volitional mediators of cognition-behavior consistency: Self-regulatory processes and action versus state orientation. In J. Kuhl & J. Beckman (Eds.), *Action control: From cognition to behavior* (pp. 101–128). New York: Springer-Verlag.

Lepper, M. R., & Hodell, M. (1989). Intrinsic motivation in the classroom. In C. Ames & R. Ames (Eds.), *Research on motivation in education* (Vol. 3, pp. 73–106). New York: Academic Press.

Maehr, M. L. (1983). On doing well in science: Why Johnny no longer excels; why Sarah never did. In S. G. Paris, G. M. Olson, & H. W. Stevenson (Eds.), *Learning and motivation in the classroom* (pp. 179–210). Hillsdale, NJ: Lawrence Erlbaum Associates.

Meece, J. L., & Holt, K. (1991). *Classification and validation of achievement-related goal patterns in elementary school children.* Unpublished manuscript, University of North Carolina Chapel Hill.

Nakamura, C. Y., & Finck, D. N. (1980). Relative effectiveness of socially oriented and task-oriented children and predictability of their behaviors. *Monographs of the Society for Research in Child Development, 45* (Nos 3–4).

Nicholls, J. G. (1984). Achievement motivation: Conceptions of ability, subjective experience, task choice, and performance. *Psychological Bulletin, 91,* 328–346.

Pervin, L. A. (1982). The stasis and flow of behavior: Toward a theory of goals. In M. M. Page (Ed.), *Personality-current theory and research* (pp. 1–53). Lincoln, NE: University of Nebraska Press.

Powers, W. T. (1978). Qualitative analysis of purposive systems: Some spadework at the foundations of scientific psychology. *Psychological Review, 85,* 417–435.

Sivan, E. (1986). Motivation in social constructivist theory. *Educational Psychologist, 21,* 209–233.

Slavin, R. E. (1984). Students motivating students to excel: Cooperative incentives, cooperative tasks, and student achievement. *The Elementary School Journal, 85,* 53–63.

Veroff, J. (1969). Social comparison and the development of achievement motivation. In C. P. Smith (Ed.), *Achievement-related motives in children* (pp. 46–101). New York: Russell Sage.

Wentzel, K. R. (1989). Adolescent classroom goals, standards for performance, and academic achievement: An interactionist perspective. *Journal of Educational Psychology, 81,* 131–142.

Wentzel, K. R. (1991a). Social competence at school: Relations between social responsibility and academic achievement. *Review of Educational Research, 61,* 1–24.

Wentzel, K. R. (1991b). *Motivation and achievement in early adolescence: The role of multiple classroom goals.* Unpublished manuscript, University of Maryland, College Park.

Wentzel, K. R. (1991c). Relations between social competence and academic achievement in early adolescence. *Child Development, 62,* 1066–1078.

Wentzel, K. R. (1991d). Social and academic goals at school: Motivation and achievement in context. In M. Maehr & P. Pintrich (Eds.), *Advances in motivation and achievement* (Vol. 7, pp. 185–212). Greenwich, CT: JAI.

Wentzel, K. R. (1991e). [Classroom behavior, student goals, and achievement outcomes]. Unpublished raw data.

14

The Effects of Task Involvement and Ego Involvement on Achievement-Related Cognitions and Behaviors

CAROLYN M. JAGACINSKI
Purdue University

Current theoretical perspectives on achievement motivation suggest that achievement-related cognitions and behaviors depend on the individual's achievement goals and that achievement goals can vary as a result of both situational and dispositional factors (e.g., Ames, this volume; Ames & Archer, 1988; Dweck, 1986; Elliott & Dweck, 1988; Nicholls, 1984, 1989, this volume). Two types of goal states are distinguished—task involvement and ego involvement. When individuals are task involved, their goal is to demonstrate ability through learning or task mastery (Nicholls, 1984). In task involvement, there is a focus on improvement through effort. On the other hand, when individuals are ego involved, their goal is to demonstrate superior ability by outperforming others (Nicholls, 1984). In this case, improvement is not sufficient to demonstrate high ability.

According to Nicholls (1984), differences in achievement goals are related to differences in the conception of ability the individual employs. There are at least two different meanings of ability that the individual can adopt (Nicholls, 1978, 1984; Nicholls & Miller, 1984). In some cases we judge our ability in a self-referenced manner, in which improvement through effort implies competence. This is the conception of ability used by young children. For young children, mastery of a task through high effort implies more ability than task mastery through low effort. Ability and effort are not clearly distinguished. This is the conception of ability employed with task involvement. Adults typically employ a more differentiated conception of ability, wherein high ability means above average. With this conception of ability, it is recognized that high effort leads to improvement, but this is not sufficient to imply high ability. Instead, high effort can imply low ability if others achieve the same level of performance with less effort. This is a less subjective conception of ability and requires a comparison of one's effort and performance with those of others. The differentiated conception of ability is used in ego involvement.

Research suggests that when adults are asked about the meaning of ability they typically use the more differentiated conception (Jagacinski & Nicholls, 1984). However, adults can adopt different conceptions of ability in different achievement situations. That is, the individual's achievement goals will determine which conception of ability is employed. When they are task-involved, adults judge their ability in the self-referenced manner typically employed by young children, and when they are ego-involved they use the more differentiated conception.

Although individual differences should influence whether an individual is likely to be task-involved or ego-involved, research suggests that situational factors are highly influential. Ego involvement is most likely to be induced when tasks are described as tests of valued abilities (e.g., intelligence), when interpersonal competition is emphasized, or when feedback stresses normative performance (Nicholls, 1984; Nicholls, Cheung, Lauer, & Patashnick, 1989). In contrast, task involvement is promoted when evaluation is not emphasized and when the task interests the individual and presents a moderate level of challenge.

In this chapter, I review the research on the effects of task- and ego-involving conditions on students' achievement-related cognitions and behaviors. I focus primarily on situational factors, but I also briefly address individual differences in the types of activities students find task- or ego-involving and differences in students' goal orientations in the classroom. I conclude the chapter with suggestions for future research and a discussion of how the research findings should apply to classrooms.

COGNITIVE AND AFFECTIVE CORRELATES OF TASK INVOLVEMENT AND EGO INVOLVEMENT

In collaboration with John Nicholls, I conducted a series of studies that examined college students' reactions to successful performance with high or low effort under task- and ego-involving conditions (Jagacinski

& Nicholls, 1984). In each study, college students read a scenario that described a task-involving or ego-involving situation. Task involvement was depicted as enjoyment of learning for its own sake. Testing and competitive conditions were used to describe ego involvement. For each situation, success was achieved through low effort for half of the students and through high effort for the rest. In these initial studies social comparison information was also provided in ego involvement, but not in task involvement. Students reading the ego-involving scenario that described success through high effort were told that others had done as well with less effort. The ego-involving scenario describing success with low effort indicated that others required more effort to achieve the same level of performance.

As expected, in the task-involving condition, effort was positively associated with feelings of competence, pride, and a sense of accomplishment, but the reverse was true in ego involvement. In the ego-involving condition, low effort was associated with greater feelings of competence, pride, and a sense of accomplishment than high effort. In both conditions, greater guilt was associated with low effort than with high. In addition, in ego involvement, but not task involvement, high effort was associated with more embarrassment than low effort. Brown and Weiner (1984) have noted similar effects for guilt and embarrassment in ego-involving conditions. That is, they found greater guilt associated with low effort as compared to high and greater embarrassment associated with high effort in contrast to low. Effort does appear to represent a double-edged sword (Covington & Omelich, 1979) in ego involvement—students risk guilt from not trying hard or embarrassment from trying too hard. This dilemma does not occur in task involvement where high effort maximizes positive affect and minimizes negative affect.

The differences that were found in the implications of effort for feelings of competence and positive affects are consistent with evidence from Ames and her colleagues that contrast competitive and individualistic goal structures (Ames, 1984; Ames, Ames, & Felker, 1977). In the competitive goal condition, two students were asked to compete with each other to see who could solve more puzzles. The explicit goal in this condition was to outperform others and should have induced ego involvement. In the individualistic goal condition, students worked alone and were told to solve as many puzzles as possible. These instructions would be unlikely to induce ego involvement. Ames et al. (1977) found that in a competitive setting satisfaction was related to self-perceptions of ability. This was not the case in an individualistic setting where effort attributions played a more causal role in determining satisfaction. This is additional evidence that ego-involving conditions lead students to focus on their perceptions of normative ability. In ego-involving conditions there are losers as well as winners—not everyone can be above average. These conditions are particularly detrimental to students with low perceived ability who often demonstrate impaired performance in ego-involving contexts (Nicholls, 1984). However, in task-involving conditions high and low perceived ability students perform similarly.

THE ROLE OF SOCIAL COMPARISON INFORMATION IN TASK INVOLVEMENT AND EGO INVOLVEMENT

The studies conducted by Jagacinski and Nicholls (1984) were designed to contrast the extremes of task and ego involvement. Social comparison information was intentionally confounded with ego involvement. However, this approach left some important questions unanswered. Would the mere presence of social comparison information induce the more differentiated conception of ability for individuals in task-involving conditions? Would effort be positively associated with feelings of competence and positive affects in ego-involving conditions if no social comparison information were provided? Two additional studies were conducted to explore these issues (Jagacinski & Nicholls, 1987). In order to take into account individual differences in the types of activities students might find task- or ego-involving, college students were asked to supply their own activities. In the task-involving condition students were asked to name activities involving skills that they enjoyed doing for their own sake and liked to do in their spare time. In the ego-involving case the activities were ones at which the students felt it was very important to be outstanding and where they would feel terrible if they were below average.

The first study involved the following effects: involvement (task vs. ego), effort (high vs. low), and social comparison information (absent vs. present). As in the previous studies, the scenario described success with high or low effort at the activity the student had named. When social comparison information was provided, students imagining success with high effort were told that others had performed the activity with less effort. For students imagining success with little effort, others were said to require more effort.

Without social comparison information, high effort was associated with greater competence than low effort in both the task- and ego-involving situations, although the difference did not achieve statistical significance in the ego-involving case. With the addition of social comparison information, there was no significant difference in competence judgments for students imagining success with high or low effort in the task-involving condition. However, among students in the ego-involving condition there was a tendency for competence judgments to be greater with low effort than high. In the absence of social comparison information, high effort was associated with a greater sense of accomplishment than low effort for both task- and ego-involving conditions. When social comparison information was provided the relationship still held for task involvement, but was no longer significant for ego involvement. The results suggested that the mere presence of social comparison information had a much stronger effect in ego involvement than in task involvement. Although the presence of social comparison information moderated judgments of competence in task involvement, positive affects were still associated with high effort.

A second study was conducted to draw more attention to the social comparison information (Jagacinski & Nicholls, 1987, Study 2). Students imagining task- or ego-involving scenarios first made judgments following success with high or low effort without any social comparison information. They were then given the social comparison information and were asked to make the judgments again. In effect, we asked students to what extent they would revise their judgments in the light of the new information. In this case the responses in task and ego involvement were very similar. In the absence of social comparison information, greater feelings of competence and more positive affects were associated with high effort than with low effort. When social comparison information was provided, competence was judged lower and embarrassment was judged higher following success with high, as compared to low, effort. Learning that others had performed as well with less effort led to a reduction in judged competence and positive affects and to a significant increase in embarrassment for task-involving, as well as ego-involving, conditions.

The mere presence of social comparison information was not detrimental to the sense of accomplishment of students imagining the task-involving situation. However, when the social comparison information was emphasized, even these students adopted the more differentiated conception of ability.

DIFFERENCES IN TASK-INVOLVING AND EGO-INVOLVING ACTIVITIES

In the experiments described in the previous section (Jagacinski & Nicholls, 1987), students were asked to describe activities that they found task- or ego-involving. Students in the task-involving condition were asked to name an activity that they really enjoyed and liked to do in their spare time. In the ego-involving condition, students named an activity at which they felt it was very important to be outstanding and in which they would feel terrible if they were below average. Thus, students in the task-involving condition all imagined activities they enjoyed doing for their own sake, but many different activities were named. Likewise, a variety of activities were named by students in the ego-involving condition but for each student it was an activity at which they wanted to be superior.

In order to investigate differences in the types of activities students find task- or ego-involving, the activities students named were classified into categories. The most frequently occurring categories are presented in Table 14.1. Students in the ego-involving condition were most likely to name academic courses or skills such as mathematics and engineering or test-taking and getting good grades. None of the students in the task-involving condition named academic tasks. However, it is not surprising that college students do not like to spend their free time working on courses. A large percentage of students in both the task- and ego-involving conditions named sports. Of the students in the task-involving condition, 23% mentioned competitive sports as did 21% of the students in the ego-involving condition. Students in the task-involving condition were more likely to mention noncompetitive sports (34%) than competitive sports, whereas the opposite was the case for students in the ego-involving condition (5% noncompetitive sports). Many of the students in the ego-involving condition (22%) named skills that are vocationally relevant such as leadership, communication, or writing. A much smaller percentage (3%) of students in the task-involving condition mentioned these activities.

In addition to naming the activity, students wrote a short paragraph

Table 14.1
Percentages of Students Naming Different Types of Activities as Enjoyable in Their Free Time (Task-Involving) or as Important to be Superior to Others (Ego-Involving)

Type of Activity	Task-Involving ($n = 146$)	Ego-Involving ($n = 141$)
Academic courses & skills (e.g., mathematics, test taking)	0%	34%
Vocationally relevant valued skills (e.g., communication, writing, leadership)	3%	22%
Competitive sports	23%	21%
Noncompetitive sports & leisure physical activities	34%	5%
Art, music, dance	15%	11%

describing why they enjoyed the activity (task involvement) or why it was important to be outstanding at the activity (ego involvement). Students' responses were coded in terms of the presence or absence of some specific concerns. These concerns included skill development, competition, relaxation or escape from problems and pressures, physical fitness, importance to future career goals, artistic or creative expression, and personal goals such as being the best you can be. Each response could be coded as expressing more than one concern. Differences between the frequencies with which these concerns were expressed suggest differences in the way students think about task- and ego-involving activities. Table 14.2 presents the percentage of students in the task- and ego-involving conditions expressing each concern. Students in the task-involving condition were more likely to be concerned with skill development, relaxation, and physical fitness than were students in the ego-involving condition. These concerns tend to focus on the process of doing the activity itself. Students in the ego-involving condition were more likely to mention a concern with meeting a personal standard of excellence and with the utility of the skill for the attainment of future career goals than were students in the task-involving condition. Hence, in the ego-involving condition, success at the activity was more likely to be instrumental to the achievement of some higher level goal than was the case in the task-involving condition.

Only a small percentage of students mentioned a concern with competition and beating others. Interestingly, students in the task- and ego-involving conditions were not significantly different in their likelihood of mentioning a concern with competition. In order to further explore this issue, additional analyses were conducted on the subset of students who named competitive sports as their task- or ego-involving activity. A sizable number of students in the task-involving ($n = 34$)

Table 14.2

Percentages of Students in Task- and Ego-Involving Conditions Expressing Various Concerns in Explaining the Importance of the Activity They Named

Concern Expressed	Task-Involving ($n = 146$)	Ego-Involving ($n = 141$)	Chi-square ($df = 1$)
Skill development	23%	1%	28.86**
Competition	12%	7%	1.74
Relaxation, escape from problems	40%	1%	65.16**
Physical fitness	33%	1%	49.34**
Importance to career goals	1%	31%	49.11**
Artistic or creative expression	8%	2%	5.37*
Personal standards of excellence	0%	18%	29.60**

$*p < .05; **p < .001$

and ego-involving ($n = 30$) conditions named competitive sports as their activity. The results were quite similar to those for the total sample. Students in the task-involving condition were more likely to mention skill development (24%) than were students in the ego-involving condition (3%). Although competition was mentioned a lot among this subset of students, it still did not distinguish task-involving activities (44%) from ego-involving activities (27%). If anything, the students naming task-involving activities had a greater tendency to mention competition. An additional comparison was made to see if students who were concerned with competition would be less likely to be concerned with skill development than those who did not mention competition. No relationship was found. Students who expressed a concern with competition were as likely as students who did not to express a concern with skill development (17% vs. 12%). Thus, in this context, skill development and competition are not seen as incompatible concerns. This was also noted by Duda (1988) in her study of goal orientations among college recreational sports participants. She found that participants who were high on mastery goal orientation (and high or low on competitive goal orientation) had been involved in the sport for more years and practiced more during their free time than participants who were low in terms of mastery goal orientation. Nearly half of the men (47.4%) in her study were high on both mastery and competitive goal orientations.

In the context of sports, the role of competition may be quite complicated. For some sports, the challenge is provided by the competition. For example, in order to improve your tennis game, you need a partner who is at least matched to your level of skill. Thus, competition may be necessary to provide the appropriate level of challenge and to judge improvement. In a sense, the competition is inherent in the activity. On the other hand, competition may play a different role in other areas such as academics or vocational skills where it is not really inherent to the task. In such cases, competition may focus attention on normative ability and promote ego involvement. Competition has been found to reduce intrinsic motivation for puzzle construction. Deci, Betley, Kahle, Abrams, and Porac (1981) reported that subjects instructed to try to complete a puzzle faster than another subject subsequently demonstrated less intrinsic interest in the task than subjects not instructed to compete.

THE EFFECTS OF COMPETENCE FEEDBACK IN TASK INVOLVEMENT AND EGO INVOLVEMENT

Because the conception of ability individuals use can vary with their achievement goals, it seems logical that the effectiveness of feedback in sustaining engagement in the activity would depend on the relevance of the feedback to the conception of ability employed. When individuals are task-involved, they are interested in assessing their improvement and mastery of the task. Often this type of information is inherent in the task itself if there are repeated trials at the same activity and changes in performance are obvious. However, if this information is not inherent in the task, social comparison information (e.g., finding out that you are performing above average) is not relevant to assessing performance improvement and would be unlikely to sustain interest in the task. On the other hand, when individuals are ego-involved their goal is to perform better than others. Social comparison information that indicates success in outperforming others is likely to result in persistence at the task, but simple performance feedback may not. Some support for these hypotheses is found in Ryan's (1982) study in which intrinsic motivation was reduced for subjects given ego-involving instructions as compared to subjects given task-involving instructions when informational feedback was provided. Under neutral conditions, Pittman, Davey, Alafat, Wetherill, and Kramer (1980) found that feedback indicating that the subject was doing well increased intrinsic motivation relative to no informational feedback.

To further explore the effectiveness of different types of feedback in sustaining task interest in task and ego involvement, I conducted an experiment that varied the type of feedback provided to college students performing a computer game under task- and ego-involving instructions (Jagacinski, 1983). One-half of the students were led to believe that their performance on the computer game was an assessment of intelligence through psychomotor performance (ego-involving instruction). The rest of the students were told that I was interested in finding out how interesting and enjoyable college students found different versions of a computer game (task-involving instruction). The task was a modified version of the Little Brick Out Game designed for Apple Computers. Students scored points by deflecting a ball off of the paddle on the right side of the screen and knocking bricks out of a wall on the left side of the screen. In the modified version of the game each trial lasted for 1 minute with the student receiving as many balls as were required during that time (a new ball was served whenever the student missed one). Nonveridical feedback messages appeared on the screen after Trials 1, 3, 5, and 7. Students were told that a score was derived as a function of the speed and accuracy of their responses, the total score, and the number of balls used in each trial.

Half of the students in the task- and ego-involving conditions were given social comparison information reported in terms of percentiles. The rest of the students were given self-referent feedback that displayed improvement or decline in performance. All students received positive feedback regardless of their performance. Students were given an opportunity to play extra trials after the seven experimental trials were completed.

The task turned out to be more interesting and enjoyable for women than for men. Men in the experiment had much more experience with computer games and perhaps found this one too simplistic. A significant triple interaction was found for involvement, gender, and feedback on task persistence. Women given task-involving instructions were more likely to persist following self-referent feedback than social comparison feedback, whereas the opposite pattern was obtained for women given ego-involving instructions. In the latter case there was greater persistence following social comparison feedback than following self-referent feedback. For men, differences among the feedback by involvement groups were not statistically significant. The pattern of results for women suggests that the feedback needs to be relevant to the subject's conception of competence in order to enhance persistence. Hence, self-referent feedback is not relevant when your goal is to perform better than others, and knowing that you are performing better than others is not relevant if your main concern is improvement.

Similar evidence of the effect of matching the feedback to the student's achievement goal was found in a study by Sansone (1986). In this experiment subjects given ego-involving instructions expressed greater task enjoyment following positive normative feedback than when simply given information about the correct answers. In addition, perceptions of ability assessed in a normative sense were positively related to task enjoyment in an ego-involving context, but not in a neutral context.

Butler (1987) investigated the effects of different types of feedback on task interest, performance, perceived success, and requests for additional tasks. Fifth- and sixth-grade students performed a divergent thinking task and were given different types of feedback. Students who were given normative grades expressed less interest in the activity, requested fewer additional tasks, and performed less well than students given comments on their performance. The comments consisted of single phrases including a reinforcing and a goal-setting component. There was no significant difference in task interest of high and low achievers in the normative grades condition. One might expect high achievers to get high grades that would enhance their competence and increase task interest. In fact, the high achievers did get higher grades, but both the high and low achievers expressed lower perceived success than subjects who received comments. This suggests that the grades were not interpreted as being that positive by the high achievers.

Butler (1988) also found that combining grades and comments did not improve performance. Students who received both grades and comments performed less well and expressed less task interest than students who only received comments. Furthermore, students who received praise did not perform as well as students receiving comments (Butler, 1987).

Koestner, Zuckerman, and Koestner (1987) investigated the effects of effort and ability feedback in the context of ego-involving versus task-focused instructions. The effort feedback suggested that the subject worked very hard at the task and seemed to work harder than others. The ability feedback informed subjects that they were above average and seemed to have a knack for the puzzles. With ego-involving instructions, there was less task persistence following effort feedback than ability feedback. This makes sense in that success through higher effort than others implies lower ability for ego-involved subjects. In the task focus condition, there was no difference in task persistence for subjects receiving ability and effort feedback. The same pattern of results was found for performance scores on a related task following the feedback.

These studies highlight the importance of different types of evaluation for performance and task interest. Under neutral or task-involving conditions normative feedback that should promote ego involvement tends to lead to decreased task interest and in some cases poorer performance than feedback that is relevant to improvement.

EFFECTS OF EGO-INVOLVING INSTRUCTIONS ON PERFORMANCE

There is also evidence that ego-involving instructions tend to result in poorer performance than task-involving instructions. In most studies that investigate this instructional effect, the ego-involving instructions suggest that performance on the task represents a valid assessment of intelligence. Graham and Golan (1991) investigated fifth and sixth graders recall of words that had been processed at a deep or shallow level following task- or ego-involving instructions. Students were presented with 60 nouns, one at a time, each with an encoding question to which they answered "yes" or "no." For shallow processing, the encoding question concerned whether or not the word rhymed with another. For deep processing, the question asked if the noun was an exemplar of a particular category or if it would fit in a given sentence. An unexpected recall test followed the task. Although the instructions did not lead to differences in the recall of words processed at a shallow level, ego-involving instructions led to poorer recall of words that had been processed at a deep level than did task-involving instructions.

Elliott and Dweck (1988) investigated the performance of fifth graders on a discrimination task following failure. Half of the students were given ego-involving instructions and half were given task-involving instructions. In addition, one half of the students in each group were led to believe that they had high ability for the task, whereas the rest were told that they had low ability. Under the ego-involving instructions, the low-ability group used less appropriate strategies and made verbal attributions for their performance to uncontrollable causes to a greater extent than did the high-ability group. Under task-involving instructions both the high- and low-ability groups maintained their performance after failure and did not tend to make attributional statements about their performance.

Hall (1988) found a similar result for college students engaged in balancing on a stability platform. Based on a series of practice trials, half of the subjects were told that they were very good at the task, whereas the rest were told that they were not very good. During the experimental trials subjects were instructed to try to improve their performance by 60%. All received feedback indicating that they were improving. In addition, half of the subjects were told that compared to others their performance was well below average. Subjects who had been told that they were good at the task performed equally well given improvement feedback or improvement feedback plus negative social comparison information. However, among the subjects who were told that they were not very good at the task, the negative social comparison information led to poorer performance than did the simple improvement feedback.

THE NATURE OF TASK- AND EGO-INVOLVING CONDITIONS

What is it about ego-involving instructions that affects students' achievement-related cognitions and behaviors? Several studies have contrasted affects and attributions under task- and ego-involving instructions. I have found that subjects given ego-involving instructions report feeling more anxious and tense while performing a task than subjects given task-involving instructions (Jagacinski, 1983). In addition, Ryan (1982) and Plant and Ryan (1985) found that subjects report greater tension and pressure following ego-involving, as compared to task-involving, instructions.

Butler (1987) investigated the effects of different types of feedback on students attributions for their effort and attributions of success. Students who received comments on their performance were more likely to attribute their effort to interest and a desire to improve their performance than students who received normative grades. The students who received normative grades were more likely to attribute their effort to a desire to do better than others and to avoid doing worse than others. In terms of attributions for success, students receiving comments were higher on interest and effort, whereas those receiving normative grades were higher on ability and other's outcomes. These results suggest that the feedback conditions activate different ways of thinking about one's performance that are consistent with the different conceptions of ability.

CLASSROOM STUDIES OF ACHIEVEMENT GOAL ORIENTATIONS

Recent research in classroom settings has assessed students' goal orientations for school in general (e.g., Nicholls, 1989; Nicholls, Patashnick, & Nolen, 1985) or for specific classes (e.g., Meece, Blumenfeld, & Hoyle, 1988). A task or mastery orientation has been distinguished from an ego orientation. Students high in task orientation endorse items expressing a concern with learning and understanding. An ego orientation is characterized by a concern with being superior to others and demonstrating how smart one is. In general, scales assessing these orientations have been found to be uncorrelated. That is, students are as likely to be characterized as high or low in both task and ego orientations as they are to be high in one and low in the other. This indicates that task and ego orientations do not represent opposite ends of a continuum, but rather two separate dimensions. Furthermore, correlations between the orientations and perceived ability typically are quite small or not statistically significant.

Students' achievement goal orientations have been found to relate to beliefs about the causes of success. A task orientation is associated with beliefs that interest and effort determine success, whereas an ego orientation is associated with a belief in the importance of ability and competition for academic success (Nicholls et al., 1989). Thus, there is a consistency between students' goal orientations and their beliefs about the causes of success in school. In addition, task orientation, but not ego orientation, is positively related to satisfaction with school.

Students' goal orientations have also been found to relate to their learning behaviors. Nolen (1988) reported that task orientation, but not ego orientation, is related to the use of deep-processing strategies by junior high school students when reading science materials. Meece et al. (1988) have also found that a task orientation, more than an ego orientation, is related to the use of active cognitive engagement strategies in science learning activities for fifth and sixth graders. In addition, Ames and Archer (1988) reported a positive relationship between mastery orientation for a specific class and the number of learning strategies the students used.

Students' goal orientations have been treated as individual difference variables. However, it seems more likely that they are affected by both situational factors and dispositional factors. Several classroom-based studies have suggested that the situation can influence the students' goal orientations. Two research programs present results relevant to this issue.

Cobb, Yackel, and Wood (1989) reported on a field-based experiment in which a cooperative problem-solving approach to learning mathematics was attempted in a second-grade class. Students worked together in small groups to try to solve problems. The groups later came together to discuss their solutions and to resolve conflicts. Students knew that they would have to justify their answers and that thinking was more important than getting the right answers. Children in this class became quite excited when they were able to solve a problem regardless of whether or not other groups had already solved it. An assessment of the goal orientations of the students in this class relative to other second-grade classes revealed that these students were higher on task orientation and lower on ego orientation (Nicholls, Cobb, Wood, Yackel, & Patashnick, 1990). In addition, they were more likely to rate understanding and cooperation as causes of success than students in other classes. These results suggest that the classroom experiences can have an effect on the students' motivational orientations.

Additional evidence is presented by Meece (in press) in a descriptive study that examines differences in fifth- and sixth-grade science classes in which students were high or low in task orientation. In classes where students were high in task orientation, there was less emphasis on grades and formal evaluation. In fact, one of the teachers wrote comments on students daily assignments, but did not grade them. There was also more emphasis on cooperation and group projects in the high task-orientation classes. In addition, teachers of high task orientation students placed greater emphasis on the intrinsic value of learning and attempted to relate scientific concepts to students' experiences.

Both of these classroom-based studies find higher task orientation when the process of learning is emphasized and normative evaluation is minimized (see also Ames, this volume). Students are less concerned with how many worksheets they can complete and more concerned with gaining an understanding of new concepts. These findings are consistent with the experimental results reviewed earlier in the chapter.

SUGGESTIONS FOR FUTURE RESEARCH

There is ample evidence now that students react differently to task- and ego-involving conditions. Numerous studies have investigated the effects of task- and ego-involving instructions on students' perceptions of competence, affective reactions, task persistence, and performance. Observed differences are consistent with the hypothesis that students employ a different conception of ability in task involvement and in ego involvement. Anticipated affects following success have been found to be a function of how ability is defined. Persistence and performance have been found to be related to the extent to which different types of feedback enhance feelings of competence for the conception of ability employed.

Research on students' achievement goal orientations has demonstrated that students can interpret the same situation differently. Hence, some students have a task orientation for school and expect success in school to be a function of effort and mastery. Other students have an ego orientation and expect success to be more a function of normative ability. Because these different orientations have been found to be unrelated, students may espouse both viewpoints, or neither. An important area for future research is to examine how different combinations of motivational orientations relate to affects and performance. Some work in this area has already been reported by Meece and Holt (1990). Fifth- and sixth-grade science students who were high in task orientation and low in ego orientation were compared to students who were high on both of these orientations. The results revealed that students with the high task/low ego combination were higher in science grades, achievement test scores, attitudes toward science, intrinsic motivation, and cognitive competence than students high in both orientations.

Current research trends suggest that some researchers deal primarily with self-perceived motivational orientations without examining strong situational factors, whereas other researchers focus on strong situational manipulations without assessing self-perceived motivational orientations. Research is needed that examines how differences in achievement orientations interact with situational demands. How does a student high in both task and ego orientations react in a task- or ego-involving context? Past studies have suggested that students low in perceived ability tend to perform poorly in ego-involving situations, but students high in perceived ability do not. Yet, perceived ability has been found to be only slightly related to achievement orientations for school. Perhaps the performance of low perceived ability students in ego-involving situations will vary with their achievement orientations. Would students with a strong task orientation perform better in such situations than students low in task orientation? Do students who are high in ego orientation but low in task orientation perform well in task-involving conditions? The interface of dispositional factors and strong situational factors has yet to be systematically explored.

The effects of competition on task- and ego-involving activities also need to be explored more thoroughly. How the individual interprets competition may be important. Perhaps when it is viewed as an inherent part of the activity or the norm for the activity it will not be detrimental. It does appear that competition in and of itself does not necessarily produce ego involvement. This is most obvious in the area of sports. It is clear that normative evaluation which is related to competition can have a negative impact on performance particularly for students with low perceived ability. The salience of this type of evaluation may lead students to seek out and attend to social comparison information. However, does interest in working on a project for a science fair decline because someone will be declared a winner? The effects of different types of competitive situations need to be examined more closely.

APPLICATIONS

The research reviewed in this chapter suggests that it would be most beneficial to promote task involvement in the classroom. Although we have very clear ideas on how to promote ego involvement, fostering task involvement may be less straightforward. The research reviewed here suggests that task involvement can be fostered by avoiding normative comparisons and by developing an interest in learning for its own sake.

The classroom environment needs to support a focus on the less differentiated conception of ability. This can be achieved in part by avoiding evaluation in the normative sense. Butler (1987, 1988) noted that normative grading even when accompanied by comments tended to reduce student performance and intrinsic interest relative to simply providing comments. Personalized comments that included a goal were very effective. Butler also found that simple praise (e.g., "very good") was quite similar to normative grades in its effects on performance and affective reactions. Meece (in press) noted that in a classroom where students were high in task orientation, the teacher never graded homework but simply provided comments. Other techniques used in classrooms with high task-oriented students included using quizzes for review rather than evaluation and providing opportunities to retake tests. Classrooms where students were lower in task orientation demonstrated much more emphasis on normative evaluation (Meece, in press). Grades were often posted and frequent references were made to learning the material for a test or quiz.

It is also important to foster a concern with learning for its own sake. This can be achieved in part through the types of classroom norms that are developed. For example, in the second-grade mathematics class described in Cobb et al. (1989), there was an emphasis on the thinking process. Whether the answer was correct or not was less important than the thinking process used to get the answer. There was also a classroom norm that banned the use of the phrase "that's easy" because it could hurt people's feelings. Both of these techniques are designed to allow students to make mistakes and to learn from them without feeling incompetent. The students also recognized that figuring things out for yourself is fun. Students were visibly excited when they solved a problem even if others had already figured it out.

Cooperative learning activities have also been found to promote task involvement. This approach typically involves an interdependent reward system so that students become less concerned with evaluation. In addition, students help each other and learn to justify their answers in the process. These activities also offer opportunities for students to exert more control over the learning process which tends to increase their sense of involvement and their interest.

Self-directed learning can also be promoted by providing students with sources of feedback other than the teacher. Meece (in press) noted that in classrooms where students were high in task-orientation feedback was provided either inherently in the task or from some external source other than the teacher. On the other hand, in classrooms where students were low in task orientation most feedback was provided directly by the teacher.

Another factor that can foster task involvement is the incentives the teacher offers for learning. Ego involvement is most likely to occur if students are told they are learning material for a test. The classroom-based studies reviewed here find that students are higher in task orientation when their teachers stress the importance of understanding concepts, pose meaningful problems, and attempt to relate new concepts to the students' personal lives. Also, to ensure opportunities for success, these teachers adapted the difficulty level of the material to the abilities of the students.

The goal of promoting task involvement in the classroom is clearly not a simple one (see Ames, this volume). Little of the research reviewed in this chapter directly addresses the role of the teacher in promoting task involvement, yet the teacher is obviously the key factor. The situational factors discussed in this chapter can be manipulated by the teacher. Clearly the teacher sets the tone and goals of the class and the teacher's interests and values are communicated to the class.

REFERENCES

Ames, C. (1984). Competitive, cooperative, and individualistic goal structures: A motivational analysis. In R. Ames & C. Ames (Eds.), *Research on motivation in education: Student motivation* (pp. 177–207). New York: Academic Press.

Ames, C., Ames, R., & Felker, D. (1977). Effects of competitive reward structure and valence of outcome on children's achievement attributions. *Journal of Educational Psychology, 69,* 1–8.

Ames, C., & Archer, J. (1988). Achievement goals in the classroom: Student learning strategies and motivation processes. *Journal of Educational Psychology, 80,* 260–267.

Brown, J., & Weiner, B. (1984). Affective consequences of ability versus effort ascriptions: Controversies, resolutions, and quandaries. *Journal of Educational Psychology, 76,* 146–158.

Butler, R. (1987). Task-involving and ego-involving properties of evaluation: Effects of different feedback conditions on motivational perceptions, interest and performance. *Journal of Educational Psychology, 79,* 474–482.

Butler, R. (1988). Enhancing and undermining intrinsic motivation: The effects of task-involving and ego-involving evaluation on interest and performance. *British Journal of Educational Psychology, 58,* 1–14.

Cobb, P., Yackel, E., & Wood, T. (1989). Young children's emotional acts while engaged in mathematical problem solving. In D. B. McLeod & V. M. Adams (Eds.), *Affect and mathematical problem solving: A new perspective* (pp. 117–148). New York: Springer-Verlag.

Covington, M. V., & Omelich, C. L. (1979). Effort: The double-edged sword in school achievement. *Journal of Educational Psychology, 71,* 169–182.

Deci, E. L., Betley, G., Kahle, J., Abrams, L., & Porac, J. (1981). When trying to win: Competition and intrinsic motivation. *Personality and Social Psychology Bulletin, 7,* 79–83.

Duda, J. L. (1988). The relationship between goal perspectives, persistence and behavioral intensity among male and female recreational sport participants. *Leisure Sciences, 10,* 95–106.

Dweck, C. S. (1986). Motivational processes affecting learning. *American Psychologist, 41,* 1040–1048.

Elliott, E. S., & Dweck, C. S. (1988). Goals: An approach to motivation and achievement. *Journal of Personality and Social Psychology, 54,* 5–12.

Graham, S., & Golan, S. (1991). Motivational influences on cognition: Task involvement, ego involvement, and depth of information processing. *Journal of Educational Psychology, 83,* 187–194.

Hall, H. K. (1988, June). *Goal setting in sport: A social cognitive interpretation.* Paper presented at the annual meeting of the North American Society for the Psychology of Sport and Physical Activity, Knoxville, TN.

Jagacinski, C. M. (1983, August). *Effects of feedback on intrinsic motivation in different achievement contexts.* Paper presented at the meeting of the American Psychological Association, Anaheim, CA.

Jagacinski, C. M., & Nicholls, J. G. (1984). Conceptions of ability and related affects in task involvement and ego involvement. *Journal of Educational Psychology, 76,* 909–919.

Jagacinski, C. M., & Nicholls, J. G. (1987). Competence and affect in task involvement and ego involvement: The impact of social comparison information. *Journal of Educational Psychology, 79,* 107–114.

Koestner, R., Zuckerman, M., & Koestner, J. (1987). Praise, involvement and intrinsic motivation. *Journal of Personality and Social Psychology, 53,* 383–390.

Meece, J. L. (in press). The classroom context and children's motivational goals. In M. Maehr & P. Pintrich (Eds.), *Advances in achievement motivation research* (Vol. 7). New York: Academic Press.

Meece, J. L., Blumenfeld, P., & Hoyle, R. (1988). Factors influencing students' goal orientation and cognitive engagement in classroom activities. *Journal of Educational Psychology, 80,* 514–523.

Meece, J. L., & Holt, K. (1990). *Classification and validation of achievement goal patterns in elementary school.* Unpublished manuscript.

Nicholls, J. G. (1978). The development of the concepts of effort and ability, perception of own attainment, and the understanding that difficult tasks demand more ability. *Child Development, 49,* 800–814.

Nicholls, J. G. (1984). Achievement motivation: Conceptions of ability, subjective experience, task choice, and performance. *Psychological Review, 91,* 328–346.

Nicholls, J. G. (1989). *The competitive ethos and democratic education.* Cambridge, MA: Harvard University Press.

Nicholls, J. G., Cheung, P. C., Lauer, J., & Patashnick, M. (1989). Individual differences in academic motivation: Perceived ability, goals, beliefs, and values. *Learning and Individual Differences, 1,* 63–84.

Nicholls, J. G., Cobb, P., Wood, T., Yackel, E., & Patashnick, M. (1990). Assessing students' theories of success in mathematics: Individual and classroom differences. *Journal of Research in Mathematics Education, 21,* 109–122.

Nicholls, J. G., & Miller, A. T. (1984). Development and its discontents: The differentiation of the concept of ability. In J. G. Nicholls (Ed.), *The development of achievement motivation* (pp. 185–218). Greenwich, CT: JAI Press.

Nicholls, J. G., Patashnick, M., & Nolen, S. B. (1985). Adolescents' theories of education. *Journal of Educational Psychology, 77,* 683–692.

Nolen, S. B. (1988). Reasons for studying: Motivational orientations and study strategies. *Cognition and Instruction, 5,* 267–287.

Pittman, T. S., Davey, M. E., Alafat, K. A., Wetherill, K. V., & Kramer, N. A. (1980). Informational versus controlling verbal rewards. *Personality and Social Psychology Bulletin, 6,* 228–233.

Plant, R. W., & Ryan, R. M. (1985). Intrinsic motivation and the effects of self-consciousness, self-awareness, and ego-involvement: An investigation of internally controlling styles. *Journal of Personality, 53,* 435–449.

Ryan, R. M. (1982). Control and information in the intrapersonal sphere: An extension of cognitive evaluation theory. *Journal of Personality and Social Psychology, 43,* 450–461.

Sansone, C. (1986). A question of competence: The effects of competence and task feedback on intrinsic interest. *Journal of Personality and Social Psychology, 51,* 918–931.

15

Achievement Goals and the Classroom Motivational Climate

CAROLE AMES
University of Illinois at Urbana-Champaign

Although achievement motivation has traditionally been construed as goal-directed behavior, the recent literature (Dweck, 1986; Dweck & Elliott, 1983; Dweck & Leggett, 1988; Eliott & Dweck, 1988) has moved toward defining a broad conceptual framework for organizing both the cognitive and affective components of motivation. This framework has been identified as a theory of achievement goals (Ames & Ames, 1984; Dweck, 1986; Maehr, 1984; Maehr & Nicholls, 1980; Nicholls, 1979, 1984a, 1989, this volume). Achievement goals define patterns of motivation that represent different ways of approaching, engaging in, and responding to achievement-related activities. According to Elliott and Dweck (1988), the adoption of a particular achievement goal serves to trigger a "program" of cognitive processes that are related to how individuals attend to, interpret, and respond to informational cues and situational demands. Others (Ames & Ames, 1984; Butler, 1987, in press; Corno & Rohrkemper, 1985; Nicholls, 1984b, this volume) describe how cognitions about self, tasks, and others are impacted by how an individual interprets situational demands.

Considerable research (for reviews see Brophy, 1983; Covington, 1984; Covington & Beery, 1976; Dweck, 1986; Nicholls, 1984b) has focused on distinguishing positive or adaptive from negative or maladaptive patterns of motivation and defining them in terms of a number of cognitive and affective processes. A positive motivational pattern, for example, involves a belief that effort and outcome covary, and it is this belief that maintains achievement-directed behavior over time and in the face of obstacles. According to Dweck (1986), an adaptive or "mastery-oriented" motivational pattern is also characterized by the use of effective task strategies, a belief in one's ability to improve, a preference for challenging tasks, and feelings of satisfaction when effort is applied to difficult tasks and when effort leads to personal success.

In contrast, a maladaptive or "helpless" pattern (Diener & Dweck, 1978, 1980; Dweck & Repucci, 1973) is evident when children engage in ineffective task cognitions and negative self-evaluations in the face of difficulty. Covington (e.g., 1984) argued that a negative motivational pattern occurs when an individual's self-worth is threatened by an overemphasis on ability and performance, the presence of competition and social comparison, and unrealistic expectations. In fact, considerable evidence suggests that social comparison may be among the most potent factors contributing to a negative motivation pattern (e.g., Ames & Ames, 1984; Covington & Omelich, 1984; Nicholls, 1989).

In this chapter, I first describe how achievement-goal theory provides a viable framework for understanding motivational processes within the context of the classroom. Second I discuss how these achievement goals translate into specific classroom processes and describe a paradigm for studying the motivational climate of the classroom.

ACHIEVEMENT GOALS: OVERVIEW

The research literature now suggests that positive and negative patterns of cognition and affect may be elicited by different reasons for task engagement, that is, different goals or purposes for achievement activity (Ames, in press; Ames & Ames, 1984; Dweck, 1986; Maehr, 1984; Nicholls, 1984b, 1989). A positive pattern is more likely to evolve when individuals adopt a mastery goal orientation (Ames & Archer, 1988). When mastery-oriented, individuals are focused on developing new skills, improving their present level of skill or competence, or attaining a sense of mastery based on an internalized set of standards. Intrinsic value is attached to involvement and participation in the achievement activity itself. Effort is viewed as the means for achieving success and personal satisfaction, and achievement behavior is guided by a belief that effort will lead to success or mastery.

A negative pattern, on the other hand, occurs when individuals are focused on their ability to perform and when interpersonal competition, normative standards, or public evaluation are emphasized. In these situations, individuals adopt a performance goal orientation where demonstrating or protecting one's self-worth is of primary concern (Dweck & Leggett, 1988; Jagacinski, this volume; Nicholls, 1979, 1984, this volume). With a performance goal orientation, individuals are concerned with being judged as able, and ability is evidenced by being successful, by doing better than others, or by succeeding with little effort. Effort can become the double-edged sword when trying hard does not lead to success (Covington & Omelich, 1979).

These two goal constructs that I have contrasted as mastery and performance have been similarly described and elaborated by others and labeled as learning and performance goals (Dweck, 1986; Dweck & Leggett, 1988; Elliott & Dweck, 1986) and as task involvement and ego involvement (Maehr & Nicholls, 1980; Jagacinski, this volume; Nicholls, 1979, 1984a, this volume). In addition, Brophy's (1983) description of "motivation to learn" where the goal is to master new skills or content is compatible with a mastery goal as defined here. Certainly, there are other reasons for achievement-directed behavior as when individuals strive for extrinsic rewards (see, e.g., Nicholls, Patashnick, & Nolen, 1985; Wentzel, this volume). Nevertheless, children are more likely to exhibit a positive motivational pattern when they adopt a mastery goal orientation (see, e.g., Ames, 1990; Ames & Archer, 1988; Dweck, 1986; Meece, Blumenfeld, & Hoyle, 1988; Nicholls et al., 1985).

Nicholls (1979; see also Ames & Ames, 1984) described a set of cognitions that accompany a mastery (task-involving) orientation that involve a focusing on the task "How can I understand this?" (p. 1078). Task-related cognitions such as problem-solving strategies, self-instructions, and self-monitoring have been found to occur when children are focused on their progress toward goals and mastering new skills (Ames, 1984a; Ames & Archer, 1988; Diener & Dweck, 1978; Meece et al., 1988; Nolen, 1987, 1988; Stipek & Kowalski, 1989). When task engagement is guided by a mastery goal, engagement appears to be accompanied by a range of self-guiding thoughts that facilitate high quality involvement in learning (Brophy, 1986; Corno & Mandinach, 1983; Corno & Rohrkemper, 1985). The belief that effort is necessary for success or improvement and a willingness to apply such effort is the impetus for this type of task engagement. As a consequence, positive affect is linked to effort utilization, successful effort, and to the activity itself.

ACHIEVEMENT GOALS AND CLASSROOM FACTORS

Considerable research has focused on linking specific motivation patterns with different goal orientations (Dweck & Leggett, 1988;

Elliott & Dweck, 1988; Meece & Holt, 1990; Nicholls et al., 1985; Wentzel, 1989). This work continues to provide valuable insights about clusters of motivation-related variables that are associated with different goals. Moreover, research from both experimental and field studies suggests that situational factors and instructional demands can influence the salience of a particular goal and, hence, its adoption (Ames & Archer, 1988; Grolnick & Ryan, 1987a; Jagacinski, This volume; Meece, in press). If we want to enhance the quality of students' involvement in learning, increase the likelihood that they will opt for and persevere in challenging learning activities, and develop an interest in learning, positive attitudes toward school, and confidence in themselves as a student and learner, we need to ask how we can translate a mastery goal orientation into actual classroom processes. Can we define a set of principles as well as instructional strategies and practices that can serve to enhance a mastery orientation in the classroom?

Brophy (1983) suggested that if we are serious about the need for enhancing student motivation, we need to focus on classrooms and examine how the classroom can be structured to optimize student motivation. Nicholls et al. (1989; see also Nicholls, 1989, this volume) additionally argued that changing motivation may involve changing students' views about society, the purposes of learning, and what school should and can do (p. 78). It has also been suggested that beliefs about the nature of ability and conceptions of intelligence may be precursors to achievement goals and resulting motivation patterns (Dweck & Elliott, 1988; Elliott & Dweck, 1988; Jagacinski, this volume; Nicholls, 1984b, this volume). Nevertheless, there is now a literature converging on the critical role the classroom structure plays in influencing student motivation. Teachers' roles and instructional practices may have to be modified or changed if we want to elicit a mastery goal orientation and positive motivational patterns in students (Brophy, 1986, 1987; de Charms, 1976; Johnson & Johnson, 1984; Lepper, 1989).

Some literature (Blumenfeld, Pintrich, Meece, & Wessel, 1982; Good & Brophy, 1987) suggests that the mastery orientation of many elementary school classrooms is weak at best. Students often pay little attention to the purposes of specific learning activities (Brophy, 1986). Uniform tasks, few opportunities for choice, normative evaluation, and public social comparisons are commonplace. Extrinsic rewards and incentive programs are pervasive and are used with little or no attention to children's level of interest or capability. Within-class ability grouping has become the venue for instruction. Students often pay little attention to the purposes of specific learning activities (Brophy,

1986). Many children, especially those who are low achieving, are faced with a repetition of drill and practice tasks, rarely see their effort as increasing their competence at school tasks, and as a result, they tend to view school as "joyless" and "arduous" (Levin, 1990).

How, then, can a mastery goal be conceptualized in relation to specific classroom processes? And, can we begin to define how teachers can enhance the mastery orientation of their classroom? The literature points to a number of classroom variables and instructional practices that can influence whether or not students adopt a mastery goal orientation. Meece (in press), for example, suggests that a mastery goal orientation becomes evident when the teachers' instructional approach is designed to promote meaningful, rather than rote, learning, is adapted to students' interests, promotes positive peer relationships, and emphasizes the intrinsic value of learning. Evaluation practices, task design, and grouping arrangements have been consistently identified as structural features of classrooms that influence a wide range of motivational processes including task preferences, self-concept of ability, interest in learning, and persistence (see e.g., Covington & Beery, 1976; Mac Iver, 1988; Marshall & Weinstein, 1984, 1986; Rosenholtz & Simpson, 1984a, 1984b; Stipek & Daniels, 1988). According to Corno and Rohrkemper (1985; see also Brophy, 1983), students are more likely to exhibit a motivation to learn when the teacher provides instructional support, establishes realistic, but challenging goals, and encourages effort. Finally, Stipek and Daniels (1988; see also Rosenholtz & Rosenholtz, 1981) suggest that teachers' practices for evaluation, grouping, assigning uniform or differentiated tasks, and involving students in decision making can influence the structure of the learning environment and the potency of different achievement goals.

As discussed, there is now a broad base of literature in the field of motivation that provides a conceptual framework for defining a mastery goal orientation. Furthermore, much related research literature (see earlier) identifies specific classroom parameters that should reflect a mastery goal structure. And, finally, the literature on achievement motivation offers both general and specific principles that, on the one hand, have been linked to adaptive motivation processes and, on the other, are conceptually consistent with a mastery goal orientation. Although there are several classroom studies (Ames & Archer, 1988; Mac Iver, 1988; Meece & Holt, 1990; Stipek & Daniels, 1988) that have linked some specific elements of a mastery goal orientation to positive motivational patterns, there is little experimental research that has actually attempted to change the motivational goal orientation of the classroom.

ACHIEVEMENT GOALS: CLASSROOM INTERVENTION

Our current and ongoing research (e.g., Ames, 1990; Ames & Maehr, 1989) is focused on this latter issue, that is, changing the climate of elementary school classrooms by enhancing a mastery goal orientation. This project involves evaluating an intervention program that we have designed to stimulate adaptive patterns of motivation in elementary school-age children. In this work, we first defined a mastery goal orientation in terms of actual classroom parameters and then focused on six highly salient dimensions of the classroom learning environment that can be structured to emphasize a mastery goal orientation. These dimensions include task design, distribution of authority, recognition of students, grouping arrangements, evaluation practices, and time allocation. These six areas were initially identified and described by Joyce Epstein (1988, 1989) as manipulable structures of both school and home learning environments that relate to children's motivation and development. She used the acronym TARGET to represent the six structures: task, authority, recognition, grouping, evaluation, and time.

The research literature on motivation offers a wide range of motivational principles and strategies that relate to each of these TARGET areas and that are consistent with a mastery goal orientation. An underlying assumption guiding this research has been that a mastery goal orientation must be integrated within all dimensions of the classroom structure. Epstein's TARGET structures provided a comprehensive framework for organizing these principles and strategies. Thus, our task has involved mapping these strategies onto the TARGET areas. As part of the intervention, we have additionally compiled specific techniques and actual instructional practices used by teachers that served to operationalize these principles and strategies. The intervention, therefore, has involved teachers implementing these strategies through a wide variety of instructional practices on a day-to-day basis.

In the remainder of this chapter, I describe how each of these six TARGET areas relates to a mastery goal orientation, first by identifying specific motivational principles and strategies within each area that enhance a mastery orientation, and second by describing supporting research evidence. For a rich description of each Target structure, the reader is referred to Epstein (1988, 1989).

TARGET Areas of the Classroom

Task Dimension.   The TASK area of the classroom concerns the design of learning activities, tasks, and assignments (Epstein, 1988).

There are a number of motivational strategies concerning the design of tasks which are consistent with a mastery orientation. The purpose of these strategies is to increase children's involvement and interest in learning as well as the quality of their engagement (Epstein, 1988). Some of these strategies include:

1. Designing activities that make learning interesting and that involve variety and personal challenge. Children should understand the reasons for engaging in learning tasks and classwork (Brophy, 1986).
2. Helping students establish realistic goals. With short-term goals, students view their classwork as manageable, and they can focus on their progress and what they are learning (Schunk, 1989).
3. Helping students develop organizational and management skills and effective task strategies. Students, especially those with learning difficulties, need to develop and apply strategies for planning, organizing, and monitoring their work (Corno & Mandinach, 1983; Corno & Rohrkemper, 1985).

A number of researchers have argued effectively for diversity, variety, and novelty in the design and structure of classroom tasks (Brophy, 1986; Lepper & Hodell, 1989; Marshall & Weinstein, 1984, 1986; Rosenholtz & Simpson, 1984b). Brophy and Merrick (1987) have defined a rather comprehensive scheme for organizing both general and specific motivational principles as they apply to classroom learning and have tested them in an intervention in junior high school classrooms. In this intervention, they used variety, novelty, and active participation as descriptors of how tasks and learning should be structured. In the area of task design, their list of recommended motivational strategies included both general (e.g., "structure activities as learning experiences") and more specific (e.g., "induce task interest for appreciation") elements. Three components of intrinsic motivation—challenge, curiosity, and personal control—as outlined by Malone and Lepper (1987) also have important implications for the structure and design of tasks in the classroom. According to Malone and Lepper (1987; see also Lepper & Hodell, 1989), "motivating" tasks should offer personal challenge, include variety, and appeal to students' interests. Similarly, Corno and Rohrkemper (1989) described "meaningfulness" and "variety" as task conditions that facilitate an interest in learning.

The design of tasks can influence students' perceptions of their own and others' ability. Rosenholtz and Simpson (1984a, 1984b) defined uniformity of tasks as one factor that contributes to what they labeled as an *unidimensional classroom structure.* In classrooms of this type, students tend to use the same materials and have the same assignments. Within a unidimensional structure, students are likely to translate performance differences into ability differences. By contrast, in *multidimensional classrooms,* students tend to work on different kinds of tasks or have different assignments, and there is less opportunity or need for students to compare their performance with others. Hence, students develop a sense of their own ability that is not dependent on social comparison. In their work, diversity in tasks diminished the likelihood that students perceived a hierarchy of ability in the classroom. Variety, as well as choice, of tasks can reduce social comparison among students and the use of comparative information in the process of self-evaluation (Marshall & Weinstein, 1984, 1986).

The reasons students are given for learning can increase the quality of their involvement and affect their selection of learning strategies. Benware and Deci (1984), for example, found that the quality of learning increased when students were told to learn material in order to teach it to another than when they were told to learn the material to take a test. Students who are focused on trying to understand what they are learning tend to report greater satisfaction with school learning in general (Nicholls, et al., 1985). Reasons for learning that emphasize understanding, gaining and improving skills, and task introductions that elicit students' interest are likely to foster a view of "the experience of learning as inherently valuable" (Nicholls et al., 1985, p. 691).

When tasks are structured in such a way that students are involved in goal setting, they are more likely to experience a sense of self-efficacy (for review see Schunk, 1989). Whether the goals are established by the student or the teacher, when they are specific and short-term, the result is enhanced effort on the part of the student (Schunk, 1985). Students' confidence in their ability to do the work is reinforced as they observe their progress toward the goal. At the elementary-school level, a long-term goal might involve an assignment that is given on Monday and due on Friday. Even when time is set aside each day to work on the assignment, some children are likely to become overwhelmed with the whole task in front of them and still others may approach the assignment without any plan or organization in mind. For these children, the assignment typically isn't completed at the end of the week, and the teacher blames the child because he or she had the entire week to complete it. Breaking down the week-long assignment into short-term goals is likely to enhance work completion and children's beliefs that they can do the tasks (see Schunk, 1989).

Finally, Corno and Mandinach (1983) contended that the quality of students' cognitive engagement is determined by their ability to utilize organizing, planning, and monitoring strategies. Children with learning difficulties are often unable to organize their work, plan for its completion, and monitor their progress toward completion. Task design, instructions, and modeling can facilitate the development and application of these skills (Corno & Rohrkemper, 1989).

Authority Dimension. The AUTHORITY area involves students' opportunities to take leadership roles, develop a sense of personal control and independence in their learning. The goals of motivational strategies in this area are to foster active participation and a sense of ownership in the learning process.

1. Giving students opportunities to participate actively in the learning process via leadership roles, choices, and decision making (Epstein, 1988; Ryan, Connell, & Deci, 1985).
2. Helping students develop the skills that will enable them to take responsibility for their learning.

Evidence (Grolnick & Ryan, 1987a, 1987b; Ryan et al., 1985; Ryan & Grolnick, 1986) suggests that children's feelings of self-competence tend to be higher in classrooms that are "autonomy-oriented." This autonomy-oriented climate is described as one where teachers involve students in the learning process by giving them choices (Grolnick & Ryan, 1987a). Giving more responsibility to low-achieving students, in particular, may reduce or eliminate the potentially harmful effects of teachers' low or negative expectations of these students (Marshall & Weinstein, 1984). The strategies teachers use to encourage students to take on challenging tasks and to participate affect children's attitudes toward their own ability, toward school, and toward the learning process (Ryan et al., 1985).

The positive relationship between an autonomy-oriented environment and students' mastery motivation and perceived competence has been supported across numerous studies. Deci, Schwartz, Sheinman, and Ryan (1981), for example, found that elementary school teachers' orientations toward autonomy were related to children's perceived competence and mastery motivation. Moreover, positive changes in children's motivation over time have been related to teachers' orientations toward autonomy (Deci, Nezlek, & Sheinman, 1981). Children have been found to make significant gains in feelings of self-determination when in classrooms of autonomy-oriented teachers (Grolnick & Ryan, 1987b). In his large-scale classroom study, de Charms (1976) attempted to create "origin-like" environments by having teachers use instructional practices that would support student autonomy. These practices involved giving students choices and involving them as active participants in all phases of the learning process. The project findings were indeed complex but provided much support for the argument of involving students in meaningful decision making.

Classroom structures that provide students with choices and opportunities for decision making appear to increase the quality of student engagement in learning (Grolnick & Ryan, 1987b; Ryan et al., 1985). When students are given choices, however, they must perceive the choice as "real." In some instances, telling students that they can choose any book they wish for a book report may only result in some students choosing books that are much too difficult and others choosing books that are too easy. This is especially likely to occur when the students anticipate normative evaluation of their work. If children's choices are motivated by a "failure avoidance" (Covington & Beery, 1976; Covington & Omelich, 1985), feelings of "self-determination" (Ryan et al., 1985) or personal control are not likely to be enhanced. Choices must be perceived as "equal" choices such as giving students a choice among a range of equally difficult books or a choice of equally desirable activities or assignments. The student's choice, then, is guided by his or her interest and not by efforts to protect feelings of self-worth. These constraints are noted by Ryan et al. (1985) when they recommend "providing structure" for children's choices.

Grolnick and Ryan (1987a) further suggest that increased autonomy in learning can also enhance the quality of learning. In one study, Grolnick and Ryan (1987b) found that when children were given a task focus (i.e., minimizing external controls and presumably creating a situation where children should feel a sense of autonomy), conceptual learning was enhanced. Moreover, retention of the material was greater than when students were told they were to be tested and evaluated at a later point in time. This point, of course, is closely related to the evaluation area; and it is well to note here that the TARGET areas naturally overlap but, in that way, they provide a integrated approach to studying classroom processes.

Recognition Dimension. The RECOGNITION area concerns the formal and informal use of rewards, incentives, and praise in the classroom. The types of rewards, reasons for rewards, and the distribution of rewards have important consequences for whether children develop an interest in learning, feelings of self-worth, and a sense of satisfaction with their learning. Recognition and rewards when focused on individual gains, improvement, and progress provide all students with opportunities for recognition (Covington & Beery, 1976). The guidelines for strategies in this area are:

1. Recognizing individual student effort, accomplishments, and improvement.
2. Giving all students opportunities to receive rewards and recognition.
3. Giving recognition and rewards privately so that their value is not derived at the expense of others (Covington & Beery, 1976).

It is well recognized that rewards and incentives can have paradoxical effects on student motivation, interest, and participation (see, e.g., Lepper & Hodell, 1985). Lepper and Hodell chronicled the negative short and long-term consequences that extrinsic rewards can have on children's intrinsic interest in learning. When perceived as "bribes," extrinsic rewards can serve to undermine children's interest and participation over the long term (Lepper & Hodell, 1985). Rewards can become the reason for one's engagement and participation, and when they are perceived as such, the rewards are controlling and detract from the intrinsic value of the task (see Ryan et al., 1985). Ryan et al., however, also suggest that intrinsic interest may not be threatened when rewards are perceived as informative, that is, when they are tied to specific aspects of a child's performance.

The use of incentives in the classroom proves problematic because they are typically applied to all the children (i.e., those whose low participation may require some external incentive as well as those whose participation is moderate or high and voluntary) in the classroom (Lepper & Hodell, 1985). Recent research by Boggiano and her colleagues (Boggiano, Barrett, Weiher, McClelland, & Lusk, 1987) suggests that adults tend to prefer the use of extrinsic reinforcements over other strategies for motivating children. In their study, Boggiano et al. presented a number of scenarios to adults that described children in high and low interest activities. When asked to select a strategy either for increasing or for maintaining the child's interest, the adults preferred extrinsic rewards over other less invasive strategies (e.g., reasoning, noninterference). Moreover, adults paid little attention to information about whether or not children were interested in the activity, participated in the activity, or were capable in the activity.

Programs involving extrinsic rewards (e.g., reading incentive programs) are pervasive in our schools. Even goals established so that everyone can earn a reward or rewards given to recognize individual goals can have negative effects on children's feelings of competence and interest in learning when the goals are viewed as externally imposed and when recognition is made public (Covington & Beery, 1976). Bulletin boards and charts, for example, that display children's accomplishments, work, or progress toward goals invite social comparisons. Even when the progress is toward an individual goal (e.g., a certain number of books to be read), the public forum guarantees that many children will feel a negative form of recognition. Similarly, emphasizing and rewarding perfection (e.g., charting 100% in spelling, redoing work to attain 100%, posting of perfect papers or papers with A's) especially in public makes ability a highly salient dimension of the classroom learning environment. When recognition for accomplishments or progress is private, between the teacher and the child, feelings of personal pride and satisfaction do not derive from doing better than others. Recognizing student effort can also be an important way of enhancing students' feelings of efficacy when they begin new tasks (Schunk, 1989).

In an analysis of teacher praise, Brophy (1981) showed how verbal reinforcements can convey a range of different (and, sometimes unintended) information to a student. According to Brophy, praise is too often directed toward the very general and unimportant aspects of a child's work. When given, praise can also have negative effects on student's motivation when it is used in such a way that elicits social comparison. "Praise can provide encouragement and support when made contingent on effort, . . . when it directs students' attention to genuine progress or accomplishment" (Brophy, 1983, p. 21).

Grouping Dimension. The GROUPING area focuses on students' ability to work effectively with others on school tasks. The goal is to establish an environment where individual differences are accepted and all students develop a feeling of "I belong here." Differences in ability, then, do not translate into differences in motivation. The strategies in this area include:

1. Providing opportunities for cooperative group learning and peer interaction.
2. Using heterogeneous and varied grouping arrangements

The classroom is a social environment, and student relationships and social organizational features of the environment impact student motivation (Corno & Rohrkemper, 1989; Johnson & Johnson, 1985). Consider, for example, a teacher who begins each math class by presenting a challenging problem to the students. The teacher gives the students 5 minutes to think about it and then asks for volunteers to "try it on the board." The activity itself is rather low key, and the teacher is very encouraging even when students make mistakes. Nevertheless, few students volunteer to "try it" and almost none remember the problem when the class period is over. This "individual" activity could elicit more student participation if the students were given 10 minutes to tackle the problem in small groups of three students. Instead of individual students being called upon to share their answer and strategy, one or more small groups could volunteer to share their approach. A small group approach has the advantage of eliciting more student involvement, and "active" learning because it poses substantially less risk for individual students (see Johnson & Johnson, 1985).

Classrooms can be structured so that students work competitively, cooperatively, or individually and each type of structure has different consequences for students' learning and motivation (Ames, 1984b). Classroom structures that emphasize competition or social comparison have been found to elicit thought processes that quite likely impede learning and subsequent motivation (Ames & Ames, 1984). When social comparison is made salient, children tend to focus on their ability and often engage in debilitating self-evaluations and cognitions (Ames, 1984a). By contrast, when students work toward individual goals or within a cooperative structure, children tend to focus more on their effort and positive affect derives from trying hard or working successfully with another (Ames & Ames, 1984).

Low-achieving students, in particular, appear to benefit from cooperative structures (Johnson & Johnson, 1985; Slavin, 1983). Differential ability is not the focus of attention (Ames, 1981) and differential teacher treatment is less visible to students (Marshall & Weinstein, 1984, 1986). As a consequence, individual differences in ability and performance do not translate into peer rejection. Self as well as interpersonal evaluations have been found to be less discrepant as well as more favorable when students experience some success on small group tasks (Ames, 1981). According to Johnson and Johnson's (1985) analysis, cooperative structures promote an interest in learning and a focusing on the value of joint effort.

Small group learning typically allows students to assume more control over their learning (and, in this way, it relates to the Autonomy area) which fosters task involvement (Meece et al., 1988). Corno and Mandinach (1983), however, warn us that cooperative structures can also lead to "recipience" on the part of students. That is, students may become quite willing or even eager to let others take responsibility for the work. Slavin's (1983) emphasis on the importance of individual accountability within cooperative learning models reduces the likelihood that student engagement will be characterized by recipience.

There are many models of cooperative learning (Johnson & Johnson, 1985; Slavin, 1983), and it is beyond the scope of this chapter to review these alternative methods. Research evidence is robust in documenting the benefits of cooperative learning, and in general, cooperative learning appears to facilitate a wide range of processes that contribute to and enhance active engagement in learning.

Evaluation Dimension. The EVALUATION area involves the methods that are used to assess and monitor student learning (Epstein, 1988). Because evaluation is one of the most salient features of the classroom, students' motivation to learn can be easily undermined by how evaluation occurs (Covington & Beery, 1976). Within a mastery goal orientation, students need to feel that it's okay to make mistakes (or that mistakes are a part of learning and not a measure of failure), that they have opportunities to improve, and satisfied when they have applied reasonable effort or when they have achieved mastery, or personal improvement. Some strategies that have been identified within this area are:

1. Evaluating students for individual progress, improvement, and mastery.
2. Giving students opportunities to improve their performance.
3. Varying the method of evaluation and making evaluation private.

It is not only a matter of whether evaluation occurs or doesn't occur, of particular concern is the type, form, and purpose of evaluation; and more importantly, students' perceptions and interpretations of the meaning or intent of the evaluation (Mac Iver, 1987). Evaluation practices can establish very different motivational climates, can orient children toward different goals, and, as a result, can elicit different systems of motivation.

Much literature (Butler, 1987, in press; Covington, 1984; Covington & Omelich, 1984; Crooks, 1988; Jagacinski, this volume; Jagacinski & Nicholls, 1984, 1987) suggests that evaluation practices can have deleterious effects on student motivation when they are normatively based, public, and linked to ability. Evaluation systems that emphasize social comparison tend to lower children's perceptions of their competence when they don't compare favorably and cause them to engage in many self-defeating cognitions and experience considerable negative affect (Ames & Ames, 1984). The negative effects of social comparison and competition have been repeatedly noted in sports settings (Duda, 1989; Roberts, 1984) and the parallels between sport and classroom settings has been elaborated elsewhere (Ames, in press).

Normative evaluation establishes a performance goal orientation that focuses children on evaluating their ability. Children's self-worth becomes linked to ability, and as a consequence, they often engage in failure-avoiding behaviors to protect their feelings of worth (Covington, 1984). Normative-based grades, the most common form of evaluation in school, have been found to reduce children's interest in learning even when the evaluation conveys positive feedback (Butler, 1987; Butler & Nisan, 1986). Covington and Beery (1976) described evaluation as a pervasive phenomenon in most schools and classrooms, and children discover that only work and assignments that are to be graded are important. Finally, evaluation, when it occurs, is often public (e.g., honor rolls are announced, Math Wizzards are posted, perfect papers are displayed, and highest and lowest grades are announced when returning papers), inviting social comparison and, for many students, negative self-evaluations.

Children are more likely to adopt a mastery goal orientation when evaluation is based on personal improvement, progress toward individual goals, participation and effort (Ames, 1984a). Children tend to focus on their effort, rather than ability, and utilize specific task strategies that will contribute to improvement and mastery. Covington and Omelich (1984) found that when students were given opportunities to improve their performance and grades on tests, the connection between ability and feelings of self-worth was severed (see also Covington, 1984). Offering students opportunities to improve their grades suggests to students that mistakes and errors are part of the learning process and not indicative of failure to learn. According to Brophy (1987), evaluation and testing practices should help students assess their own progress and should not be viewed as a way of finding out who is less able.

Evaluation practices that are public, rather than private, and that emphasize social comparison, rather than individual progress, can promote what Marshall and Weinstein (1984) label as a "high differential treatment" classroom. Similarly, the unidimensional classroom described by Rosenholtz and Rosenholtz (1981) is one where grades are frequent, public, and emphasized. In these classrooms, there is much opportunity for students to question their ability and judge their ability as inadequate. Finally, research suggests that we should consider a range of different practices in evaluating students. When Butler and Nisan (1986) compared the effects of different forms of evaluation on student interest in learning, they found that task-specific comments had a more positive influence on interest and commitment than did praise or grades.

Using a variety of evaluation practices and incorporating methods that deemphasize the appearance of an ability hierarchy reduces students' opportunities for social comparison. Mac Iver (1988) studied the impact of grade dispersion in classrooms on students' perceptions of their own and other's ability and found that high dispersion of grades increased the variability in perceived ability among the students. His findings additionally suggest that the frequency of giving grades may be less important than the actual dispersion of grades in the classroom. This dispersion, then, can easily contribute to an hierarchy of perceived ability which translates into motivational inequities (see also Nicholls, 1989).

Time Dimension.   The TIME area concerns the appropriateness of the workload, the pace of instruction, and the time allotted for completing learning activities and assignments (see Epstein, 1988). The TIME area is closely related to the design and structure of tasks because the design of assignments and time allotted for completion must accommodate different entry skills, attention spans, and capabilities. Priorities in the workload and assignments need to be adapted for individual student's skill level, learning rate, and available time for out-of-class learning. The strategies in this area include the following:

1. Adjusting task or time requirements for students who have difficulty completing their work.
2. Allowing students opportunities to plan their schedules, and progress at an optimal rate.

Good (1983) suggested that students' perceptions of tasks and instructions affect how time is used in the classroom. He pointed out that we need to attend to how classroom learning activities can be designed to optimize student rate of learning and achievement. Unfortunately, even when available time is optimized, quality of task engagement may not be affected. Students' opportunity to learn, the quality of that time, and students' ability to apply quality effort are all considerations in this area. Diversity among students in their skills, learning rates, and motivation is evident even in the early school years; as a consequence, schedules, assignment priorities, and time allocations must be flexible to deal with this diversity (Epstein, 1988).

The time structure is closely related to other TARGET areas such as task (e.g., how much children are asked to accomplish within specific time periods), authority (e.g., whether children are allowed to schedule the rate, order, or time of completion of their assignments and activities), grouping (e.g., whether quality of instructional time is equitable across groups), and evaluation (e.g., time pressure on tests, whether the amount of work or criteria for mastery is same for all students). In many classrooms, some children are overwhelmed when confronted with the assignments for the day and as a result, quality of work becomes secondary to quantity of output. In addition, some children see themselves as having few options when they are given the requirements and schedule, and they feel a lack of personal control.

Time limits and pressures during testing even on classroom tests have been found to have debilitating effects on children who become anxious when taking tests (Hill, 1984). By relaxing time limits on tests, the test-taking strategies and actual test performance of middle and high anxious children has been found to improve (Hill, 1984). Hill argued for "optimizing" testing procedures in classrooms to reduce the negative motivational effects of failure. These optimizing conditions included relaxed time limits, providing children with information about the difficulty of the test as well as adjusting the length and frequency of tests. At other times, however, imposing time limits on assignments may provide the necessary structure for completing work. For example, if students are given a certain amount of time to spend on an assignment (without negative consequences if the assignment is completed), told how much time an assignment should require, or asked to give quality effort to a task for a certain amount of time, a willingness to apply effort may be enhanced.

CONCLUSIONS

The TARGET structures provide a framework for integrating specific motivational strategies that are consistent with a mastery goal orientation and for applying achievement goal theory to classroom processes. The goal orientation of a classroom is shaped by how learning is structured and how teachers' instructional practices relate to each of the six TARGET structures. And, more importantly, the goal orientation is dependent on how individual students experience these "structures" in the classroom.

These six structures or dimensions of classroom learning are related to each other and, to some extent, desirably overlap. Moreover, if these dimensions are not coordinated, the positive impact on student motivation of one structure (e.g., adding variety, challenge and short-term goals to the design of tasks) may be undermined or negated by the lack of attention to another structure (e.g., using evaluation practices that emphasize social comparison). In fact, the success of many cooperative learning models in enhancing students' feelings of esteem and learning may be a function of the attention given to all, or most, of the TARGET structures. The guidelines and parameters for cooperative learning are typically quite compatible with the TARGET-defined strategies and with a mastery goal orientation, in general.

To date, our findings (Ames, 1990) suggest that those children who may be most likely to benefit from an enhanced mastery climate are those who are often considered as "at-risk." These are the children who lack confidence in their ability, avoid challenges, do not use effective learning strategies, and have negative affect toward school and classroom learning. As noted by Dweck (1986), many interventions and practices that are used to alleviate poor self-image and lack of confidence often emphasize tangible reinforcements and external incentives for achieving success. These practices, however, do not serve to enhance a mastery goal orientation and, instead, may only increase the perceived importance of ability and performance in the classroom. Within an achievement goal framework, an adaptive or positive goal orientation is not dependent on a single set of strategies or single instructional method. As suggested here, a mastery goal orientation may require a comprehensive view of the classroom processes and an approach that influences a wide range of children's classroom experiences.

Our research on the TARGET structures is ongoing but our findings from the first year of the project (Ames, 1990) suggest that the mastery climate of the elementary school classroom may be increased when teachers implement strategies in the TARGET areas over time. The intervention program has provided promising results in influencing children's interest in learning, use of effective learning strategies, attitudes toward learning, and self-concept of ability.

Finally, we will need to attend to the impact of interventions over time. What happens when children are in mastery-oriented classrooms for one, two, or even three years? Do stable patterns of motivation processes evolve as a result of certain kinds of experiences over time? We also need to move beyond the classroom and examine school-level policies and practices that may undermine teachers' efforts to establish a mastery motivational climate in the classroom. On the positive side, we need to study school-level practices (incentive programs, ways of recognizing students) that can serve to enhance the mastery climate of school, classroom, and even home environments.

ACKNOWLEDGMENT

The research program described herein has been supported by Research Grant DE-H023T80023 from the Office of Special Education and Rehabilitative Services, U.S. Office of Education

REFERENCES

Ames, C. (1981). Competitive versus cooperative reward structures: The influence of individual and group performance factors on achievement attributions and affect. *American Educational Research Journal, 18,* 23–287.

Ames, C. (1984a). Achievement attributions and self-instructions under competitive and individualistic goal structures. *Journal of Educational Psychology, 76,* 478–487.

Ames, C. (1984b). Competitive, cooperative, and individualistic goal structures: A motivational analysis. In R. Ames & C. Ames (Eds.), *Research on motivation in education* (Vol. 1, pp. 177–207). New York: Academic Press.

Ames, C. (1990). *Achievement goals and classroom structure: Developing a learning orientation.* Paper presented at the Annual Meeting of the American Educational Research Association, Boston, MA.

Ames, C. (in press). Achievement goals and adaptive motivation patterns: The role of the environment. In G. Roberts (Ed.), *Motivation in sport and exercise.* Champaign, IL: Human-Kinetics.

Ames, C., & Ames, R. (1984). Systems of student and teacher motivation: Toward a qualitative definition. *Journal of Educational Psychology, 76,* 535–557.

Ames, C., & Archer, J. (1988). Achievement goals in the classroom: Student learning strategies and motivation processes. *Journal of Educational Psychology, 80,* 260–267.

Ames, C., & Maehr, M. (1989). *Home and school cooperation in social and motivational development.* Research funded by the Office of Special Education and Rehabilitative Services, Contract No. DE-H023T80023.

Benware, C., & Deci, E. L. (1984). Quality of learning with an active versus passive motivational set. *American Educational Research Journal, 21,* 755–766.

Blumenfeld, P., Pintrich, P., Meece, J., & Wessel, K. (1982). The role and formation of self-perceptions of ability in elementary school classrooms. *Elementary School Journal, 82,* 401–420.

Boggiano, A., Barrett, M., Weiner, A. W., McClelland, G. H., & Lusk, C. M. (1987). Use of maximal-operant principle to motivate children's intrinsic interest. *Journal of Personality and Social Psychology, 53,* 866–879.

Brophy, J. (1981). Teacher praise: A functional analysis. *Review of Educational Research, 51,* 5–32.

Brophy, J. (1983). Conceptualizing student motivation. *Educational Psychologist, 18,* 200–215.

Brophy, J. (1986). On motivating students. (Occasional paper No. 101). East Lansing, MI: Institute for Research on Teaching.

Brophy, J., & Merrick, M. (1987). *Motivating students to learn: An experiment in junior high social studies classes.* East Lansing, MI: Institute for Research on Teaching.

Butler, R. (1987). Task-involving and ego-involving properties of evaluation: Effects of different feedback conditions on motivational perceptions, interest and performance. *Journal of Educational Psychology, 79,* 474–482.

Butler, R. (in press). Task involving and ego involving properties of evaluation on interest and performance. *Journal of Educational Psychology.*

Butler, R., & Nisan, M. (1986). Effects of no feedback, task-related comments, and grades on intrinsic motivation and performance. *Journal of Educational Psychology, 78,* 210–216.

Corno, L., & Mandinach, E. B. (1983). The role of cognitive enjoyment in classroom learning and motivation. *Educational Psychologist, 18,* 88–108.

Corno, L., & Rohrkemper, M. M. (1985). The intrinsic motivation to learn in the classroom. In C. Ames & R. Ames (Eds.), *Research on motivation in education* (Vol. 2, pp. 53–90). New York: Academic Press.

Covington, M. C. (1984). The motive for self worth. In R. Ames & C. Ames (Eds.), *Research on motivation in education: Student motivation* (pp. 77–113). New York: Academic Press.

Covington, M. C., & Beery, R. G. (1976). *Self worth and school learning.* New York: Holt, Rinehart & Winston.

Covington, M. C., & Omelich, C. (1979). Effort: The double-edged sword in school achievement. *Journal of Educational Psychology, 71,* 169–182.

Covington, M. C., & Omelich, C. (1984). Task-oriented versus competitive learning structures: Motivation and performance consequences. *Journal of Educational Psychology, 76,* 1098–1050.

Covington, M. C., & Omelich, C. (1985). Ability and effort valuation among failure-avoiding and failure-accepting students. *Journal of Educational Psychology, 4,* 446–459.

Crooks, T. J. (1988). Classroom evaluation practices. *Review of Educational Research, 58,* 438–481.

de Charms, R. (1976). *Enhancing motivation: Change in the classroom.* New York: Irvington.

Deci E. L., Nezlek, J., & Sheinman, L. (1981). Characteristics of the rewarder and intrinsic motivation of the rewardee. *Journal of Personality and Social Psychology, 40,* 1–10.

Deci, E. L., Schwartz, A. J., Sheinman, L., & Ryan, R. M. (1981). An instrument to assess adults' orientations toward control versus autonomy in children: Reflections on intrinsic motivation and perceived competence. *Journal of Educational Psychology, 73,* 642–650.

Diener, C. I., & Dweck, C. S. (1978). An analysis of learned helplessness: Continuous changes in performance, strategy, and achievement cognitions following failure. *Journal of Personality and Social Psychology, 36,* 451–462.

Diener, C. I., & Dweck, C. S. (1980). Analysis of learned helplessness II: The processing of success. *Journal of Personality and Social Psychology, 39,* 940–952.

Duda, J. (1989). Goal perspectives and behavior in sport and exercise settings. In M. L. Maehr & C. Ames (Eds.), *Advances in motivation and achievement* (Vol. 6, pp. 81–115). Greenwich, CT: JAI.

Dweck, C. S. (1986). Motivational processes affecting learning. *American Psychologist, 41,* 1040–1048.

Dweck, C. S., & Elliott, E. S. (1983). Achievement motivation. In P. Mussen & E. M. Hetherington (Eds.), *Handbook of child psychology.* New York: Wiley.

Dweck, C. S., & Leggett, E. L. (1988). A social cognitive approach to motivation and personality. *Psychological Review, 95,* 256–273.

Dweck, C. S., & Reppucci, N. D. (1973). Learned helplessness and reinforcement responsibility in children. *Journal of Personality and Social Psychology, 25,* 109–116.

Elliott, E., & Dweck, C. (1988). Goals: An approach to motivation and achievement. *Journal of Personality and Social Psychology, 54,* 5–12.

Epstein, J. L. (1988). Effective schools or effective students: Dealing with diversity. In R. Haskins & D. MacRae (Eds.), *Policies for America's public schools: Teacher equity indicators.* Norwood, NJ: Ablex.

Epstein, J. L. (1989). Family structures and student motivation: A developmental perspective. In C. Ames & R. Ames (Eds.), *Research on motivation in education* (Vol. 3, pp. 259–295). New York: Academic Press.

Good, T. (1983). Classroom research: A decade of progress. *Educational Psychologist, 18,* 127–144.

Good, T., & Brophy, J. (1987). *Looking in classrooms.* New York: Harper & Row.

Grolnick, W. S., & Ryan, R. M. (1987a). Autonomy in children's learning: An experimental and individual difference investigation. *Journal of Personality and Social Psychology, 52,* 890–898.

Grolnick, W. S., & Ryan, R. M. (1987b). Autonomy support in education: Creating the facilitating environment. In N. Hastings & J. Schwieso (Eds.), *New directions in educational psychology: Behavior and motivation.* (pp. 213–232). London: Falmer Press.

Hill, K. T. (1984). Debilitating motivation and testing: A major educational problem. In R. Ames & C. Ames (Eds.), *Research on motivation in education: Student motivation.* New York: Academic Press.

Jagacinski, C. M., & Nicholls, J. G. (1984). Conceptions of ability and related affects in task involvement and ego involvement. *Journal of Educational Psychology, 76,* 909–919.

Jagacinski, C. M., & Nicholls, J. G. (1987). Competence and affect in task involvement and ego involvement: The impact of social comparison information. *Journal of Educational Psychology, 79,* 107–114.

Johnson, D. W., & Johnson, R. T. (1985). Motivational processes in cooperative, competitive, and individualistic learning situations. In C. Ames & R. Ames (Eds.), *Research on motivation in education* (Vol. 2, pp. 249–286). New York: Academic Press.

Lepper, M. R., & Hodell, M. (1989). Intrinsic motivation in the classroom. In C. Ames & R. Ames (Eds.). *Research on motivation in education* (Vol. 3, pp. 73–105).

Levin, H. (1990). Presentation at the Illinois site-based management: Accelerated schools project, University of Illinois, Champaign, IL.

Mac Iver, D. (1987). Classroom factors and student characteristics predicting students' use of achievement standards during self-assessment. *Child Development, 58,* 1258–1271.

Mac Iver, D. (1988). Classroom environments and the stratification of pupils' ability perceptions. *Journal of Educational Psychology, 80,* 495–505.

Maehr, M. L. (1984). Meaning and motivation: Toward a theory of personal investment. In R. Ames & C. Ames (Eds.), *Research on motivation in education* (Vol. 1, pp. 39–73). New York: Academic Press.

Maehr, M. L., & Nicholls, J. G. (1980). Culture and achievement motivation: A second look. In N. Warren (Ed.). *Studies in cross cultural psychology* (Vol. 3, pp. 221–267). New York: Academic Press.

Malone, T. W., & Lepper, M. R. (1987). Making learning fun: A taxonomy of intrinsic motivation for learning. In R. E. Snow & M. J. Farr (Eds.), *Aptitude, learning, and instruction* (Vol. 3). Hillsdale, NJ: Lawrence Erlbaum Associates.

Marshall, H. H., & Weinstein, R. S. (1984). Classroom factors affecting students' self-evaluations: An interactional model. *Review of Educational Research, 54,* 301–325.

Marshall, H. H., & Weinstein, R. S. (1986). Classroom context of student-perceived differential teacher treatment. *Journal of Educational Psychology, 78,* 441–453.

Meece, J. (in press). The classroom context and children's motivational goals. In M. Maehr & P. Pintrich (Eds.). *Advances in achievement motivation research* (Vol. 7). Greenwich, CT: JAI Press

Meece, J. L., Blumenfeld, P., & Hoyle, R. (1988). Students' goal orientations and cognitive engagement in classroom activities. *Journal of Educational Psychology, 80,* 514–523.

Meece, J. L., & Holt, K. (1990). *Classification and validation of task-related goal patterns in elementary school children.* Unpublished manuscript, University of North Carolina, Chapel Hill.

Nicholls, J. G. (1979). Quality and equality in intellectual development: The role of motivation in education. *American Psychologist, 34,* 1071–1084.

Nicholls, J. G. (1984a). In R. Ames & C. Ames (Eds.), *Research on motivation in education* (Vol. 1). New York: Academic Press.

Nicholls, J. G. (1984b). Achievement motivation: Conceptions of ability, subjective experience, task choice, and performance. *Psychological Review, 91,* 328–346.

Nicholls, J. G. (1989). *The Competitive Ethos and Democratic Education.* Cambridge, MA: Harvard University Press.

Nicholls, J. G., Patashnick, M., Cheung, P. C., Thorkildsen, T. A., & Lauer, J. M. (1989). Can achievement motivation theory succeed with only one conception of success. In F. Halisch & J. H. L. van der Bercken (Eds.), *International Perspectives on Achievement and Task Motivation.* (pp. 187–208). Amsterdam: Swets & Zeitlinger.

Nicholls, J. G., Patashnick, M., & Nolen, S. B. (1985). Adolescents' theories of education. *Journal of Educational Psychology, 77,* 683–692.

Nolen, S. B. (1987, April). *The influence of task involvement on use of learning strategies.* Paper presented at the annual meeting of the American Educational Research Association, Washington, DC.

Nolen, S. B. (1988). Reasons for studying: Motivational orientations and study strategies. *Cognition and Instruction, 5,* 269–287.

Roberts, G. C. (1984). Achievement motivation in children's sport. In J. G. Nicholls (Ed.), *Advances in motivation and achievement: The development of achievement motivation* (Vol. 3). Greenwich, CT: JAI.

Rosenholtz, S. R., & Rosenholtz, S. J. (1981). Classroom organization and the perception of ability. *Sociology of Education, 54,* 132–140.

Rosenholtz, S. J., & Simpson, C. (1984a). Classroom organization and student stratification. *The Elementary School Journal, 85,* 21–37.

Rosenholtz, S. J., & Simpson, C. (1984b). The formation of ability conceptions: Developmental trend or social construction? *Review of Educational Research, 54,* 31–63.

Ryan, R. M., Connell, J. P., & Deci, E. L. (1985). A motivational analysis of self-determination and self-regulation in education. In C. Ames & R. Ames (Eds.), *Research on motivation in education* (Vol. 2, pp. 13–51). New York: Academic Press.

Ryan, R. M., & Grolnick, W. (1986). Origins and pawns in the classroom: Self-report and projective assessments of individual differences in children's perceptions. *Journal of Personality and Social Psychology, 50,* 550–558.

Schunk, D. (1985). Self efficacy and classroom learning. *Psychology in the schools, 22,* 208–223.

Schunk, D. (1989). Self-efficacy and cognitive skill learning. In C. Ames & R. Ames (Eds.), *Research on motivation in education* (Vol. 3, pp. 13–44). New York: Academic Press.

Slavin, R. E. (1983). *Cooperative learning.* New York: Longman.

Stipek, D. J., & Daniels, D. H. (1988). Declining perceptions of competence: A consequence of changes in the child or educational environment. *Journal of Educational Psychology, 80,* 352–356.

Stipek, D. J., & Kowalski, P. S. (1989). Learned helplessness in task orienting versus performance orienting testing conditions. *Journal of Educational Psychology, 81,* 384–391.

Wentzel, K. R. (1989). Adolescent classroom goals, standards for performance, and academic achievement: An interactionist perspective. *Journal of Educational Psychology, 81,* 131–142.

Author Index

349

Subject Index

A

Ability grouping, *see* Grouping
Academic achievement (performance),
    56, 69, 165–166, 235–237, 239,
    292, 294–297, 301, 317–318
Academic choice, 209–216
Academic outcomes, 188–189
Academic self-concept, *see* Self-concept
Academic self-regulation, *see* Self-
    regulated learning
Achievement
  domains, 103, 106, 109–110
  mathematics, 213, 217, 221, 224, 243
  motivation, 9, 62, 69, 100–101, 270,
      307, 327, 331
  science, 217, 224, 235–236, 243
  values, 101–107
Achievement beliefs
  age differences, 106–107
  gender differences, 106–107, 211–220,
      316
Affect, 318, 344
African-American youth, 75–76, 82–90,
    92
Aggression
  antecedents of, 12, 76–77
  and attributions, 78–86

and perceived intentionality, 12–13,
    78, 81–90
  proactive, 90
  reactive, 90
Anger, 12–13, 81–92
Anxiety, 212, 215, 240, 242–243, 318,
    343
Attitude toward mathematics, 235, 242
Attribution theory, 10, 20, 78–80, 268
Attributions
  ability, 10, 79, 192, 248, 250–251,
      254, 273, 319
  attributional change programs, 86–92,
      260
  causes and dimensions, 10, 79–80,
      272
  effort, 10, 79, 128, 192–193, 250–251,
      254, 309, 319
  and emotion, 81–86
  strategy, 128, 175, 186, 188, 191–194
Autonomy, *see* Perceptions

B,C

Behaviorism, 6–7
Career
  choice, 230–234, 239
  decision making, 15–16, 237–238, 240